FOR Dummies™
BESTSELLING
BOOK SERIES

Canadian Wine For Dummies®

by Tony Aspler and Barbara Leslie

RETI Cheat Sheet

Canadian Wine Regions at a Glance

Ontario*
- ✔ Niagara Peninsula*
- ✔ Lake Erie North Shore*
- ✔ Toronto GTA
- ✔ Pelee Island*
- ✔ Prince Edward County

British Columbia*
- ✔ Okanagan Valley*
- ✔ Similkameen Valley*
- ✔ Fraser Valley*
- ✔ Vancouver Island*

Québec
- ✔ Montérégie
- ✔ Eastern Townships
- ✔ Québec City

Nova Scotia
- ✔ Annapolis Valley
- ✔ Northeast Shore

*Regions entitled to Vintners Quality Alliance designation (VQA)

Canada's Ten Most Popular Grape Types

White	Red
1. Chardonnay	6. Cabernet Franc
2. Pinot Blanc	7. Cabernet Sauvignon
3. Pinot Gris	8. Maréchal Foch
4. Riesling	9. Merlot
5. Vidal	10. Pinot Noir

Ten Milestones in Canadian Wine

- ✔ **1668:** Jesuit Father Jacques Bruyas encourages settlers to become wine growers. In a letter he writes, "If one were to take the trouble to plant some vines and trees they would yield as well as they do in France…and (properly pruned) the grapes would be as good as those of France."

- ✔ **1811:** Johann Schiller, a retired corporal, plants the first commercial vineyard in Cooksville, Ontario (now Mississauga).

- ✔ **1916:** Prohibition is introduced (within a year all provinces but Québec proscribe the sale of beverage alcohol. Wine is exempt from the Act).

- ✔ **1927:** Prohibition is repealed. The provincial liquor board system is instituted.

- ✔ **1937:** Brights sends their winemaker to France to learn about European grapevines.

- ✔ **1955:** Brights produces the first Chardonnay from cuttings brought back from France.

- ✔ **1974:** The first winery licence since Prohibition is issued to Inniskillin.

- ✔ **1979:** The first estate winery in British Columbia, Claremont, opens its doors.

- ✔ **1988:** Introduction of the Vintners Quality Alliance (VQA) in Ontario.

- ✔ **1997:** Canada's first wine school founded at Brock University in Ontario.

...For Dummies®: Bestselling Book Series for Beginners

Canadian Wine For Dummies®

White Wine and Food Matching Chart

Grape Type	Best Food
Chardonnay (white Burgundy)	Fish, shellfish, deep-fried fish, poultry, rabbit, veal, pork, cream sauces, egg dishes, snails
Chenin Blanc (dry Vouvray)	Shellfish, sole, chicken, pork, light cream dishes, soy dishes
Gewürztraminer	Oriental dishes (Thai, Japanese), light curries, smoked fish
Riesling (dry)	Fish, shellfish, game birds, pork, veal, Thai dishes, Chinese food
Sauvignon Blanc	Shellfish, fish, chicken, spicy sausage, prosciutto, vegetarian dishes

Red Wine and Food Matching Chart

Grape Type	Best Food
Cabernet Sauvignon (red Bordeaux)	Full-flavoured meats (steak, roast, lamb, duck, game birds)
Gamay (Beaujolais)	Light meat dishes (ham), sausages, hamburger, pizza
Merlot (St. Emilion/ Pomerol)	Lamb, venison, game, turkey, meat casseroles
Pinot Noir (red Burgundy)	Grilled meats, game birds, veal, roast chicken, rabbit, salmon
Syrah (red Rhône)/ Shiraz	Highly-spiced meat dishes, game, garlicky casseroles
Sangiovese (Chianti)	Casseroles, spicy sausage, tomato-based meat dishes, pasta, pizza
Zinfandel	Rich meat dishes, venison, game, roast turkey, spicy pastas

...For Dummies®: Bestselling Book Series for Beginners

Praise for Tony Aspler

"Everyone learns about wine in his or her own way. Tony's way has been…extremely human; richly mixed with real life, literary life, incident and accident in some unexpected parts of the world . . . Tony Aspler is one of the frankest and funniest…"
— *Hugh Johnson*

"It's always a happy circumstance when somebody who knows a subject can also bring that expertise alive with good writing."
— *Ottawa Citizen*

"[Tony Aspler] is the wine expert's Canadian wine expert. Aspler is the drinking companion we'd all like to invite 'down to the cellar'."
— *Eye Weekly (Toronto)*

Praise for Vintage Canada

". . . a masterful cross-Canada survey of wineries . . ."
— *The Toronto Sun*

". . . Superb."
— *The Montreal Gazette*

Praise for Tony Aspler's Wine Lover's Companion

"Outstanding! . . . 37 years as a wine judge and I learned something new in each chapter."
— *David G. Male, President, InterVin International*

"Only a handful of writers . . . combine authoritative knowledge . . . with an easy-reading, fluid style. Tony Aspler is one of them. The Wine Lover's Companion makes for delightful reading, and yet is an authentic wine reference. Well done!"
— *Ed McCarthy, Wine For Dummies®*

". . . full of information that presupposed nothing, and explains simply, without pretension."
— *The Globe and Mail*

Canadian Wine FOR DUMMIES®

by Tony Aspler
and Barbara Leslie

CDG BOOKS CANADA

CDG Books Canada, Inc.

◆ Toronto, ON ◆

Canadian Wine For Dummies®

Published by
CDG Books Canada, Inc.
99 Yorkville Avenue
Suite 400
Toronto, ON M5R 3K5
www.cdgbooks.com (CDG Books Canada Web Site)
www.idgbooks.com (IDG Books Worldwide Web Site)
www.dummies.com (Dummies Press Web Site)

Canadian Cataloguing in Publication Data

Aspler, Tony, 1939–

Canadian wine for dummies

Includes index.
ISBN: 1-894413-18-0

1. Wine industry — Canada — History. 2. Wineries — Canada. 3. Wine and wine making — Canada.
I. Leslie, Barbara. II. Title.

TP559.C3A855 2000   338.4'76332'00971   C00-932603-0

Printed in Canada

1 2 3 4 5 TRI 04 03 02 01 00

Distributed in Canada by CDG Books Canada, Inc.

For general information on CDG Books, including all IDG Books Worldwide publications, please call our distribution center: HarperCollins Canada at 1-800-387-0117. For reseller information, including discounts and premium sales, please call our Sales department at 1-877-963-8830.

This book is available at special discounts for bulk purchases by your group or organization for resale, premiums, fundraising and seminars. For details, contact CDG Books Canada, Special Sales Department, 99 Yorkville Avenue, Suite 400, Toronto, ON, M5K 3K5; Tel: 416-963-8830; Email: spmarkets@cdgbooks.com.

For press review copies, author interviews, or other publicity information, please contact our Marketing department at 416-963-8830, fax 416-923-4821, or e-mail publicity@cdgbooks.com.

For authorization to photocopy items for corporate, personal, or educational use, please contact Cancopy, The Canadian Copyright Licensing Agency, One Yonge Street, Suite 1900, Toronto, ON, M5E 1E5; Tel: 416-868-1620; Fax: 416-868-1621; www.cancopy.com.

is a trademark under exclusive license to CDG Books Canada, Inc., from International Data Group, Inc.

About the Authors

Tony Aspler is the most widely read wine writer in Canada. He is recognized as the leading authority on Canadian wines and is the creator of the annual Air Ontario Wine Awards competition. Author of *Travels with My Corkscrew*, *Vintage Canada*, *Tony Aspler's Wine Lover's Companion*, and many other books on wine and food, Tony is the wine columnist for the *Toronto Star*. He has also published nine novels, including a series of wine lover's mysteries featuring wine writer-detective Ezra Brant.

Tony is on the advisory board of Masters of Wine (North America) and is co-founder of the charitable foundation Grapes for Humanity.

Barbara Leslie lucked into one of the world's greatest jobs working for *Winetidings*, Canada's oldest continually published wine magazine. Over the course of a 15-year career with the magazine, she did just about everything from tasting wine, to writing and editing, to typesetting and layout. When she retired from the *Winetidings* staff in 1999, she held the title of publisher. Barbara is currently pursuing her freelance career in the Niagara Peninsula, where she lives around the corner from of some of Canada's greatest wineries.

Barbara grew up in Montréal and studied at McGill University, where she majored in Italian. This was quite helpful when she guided a group of wine lovers through the vineyards of northern Italy on behalf of the Opimian Society. She has also led a number of tastings and introductory wine seminars, albeit in English and French. She has yet to lead one in Italian, but she's working on it!

Barbara has known and worked with Tony Aspler for many years. She shares both Tony's appreciation of wine and his affection for cats.

ABOUT CDG BOOKS CANADA, INC. AND
IDG BOOKS WORLDWIDE, INC.

Welcome to the world of IDG Books Worldwide and CDG Books Canada.

IDG Books Worldwide, Inc., is a subsidiary of International Data Group, Inc., the world's largest publisher of computer-related information and the leading global provider of information services on information technology. IDG was founded more than 30 years ago and now employs more than 9,000 people worldwide. IDG publishes more than 295 computer publications in over 75 countries (see listing below). More than 90 million people read one or more IDG publications each month.

Launched in 1990, IDG Books Worldwide is today the #1 publisher of best-selling computer books in North America. IDG Books Worldwide is proud to be the recipient of eight awards from the Computer Press Association in recognition of editorial excellence and three from *Computer Currents'* First Annual Readers' Choice Awards. Our best-selling *...For Dummies*® series has more than 55 million copies in print with translations in 31 languages. In record time, IDG Books Worldwide has become the first choice for millions of readers around the world who want to learn how to better manage their businesses.

In 1998, IDG Books Worldwide formally partnered with Macmillan Canada, a subsidiary of Canada Publishing Corporation, to create CDG Books Canada, a dynamic new Canadian publishing company. CDG Books Canada is now Canada's fastest growing publisher, bringing valuable information to Canadians from coast to coast through the introduction of Canadian *...For Dummies*® and *CliffsNotes*™ titles.

Every one of our books is designed to bring extra value and skill-building instructions to the reader. Our books are written by experts who understand and care about our readers. The knowledge base of our editorial staff comes from years of experience in publishing, education, and journalism — experience we use to produce books to carry us into the new millennium. In short, we care about books, so we attract the best people. We devote special attention to details such as audience, interior design, use of icons, and illustrations. And because we use an efficient process of authoring, editing, and desktop publishing our books electronically, we can spend more time ensuring superior content and spend less time on the technicalities of making books.

You can count on our commitment to deliver high-quality books at competitive prices on topics you want to read about. At IDG Books Worldwide and CDG Books Canada, we continue in the IDG tradition of delivering quality for more than 30 years. You can learn more about IDG Books Worldwide and CDG Books Canada by visiting www.idgbooks.com, www.dummies.com, and www.cdgbooks.com.

Eighth Annual
Computer Press
Awards ≫ 1992

Ninth Annual
Computer Press
Awards ≫ 1993

Tenth Annual
Computer Press
Awards ≫ 1994

Eleventh Annual
Computer Press
Awards ≫ 1995

IDG is the world's leading IT media, research and exposition company. Founded in 1964, IDG had 1997 revenues of $2.05 billion and has more than 9,000 employees worldwide. IDG offers the widest range of media options that reach IT buyers in 75 countries representing 95% of worldwide IT spending. IDG's diverse product and services portfolio spans six key areas including print publishing, online publishing, expositions and conferences, market research, education and training, and global marketing services. More than 90 million people read one or more of IDG's 290 magazines and newspapers, including IDG's leading global brands — Computerworld, PC World, Network World, Macworld and the Channel World family of publications. IDG Books Worldwide is one of the fastest-growing computer book publishers in the world, with more than 700 titles in 36 languages. The "...For Dummies®" series alone has more than 50 million copies in print. IDG offers online users the largest network of technology-specific Web sites around the world through IDG.net (http://www.idg.net), which comprises more than 225 targeted Web sites in 55 countries worldwide. International Data Corporation (IDC) is the world's largest provider of information technology data, analysis and consulting, with research centers in over 41 countries and more than 400 research analysts worldwide. IDG World Expo is a leading producer of more than 168 globally branded conferences and expositions in 35 countries including E3 (Electronic Entertainment Expo), Macworld Expo, ComNet, Windows World Expo, ICE (Internet Commerce Expo), Agenda, DEMO, and Spotlight. IDG's training subsidiary, ExecuTrain, is the world's largest computer training company, with more than 230 locations worldwide and 785 training courses. IDG Marketing Services helps industry-leading IT companies build international brand recognition by developing global integrated marketing programs via IDG's print, online and exposition products worldwide. Further information about the company can be found at www.idg.com.   8/24/99

Dedication

Tony Aspler dedicates this book to his friend and colleague Jacques Marie, whose love of wine has communicated itself to thousands of Canadians over some 30 years of education.

Barbara Leslie dedicates this book to Mike Blakely, her son and arbiter of good taste.

Authors' Acknowledgements

Writing a wine book of this nature is a co-operative effort. We did not simply sit in front of our word processors and bash it all out from memory. We relied on the expertise, experience, and good nature of dozens of people in all areas of Canadian wine — from the winemakers themselves to the organizations and institutions that support them, the liquor boards who purvey their products, and the hospitality industry that serves Canadian wines in their restaurants.

Special thanks to the Wine Council of Ontario, who patiently answered all our inquiries, in spite of our endless requests for background on the newest wineries right up to press time, as we strove to keep the information as fresh and lively as the wines it represents. Thanks to VQA Canada, and both its arms in British Columbia and Ontario for their generous help whenever we asked — which was frequently. We would be remiss if we did not single out certain individuals who gave freely of their time and advice: Dave Gamble, Publisher/Editor of *BC Wine Trails*, wine writers Tim Pawsey in Vancouver and Linda Bramble in St. Catharines, Ontario.

Once we had the raw data, we had to put it into a unique form, unlike any other wine book we had written. Guiding us through the technique and the technology were Joan Whitman and Melanie Rutledge at CDG Books in Toronto. They kept us in the information highway's fast lane in spite of ourselves. Thank you both for your support and for having the vision to see that this was a book that would introduce a whole new generation to the fascinating world of Canadian wine.

We would also like to thank our agent, Dean Cooke, of Livingston Cooke, who cosseted us through the project and showed us there was light at the end of the information tunnel.

Lastly, we'd like to thank you for buying this book. It may not be the only wine book you will ever purchase, but it *will* be the only one that gives you a comprehensive view of Canadian wine, the people who make it, and its place in the global scheme of things. Cheers!

Publisher's Acknowledgments

We're proud of this book; please register your comments through our IDG Books Worldwide Online Registration Form located at `http://my2cents.dummies.com`.

Some of the people who helped bring this book to market include the following:

Acquisitions and Editorial

Editorial Director: Joan Whitman

Associate Editor: Melanie Rutledge

Assistant Editor: Kim Herter

Copy Editor: Pamela Erlichman

Editorial Assistant: Stella Partheniou

Production

Director of Production: Donna Brown

Production Editor: Rebecca Conolly

Layout and Graphics: Kim Monteforte, Heidy Lawrance Associates; Shelley Norris; Brent Savage; Rashell Smith

Special Art: Jane Whitney (cartographer)

Proofreader: Kelli Howey

Indexer: Belle Wong

Special Help

Amy Black, Michael Kelly

General and Administrative

IDG Books Worldwide, Inc.: John Kilcullen, CEO; William Barry, President

CDG Books Canada, Inc.: Ron Besse, Chairman; Tom Best, President; Robert Harris, Vice President and Publisher

IDG Books Technology Publishing Group: Richard Swadley, Senior Vice President and Publisher; Walter Bruce III, Vice President and Associate Publisher; Mary Bednarek, Branded Product Development Director; Mary Corder, Editorial Director

IDG Books Consumer Publishing Group: Roland Elgey, Senior Vice President and Publisher; Kathleen A. Welton, Vice President and Publisher; Kevin Thornton, Acquisitions Manager; Kristin A. Cocks, Editorial Director

IDG Books Internet Publishing Group: Brenda McLaughlin, Senior Vice President and Publisher; Diane Graves Steele, Vice President and Associate Publisher; Sofia Marchant, Online Marketing Manager

IDG Books Production for Dummies Press: Michael R. Britton, Vice President of Production; Debbie Stailey, Associate Director of Production; Cindy L. Phipps, Manager of Project Coordination, Production Proofreading, and Indexing; Tony Augsburger, Manager of Prepress, Reprints, and Systems; Laura Carpenter, Production Control Manager; Shelley Lea, Supervisor of Graphics and Design; Debbie J. Gates, Production Systems Specialist; Robert Springer, Supervisor of Proofreading; Kathie Schutte, Production Supervisor

Dummies Packaging and Book Design: Patty Page, Manager, Promotions Marketing

◆

The publisher would like to give special thanks to Patrick J. McGovern, without whom this book would not have been possible.

◆

Contents at a Glance

Cartoons at a Glance

By Rich Tennant

page 323

page 203

page 141

page 97

page 5

page 51

page 341

Fax: 978-546-7747

E-mail: richtennant@the5thwave.com

World Wide Web: www.the5thwave.com

Table of Contents

Introduction

*W*ine is more than the sum of its grapes. Wine has inspired poets to write sonnets, musicians to compose symphonies, and lovers to propose marriage. A bottle of wine can turn a simple dinner into a night to remember — but two nights later, that very same wine makes you wonder why you thought it was so special in the first place. What happened? Where did the magic go?

That's one of wine's mysteries. Well, we demystify wine for you in this book, and tell you a lot more about it besides, including how to hold on to the romance of that first night's dinner. With a little bit of knowledge, you need never be disappointed in your wine again.

To uncork many of the things you need to know, we take a look around wine country — no, not in France, not in Italy, not even in California — we find just about everything we need to know here at home, in Canada.

"Only in Canada?" you ask, disbelieving. Well, not entirely. There are lots of countries around the world that have made wine for centuries. Canada has only just woken up to the fact that it's possible to make really great wine here. But that's what makes it exciting. We show you what Canadian winemakers are doing now, and how, over the course of about 30 years, they've changed "no class" wines into "world-class" award-winning ones.

So, take a step with us into the world according to Canadian wine. It won't be long before you can take on any waiter in any restaurant and end up with a really great bottle.

We have all, at one time or another, been absolutely baffled by wine. There are so many choices. So many labels. Dozens of countries around the world make wine. And every year, thanks to different weather patterns, they all produce a different style. Are you overwhelmed when you walk into a wine store? Are you reduced to a dithering mass of indecision when:

- Facing seemingly endless rows of bottles at the liquor store?
- Choosing a wine to serve with the Thanksgiving turkey?
- Storing that bottle of vintage Canadian red your uncle gave you?
- Buying the right wineglasses for a wedding gift?
- Accepting an invitation to a wine tasting?
- Ordering wine in a restaurant?
- Reading a wine label?

- ✔ Preparing a dish that requires wine?
- ✔ Asked to open a bottle of sparkling wine?

If you answer "Yes!" to any of these questions, then *Canadian Wine For Dummies®* is the book for you. We have tried to simplify a complex subject because we want to share our own passion for wine with you — particularly wines made in Canada from locally grown grapes.

There's a tendency in the wine world to make the subject exclusive; to cloak the immediate pleasure that a well-made wine gives in language that intimidates the novice.

This book is meant to inspire, not intimidate. It's a practical handbook for those who want to understand and enjoy wine but are maybe put off by all the snobbery, affectation, and arcane ritual surrounding it.

We guide you through the wine world from a decidedly Canadian perspective, simply and easily. You discover how to appreciate wine; how to taste, buy, store and serve it. It's a magic carpet ride with plenty of stops to ferret out the best producers and best values.

And all this with a sense of fun.

So, what are you waiting for? Uncork this book for a lifetime of wine enjoyment!

How to Use This Book

You can, of course, read this book from cover to cover, like an instruction manual. But you don't have to. There's no exam at the end; only the satisfaction of knowing you've completed the course — and by so doing, have developed a pretty solid grounding in wine knowledge.

Or, you can dip and sip, treating the book like a reference. Scan the table of contents. You can readily access topics you may need at a moment's notice (such as wines to lay down and wines *not* to lay down, how to decant, how to score wines, what wines to serve with goat cheese . . .). These pages have all the basic information you need to become stirred up — not only about Canadian wines, but wines of the world.

Part I: What Is Wine?

There's a little bit of magic involved in turning grapes into wine, but there are some basic, practical elements, too. This part takes you into the vineyard and the winery and explains the many variables that make one wine taste so different from another.

Part II: Appreciating Wine

This part is all about looking, smelling, and tasting, and how all your senses play a part in your enjoyment of wine. We also explain why some people wave their wineglasses around in the air before drinking. Yes, they do it for a reason.

Part III: Enjoying Wine

There's a multitude of ways to enjoy wine. This part gives you some tips on ordering wine in restaurants (like when to send the bottle back) as well as on serving wine at home. You also find out which part of your basement is best for storing your wine and where to buy great wine to store there.

Part IV: Wine and Food

Wine and food go hand in hand, but have you ever wondered what wine goes best with what food? This part shows you how different foods affect the way you taste wine and how to become a successful matchmaker. We also tell you how to take your wine into the kitchen and come out with some superb dishes.

Part V: Wineries across Canada

This part takes you back in time to find out how the Canadian wine industry began. Then we take you on a cross-country tour of Canada's wine regions. You find out how the Canadian climate is a constant challenge for our winemakers, and what choices they have to make to stack the odds in their (and our) favour.

Part VI: The Part of Tens

In this uniquely . . . *For Dummies*® part are answers to ten frequently asked questions about wine. We also count down the top ten winemakers currently working in Ontario and British Columbia, to give you a heads up when you confront all that choice in the liquor store.

Part VII: Appendixes

If you find some of wine's more technical terms a bit tricky, flip to the glossary in this part. Or, if you're looking for a particular winery in Canada, check in the directory for addresses and informative Web sites. If you need a new corkscrew, are looking for a gift, or would like to build a wine cellar, then the list of stores specializing in wine accessories is where you want to be.

Icons Used in This Book

This little guy is our wine nerd. He loves to know about all the little details that go into winemaking (and he'll bore you to death if you let him go on as long as he would like to). If you don't want to go into that much detail, just skip over the text where he appears. Your enjoyment of wine won't suffer one bit — and you can always refer back to him if there's some nagging doubt in your mind.

The bull's eye tells you where to look for snippets of information to help you make better wine choices. It'll help speed you on your way to becoming a real wine connoisseur. You can pick these tips out and apply them immediately to your wine buying and appreciation.

Some issues in wine are so fundamental that they bear repeating. Just so you don't think we repeated ourselves without realizing it, we'll mark the repetitions with this symbol. It's today's equivalent of tying a knot in your handkerchief (a memory aid your mother used to tell you to do, if you're of a certain age).

To put Canadian wine in context, we include information about wines from other countries as well. This icon points you in the direction of some terrific international wines we suggest you try. We like them, and we think you will too. This icon also pops up in reference to particularly scrumptious foods — our other consuming passion.

This shines the spotlight on some of Canada's best wines. And, it's not just Tony and Barb who think so. We're proud to say that most of the wines we indicate with this symbol have won awards in national and international wine competitions. We also use this icon to indicate a relevant aspect of our national wine industry.

Part I
What Is Wine?

The 5th Wave   By Rich Tennant

"Wine reminds me of opera. I enjoy it even though I don't always understand what's being said."

In this part . . .

Before you pour your first glass of wine and begin to explore its complexity, it helps if you understand exactly how grapes become wine and why different varieties of wine grapes, planted in different regions, taste the way they do.

You may not recognize it at first, but each grape has its own flavour, and that flavour changes in subtle or sometimes not so subtle ways, depending on a variety of factors, including the soil in which the grape grows, its cultivation in the vineyard, and what the winemaker does to it in the winery.

Chapter 1

What Makes a Wine

In This Chapter

▶ Knowing what makes a wine "Canadian"

▶ Realizing that air has something to do with it

▶ Recognizing what grapes have to do with it

▶ Explaining winemaking standards

Making wine is both an art and a science. Anyone can make wine. You only need grapes (or grape juice) and yeast. Which is rather like saying all you need to write *Hamlet* is pen and paper or you can paint the *Mona Lisa* if you've got canvas, oil paints, and a brush.

You can have these elements, as well as the most sophisticated presses, fermentation tanks, and new oak barrels at your disposal for winemaking; but unless you know how to select your grapes and what each piece of equipment is capable of, you'll probably end up with something more akin to vinegar than wine. Reading this chapter won't turn you into a winemaker instantly, but it will give you the basic information about how winemakers produce a nectar out of grape juice and the decisions they make along the way.

Understanding What Wine Is

Simply put, wine is fermented grape juice. It can be white, red, pink — and it can be sparkling in all these colours. A *fermentation* occurs when grape sugar is attacked by yeast. The sugar is converted into alcohol and the grape juice "magically" becomes young wine. Some enthusiasts extend the definition of wine to include other fruits, such as strawberries, peaches, or pears. Chapter 21 looks at the production of fruit wine in Canada.

Canadian wine is made from grapes that are grown in 100 percent Canadian soil. Is it possible, then, to have grapes that are less than 100 percent Canadian-grown? Well, under federal wine regulations, it is permissible to blend wines from other countries into Canadian-grown wines. The Canadian government legislated the Wine Content Act following the Free Trade Agreement with the United States in 1988 to help winemakers adjust to the highly competitive open market. It permits winemakers to identify their wines as "Product of Canada" with as little as 30 percent Canadian content as long as they incur the cost of processing and bottling in Canada. Most of the wines in this category compete at the high volume/low end of the market.

Such products, however, cannot be labelled with the symbol VQA (*Vintners Quality Alliance*), a specification reserved for wines whose grapes grow entirely in designated vineyard areas across the country. The VQA is an important winemaking organization, and we give you more details about it later in this chapter.

If you want to be sure the wine you buy is 100 percent Canadian, look for the VQA symbol on the label or the *capsule*, the metal or plastic cap that covers the top of the bottle. This is your guarantee that the wine comes from the geographical location stated on the label.

Winemaking Basics

You can make wine using two basic methods. You crush the grapes and ferment the resulting *must* (juice and grape pulp) in either:

- Stainless steel tanks without air

  or

- Oak vats or barrels with oxygen present

Wines made in stainless steel tanks are fresh and fruity. It's rather like canning peas. What you put into a tank comes out with pretty much the same flavour because no oxygen is present — this is what ages a wine. Most white wines are made this way to preserve their freshness. Wines made in stainless steel tanks are destined for early drinking within a year or two of their *vintage*, the year the grapes were harvested, stated on the label.

If no vintage date is stated on a bottle of wine, you know it's a blend of two or more vintages. A good example is champagne. Most champagnes are blends of two or more years. Those champagnes that carry a single year on the label were made in good vintages when the grapes ripened fully.

Red wine is often fermented in oak barrels, as its hard *tannins* — the substance derived from the skin, seeds, and stalks of the grape that tastes harsh — benefits from the softening properties of the wood. White wines can also be barrel-aged. Some of the best white wines capable of aging are fermented in oak barrels — but for a shorter time than the reds. Not only is there air inside the barrel, but there is also an exchange of air through the *staves* (narrow slats of wood that make up the barrel).

TECHNICAL STUFF

The fermentation formula

Winemakers work with the following equation:

Sugar + Yeast = Alcohol + Carbon dioxide gas (in almost equal proportions). The word *fermentation* comes from the Latin verb *fervere*, meaning to boil. If you watch a fermentation in progress, the juice appears to be boiling violently in the vat.

The more sugar in the grapes, the higher the potential alcohol in the finished wine. If the grapes contain a large amount of sugar, which can happen when the weather is very hot and sunny, the fermentation may suddenly stop and the wine turns out sweet. Some strains of yeast can eat more sugar than others and winemakers can control the sweetness of the wine by choosing special yeasts (researchers have developed a whole range specifically for wine-making). These "farmed" yeast strains can overwhelm the yeast that develops naturally on the grape skins. Some winemakers choose to use additional yeast whereas others prefer to take the natural route and let the wine develop without introducing farmed yeasts.

White wines are usually fermented at low temperatures (around 20° Celsius) to extract floral and fruit flavours. Red wines are generally fermented at higher temperatures, and for a shorter time, to extract colour from the skins and to inhibit the extraction of tannins (harsh, bitter components in the stalks, pits, and skins of grapes).

The importance of air

Oxygen is both a friend and an enemy of wine. In small amounts, it has a beneficial effect — maturing the wine, deepening its colour, softening its *mouth feel* (tactile sensations of the wine in your mouth) and intensifying its *bouquet* (odours derived from the winemaking process) and flavour. Too much oxygen, though, turns the wine into acetic acid, which tastes like vinegar. If you leave a small amount of wine in a glass overnight, you'll be greeted with a sharp vinegar smell the next morning. The wine *oxidizes* — the same browning process that happens to an apple you cut in half and leave exposed to the air. Just as the exposed apple tastes a little "rusty," so too will wine that has been left open to the air for too long.

The grape's goodness

When you hear the expression, "It's a vintage year," it means that the grapes have come into the wineries in good condition.

- **They have achieved the proper degree of ripeness.**
- **The sugars and acids are in balance.**

✔ They are free of rot and other diseases.

✔ They have escaped rain that might have swelled the berries and diluted their flavours.

✔ They have arrived at the press without oxidizing.

When these conditions are met, the winemaker has the raw material with which to make a potentially fine wine. What happens next — the whole wine-making process — ultimately determines the quality of the wine that reaches your table. You'll find more about winemaking in Chapters 2 and 3, but we've pared it down here to seven key stages:

1. **Crushing:** The grape skins are broken to allow the yeast to come in contact with the juice.

2. **Soaking:** The crushed berries are left in their juices to extract colour.

3. **Fermenting (time and temperature):** White wines usually undergo fermentation for more time at a lower temperature; red wines spend less time at a higher temperature.

4. **Aging:** This is done in stainless steel vats for whites, and in oak barrels for reds, though some white wines that do well when aged also end up in oak barrels.

5. **Fining:** Agents such as egg whites and gelatin are added to separate solid particles from the wine.

6. **Filtering:** The wine is strained through a filter to remove any solid particles that escaped the fining.

7. **Bottling:** The wine is transferred from storage containers into bottles for sale to the public.

We don't want to take all the magic out of wine by being too technical. Sometimes things just all come together to make one of those fantastic, unforgettable wines. No one knows how to make it happen all the time. An element of chance exists in every vintage.

You can pitch yeast into sugared water and you *will* get an alcoholic beverage. You can do the same with fruit juice and get any number of fruit wines — so why is it that people become so enamoured of wine from the grape?

A fascination for thousands of years

Grape wine has been revered for its restorative, curative, and antiseptic qualities, and reviled for stirring up temptations to excess. It has been offered to various gods of innumerable religions and is still used today in many sacred rites. No other wine has ever come close to its high profile.

A widespread appeal

The grape's components come together in a fermented beverage that appeals to just about everyone. The grape is so favoured for this purpose that over three-quarters of grape production around the world results in wine. The remainder is divided up among several products including table grapes, raisins, juice, and concentrate.

An astonishing array of colours and sizes

There's a dizzying number of grape varieties — each with its own unique characteristics. So what's the grape made of anyway? Pulp, which is mostly water, skin, and some seeds. The most important part of the grape is the fleshy pulp that, when crushed, releases a sweet juice. If the skins are allowed to remain in contact with the juice, they impart colour, flavour, and tannins. Natural yeasts cling to the surface of the skin just as though nature intended the grape to ferment. The seeds are of about as much interest in wine grapes as they are in table grapes. Their bitterness is unwelcome.

A knockout combination: Sugar and acid

The grape's combination of sugar and acid is what makes it really stand out among other fruit. Sugar converts into alcohol, which contributes to the wine's structure and age-worthiness. The sugar that remains in the wine after fermentation may be so slight that it's almost imperceptible, or more sugar may be retained to create a sweet dessert wine. The winemaker has control over this, and it's her prerogative.

Acidity gives wine its refreshing attributes. When well balanced, the flavour and feel of the wine and its aftertaste leave a lasting and pleasant impression. Wine's complexity and intrigue make writers like us want to share what we have learned about it with readers like you. It's a bit crazy, but it's a challenge and it's a whole lot of fun.

Setting the Standards

Do you ever have the feeling when you look at the label on a bottle of wine that it is nothing but incomprehensible words and numbers? The whole purpose of this book is to help you understand wine so that you feel more confident about choosing good wine. We decipher a wine label in Chapter 2. In this section we fill you in on international and Canadian winemaking standards — and they're nothing to sniff at!

Many wine-producing countries have appointed agencies to oversee the quality of wine and to which producers must submit their wine for testing to receive official approval. The system that is used around the world is called *appellation*, after the French word *appeler*, to name. Before a winemaker can attach a name to a wine, the wine must meet specific criteria.

You can tell if a wine has met these criteria by looking for a series of letters on the label. For Canadian wine, look for the letters VQA, which stand for Vintners Quality Alliance, the name given to the Canadian appellation system. Figure 1-1 shows the VQA logo. In France, the letters are AC (or AOC), which means *appellation d'origine contrôlée.* Italian labels display the letters DOC or DOCG, *denominazione d'origine controlata* or *denominazione d'origine controlata e garantita.* DOCG is a slightly higher level of quality. In Spain, the letters are DO or DOCa, *denominación de origen* or *denominación de origen calificada.* Again, the latter is a higher designation. These letters guarantee that the wine is made from grapes grown in the region indicated and that certain specific winemaking procedures have been followed. Rules cover such things as which grape types may be used, how many vines can be grown per hectare (or acre, depending on which system is used), how much wine can be produced from the area (any excess is ineligible for the appellation), what fertilizers or pesticides can be used in the vineyard, whether the vineyard can be irrigated, what sort of oak barrels can be used in the winery, and sometimes even what sort of cork may be used. Find out what Canada's criteria are in Appendix D, "Highlights of the Vintners Quality Alliance (VQA)."

Figure 1-1: The Vintners Quality Alliance logo: assurance that you're buying a high-quality Canadian wine.

The use of the word *origin* in most of the official terms is indicative of the importance of where the wine comes from. If you find a wine that says Bordeaux AC (*appellation contrôlée*) on the label, you have expectations of what the wine tastes like. It doesn't matter what else is written on the label. You don't need to know anything about Château Pleasantview, where the wine was made; if it has Bordeaux AC on the label, it should taste like Bordeaux wine. Château Pleasantview might have an individual flavour profile, but it would still have much in common with other Bordeaux wines. It's the same as if the grape name Merlot were written on the label; you would expect the wine to taste like Merlot. Instituted in 1935, the French *appellation contrôlée* laws are the standard on which other countries have based their own appellation systems. Appellation wines are expected to taste of the grapes used to make the wine and also to reflect the characteristics imparted by the *terroir* (the location in which they are grown), as different soils and climatic influences affect the taste of the wine. The terroir may encompass an entire region, such as Bordeaux, in which case the influence on the taste is fairly mild. At the other end of the spectrum, the terroir may be confined to a single vineyard and therefore exhibit quite distinct characteristics that are apparent to even a novice taster.

Canada's designated viticultural areas

In Canada, the VQA system is a result of our own winemakers' initiative. They recognized the importance of having standards against which they could measure their own wines and to measure Canadian wines against the wines of other countries. In 1989, winemakers in Ontario adopted a set of voluntary standards and formed a committee to oversee and develop the criteria. They used the French system as their prototype. Because the system is based on origin, the Canadians identified a number of *designated viticultural areas* (DVAs), geographic areas that have been singled out as having characteristics favourable to the cultivation of grapes. The DVA of a particular wine is stated on the label. Following Ontario's lead, British Columbia also adopted the VQA system, with some minor differences. Québec and Nova Scotia have not yet adopted the system although they have indicated interest in doing so. Table 1-1 identifies the specific DVAs in Ontario and British Columbia. Eventually, these areas will be divided into more precise zones, but the taste characteristics of the different terroirs must be methodically identified and recorded before this can be done. The Cool Climate Oenology and Viticulture Institute at Brock University has undertaken research in this area. You can read more about this institute, the first of its kind in Canada, in Chapter 4.

Table 1-1	Canada's Designated Viticultural Areas
Province	*Designated Area*
Ontario	Lake Erie North Shore
	Niagara Peninsula
	Pelee Island
British Columbia	Fraser Valley
	Okanagan Valley
	Similkameen Valley
	Vancouver Island

VQA regulations

The VQA in each province is now responsible for setting the standards by which wine is produced from the grapes of those provinces. The VQA's primary function is to identify criteria and regulate the use of specified terms, descriptions, and designations. Legislating the rules in each province is the first step to legislation under federal jurisdiction. Not having these rules approved at the federal level has blocked Canadian winemakers from gaining access to the lucrative European market. Here are some of the key winemaking standards put in place:

- **The VQA limits eligible grape types.** Only *Vitis vinifera* varieties (grape types within the species *Vitis vinifera*) are acceptable. These include such grapes as Riesling, Chardonnay, Cabernet Sauvignon, Pinot Noir, and a few premium *hybrids* (grape types developed by genetically crossing vines from different species) such as Vidal, which provide raw material for many Icewines.

- **The grapes must attain a minimum ripeness level when harvested.** Sugar content determines ripeness. Different categories of wine — for example, estate-bottled or Icewine — have different levels of sugar.

- **A wine must contain 85 percent of a particular grape in order for it to be named for its *varietal* (grape type).** Although some wines contain 100 percent of a particular grape type, a small amount of some complementary varieties can increase a wine's complexity without detracting from the principal grape's characteristics. This allowance for blending a minimal percentage is common practise in most wine-producing countries.

- **A wine must be 85 percent from a particular DVA (designated viticultural area) in order for it to carry that DVA's designation.** For example, 85 percent of a wine that carries the Okanagan Valley designation was made in that DVA. The other 15 percent can be made from grapes grown elsewhere in British Columbia.

- **A wine must be 100 percent from a particular vineyard in order for it to carry that vineyard's designation.** The vineyard itself must be within the boundaries of a recognized DVA. On the label, the VQA designation includes both the DVA where the grapes were grown and the name of the vineyard where the wine was made.

- **A wine must be 100 percent from land owned or controlled by a particular winery in order for it to be designated estate-bottled at that winery.** In this case, too, the winery must be located within the boundaries of a DVA.

- **Wineries must submit their wine to an independent tasting panel for evaluation in order to obtain a VQA designation.** Panel members, who are trained and experienced in wine tasting, taste 30 to 40 different wines at a go. The winery names are never revealed to the panel, but wines are numbered and identified by grape type and style; for example, "Late Harvest Vidal" #XXX. Tasters evaluate the wines for *typicity* (the wine must exhibit the characteristics expected of the grape type and geographic origins) and for flaws such as cloudiness, bubbling in a still wine, acetic acid (vinegar), sulphite, or oxidation. They then score the wine on a 20-point scale. A wine that is rejected by 50 percent of the panel is refused the VQA designation. A wine that is rejected by a minority of tasters will be resubmitted to a panel under a different number. Every effort is made to achieve consistency and fairness. See Chapter 7 for more on scoring wines.

Opening our doors to the world

The adoption of the Vintners Quality Alliance (VQA) standards is an important step towards the acceptance of Canadian wine by the international community and in particular the European Union (EU).

In 1998, Canada sold less than $1 million of wine in Europe. In that same year, Europe sold about $350 million of wine in Canada, much of it in Ontario. This reluctance on the part of the Europeans to import Canadian wine is related in part to the lack of a nationally regulated system of controls. This impediment should be eliminated once the VQA is legislated at the federal level.

Chapter 2

Wine in Its Elements

• •

• •

*Y*ou've heard people say it. Maybe you've said it yourself — most of us have at one time or another: "I love this wine, but I can't tell you why."

Here is where you start to understand the "why." In this chapter, we break wine down into its integral elements. As you begin to recognize wine's different parts, you can relate them to smells and tastes that you recognize, that are familiar to you. After some practise, you can identify these elements easily. And once you're a little more familiar with what's going on inside the bottle, we help you make sense of the outside — the label. The label is sort of like the wine's roadmap. In this chapter, we show you how to read it.

Breaking It Down: Wine's Key Ingredients

Wines made in stainless steel vats have four basic elements, whereas wines made in oak barrels have five.

All wines contain the following:

- ✔ **Fruit:** the sweetness you taste
- ✔ **Acidity:** the sourness or sharpness you taste
- ✔ **Alcohol:** no taste but a sensation of weight and hotness
- ✔ **Tannins:** bitterness

Most reds and some white wines have a further dimension — a quality that oak barrels, especially new barrels, impart to the wine: a range of flavours that include vanilla, spice, toast, and smoke, depending on the type of wood and length of time the wine spends in the barrel.

The smoke and toast flavours occur because the *staves,* the strips of wood that the barrel is made of, have been exposed to naked flames to shape them. Winemakers can order their barrels to the degree of "toastiness" they desire. If they want a rich barrel flavour imparted to their wine they will ask the *cooper* (barrel maker) for a heavy toast barrel.

Where's the fruit?

If you think of wine in human terms, fruit is the flesh of the wine. Wine grapes have a distinctive flavour when fermented. In certain varieties you can actually forecast what the wine will taste like from sampling the berries fresh from the vine. Muscat and Gewürztraminer are two highly aromatic grape varieties that taste spicy and floral on the vine and the same way in wine.

When you hear an experienced taster say that he or she smells grapefruit in the wine, or blackcurrant, don't take it literally. The winemaker does not add essence of grapefruit to improve the Riesling, or blackcurrant juice to round out the Cabernet Sauvignon. These flavours are already inherent in the grape and express themselves after fermentation.

Wine professionals can usually tell what grape variety a wine was made from just by sniffing it. Certain grape varieties have instantly recognizable aromas. You are a proficient wine taster if you can detect the type of fruit when you smell the bouquet of a wine. In Table 2-1 you can see a few of the more popular varieties and their fruit character.

Table 2-1	Grapes and their Flavours
Grape Variety	*Flavours*
White Grapes	
Chardonnay	Apple (in cool growing regions), pineapple-melon (in warm regions)
Gewürztraminer	Lychee nut, rose petal
Pinot Gris	Peach
Riesling	Lime, floral, petrol, grapefruit
Sauvignon Blanc	Cut grass, gooseberry, passion fruit

Grape Variety	Flavours
Red Grapes	
Cabernet Sauvignon	Blackcurrant, cedar
Gamay	Cherry, pepper
Merlot	Blueberry
Pinot Noir	Raspberry, black cherry
Syrah/Shiraz	Blackberry, pepper
Zinfandel	Plum

What's so good about acid?

Acidity, the sharp or lemony tang in dry whites, is the skeleton of the wine. Acid gives the wine its structure and energy; without it, the wine would taste flabby and sweet. Acid gives wine vitality, freshness, and balance. It also prolongs the flavour (giving the wine *length*) and refreshes your palate, setting you up for your next sip. Acidity also helps preserve colour in red wines.

Many of the acids in wine are only of interest to a chemist. However, the main ones are noted in Table 2-2 along with the flavours they bring to wine.

Table 2-2	Tasting Acids in Wine
Type of Acid	Flavour
Acetic	Sweet vinegar
Citric	Lemon
Lactic	Milk
Malic	Green apple
Succinic	Sharp sourness
Tartaric	Tongue-biting harshness

What's the degree of alcohol?

The amount of *alcohol* (ethyl alcohol, also known as *ethanol*) in a wine is registered on the label or back label of all wines. In some countries, it's expressed by volume rather than as a percentage. Wine labels will indicate the amount of alcohol in these two ways:

> ✓ **A percentage by volume, such as 12.5 percent alc./vol.**
>
> ✓ **A number of degrees by volume, such as 12.5 alc./vol.**

Alcohol is a preservative that allows a wine to age. Wines that have a high alcoholic content (13 to 16.5 percent alc./vol.) give an impression of weight in your mouth, making them feel full-bodied. Low-alcohol wines (8 to 10 percent alc./vol.) have a light-bodied feel in the mouth.

Most wines you buy in Canada fall within the 11.5 to 13.5 percent range.

You can see where to find the alcohol reading on a Canadian wine label in Figure 2-1, later, in the section on deciphering wine labels. Outside Canada, a wine's alcohol content is either on its front or back label — wineries are mandated to print it somewhere on the bottle.

What use are tannins?

Tannins can be found in all wines, but are more evident in reds. Tannins, as you can discover by chewing on the stalks, pits, and skins of grapes, taste bitter and harsh, rather like chewing on bark. They also leave your mouth feeling dry, especially on the roof of your mouth and gums.

TECHNICAL STUFF

Adding alcohol

Although it is illegal to add alcohol to a finished wine, some wine regions permit the augmentation of alcohol by adding sugar during fermentation.

This practise is called *chaptalization* (after an agricultural minister in Napoleon III's government, Jean-Antoine Chaptal, who legalized the custom in France in the latter part of the eighteenth century). When alcohol is added to fermenting wine, it kills the yeast and stops the fermentation before all the sugar is converted, leaving a sweeter wine with a higher alcohol content.

In cooler regions, such as Burgundy, Loire, and Alsace, winemakers are allowed to add sugar to the grape juice or fermenting must — but only to increase the alcohol content by a maximum of two degrees.

There is one instance when it *is* legal to add alcohol to finished wine, but it moves the wine into a different category — that of fortified wine, whose alcohol content ranges between 15 and 20 percent. This includes wines like sherry, port, and madeira. (If anyone ever says to you, "Have a madeira, m'dear," watch out — the alcohol content is usually about 18 percent.)

Oak barrels also have tannins, which are leeched out during aging. Over time, both grape and wood tannins soften up and eventually *precipitate* (fall out) into the wine as *sediment* (solids), and sink to the bottom of the container. If you see a very old bottle of red wine with what looks like dust particles in the bottom, these are tannins that have softened up to the point where they can no longer be suspended in the wine.

Like acidity, tannins provide structure to red wines that allows them to age for a long time. But tannins alone do not make for an age-worthy wine. It must have sufficient fruit extract that will remain in the wine after the tannins have softened.

Get to know these tannic titans. These four grape varieties contain copious amounts of tannins:

1. **Cabernet Sauvignon**, best known in the Bordeaux region for the aristocratic Médoc châteaux wines.

2. **Nebbiolo**, grown mostly in the Piedmont region of northern Italy and used in the great Barolos and Barbarescos.

3. **Syrah**, made famous by the regal northern Rhône appellation of Hermitage. Known as Shiraz in Australia and other New World wine regions.

4. **Tannat**, the basis of the blockbuster wines from the Madiran region in the Southwest of France.

In good vintages, wines made from these grapes can age 10 to 20 years. It is uncommon, though not unheard of, for wines to age much past 20 years.

What's this fifth element of wine?

Believe it or not, wooden barrels affect the way a wine tastes. Not only does the air in the barrel change the taste by oxidizing the wine, but also the wine's acidity draws out flavours from the wood, such as vanilla and spice. If the

Historic casks

If you visit wine cellars in Germany, Austria, Italy, or northeastern France, you may see large wooden casks that are up to 100 years old and still in use. The winemakers are proud of these ancient vessels.

However, these older barrels have scant influence on the wine's flavour because over time they become caked with potassium bitartrate crystals that form a barrier between the wine and the inside surface of the barrel. They also inhibit the passage of air between the staves.

inside of the barrel has been toasted, the wine may also pick up smoky or toasty aromas and flavours. New oak barrels impart more concentrated *vanillans* (vanilla flavours) and tannins than those that have been used for more than one harvest.

Barrel-aging helps to clarify and stabilize a wine; the smaller the barrel, the more the wood will influence the flavour of the wine. The most popular barrels currently used are the French *barriques* with a capacity of 225 or 250 litres. The wood is cut from forests in northern France with names such as Limousin, Nevers, Allier, and Vosges. When imported to Canada, the French barrels cost about C$900 apiece, so Canadian winemakers often use some American oak barrels, too. These cost about C$500 — a big savings. They make the wine smell different — but different in a good way. You can recognize a wine made in an American barrel by its spicy, ginger/clove, and peppery aromas.

A wine made in stainless steel tanks is generally less costly than one fermented and aged in oak barrels. New barrels are expensive and add greatly to the cost of a wine. Usually, winemakers employ a combination of new and used barrels to age their wines. To add complexity and freshness, they may blend wine made in stainless steel tanks with wine from oak barrels.

Deciphering a Canadian Wine Label

The purpose of the label on a bottle of wine is to tell you what is inside that bottle, what winemaking region it comes from, which winery/winemaker made it, the address of the winery, and the vintage (the year the grapes were grown) of the wine (unless it's a blend of two years, in which case no vintage date will be shown). Wherever wine is made, you'll find the same information on the label — even if you can't understand the language it's written in!

That elusive harmony

When all the elements in wine — sweetness (fruit), acidity, alcohol, and tannins — come together as intended, the wine achieves a harmony, or balance, that goes beyond the actual flavour. A well-balanced wine is one in which no single element stands out above the others. This is achieved only in the best vintages grown in ideal climates. In poor vintages, grapes are marked by either too much sunshine, or too little. An overabundance of heat and sun saps the acid from the grapes. Too little warmth diminishes the sugar content. Either can throw off the wine's balance. A winemaker who knows all the tricks of the trade may be able to compensate for these less-than-favourable conditions — but only to a certain degree.

Canadian wine labels are relatively easy to understand, for Canadians fluent in either of our two official languages! If your first and only language is anything besides English or French, it's not so easy.

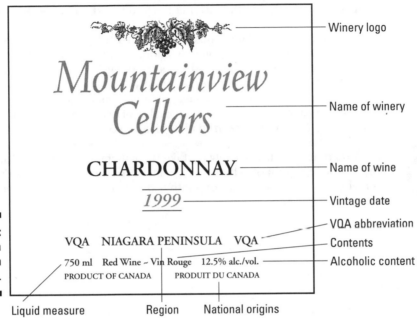

Figure 2-1:
Reading a
Canadian
wine label.

- ✔ **Winery logo:** Typically a stylized reproduction of the winery, a vineyard scene, or an abstract image.
- ✔ **Name of winery:** "Mountainview Cellars" in this case.
- ✔ **Name of wine:** Either a single grape variety (Chardonnay), two varieties (Sauvignon Blanc/Sémillon) if it's a blended wine, or a proprietary name (e.g. Hillebrand Truis Red).
- ✔ **Vintage date:** The year the grapes were harvested.
- ✔ **Vintners Quality Alliance abbreviation:** Canada's appellation system, which guarantees the grapes were grown 100 percent in the stated region.
- ✔ **Contents:** Description of what's in the bottle, in English and French.
- ✔ **Alcoholic content:** Amount of alcohol in the wine by volume.
- ✔ **National origins:** "Product of Canada" in English and French.
- ✔ **Region:** Designated Viticulture Area (DVA) where the grapes were grown.
- ✔ **Liquid measure:** 750 ml

The first thing you notice about all Canadian labels is that they are bilingual. Federal regulations demand that they be printed in both English and French. Figure 2-1 shows a typical Canadian wine label giving all the necessary information about the wine. By the way, don't go looking for a Canadian wine called Mountainview Cellars in your local wine store. It doesn't exist. Figure 2-1 is just an illustration to explain the information you'll find on Canadian wine labels.

In addition to the front label, most wineries use a back label to give more information about the wine. You may find mini history or geography lessons on the back of wine labels as producers try to entice you to purchase their wines. In many cases, the winemaker simply describes the wine (sometimes in exasperatingly convoluted language): how it tastes, how to serve it, and what foods best complement it. A back label also carries the winery's address and a bar code for computerized identification of the wine.

When reading a back label, always take the winemaker's description of his or her wine with a grain of salt. After all, wines are like the winemaker's children, and whoever heard a mother or a father describe their offspring as ugly!

Chapter 3

Getting to Know Your Berry

· ·

· ·

*T*he grape is the root of all wine, but not all grapes are created equal. Their basic structure may be the same — skin, pulp, pips, and stem, but the many varieties of grapes each have different characteristics and these become magnified and modified once the grapes have been transformed into the "elixir of the gods."

The grape itself has all that is needed to produce wine. Leave it to Mother Nature and, presto, there it is; but let a winemaker in on the act and it gets even better. Give the wine some time to age, and it might improve even more.

Some grapes make great weekday-night wine for under $10 a bottle; other grapes make even greater wine that you can buy for $1,000 a bottle about 50 years from now. And, of course, there's everything in between. That's where a grape's particular characteristics come into play.

Looking Closely at the Grape

In all wines, taste begins with the grape. The primary flavours of wine are in the juice and skins of the grape berries.

Try this simple tasting exercise:

1. Take a grape berry — any berry from a table grape to a grape grown for wine — and get up close and personal. You see it has a waxy bloom on the skin with a whitish powder sticking to it.

This powder is wild *yeast*, a natural substance that floats about in the vineyard and sticks to the bloom on the grape berries. Once these berries are crushed and the yeast comes into contact with the sweet juice inside, the fermentation starts, converting the sugar into alcohol and carbon dioxide gas in almost equal proportions. If the carbon dioxide gas is allowed to escape, the wine is *still* (without bubbles caused by carbonation). But if the gas remains trapped inside the bottle (or tank), the wine is *sparkling* (it has a bubbly appearance).

2. Detach the small stem from the berry and bite into it. Taste how bitter it is? The pits inside the berry also taste bitter and so does the grape skin once you've extracted the sweet pulp inside.

The bitter taste you experience is from the tannins. Tannins cannot be detected on the nose, but you can feel them as an astringent dryness on the roof of your mouth and gums, and you can taste it as bitterness — rather like overly strong tea.

Winemakers try to cut down the number of tannins in red wine by *destemming* the bunches of grapes before the fermentation starts. A machine is used to tear the stems and stalks away from the berries. This organic material doesn't go to waste: It's recycled in the vineyard as fertilizer along with the *pomace* (the grape skins and pits pressed out during fermentation).

Life Preservers for Wine: Tannins to the Rescue!

If tannins taste so bad and make your mouth pucker, what good are they and why would you want them in your wine? Tannins act as a preservative and give red wine the possibility of long life. It's sort of the genie in the bottle. Tannins also give the wine *structure* (a sensation of firmness on your palate). Some red wines can live for 100 years or more because of the preservative qualities of the tannins. Tony tasted a classic red Bordeaux when it was 110 years old — Château Lafite 1865 — and found it very much alive. It was somewhat pale in colour, but possessed a remarkable bouquet and flavour.

Most red wines, but not all, require aging to allow the tannins to soften. If you try to drink them too young, your mouth will tell you about it. These wines taste harsh and leave your tongue feeling like a piece of felt. The number of months or years required for aging depends on the grape variety.

In making red wine, winemakers leave the grape skins in the juice throughout the fermentation process to integrate the tannins into the liquid. At the same time, the wine absorbs its red colour from the pigment in the skins.

This technique works less well with white wine. Experience has shown that tannins cause white wines to taste bitter and astringent. Winemakers generally remove the skins from the juice of white grapes before fermentation. White wine relies on acidity to give it structure and age-worthiness.

Unfortunately, there is no hard and fast rule for the amount of time red wines need to "soften up." It depends on the grape variety, soil conditions, sunshine, rain, and the winemaking technique. In general terms, New World reds (such as wines from California, Australia, and Chile) take less time for the tannins to become supple than wines from Old World wine-growing regions, such as France, Italy, and Spain. Traditional European reds tend to need more time in the bottle to be table-ready. The many red wines that are made for early drinking, without aging, are usually less complex and less interesting than the more tannic, age-worthy wines.

There are some white wines that can age too (because of their high acidity or their residual sugar), but most of these are sweet dessert wines made from the Riesling, Sémillon, or Chenin Blanc grapes. The dry whites best known for their aging capacity come from Burgundy, the Loire Valley, and the Rhine and Mosel Valleys in Germany. These wines are based on the Chardonnay, Chenin Blanc, and Riesling grapes.

Contrasting Reds and Whites

If you press a white grape or a red grape you will get colourless (white) juice. There are a few grapes that give red juice, but virtually all the great red wines are made from grapes that contain white juice. Then there's the *Blanc de Noirs* phenomenon in champagne (a white sparkling wine that is made from two red grapes, Pinot Noir and Pinot Meunier).

Macerating makes the difference

As we indicated earlier, to produce a red wine, the juice from red grapes has to *macerate* (mix in and soak) with the skins. The acid in the grape juice breaks down the cells in the skins and releases colour. It also extracts the tannins. If the maceration period is short — 12 to 24 hours — the resulting wine is pink (*rosé*). If it's a week or two, depending on the variety, the wine is red.

During fermentation, the *must* (juice and solid bits of skin, seeds, and stems) gets hot, which encourages the absorption of colour and tannins. Some winemakers put their wine through a period of cold maceration, which changes the chemical reaction and, for some wines, improves the flavour.

Maceration can occur before, during, or after fermentation. The winemaker decides how long the maceration will last — it all depends on the type of grape and the style of wine desired. Some wines macerate for as long as four weeks.

White wines don't macerate

White wines do not usually undergo maceration, although some winemakers leave the skins of their white grapes in the juice for a period of four to eight hours before pressing, as this short soak can improve the wine's flavour without imparting any harshness.

Tannins may not be an option, but barrel fermentation and aging *on the lees* (leaving yeast solids in the wine) are techniques that can be used to promote ageability in white wine.

Carrying out fermentation in oak barrels works well for full-bodied whites, particularly Chardonnay, but not for lighter, delicate white wines. Just as red wine picks up colour and tannins from fermenting on its skins, white wine picks up a golden colour and butterscotch and vanilla flavours from the oak barrel. These strong flavours tend to kill the taste in any lighter wines.

Once fermentation is complete, solid particles start to sink to the bottom of the barrel — or fermentation vat, depending on which was used for the wine in question. Most of these bits are dead yeast cells — it doesn't sound very attractive, but that's what they are.

Eventually, these particles have to be removed from the wine so that it is clear when it goes into the bottle. But some wines increase in complexity if they are left on the lees for a few months, taking on a toasty/yeasty bouquet and flavour. Some winemakers even stir up the lees from time to time to increase the effect. Wine made in this way is often identified by the phrase "aged on the lees" or by the French term, *sur lie*, on the label.

Drinking red wine in its youth

Once fermentation has finished, how soon can you drink a red wine? In theory, right away, but in practise not for a few months or even a few years — with a few exceptions.

When wine ferments, it bubbles up and looks like it's boiling. All sorts of tiny bits of fruit and other vegetative gunk float around and it all looks really unappetizing. When fermentation stops, these bits take a while (months, actually) to sink to the bottom of the vat. The wine also stinks of yeast for quite a while and, if it's a tannic wine, a few sips may make your tongue feel like it's been rubbed with sandpaper. So, the wine needs to sit around for a time before you try to drink it.

If you are a particularly impatient person, there is one well-known red wine you *can* drink right away: Beaujolais Nouveau, a fruity wine from France made from Gamay grapes. Traditionally, this wine was rushed to the bistros in Beaujolais towns, probably because they had exhausted the last year's supply. This tradition then spread to nearby cities and even to Paris. Finally, the new wine became synonymous with a celebration of the harvest. Today, the tradition is enjoyed worldwide.

Beaujolais Nouveau undergoes a special type of fermentation process called *carbonic maceration* or *whole berry fermentation*. You can drink the wine early because of this. Here's how carbonic maceration works:

1. Whole bunches of grapes are dumped into a sealed stainless steel tank. The weight of the top grapes presses on those below and eventually breaks the skins of those at the bottom. The sugar in the juice comes in contact with the yeast and fermentation starts.

2. Once the yeast cells have consumed the sugar, they look around for more to eat, but the only available sugar is *inside* the berries — so that's where they go. Fermentation happens inside the skin of each berry as well, then, converting the sugar to alcohol. The other by-product, carbonic gas, rises up toward the top of the tank, but gets stuck at the top because the tank is, of course, sealed. The gas sits like a blanket on top of the *must* (the fermenting grapes).

3. After a matter of days, the winemaker lightly presses the grapes. The resulting wine, which is light and fruity, contains very few tannins and can be consumed with pleasure in a matter of weeks, though this rarely happens. Even Beaujolais Nouveau has to age a little longer than that.

Though Beaujolais is the most famous wine made by carbonic maceration, winemakers use this technique on other red grapes when they want to make a fruity wine for immediate consumption. Such wines are best served lightly chilled to bring out their fresh, fruity quality.

Thanks to carbonic maceration, you can satisfy your craving for fresh and fruity red wine. But this technique unfortunately contributes nothing to the wine's capacity to age. So it starts to deteriorate very quickly. As a rule of thumb, drink your Beaujolais Nouveau within six months of purchasing, though some Beaujolais Nouveaux can last up to a year.

You can buy Beaujolais Nouveau in mid-November, but quantities are usually very limited. The exact release date of the third Thursday in November is strictly regulated by the French government.

The French paradox

Red wine, taken in moderation, can be beneficial to your health. The skins of grapes contain a natural compound called *resveratrol* (pronounced rez-VER-a-trawl). It's a natural fungicide that develops in response to adverse conditions such as wet weather or infestation by insects and disease. It is present in the skins of all red grapes (though for some reason, possibly because its thin skin needs more protection, in higher concentrations in the Pinot Noir grape). Resveratrol turns up in the finished wine because the skins of the grapes remain in contact with the juice for a relatively long period of time during fermentation.

When consumed in finished wine, resveratrol acts as a kind of scrubbing agent in your arteries. It washes away low-density lipoproteins (the bad part of cholesterol that causes the sticky platelets to build up and clog blood flow, causing heart problems).

The presence of resveratrol in red wines may explain The French Paradox — how the French can eat quantities of fatty foods, such as cream, butter, cheeses, and foie gras, and yet have one of the lowest rates of heart disease in the world.

Many doctors recommend the moderate consumption of red wine to protect against heart disease.

With the popularity of Beaujolais Nouveau, wine producers other than the French wanted to get in on the act. In recent years, Italy has shipped a number of *vini novelli* (new wines), both red and white, to Canada in order to compete. They are usually a bit less expensive than the French versions. Check your wine shop in November to see what is available.

Some Canadian producers have also taken their turn at making new wines, but they are few and far between at this stage. The important thing is that the wine undergoes carbonic maceration — so if you are buying a "nouveau" wine, be sure to ask if that procedure has been followed. (If the Canadian "nouveau" is identified as a VQA wine by the symbol on the capsule, you can be sure the correct procedure has been used — that's your guarantee.)

The only Beaujolais producers to ship Beaujolais Nouveau to Canada in quantity are the large bottlers and shippers. Some reliable ones are Duboeuf, Bouchard Aîné, and Jaffelin. Italian producers include Frescobaldi, Ruffino, Folonari, and Lamberti. There are so few Canadians producing these wines at present that you should try any one you can find.

Exploring the Variety of the Grape World

You may be familiar with the names of some of the more common grape varieties, but others may seem bizarre and unpronounceable. Table 3-1 helps you decipher wine lists and labels — use it to brush up the next time you're heading for a four-star restaurant. Your effortless enunciation will make you sound like an expert!

Table 3-1	Grape Names and Pronunciation at a Glance	
Grape Variety	*Type of Wine Produced*	*Pronunciation*
Aligoté	white	Ali-got-ay
Alvarinho	white	Alvar-ee-no
Auxerrois	white	Awks-er-wah
Bacchus	white	Back-us
Baco Noir	red	Back-oh-Nwar
Barbera	red	Bar-bare-a
Cabernet Franc	red	Caburn-eh Fronk
Cabernet Sauvignon	red	Caburn-eh So-vin-non
Canaiolo	red	Can-I-owe-low
Carignan	red	Carin-yan
Carmenère	red	Car-men-air
Chardonnay	white	Shar-don-eh
Chardonnay Musqué	white	Shar-don-eh Moos-kay
Chasselas	white	Shass-el-lass
Chenin Blanc	white	Shen-in-Blonk
Cinsaut	red	San-so
Colombard	white	Col-om-bard
Cortese	white	Cor-tay-zee
Corvina	red	Cor-veen-a
de Chaunac	red	Duh-Shown-ak
Dolcetto	red	Doll-chetto
Dornfelder	red	Dorn-fell-der

(continued)

Table 3-1 *(continued)*

Grape Variety	Type of Wine Produced	Pronunciation
Durif	red	Dew-reef
Ehrenfelser	white	Aaron-fel-zer
Furmint	white	Fir-mint
Gamay	red	Ga-may
Gewürztraminer	white	Gev-ertz-tram-eener
Grechetto	white	Grey-ketto
Grenache	red	Gren-ash
Grignolino	red	Grin-yo-lean-o
Grüner Veltliner	white	Grooner-Velt-leaner
Kerner	white	Cur-ner
Limberger	red	Lim-burger
Macabeo	white	Mack-a-bayo
Malvasia	white	Mal-va-zee-a
Maréchal Foch	red	Mar-eh-shall Fosh
Marsanne	white	Mar-san
Merlot	red	Mare-low
Mourvèdre	red	Moor-ved-ra
Müller-Thurgau	white	Mewller-Tur-gow
Nebbiolo	red	Neb-ee-ollo
Petit Verdot	red	Petty-Vair-dough
Picolit	white	Pick-o-leet
Pinot Blanc	white	Pea-no Blawnk
Pinot Gris	white	Pea-no Gree
Pinot Noir	red	Pea-no Nwar
Pinotage	red	Pea-no-tage
Primitivo	red	Prima-teev-o
Prosecco	white	Pro-seck-o
Riesling	white	Reez-ling

Grape Variety	Type of Wine Produced	Pronunciation
Roussanne	white	Rue-san
Sangiovese	red	San-gee-o-vaise-ee
Sauvignon Blanc	white	Sew-veen-yon Blawnk
Sémillon	white	Say-me-yon
Silvaner	white	Sil-vahn-er
Syrah	red	See-rah
Tempranillo	red	Tem-pran-ill-o
Trebbiano	white	Tray-bee-ano
Verdicchio	white	Verdi-kee-o
Vernaccio	white	Vehr-natch-ee-o
Vidal	white	Vee-dall
Viognier	white	Vee-on-ee-eh
Zinfandel	red	Zin-fan-dell

Labelling for Variety

In Europe (known as the *Old World* in wine circles, because it has a long-established practise and style of winemaking), the tradition is to name wine based on the geographical region where the grapes are grown.

One of the best-known wines identified by geographic nomenclature is Chianti. It is named for a wine-producing region located between Florence and Siena in the Tuscany region of Italy. It would be particularly difficult to name this wine for a grape type, as the regulations state that up to 13 different varieties of grape may be used in the blend — which one would you choose?

The labels of most French wines take it one step further and give the name of the village or commune nearest to the vineyard: Chablis, Corton-Charlemagne, Pouilly-Fuissé, for example. All three of these wines are made with the Chardonnay grape in the Burgundy region, but the differing *terroirs* (soil, exposure, weather conditions) create their own local flavours and style. (See Chapter 4 for more details on vineyards and grape-growing.)

In the *New World* (the term refers to regions outside of Europe where the practise of winemaking is fairly recent, and where newer, different winemaking styles are employed), we name wines based on the grape variety from which they are produced. We call wine Chardonnay, for example, rather than Niagara-on-the-Lake, Beamsville, or Grimsby — winemaking regions in Ontario. This method of describing wine is simpler for consumers in the beginning. But when you realize that virtually all the world's wine-producing regions make a Chardonnay, it's more difficult to distinguish among them in terms of their style and taste profile by the grape name alone. A California Chardonnay has a very different taste from one grown in Ontario or British Columbia. And what about New Zealand Chardonnay? Or South African? In Chapter 6 you can find more information on comparing wines from around the world.

A varietal wine can be named for any one of the grape types in Table 3-1 — but what if there is no grape name on the label? How do you know what grape the wine is made of? Well, sometimes you don't! If the wine has a *proprietary name* (a brand name such as Grand Am in the automobile industry) like Brights' L'Oiseau Bleu or Andrés' Hochtaler, you may like the sound of the name, but you aren't any further ahead in knowing what is inside the bottle. These wines are inexpensive blends and may vary in content from batch to batch, but careful blending ensures they always taste the same.

If you find a wine that is named for a geographical region, you are much better off because that name tells you what grape or grapes have been used. It's true! If the wine is named Bordeaux, the laws in France stipulate what grapes can be used. It's the same in all the European grape-producing countries. The chart in Table 3-2 helps you get the hang of geographical names and the grapes that grow there.

Table 3-2   Geographic Regions and the Grapes That Grow There

Geographic Region Identified on the Label	What Grapes Are Used
Barolo/Barbaresco	Nebbiolo
Beaujolais	Gamay
Bordeaux (red)	Merlot, Cabernet Sauvignon, Cabernet Franc
Bordeaux (white)	Sémillon, Sauvignon Blanc
Burgundy (red)	Pinot Noir, Gamay
Burgundy (white)	Chardonnay, Aligoté
Champagne	Pinot Noir, Pinot Meunier, Chardonnay
Châteauneuf-du-Pape	Up to 13 different grape types, but the most important are Grenache, Syrah, Mourvèdre, Cinsaut
Chianti	Sangiovese, Canaiolo
Valpolicella	Corvina, Rondinella, Molinara, Negrara

Chapter 4

In the Vineyard

- -

- -

*A*ny winemaker will tell you that great wine is not made in the cellar; it's made in the vineyard. Just as a chef can only make a wonderful dish by using the freshest and most flavourful ingredients, so the winemaker must seek out the ripest grapes, free from rot, leaves, and bits of vine, to be able to produce the finest wine.

To use a cliché, you can't make a silk purse out of a sow's ear. The raw material has to be good to begin with. (You can make a sow's ear out of a silk purse, though. If winemakers are not careful, they can spoil good grapes.) In this chapter you get the scoop on how grapes are planted, pampered, and grown to become the most promising winemaking fruit.

All Grapes Are Not Created Equal

Literally thousands of different kinds of grapes are grown around the world, but not all of them are worthy of being turned into wine. The grapes you eat, for example, would make very poor wine. They may be sweet, but they lack balancing acidity that gives structure to wine. Of some 5,000 different varieties of grapes, only a few hundred are cultivated for wine production.

Most grapes fall into one of these four categories, all of differing quality:

1. ***Vitis vinifera (vitis* is Latin for vine): A species of wine grape native to Europe, now grown in many countries around the world.** These are the so-called noble varieties and include the names on labels you'll be most familiar with — Chardonnay, Sauvignon Blanc, Pinot Gris, Cabernet Sauvignon, Merlot, Pinot Noir, and so on. Indisputably, the best grapes for wine.

2. *Vitis labrusca*: **A species of table grape native to North America.** Labrusca, and some similar species (*riparia, rotundifolia,* and *aestivalis*) were discovered centuries ago growing wild in North America, Mexico, and the Caribbean. These vines are winter-hardy and disease-resistant, easy to grow, and produce a lot of grape bunches. The only problem is that the wines don't taste very good; they have a "foxy" bouquet and flavour. ("Foxy" is difficult to define but can best be described as a pungent, slightly unpleasant odour and taste. You only have to experience it once.) You've probably tasted labrusca grapes without knowing it — grape jams, jellies, and soft drinks are flavoured with such varieties as Concord (red) and Niagara (white).

3. **Hybrids: The crossing of two varieties of grape species.** To improve the flavour of North American labrusca grapes, early *viticulturists* (grape growers) crossed them with more desirable *Vitis vinifera* varieties from Europe. The resulting offspring share the best characteristics of both parents — the sturdiness of labrusca and the more refined smell and taste of vinifera. Baco Noir, for instance, is a hybrid of Folle Blanche, a vinifera grape grown in the Cognac region of France, and a North American *Vitis riparia* grape. (A French viticulturist, François Baco, made the match in 1902.)

4. **Crossings: Similar to hybrids in that they are the result of "marrying" two different grapes.** But in this case, the grapes are from the same species, that is, both *Vitis vinifera*. This is done to produce a grape that ripens early, yields more fruit, and is less prone to disease and winterkill. An example of a crossing is the German grape, Müller-Thurgau — a cross between Riesling and Silvaner (created by Dr. Hermann Müller).

Where Wine Grapes Grow — And How!

Wine grapes can thrive in moderate to warm climates. Below 10° Celsius (50° Fahrenheit), a vine closes down and will not grow. In Figure 4-1 you can see two bands across the globe indicating the temperature range and climatic conditions vines need to flourish. Areas most suited to grape-growing are shaded. Any area 30° to 50° latitude north of the equator and roughly 30° to 40° south of it can be suitable for grape-growing. Outside these zones, the weather is either too hot or too cold to support *Vitis vinifera* vines.

The temperate zones in the Northern Hemisphere run from North Africa to Germany, including parts of China and Russia. On the North American continent, the band stretches from the southern United States to Ontario in the East and from Southern California to British Columbia in the West.

In the Southern Hemisphere, the growing zones take in Chile, Argentina, Uruguay, and parts of Brazil, as well as the Cape region of South Africa, New Zealand, and the southern, coastal areas of Australia.

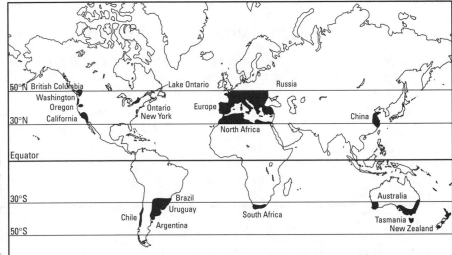

Figure 4-1:
International
grape-
growing
zones.

You can find some grapevines outside of the generally accepted grape-growing territory, such as in southern England, but these grapes don't always ripen. In hotter regions, such as Lebanon and Mexico, wine grapes are grown high in the hills where temperatures aren't so scorching.

Why vines should struggle

Unlike other fruits and crops, wine grapes do best in poor soil. This isn't as heartless as it sounds. If you plant a vine in rich soil, it gets lazy and apathetic. Rather like sitting around eating chocolates all day. For best results, grapevines have to compete. Unlike most people, grapevines must enjoy stress — they invariably do their best work under duress.

If you look at a vineyard, you'll see that it's planted quite densely; the vines are close together in rows to force them to compete with each other for nourishment from the soil. Their roots have to go straight down — and down deep — to find moisture, instead of spreading out just below the surface of the soil. By driving their roots several metres into the ground, the vines pick up trace minerals from the different soils they pass through as they seek that coveted moisture.

Trace minerals in the soil add complexity of flavour to wine and give you a sense of the wine's *terroir* when you taste it — literally the flavour of the soil. In the Champagne district of northern France, the soil is pure chalk; in the Mosel region of Germany, it's slate; in the Médoc region of Bordeaux, it's gravelly. Each soil imparts a characteristic and recognizable taste to the grapes grown in it.

When a vine is over the hill

A grapevine has a productive life of about 40 years, after which it begins to lose its vigour and produce less grape clusters. Most wineries will replant their vineyards in stages so that they have a mix of varying ages among their vines. However, some vines in warm, frost-free climates can live well beyond their allotted span. Australian Shiraz and California Zinfandel have been known to produce fruit from vines that are over 100 years old. These geriatric vines only produce a few clusters — but the fruit flavour can be extremely concentrated.

Like a tree, the older a vine grows, the fatter its trunk. A new vine is about as thick as a pencil. After 25 years, though, you won't be able to get the fingers of both hands around its trunk.

How grapes get sweet

Grapevines rely on soil, water, and sunshine to produce leaves and fruit. The leaves absorb sunlight and by *photosynthesis* (the process by which the energy of sunlight is used to synthesize carbohydrates from carbon dioxide and water) convert this energy into sugar — the sweet taste you experience in the berries.

Photosynthesis has to do with sunlight and plant growth. The energy from sunlight creates sugar in grapes through a biochemical reaction: This is effected by the combination of water in the leaves of a grapevine and the carbon dioxide in the air around it. The green chlorophyll pigments in the leaves capture the sun's energy and convert it into grape sugars.

The amount of sunlight grapes are exposed to during the growing season directly affects the amount of sugar produced in each grape. Brighter years mean sweeter grapes. More sun also means a potentially higher alcohol content. Wine regions that enjoy long growing seasons, free of cloud cover, produce grapes with a higher sugar content than those in cooler, damp climates. Think of the weather in the Champagne district of northeast France or the Rheingau in Germany. Now compare that to the climate in California or Australia. When you think of California and Australia, you think of sun and surf. When you think of France and Germany, you remember that the Europeans carry umbrellas for good reason!

If you compare a California or Australian Cabernet Sauvignon with an Ontario, British Columbia, or even a red wine from Bordeaux made predominantly from Cabernet Sauvignon, you can experience the difference that consistently warm weather has on the ripeness level of the grapes. California and Australia Cabernets show jammy, full-bodied fruit, while the cooler climate Canadian Cabernets or red Bordeaux are more elegant, leaner, and apparently acidic.

But both styles have their place on your dining-room table. It all depends on what you're serving them with. We have some suggestions for food and wine combinations in Chapter 14.

Red wines from warm climates have riper, more luscious fruit than reds grown in cool climates. For example, Cabernet Sauvignon-based wines grown in California, Australia, or Chile will be fatter and more concentrated in flavour than their counterparts grown in Bordeaux or Canada. Cooler-climate reds will be leaner and more sinewy. The style you prefer is a matter of taste. Similarly, with white wines, those grown in warm climates taste richer and rounder since the grapes are riper. But they also have less acidity than cool-climate whites, which means the winemaker may have to *acidify* the wine (add acid to the wine, usually before fermentation) to make it more balanced and give it freshness.

Give these warm-climate wines a try: In the red category, go for Rosemount Estates Cabernet Sauvignon (Australia) or Cline Zinfandel (California). As far as whites go, try Wolf Blass Chardonnay (Australia) or Fetzer Sundial Chardonnay (California). In the mood for something a little chillier? A good cool-climate red is Château Bonnet (Bordeaux, France). Try also the white Fèvre Chablis Champs Royaux (Burgundy, France).

Some Canadian cool-climate selections: Stoney Ridge Cabernet Franc (ON) (red), Mission Hill Pinot Blanc (BC) (white).

Wines from South America, South Africa, Australia, and New Zealand are six months older than wines from wine regions in the Northern Hemisphere bearing the same vintage date. South of the equator, grape harvesting is done anywhere between February, March, and April, but north of the equator, it isn't done until August, September, or October.

The cool connection

If you live in Canada, you know all about cool and cold. Most Canadians try to avoid it, or at least forget about it.

Wine grapes don't particularly like the cold either, but they are in their element if they can get a good dose of cooler temperatures. Grapes *can* grow in hot climates, but they're not necessarily that good for making wine.

Most of the world's great wines are made in what are considered cool climates. These include Bordeaux, Burgundy, Alsace, Loire, and Champagne in France, along with Germany and Austria. Many cool New World areas (non-European regions whose wine-growing activities are fairly recent) are producing some noteworthy wines. These include Oregon, parts of Washington, and even parts of regions normally considered warm climates like northern California in the U.S., southern Chile, and New Zealand's South Island.

A cool climate in winemaking terms is characterized by a long, steady period of growth with lots of sunshine. These conditions result in complex flavours and acidity. Intense heat, on the other hand, promotes rapid maturation and high sugar levels that translate into high alcohol and highly concentrated, flavourful wines with little or no subtlety.

Hot-climate wines are characterized by intense fruit flavours and full body. And they don't often have the acid needed to balance this intensity. Although these wines can be very impressive initially, they often tire the palate and lack the refreshing attributes of the lighter wines. The ideal in winemaking is to achieve good concentration of flavour with enough acid to provide structure and equilibrium.

None of the famous regions mentioned above are known for snow and cold the way Canada is, but the mean temperature during the summer growing season is cool enough that later-ripening grapes don't necessarily make it to full maturity. Fortunately, the majority of the most desirable wine grapes are either early or mid-season ripeners.

Table 4-1 lists some of the greatest early and mid-season grapes and where they earned their enviable reputation. These are the varieties that hold the most promise for the cool-climate wine industry in Canada.

Table 4-1	The Great Cool-Climate Grapes
Grape Variety	*Region*
Cabernet Franc	Bordeaux
Cabernet Sauvignon	Bordeaux
Chardonnay	Burgundy
Gamay	Beaujolais
Gewürztraminer	Alsace and Germany
Merlot	Bordeaux
Pinot Blanc	Alsace
Pinot Noir	Burgundy
Riesling	Alsace and Germany
Sauvignon Blanc	Bordeaux and Loire
Syrah	Northern Rhône

A History of Mediocrity

For many years, too few people believed that Canada could grow the grapes needed to produce decent wine. That Canada could make great wine was not even a consideration until quite recently — the mid-1970s. Before that, Canadian wine was barely fit for consumption. Up until the Second World War, Canadians had little exposure to the great wines of Europe. Most people were content to sip mediocre, sweet, highly alcoholic wines usually labelled as "sherry" or "port." (They were known as "Block and Tackle wines": You drank a bottle, walked a block, and could tackle anyone!) The vineyards that existed in Ontario and British Columbia at the time supplied a handful of wineries that were turning out a variety of table wines as well as some *fortified* (alcohol-enhanced) wines made in the style of sherry and port.

Back then, any experimentation with respect to importing European varieties and hybrids had little impact on the industry. But, finally, in 1975, a tiny groundswell of determined Canadian winemakers burst onto the scene with their limited, but promising, selection of vinifera wines. If you want to read more strange and wonderful stories about the history of winemaking in Canada, replete with equally strange and wonderful characters, look at Chapter 17.

The only real impediment to growing these fantastic grapes in Canada is the weather. Even if the best wine grapes are cool-climate grapes, Canada is usually just a little *too cool*. Vinifera vines need between 160 and 180 frost-free days to ripen, and a mean temperature of 16° Celsius during the April – October growing season. They can't survive temperatures below –23° Celsius, so don't go looking for vineyards in Nunavut or even Manitoba any time soon. Global warming has to hit new heights before vinifera grapes will survive there.

A Year in a Canadian Vineyard

Only recently has the rest of the world come to learn and appreciate that Canada is a wine-growing country, like France, Italy, Germany, and Spain. When Europeans think about Canada, the first image that springs to mind — after red-coated Mounties — is winter landscapes. It's a revelation to them that we can grow grapes and make wine. Just how do we do it? What does it take to make a vineyard flourish in Canada?

As far as you're concerned, the year begins on the first day of January. But not in the vineyard. Nothing happens during the winter months in terms of growth. All you can see are the pruned vine stocks that look like black fists sticking out of the ground, waiting to come alive again as the weather warms up.

When spring arrives, things really start happening. In Canada, as in all wine-growing regions in the Northern Hemisphere, spring starts in March. South of the equator, it's September. Table 4-2 maps out the wine-growing season in Canada, month by month, taking note of what happens to the grapes and what the *growers* (the farmers who actually grow the grapes) do to them to bring them along.

Table 4-2   The Canadian Wine-Growing Season Month by Month

Month	What the Grapes Do	What the Growers Do
March	Air temperature reaches 10° Celsius (50° Fahrenheit)	Plant new vines
		Plough between rows; spray vines to protect from insects and fungi
	Vines wake up from winter slumber	
	Buds on vines begin to swell	
	New shoots produce leaves	
April	Underground root systems begin to grow	Spray vines again (you can never be too safe)
	Weather warms up, more leaf growth	
May	New shoots grow more rapidly	Tie new shoots to *trellising wires*; sink posts into the earth at regular intervals and string with wires to support the vines
	Grape clusters begin to appear	Trim back other vegetation (leaves) so vines' energy goes into growing grapes
June	Air temperature reaches 15° Celsius (60° Fahrenheit), grape clusters burst into flower	Spray vines again (hey, why not?)
	Fruit-set period begins (fertilized flowers develop into fruit)	Perform *cluster thinning*, (removal of excess grape clusters), so that each vine produces the right amount of fruit

Month	What the Grapes Do	What the Growers Do
July	40–50 days into fruit-set period, grape berries begin to change colour and ripen (called *veraison*)	Perform a *green harvest*, cutting away some of the smaller bunches so that those remaining mature with more concentrated sugars and flavour components
August	Grapes are larger; well-defined clusters form	
	Sugar content rises through *photosynthesis*, the action of sunlight on the vines' leaves	
	Harvest begins in warmer regions	
September	Harvest period	
October – November	Harvest continues in cooler regions	
	Leaves on vines turn colour and begin to fall	
	Action moves indoors to cellars, where grapes are pressed and fermented	
December		Cut back vines significantly so that new ones can sprout next year

Many of the wineries in Canada offer vineyard tours that illustrate what happens to the vines throughout the year. You can find more information in the winery profiles in Chapters 18, 19, and 20.

The best time to visit a Canadian winery is in the late spring, summer, or fall. Don't go in winter. A vineyard under snow is not an appealing sight. All you see are cut-back vines sticking out of the frozen ground like so many exhausted soldiers on the march. Besides, you may not find the winemaker in residence in winter (probably on vacation).

The *busiest* time in a vineyard is around the harvest (September – October) and the smaller wineries may not have the personnel to show you around then as everyone will be participating in the crush.

The French have calculated from experience that 100 days pass between the flowering of the vine and the point at which the clusters of grapes are ready for picking.

The case for spraying

Spraying is done in the vineyard to protect grapevines against insects, rot, and fungi, and to control weeds.

These days, with more emphasis on environmentally friendly methods of pest and rot control, growers are using organic products and cutting the use of sulphur (which is normally used to treat the vines) to a minimum. (Sulphur is used in the vineyard as a fungicide, and in the winery as a disinfectant. It reacts with oxygen to prevent oxidation and is widely used for the preservation of fruit of all types.)

Organic wines can only be made successfully in warm regions with low humidity. Wetness in the vineyard encourages the growth of moulds, which causes the bunches to rot.

You *can* find organically grown wines though they don't have the shelf life of wines containing *sulphites*. They tend to oxidize quicker.

As a general rule, Canadian winemakers limit the use of chemicals in the vineyard and winery as much as possible, but very few wines are 100 percent organic.

Weathering the Vintage

We have painted an ideal portrait of the growing season in Table 4-2, but Mother Nature doesn't always make life easy for the grape grower or the winemaker. Weather patterns vary every year and nothing can be taken for granted.

A *vintage date*, or *vintage*, refers to the year in which the wine is harvested. The quality of the vintage results from the growing conditions over the course of that particular year up to and including the harvest itself. Weather can make or break the vintage.

All through the year, the vines stand vulnerable, exposed to Mother Nature's vengeance or benevolence. The winemaker's arsenal is strong, but never strong enough to reverse all of the damage caused by weather's devastation. When nature is cooperative wine can be sublime, but at each stage in the yearly cycle of the grapevine things can go terribly wrong.

In the winter, the vine is dormant. You'd think it would be safe. But none of the great wine grapes are winter-hardy. You can't get a Cabernet Sauvignon vine to grow in Ottawa any more than you can get a palm tree to grow there.

Even in the balmy climes of southern Ontario and southern British Columbia, the risk of heavy freeze lurks around the corner. It may happen, on average, only once every 20 years, but it can ruin the crop. Temperatures that scrape the bottom of the barrel, down around –25° Celsius, can split the trunk of the vine, opening a wound that exposes tender plant tissues and invites disease. One of the most common of these diseases is a bacteria called Crown Gall.

The bacteria cause tumours to grow over the surface of the trunk. Already weakened, the vine has little resistance. If the vine survives, its weakened condition seriously inhibits the production of grapes. In Canada and other cold climates, grape growers often allow the vines to produce two or more trunks. So if only one trunk is harmed, the others can take up the slack. Ideally, one trunk is preferred because it generally gives better-quality grapes, but having a back-up (or two) eliminates the financial loss of a ruined crop.

Frost warnings

If the vines make it to spring, more dangers await. Warming temperatures and longer hours of daylight coax the sleeping vines back to life. But in March, April, and even May, cool climates can surprise the viticulturist with a sudden cold snap. A killing frost can damage buds, young shoots, and leaves. The usual result is for the affected parts to turn brown and fall off. This is a serious problem, but not a total disaster. The vines continue to grow and replace their lost parts. However, this growth starts later and can delay ripening later on in the season. Winemakers may have to pick before optimal ripening is attained and the wines suffer from grapes lacking sugar. These less-than-excellent grapes make the wine thin and lacking in fruit flavours.

An astute vineyardist can provide a bit of a compromise. Pruning the vines in the early spring as opposed to during the winter can delay budding. This decreases the risk of frost damage but doesn't delay budding so much that ripening is compromised.

Sometimes, extreme methods are required. Growers place huge fans in the vineyard to move the air around and prevent frost from settling. Some growers hire a helicopter to perform the same function. Others install sprinkler irrigation systems to spray their vines, hoping that the heat produced as the water evaporates gives the vines that extra bit of protection. But all these methods are costly, so it's usually the larger producers that use them. In Canada, however, our climate makes this kind of treatment a necessity. Many producers, therefore, bite the bullet and go ahead with it.

Singing in the sunshine

The elements of sun and rain play a pivotal role during the growing season. Sunshine on the leaves encourages photosynthesis, the chemical reaction that causes the plant-nourishing sugars to form and the vine to grow and produce fruit. Sun also warms the soil, which can hold sufficient heat to defeat a spring frost.

The sun's perilous side is only a minor consideration in Canada. If the sun is very hot, it can burn and dry out the grape skin. Pinot Noir, with its very thin skin, is particularly susceptible to this. But even drought is welcome in Canada's vineyards. A hot dry summer results in wine with more concentrated flavours. British Columbia's Okanagan Valley, some of which is a desert, has an advantage in this respect.

Crying in the rain

Rain is not without its redeeming features. Grapevines require water to grow, particularly in the spring, which is the period of greatest growth. And, when moisture on the leaves and grapes evaporates, it releases heat that can protect against frost damage. But too much of a good thing always spells trouble, and too much rain causes all sorts of problems. It reduces the hours of sunlight, which slows the growth of the plant. If moisture remains on the leaves and grapes, it provides a marvellous environment for the growth of fungus and mould.

Very heavy rain causes water to sit in the surface of the ground, keeping the soil cool and more conducive to frost. The composition of the soil and the lay of the land are critical in preventing this sort of water retention by allowing for adequate drainage. Removing any weeds growing around the vines also helps the ground dry out and warm up.

Lots of rain favours leaf growth, and too many leaves use up the nutrients needed to develop the grapes. Leaves also create too much shade. The best situation is when each leaf on the vine is exposed to the sun. Excess foliage, by casting shadows on other leaves, hinders photosynthesis.

As harvest time approaches, rain is definitely unwelcome. The water is absorbed into the grapes, swelling the berries and diluting flavours. Even worse, the engorged grapes may split their skins. If this happens, fermentation can start right there on the vine, or fungal and bacterial infections may strike. If winemakers know rain is coming and their harvest date is imminent, many bring the grapes in early rather than risk a washed-out harvest.

Harsh lessons

In warmer climates, springtime is when the tender new growth is the most susceptible to severe weather. But the risks in cool climates exist all through the year. High winds or hail can rip the leaves and defoliate the vines, knock grape bunches to the ground, and split the skins leaving them exposed to rot and mould. Characteristically, these conditions are very localized and affect

The friendly fungus

Fungus and mould are among the most difficult problems to control in the vineyard. The least bit of moisture can provide the ideal environment for their spread. However, there is one fungal growth that is welcome: *Botrytis cinerea*, more familiarly called "noble rot." Although it is discouraged during most of the growing season, its appearance on ripe grapes destined to be made into dessert wine is an occasion for celebration. As this fungus consumes the grapes, they dehydrate and become very sweet. The wine acquires a honey-like bouquet and flavour. The grapes look really gross, but the wine tastes wonderful. This condition occurs in most years in Sauternes, the great French dessert wine region, and in Germany, where Botrytis-affected wines are called *Trockenbeerenauslese*. It occurs occasionally in Canadian vineyards, but is by no means widespread.

only part of a region. Like the aftermath of a tornado, sometimes one vineyard is decimated while its neighbour is spared. In an area like Bordeaux in France, where the Médoc is known for its Cabernet Sauvignon grape and St. Émilion for its Merlot, you can have split vintages, with excellent wines in one area and less successful ones in another. In Canada, where vines are more mixed, you can have vintages that favour either earlier-ripening varieties or later ones, depending on when the bad weather hits. The Pinot Noir and Merlot grapes might be fermenting merrily away when a storm wipes out the Cabernet Sauvignon still hanging on the vines.

Once the cool weather moves in the autumn, growth slows again and the vines are less susceptible to damage. But, if grapes are still hanging on the vine for late harvesting, or if they've been reserved for Icewine, rain, wind, and hail can still knock that precious fruit to the ground.

The Education Advantage

There is an enormous amount to learn about growing grapes and making wine. The basics are simple. Anyone can learn to ferment wine, it's not rocket science. But if you want to make great wine year after year in good vintages and bad, you might need a little help. Winemaking in the 21st century, whether in the established Old World regions of Europe or the emerging New World wine regions of the Americas and the Pacific, has shifted its emphasis away from the artistic approach and into the realm of technology. To make really good wine, you need to think like a scientist — maybe not like a rocket scientist but at least like a biochemist.

Way back when, it was the older generation that educated the younger in the family winemaking traditions. And while there is much to be said for this method, it is slow to recognize new methodology even though most children want to improve on what they learn from their parents. Or, if the parents happen to be welders or bankers, they are not much use to the child who wants to make wine.

Winemaking as a science was formalized at the end of the 19th century with the founding of several important university-based wine institutes that combined research with higher learning. There may be many schools around the world that provide courses on growing grapes and making wine, but there are only a handful that grant bachelor-level or graduate degrees. Each of these is located at the heart of a great winemaking region.

- ✔ **Bordeaux University's Institute of Oenology:** Founded in 1880, this world-renowned winemaking school grants both undergraduate and graduate degrees. The university emphasizes the importance of tasting and the analysis of flavour characteristics.

- ✔ **Geisenheim in the Rheingau, Germany:** This is one of the world's oldest wine schools, founded in 1872. Its current emphasis is on education and applied research centred on minimizing the need for fertilizers and pesticides in the vineyard.

- ✔ **Roseworthy Agricultural College in South Australia:** Founded in 1883 following the recommendations of a government commission on agriculture, this college now offers a Bachelor of Science in *Oenology* (the study of wine), a Graduate Diploma in Wine, and an Associate Diploma in Wine Marketing.

- ✔ **University of California at Davis:** Founded in 1880 by an order of state to open a research station and teach oenology, this campus gives direction to the grape and wine industries. It has earned a highly respected reputation worldwide — particularly for research. For over 100 years, Davis was the only university in North America to grant a degree in this field.

- ✔ **University of Montpellier:** Located in the south of France, the university founded its School of Agronomy in 1872 in response to problems of epidemic proportions with powdery mildew (in small-size grapes), downy mildew (causes the leaves to drop off), and phylloxera (an aphid that bores into the roots of the vine). The school is now best known for its work in viticulture, although it does offer courses in winemaking.

These institutions combine education with research and, as well, maintain experimental vineyards and nurseries. Besides book learning, students spend practical time in labs and even get right out in the fields, obtaining valuable firsthand experience.

Canada has entered this increasingly important field of education in wine production very recently. Established in 1996 at Brock University, the Cool Climate Oenology and Viticulture Institute (CCOVI) is the only institute in the world to specialize in the requirements of cool-climate wine production. Located at the heart of the Niagara Peninsula, Canada's largest wine-producing region, its creation followed on discussions with industry leaders, government agencies, and the university itself.

At the undergraduate level, students can earn an Honours Bachelor of Science degree in oenology and viticulture — the only program of its kind in Canada. While the degree's focus is scientific, students also learn about wine as it applies to marketing and tourism, and obtain practical skills during internships in vineyards and wineries. Biotechnology is the core of the program, which includes courses on fermentation technology, viticultural practises, wine microbiology, wine analysis, and sensory evaluation of wine. Students may also choose to continue their education in oenology and viticulture in Brock's postgraduate program.

To complement its degree programs, CCOVI offers non-degree options such as a certificate program in grape and wine technology and courses in wine sales and service training for the industry. Many of these classes are scheduled to accommodate the demands of seasonal work. Courses in wine appreciation are available to the general public through the Continuing Education department.

Take a tour of Canada's winemaking school

The Cool Climate Oenology Viticulture Insititute (CCOVI), at Brock University, accepted its first students in 1996 and graduated its first class in 2000. The institute is housed in a recent addition to the science complex at Brock University. Inniskillin Hall, named for Inniskillin Winery, Niagara's first "boutique" winery, comprises 24,000 square feet over three storeys. On the top floor are the labs: a viticulture research laboratory, a fermentation laboratory, two undergraduate laboratories, six temperature-controlled rooms, a sensory room (for tasting), and two offices. Experimental wine is made in very small quantities in the fermentation lab, which leads to larger-scale experiments in a pilot winery. The goals are to improve viticultural practises and winemaking technology.

The ground floor is devoted to biotechnology research and analysis of data. Research facilities include computer labs, an incubator and cold rooms for temperature-controlled situations,

the pilot winery, a conference room containing journals and books related to wine research, and offices.

The cellar houses a temperature- and humidity-controlled "Vinothèque" for the storage of wines used in teaching sensory perception, as well as some wines made by the students for the purpose of studying aging capacity. Another wine storage facility houses the Ontario Wine Library (OWL). This wine cellar contains a collection of Ontario wines that will be analyzed over a number of years to monitor aging. These studies are intended to establish a correlation between winemaking practises and the capacity for wine to age. OWL, overseen by an independent trust, is an extremely valuable benefit to the industry. With space for some 40,000 bottles, this is the first time it has been possible to monitor not only the capacity of Ontario's wines to age, but also the progression in quality as experience accumulates over the years.

Part II
Appreciating Wine

The 5th Wave   By Rich Tennant

"THIS ONE'S EARTHY BUT LIGHT, WITH UNDERTONES OF BLACKBERRY, VANILLA, AND SCOTCH-GUARD."

In this part . . .

We actually get down to the fun stuff. We analyze the wine itself and explain why wines taste the way they do. You'd be amazed what goes on inside the skin of a grape berry and the range of flavours it can produce once it's fermented.

Chapter 5

Sensing Good Wine

*W*ine appeals to three of the five senses — sight, smell, and taste, in that order. You could argue it also appeals to the sense of hearing: the "pop" of a champagne cork, for instance, and the stimulation a glass of wine gives to conversation around the dinner table! Or, you could say that a tactile element enters into the discussion as well. For instance, you can feel the bubbles in a sparkling wine and the astringency of a tannic wine on your tongue.

Each of these sense perceptions helps you understand wine. Most of the time we're so eager to get a taste of the wine that we forget about what it actually looks like and, more important, what it smells like. It's your nose, after all, that has the best capacity to size up a wine. But, let's be honest — we buy wine to drink it, that is, to taste it. If you're ready to taste you can skip to Chapter 6, but there's much more to wine than what it does to your palate. And that's what this chapter deals with — evaluating wine based on sight and smell. Think of these next two chapters as a pair: By the time you're through, you'll be able to enjoy *all* of wine's complex characteristics.

Visual Basics

The visual impact of the wine is your first clue to its quality. Don't underrate your powers of observation. Pull the cork, pour a glass, and the first thing you see is the colour of the wine. If you can tell the difference between red wine and white, you are one step closer to being a connoisseur. The secret is to keep your eyes open. Even professional tasters can sometimes confuse the colours if they can't see what they're tasting. Take a look deep into your glass and you'll start to uncover wine's secrets. Once you have a practised eye, you can determine if it's a young wine or an older one, whether it's light-bodied or full-bodied, and whether it was grown in a cool or a warm climate. And, above all, if it's in good condition.

Judging colour

Figure 5-1 shows you the shape of typical white and red wineglasses. While you don't *have* to have white wine in a white wineglass and red wine in a red wineglass, the shape and characteristics of each do in fact enhance the experience of the wine they were designed to contain. Once you've chosen your glass and poured your wine, hold it up to a light source (daylight is best; candlelight is more romantic, but even fluorescent or incandescent will do) and view it against a white background (a tablecloth or even a piece of white paper held up behind the glass). This way you'll get a true reading of the colour and its depth without the distraction of other colours in the room. If you were to hold your glass up to a window that is framed by brightly coloured curtains, you would find distorted reflections of colour in your wine.

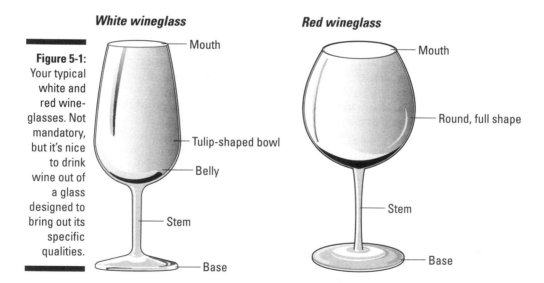

White wineglass — Mouth — Tulip-shaped bowl — Belly — Stem — Base

Red wineglass — Mouth — Round, full shape — Stem — Base

Figure 5-1: Your typical white and red wineglasses. Not mandatory, but it's nice to drink wine out of a glass designed to bring out its specific qualities.

When you look at the wine, tip the glass away from you and see how the colour graduates towards the edge. This helps you identify different nuances of colour, from the most concentrated in the bowl of the glass out to the palest near the rim.

Once you have considered the colour, its intensity and its nuances, you should check the wine for faults. The wine you are examining should be clean and bright. If it's murky or has anything floating in it, this is not a good sign. Some texture to the wine is fine. This is probably only bits of very fine fruit particles suspended in the liquid. These appear uniform and attractive in colour, not murky or cloudy.

Most wines are filtered to give them a brilliant, polished look and, to be perfectly honest, an unfiltered white wine can look pretty unappealing. But today, many winemakers are opting not to filter their reds to maintain as much flavour and aroma in the wine as possible. Just because you can't see through a wine does not mean that it isn't totally clean.

Looking at whites

White wines range in colour from water white with a tint of green to golden amber. Anything outside this spectrum is suspect. Browning edges suggests oxidation, the same effect as leaving a cut apple exposed to air. This is an indication that your wine may have been overheated or is "over the hill" (getting too old) and losing its pleasant, fresh flavours.

Sometimes you can see a tinge of pink in a white wine, but not enough to make you think it is a rosé. This could be a wine made from a white grape with a pinkish skin like Pinot Gris or Gewürztraminer. Or, it could be that a white wine was made from red grapes but not allowed to remain in contact with the skin. You can often see this pink tone in champagne, as the red Pinot Noir is a favoured grape in making this sort of wine. Whether *sparkling* (with bubbles) or *still* (without bubbles), these wines may be called *Blanc de Noirs* (white wine made from red grapes).

If you are now completely confused about what you might see in your glass of white wine, try some of these typical descriptors:

- Pale straw (perhaps with green or gold highlights)
- Straw gold
- Burnished gold
- Amber
- Pink-tinged

Except in the case of a professional technical tasting, a bit of creativity is normal in wine descriptions. More on describing wines in Chapter 7.

White wines are for the most part consumed younger than red wines. If you find a white wine that has started to look brown, it is natural to be suspicious that it may have been left too long. Important exceptions to this rule are fine Riesling wines (usually the sweeter ones) and Sauternes, the great French dessert wine. In dry whites, Chardonnay does have aging capacity, but it is often given some oak treatment, which deepens its colour to begin with. So, to confirm your visual impression, you need to smell the wine and taste it.

Seeing red

Red wines start off life purple and lose colour as they age; by contrast, white wines get deeper in colour as they age. Reds range from bright cherry to almost black in colour, depending on the grape variety and the region they're from. Wines from warmer climates are more deeply, densely coloured than wines from cooler climates. A wine made from Gamay grapes in the cool region of Beaujolais looks cherry red in the glass and graduates to pink at the rim. A Zinfandel from California is usually densely coloured and blackish red. As a young wine, the rim will appear reddish pink. As it ages, the browning will show up in a brick-coloured rim.

Again, if you are groping for the right words to describe the appearance of your red wines, here are some helpful expressions:

- Bluish/purple
- Cherry/pink
- Ruby or ruby with garnet highlights
- Brick-coloured
- Inky or black (wines that are particularly dense and opaque elicit descriptions like this)

Pink wines are usually identified by the term *rosé*. They range in colour from the merest blush to rose or cherry, with a range of pink hues that embrace salmon (orangey pink) to bluish pink. And those are pretty well the same expressions used in discussing their colour.

To get a sense of the density of a red wine, place two fingers behind the bowl (the round globe of the glass) and look through it. If you can see your fingers, the wine is probably from a cool climate. Red wines grown in warm climates tend to be dense and opaque in colour. A wine you can't see through will probably be more intense in flavour than one you can.

Checking out those legs!

The wine's *legs* (fluid that clings to the side of the glass) can tell you something about its alcohol content.

Hold the glass by the stem or the base and swirl the wine a few times by rotating your wrist. Look at the transparent wet effect the wine leaves on the side of the glass — its legs. This is actually alcohol clinging to the glass. The liquid soon starts to fall back to the level of the wine in a series of tears. The thickness of these tears as they slide back to the surface of the wine gives you an indication of the alcoholic strength. The heavier and slower moving the legs, the higher the amount of alcohol. Low-alcohol wines will virtually evaporate on the side of the glass.

It's interesting to note that while the French call this phenomenon "legs," as we do in this book, the Germans interpret this arching effect on the side of the wineglass as "church windows," which suggests a different national perspective in these matters.

If you find swirling your wine difficult to do while holding the glass in the air, place it on a tabletop and with your hand firmly on the base, swirl the glass until the wine rides up the sides in whirlpool fashion. With a little practise you'll get proficient at swirling without splashing your dining companions!

The tearing effect has to do with how molecules of liquid cling to the surface of a glass and the fact that the alcohol in the wine evaporates more quickly than the water. (Nobody watered down your wine, water is just a natural component in wine as it is in the grapes and in the human body.) Try this experiment: Swirl the glass (on the table or in the air, it doesn't matter) to cause the tears to form, then cover the glass tightly. The tearing stops because there is no evaporation. Remove the cover and watch the tears start to flow again. The higher the alcohol content of the wine, the faster the evaporation and the more evident the tears. They show up best in wines of over 12 percent alcohol.

Sending wines back: Five unsightly reasons to do so

It is actually quite rare to find visual faults in wine, but you should always check for the following problems nonetheless. All the conditions below apply equally to white, red, and rosé.

1. Haziness in appearance
2. Excessive browning in colour
3. Sparkling (or bubbling) when the wine is meant to be still
4. Flotsam and jetsam floating on the surface
5. Glass shards

Shards of glass do occasionally turn up in wine but usually occur when the bottle is being opened. It is a good idea to check the top of the bottle once the cork is out. You can sometimes chip the glass when you are manipulating the corkscrew.

Wine diamonds

You may find tiny crystals at the bottom of the bottle or clinging to the business end of the cork (the end that comes into contact with the wine). This happens particularly with white wines and is no cause for alarm. The trade calls these crystals *wine diamonds*. They are harmless bits of potassium bitartrate, a natural salt in wine, that precipitate out in crystalline form when the wine has been chilled down too quickly.

The presence of wine diamonds in a wine is no cause to send it back. They do not affect the taste or smell in any way. They are merely unsightly for those who look for crystal-clear wines. Ironically, these "foreign bodies" in a wine are a mark of the wine's quality.

Nuancing the Nose

One of the most challenging aspects of wine is how to describe the smell of what's in your glass. You can take the easy route out and say, yes, it smells like wine. But with a little practise, you'll be able to recognize that each wine style has its own particular perfume. And if you store that information in your sensory memory bank, you'll be able to detect it the next time you have that particular wine.

Believe it or not, your nose is the most important organ you have when it comes to assessing the quality of a wine. It will tell you at least 80 percent of what you want to know. It is much more acute than your palate; in fact, you virtually *taste* with your nose rather than your tongue. Figure 5-2 shows you how this works.

Figure 5-2:
Most wine flavours are actually aromas that are vapourized in the mouth and perceived through the rear nasal passage.

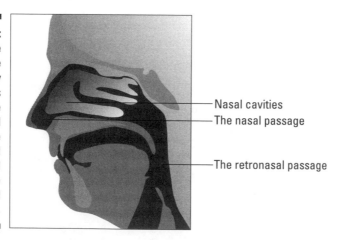

Nasal cavities
The nasal passage

The retronasal passage

Try this experiment to see just how important your nose is when you taste a wine:

1. Pinch your nostrils shut and take a swig of wine.

2. Hold your nose closed for five seconds after you've swallowed and then release it.

What do you notice? You can only taste the wine when your nasal passages are open. Your taste buds merely confirm what your nose tells you.

If you have a cold or your nasal passages are congested, not only will you not smell, but you also won't be able to taste. That's why mothers tell you to hold your nose when giving you some evil-tasting medicine.

By the same token, imagine you're cooking for a child and you decide that you want to put something down in front of little Johnny that is not macaroni and cheese. Just to break the monotony (for you), you prepare grilled fish. You place the dish lovingly in front of Johnny who immediately turns up his nose and tells you he doesn't like it. You, the exasperated parent, reply, "What do you mean, you don't like it? You haven't even tasted it!"

But he has. Little Johnny has smelled that grilled fish; he now knows what this foreign matter tastes like and he doesn't want it.

The nose is much more powerful a sensor than the *palate* (your tongue and gums). You can smell as few as 400 molecules of a substance but to taste that substance you need at least 25,000 molecules of it dissolved in the saliva of your tongue. Tiny little hairs at the top of your nose interpret the signals transmitted by your taste buds and explain to your brain what you are tasting. Your tongue only registers four basic tastes: sweet, salt, sour, and bitter. The real work in fanning out these four tastes is done by the nose.

Getting swirling again (it's worth it)

If you swirl the wine in the glass, you get a more concentrated bouquet. The act of swirling causes friction that allows the wine's *esters* (chemical compounds that result from mixing organic acids with alcohol) to evaporate and rise. These esters carry the wine's *aromatics* — a complex smell of fruit, acids, and oak.

The smell of the wine — its *bouquet* — tells you almost everything you need to know to judge whether you will like it or not. If it smells good, it will taste good. If it smells of oak, it will taste oaky. The only things your nose will not tell you about in advance are the *body* of the wine (its feel in your mouth) and how long the flavour will linger on your palate (a lengthy amount of time is the mark of a good wine).

Finding the right partners

Wine appreciation can be like choosing a spouse. You may start off with a negative attitude, looking for faults. When you can't find anything wrong, you then praise the virtues you observe. When smelling a wine, be critical. Look for flaws. Is there an off odour? A wine in good condition should smell fresh and lively — of fruit (especially berries, citrus fruits, and, in warm growing regions, tropical fruits), flowers, sometimes vegetables (especially in Sauvignon Blanc), and vanilla (from oak).

Older wines take on more organic bouquets of caramel, coffee beans, chocolate, leather, or truffles.

In better wines you will be able, with practise, to detect a range of different smells.

If you are doing an analytical tasting — that is, more than just checking that the wine is okay for dinner, don't wear perfume, cologne, aftershave, fragrant lotion, or hairstyling products. These odours interfere with your ability to identify different olfactory characteristics in the wine. Actually, you probably won't notice your fragrance as much as your tasting buddies will. For the same reason, don't start to cook dinner or serve that smelly cheese until you've done your tasting.

Chemical, fruity, or vegetable?

In the 1980s, Ann C. Noble, a researcher at the University of California at Davis, identified at least 95 different odours in wine alone. Your sense of smell probably perceives close to 10,000 odours, not that you can name them all. Your poor, challenged sense of taste can only identify a cast of four — which explains why you lose your taste when your nose is out of commission.

Noble divided the odours up into various categories to enable tasters to better describe what they smelled. The three most recognized categories are chemical, fruity, and vegetable. Examples of chemical smells like sulphur include burnt match, hydrogen, and wet dog. Fruity smells are far more appealing and are exemplified by citrus (grapefruit and lemon are quite common), berry (like strawberry and blackcurrant) and tropical fruit (like melon and banana). Freshly cut lawn, green pepper, tea, and tobacco typify vegetable smells.

Your own life experiences influence how you perceive odours in wine. For instance, if you enjoy fruit, you are quite likely to identify fruit smells in wine. Garage mechanics may relate more to Riesling, which is often characterized by a sometimes not too subtle odour of diesel fuel along with fruit and floral smells.

If a taster speaks to you about aroma and bouquet, you should know that in wine terms these are quite different. Aroma refers specifically to grape smells and is most common in young wines. Bouquet refers to the odours that result from a wine's aging process and from winemaking influences such as fermentation oak aging. Unfortunately, there is no precise explanation of where aroma ends and bouquet begins, but thinking in these terms is simply a way to help you divide up your sensory perceptions.

Wake up and smell the coffee. The best way to improve your wine appreciation skills is to smell EVERYTHING — take things out of the fridge and smell them, go outside and smell the roses, even smell your sneakers! All this will help train your sense of smell and expand your sensory repertoire.

Smelling something fishy: Avoiding bad wine days

"Good taste," wrote the English novelist Arnold Bennett in 1930, "is better than bad taste, but bad taste is better than no taste at all."

True, in all things except wine.

Many wine drinkers don't recognize certain olfactory warning signs and therefore consume wines that are *corked* (tainted by a musty taste from a faulty cork), oxidized, or suffering from faults that make them smell like a beaver's armpit or a tire fire.

Bottle stink and other problems

There are a few smelly conditions that occur quite commonly in wine and most are good reason to reject the bottle. Take it back to the store where you bought it or, if you're in a restaurant, ask the waiter to bring you another. See Chapter 9 for more on ordering wine in restaurants.

The term *bottle stink* is sometimes used to describe a sulphurous odour that wafts up from the depths of the bottle in question. Sulphur is used in the vineyard as a fungicide and in the winery as a disinfectant. Sometimes a tiny bit of residue gets into the wine, causing an off odour. This smell usually dissipates as the wine sits in your glass. You can even hurry it along with some energetic swirling or by *decanting* the wine (pouring it into another container before you pour it into your glass). If the smell persists, return the bottle.

Oxidation

Oxidation and "corkiness" are the most common faults found in wine. Oxidation occurs when the wine deteriorates because of exposure to air. It could simply be because the wine is too old, so make sure you check the vintage date on the label. Only a few wines really improve with age. All wines change over time and eventually they change for the worse. If you have an $8 to $10 bottle of wine that's five years old or more, it is probably well past its prime. As it starts to oxidize it smells more like sherry, which is okay for sherry, but not for regular table wine. When you taste an oxidized wine, it is bland and sour.

Sometimes a wine oxidizes prematurely, usually as a result of excessive heat (from being left in the sun or in heated storage) or a faulty cork. Your wine store will refund or exchange a prematurely oxidized wine but not one you have kept for too long. If you are served an oxidized wine in a restaurant, ask the waiter to take it back.

Eventually, if a wine is left exposed to air long enough, it will go beyond oxidation and turn to vinegar. If your wine smells too much like your salad, it has turned.

You can train your nose to these off odours by leaving a tiny amount of wine in a glass overnight. By morning it will smell oxidized and vinegary.

Corkiness

A wine that is stoppered with a cork is, technically, a corked wine. But the term *corked* used in the industry refers to a wine that has been adversely affected by a faulty cork and taken on a bad smell and taste. A corked wine may be a bit difficult to recognize until someone points one out to you, but the odour typically resembles a particularly pungent, mouldy cork. Try sniffing a clean cork; it has a mild corky smell. If a similar but strong odour interferes with the fruity aroma of your wine, then it is quite likely corked.

The cork stopper in wine bottles comes from the bark of a tree. To clean cork once it has been cut, it is bathed in a strong chlorine solution that can react with mould to produce TCA (trichloranisole). This chemical can become trapped in the crevices of the cork and "turn" the wine, giving it an unpleasant flavour and smell.

More stinky reasons for sending wines back

Chemical smells like turpentine and nail polish remover usually indicate a winemaking problem, but it takes a trained nose to match the bad smell to the specific problem. Table 5-1 lists various suspicious odours and the associated problem with the wine. If you notice any of the following odours when you smell a wine, something's not right:

Table 5-1	Bad Odours and Their Causes
Odour	*Cause*
Asparagus, garlic, cabbage	Excessive use of sulphur
Basement smells, mould	Cork problem
Burnt matches	Overly sulphured
Dill pickle or sauerkraut	Fermentation problem
Egg salad	Excessive hydrogen sulphide
Geranium	Bacterial problem
Horsey, barnyard	Yeast sulphur dioxide problem
Mousey	Yeast problem
Nail polish	Too much acetic acid
Sherry	Oxidation
Vinegar	Acetic acid caused by microbiological activity

How can you tell if a wine is off at that critical moment when the waiter pours you a sample and hovers over you waiting for you to sniff it, taste it, and give your approval? Don't be intimidated. Take your time. Look at the wine and check for faults. Then smell it once, swirl it, and smell it again. Finally, take a sip. No visual faults? No off odours? No offending taste? (More about tasting wine in Chapter 6.) Smile with confidence and instruct the waiter to pour the wine.

Chapter 6

Pleasing Your Palate

●●●

●●●

*Y*ou can sit around studying the colour of wine and sniffing its bouquet, but ultimately the main event is its taste. That's why you pulled the cork — to enjoy the wine with a meal or as an apéritif.

Your tongue, as we explain in Chapter 5, is a fairly blunt instrument. Your taste buds are neanderthal in their response compared to the acuity of your nose. But you can't spend your life just swirling and sniffing a glass of wine and then pushing it away when your nose has had enough.

The best way to learn about wine is to taste it. Now, that statement might seem obvious, but ultimately it is your palate and your taste memory that enlarges your understanding of wine. Reading about wine in a book is a mental exercise. You can learn the theory of wine appreciation, but the practise is much more fun. Lifting a glass of wine, studying its colour, sniffing its bouquet, and savouring its taste is a powerful sensory experience — if you like the taste, it's a hedonistic one as well.

Getting to Know Your Tongue

Your tongue registers the four basic taste sensations of sweet, salt, sour (acid), and bitter on different parts of the *palate* (the whole mouth). The immediate impression we get of a wine is sweetness, because the taste buds that register sweet are at the tip of the tongue. See Figure 6-1 for an illustration of your tongue's sensitive areas. As the wine works its way to the back of your mouth, you experience its acidity as a tingling sensation on the inside of your cheeks. Tannins (bitterness) are also experienced at the back of the mouth and along your gums. Salt is non-existent in wine, though some wines may taste slightly salty nevertheless.

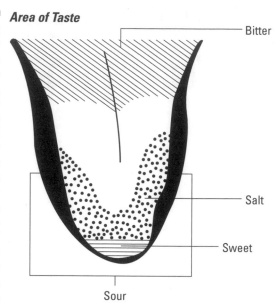

Area of Taste

Bitter

Salt

Sweet

Sour

Figure 6-1: The four basic tastes — sweet, salt, sour, and bitter — are transmitted from your tongue up to the bridge of your nose where they are "interpreted" into all the tastes we recognize.

As you're drinking a wine you should notice three stages of taste:

1. The *initial taste* when the wine hits your tongue.

2. The *secondary taste* when the wine warms up in your mouth, covering your entire palate.

3. The *aftertaste* when you swallow the wine.

The mark of a good wine is how long the taste of fruit lingers in your mouth once you have swallowed it.

A wine taster's trick to get the maximum flavour out of a wine is to pucker up with a mouthful and suck in air while you "chew" the wine. The principle is similar to extracting more bouquet by swirling the wine in your glass. Practise this at home before you try it in public. It's not recommended at smart dinner parties since it sounds like gargling!

Putting Your Palate to the Test

Comparative tasting is tasting one wine against another to illuminate the differences between them. Since wine is a social beverage that is best shared, try these simple comparisons in your own home with a group of friends. See Chapter 8 for more on creating just the right ambience for a wine tasting at home.

Purchase two bottles of wine produced from the same grape but from different regions, preferably one in the Old World style (traditional European appellations) and one from the New World (for example, California, Australia, or Chile). This will give you the most marked of contrasts. Or you might like to compare a wine from Ontario with one from British Columbia.

Comparing whites

White wines are generally easier to appreciate than reds, but if you're a die-hard red drinker, skip to the end of the chapter for pointers on doing comparative tastings with red wines. Well, we suggest you do both!

For starters, buy a couple of bottles of white wine, say a 1998 Chablis (made from Chardonnay grapes grown in the Burgundy region of France) and a bottle of 1998 Chardonnay from the Napa Valley in California. Prices for wines of this calibre vary across Canada but should fall in the $20 to $25 range.

Try this exercise on our own wines by comparing products from British Columbia and Ontario. For a fair comparison, choose the same grape type — Chardonnay or Pinot Blanc, for example — from the same vintage, in a similar price range, and taste them against each other. Try to choose wines that have not been barrel-aged, as the oak will change the character of the wine. Such a comparison will give you a real sense of how the two different climates and soils affect the bouquet and taste of the wines grown in western and central Canada. You could try comparing Strewn Chardonnay Unwooded, from the Niagara region, with Gray Monk Cellars Unwooded Chardonnay, from the Okanagan Valley.

Chill both bottles for about an hour in the refrigerator. Take clean glasses of the same size and shape and pour equal measures of the two wines. A two-ounce pour is sufficient for tasting purposes (most standard wine bottles contain 750 ml, which is 26 ounces, so you can invite up to 12 friends to the party).

You compare these white wines on the basis of the impact they make on all three key senses: eyes, nose, and mouth.

That glowing colour

In a well-lit room, place the glasses side by side against a white background, either a tablecloth or a piece of paper. Consider the colour of the Burgundy Chablis and compare it to the California Chardonnay.

This is what you can expect from the two samples:

- Chablis: The palest straw colour with a tint of green.
- Chardonnay: A golden yellow tone, much deeper in colour.

The intensity of colour tells you a lot about the wine. Tilt each glass and study it. Look directly down on the wine and note the colour. Now lift each glass and tilt it at an angle away from you so that you can see the rim where the wine touches the glass. You can note three things from the colour of white wines:

1. Older white wines have varying shades of colour from the centre to the rim. A young wine's colour is constant throughout.

2. When they're first made, white wines are very pale and greenish, almost the colour of water. They take on a deeper hue as they age.

3. White wines matured in stainless steel tanks without the presence of oxygen have a lighter colour than those aged in wood barrels. Barrel maturation deepens the colour of whites because of the oxygen present.

Sweet wines are in most cases deeper in colour than dry wines. Really old dessert wines like Sauternes turn the colour of brown shoe polish after several decades because of the effect of the residual sugar in the wine. While the idea of drinking liquid shoe polish might not attract you, these venerable old wines can taste magnificent. Just try a 1937 Château d'Yquem and you'll see what we mean.

Those revealing legs

Swirl the wine in your glass a few revolutions and watch as the tears or "legs" fall down the sides of the glass to the surface of the wine. Note the thickness of these tears and the speed at which they move. Refer to Chapter 5 for an explanation of the tears phenomenon.

The thicker the tears and the slower they roll down the side of your glass, the higher the alcohol content of the wine. A low-alcohol wine, such as a dry Riesling from Germany's Mosel region, almost evaporates on the side of the glass; whereas Chardonnay from a warm growing region such as the Murray River area of Australia has mighty legs.

When you compare your Burgundy Chablis and California Chardonnay, the California wine typically has "better legs," because of its higher alcohol content, though the difference won't be as striking as between the Mosel Riesling and the Murray River Chardonnay.

Since alcohol is fermented sugar, a sweet wine with a comparatively low degree of alcohol (such as Canadian Icewine) also exhibits stout, slow-moving legs.

The nose knows

Don't forget to compare the bouquets of the wines. First, take the Chablis and swirl the wine. When it has settled in the glass, take a small sniff with your nostrils about two inches above the opening of the glass. Swirl it again and put your nose closer into the glass. Repeat this process with the Chardonnay.

Your samples should offer the following bouquets:

- ✔ Chablis: It smells of crisp green apple and lemon.
- ✔ Chardonnay: Combines the odours of butter, vanilla, and tropical fruit with citrus notes.

Once you take in the appearance and scent of the wines, you've done most of the work towards identifying what the wines will taste like. You can pour them down the sink at this point if you're driving, if you're prohibited alcohol for religious reasons, or if you're a teetotaller. Your eyes and nose tell you virtually all you need to know about the wines, except for how long the flavours you have identified with your nose will last on your palate.

But stopping the exercise at this point would be an affront to Dionysius (the Greek god of wine), to say nothing of denying yourself the pleasure of two of the world's great wines.

The proving of your palate

Tasting the wines will confirm what your nose tells you. You also gain an idea of the *weight* of the wine on your palate. In other words, tasting reveals the *body* of the wine.

Body is a term that denotes the amount of dry extract from the grapes, the amount of alcohol in the wine, and the measure of residual sugar left in the wine after fermentation.

Take a sip of the Chablis. Let it roll over your tongue so that it comes in contact with every part of your mouth. Feel how your mouth reacts to the wine on entry and how that changes when the wine reaches the back of your mouth. Do the same with the Chardonnay.

Your first impression (initial taste) suggests the weight of the wine, how it feels on your tongue:

- ✔ *Light-bodied:* Wines with low alcohol (7 to 11.5 degrees of alcohol) and light extract, invariably pale in colour.
- ✔ *Medium-bodied:* Wines with moderate alcohol (12 to 12.5 degrees of alcohol), good colour, good weight.
- ✔ *Full-bodied:* Wines that are densely coloured, generous and full-flavoured, with lots of extract (13 to 16 degrees of alcohol).

You experience a sweetness as the wine first touches your tongue. It comes in contact with the taste buds on the tip of your tongue, which register it. So, your initial taste of the wine is its fruitiness. As the liquid glides over your tongue, it comes in contact with the receptors that detect sourness or bitterness. You experience the wine's secondary taste at this point. These taste buds register the acidity and tannin in the wine. The third tasting stage is the aftertaste, the wine's final, lingering taste on your palate. Refer to Figure 6-1 for a diagram of the tongue and the location of the different taste receptors. Your tasting will resemble the following:

- ✔ Chablis: Initially an apple flavour that gives way to a citrus, lemony finish. Medium weight and sinewy, with good length and a lively, acidic end.

- ✔ Chardonnay: First sensation is the sweet, tropical fruit flavour and behind it, a spicy, toasty note from the oak. It has a fuller-bodied, softer, and rounder feel on the palate, with a sweeter finish.

If you want to find a really dry white wine, choose one from a cool growing climate, such as the Loire Valley, northern France, northeastern Italy, Switzerland, Ontario, British Columbia, New York State, or New Zealand. Nine times out of ten, wine professionals use the example of Muscadet from the Loire to illustrate dryness in wine.

Examples of Canadian dry whites are Konzelmann Chardonnay from Ontario and Mission Hill Pinot Blanc from British Columbia.

If you're considering what you would like to eat with both wines, skip forward to Chapter 14 to discover the best food matches for these particular wine styles.

The term *organoleptic* is a fancy word meaning the total tasting experience — the sight, smell, and taste of a wine. Drop that one at a dinner party and your fellow guests will either take you to be an oenologist or a wine geek.

Comparing reds

If you're not a white wine fan, perhaps you'd rather try comparative tasting using red wines. You have to purchase two wines with sufficiently different characteristics. Let's say, a 1999 Beaujolais-Villages from France and a 1998 Australian Shiraz.

Make sure that both bottles are at the same room temperature (even though Beaujolais is best tasted slightly chilled to bring out its freshness). Pour equal amounts (about two ounces) into two similar-shaped glasses and study the colour of each. Look at the wine from the top, the side, and then tilt the glass and study the rim (where the wine touches the glass when you tilt it). Compare the two colours. Then swirl and look at the legs. You will likely notice the following:

- ✔ Beaujolais: Medium ruby colour, paler to the rim where it meets the glass. The coating is light on the sides of the glass and the legs move relatively quickly down the sides.

- ✔ Shiraz: Purple-ruby colour, dense, almost opaque, with consistent colour to the rim. The coating is thick and viscous — so thick that it almost leaves a purple stain on the side of the glass.

Sugary secrets

There is no such thing as a totally dry wine. Some residual sugar remains in all wines because, during fermentation, yeast cannot convert 100 percent of the sugar into alcohol. The driest wines you will ever taste have about 3 grams per litre of residual sugar. Some of our Canadian wines taste very dry, but the most often used example of an ultra dry-tasting wine is Muscadet, from the Loire in France.

The acidity in wine is what makes it taste dry. The sugar codes (or ratings) that you see in liquor stores in Ontario are helpful to a point in directing you to the driest style of wine. The sugar rating is rarely displayed on the bottle or label; however, the liquor boards and wineries do have this information, so just ask.

Within the zero-designated sugar code (0) there is a significant range in perceptible sweetness. Some (0) wines will taste sweeter than others because of their acid balance. If a wine has high acidity, the sweetness of the fruit is masked and the wine tastes tart. A Sauvignon Blanc from the Loire Valley rated (0) (but with high acidity) will seem much drier than a lower-acidity Chilean Sauvignon Blanc similarly rated. For this sugar coding, only the residual sugar in the wine is measured — not the level of acidity.

A zero sugar code (0) wine can actually contain up to a maximum of 4.9 grams per litre of residual sugar. Some zero-rated wines contain less.

✔ A wine rated (1) contains between 5 and 14.9 grams per litre of residual sugar.

✔ A wine rated (2) contains between 15 and 24.9 grams per litre

✔ A wine rated (3) contains between 25 and 34.9 grams per litre

✔ A wine rated (4) contains between 35 and 44.9 grams per litre

✔ A wine rated (5) contains between 45 and 54.9 grams per litre

✔ A wine rated (6) contains between 55 and 64.9 grams per litre

✔ A wine rated (7) contains between 65 and 74.9 grams per litre

✔ A wine rated (8) contains between 75 and 84.9 grams per litre

✔ A wine rated (9) contains between 85 and 94.9 grams per litre

A wine rated either (0) or (1) on the sugar code will be dry to relatively dry.

A wine rated either (2) or (3) will be off-dry or medium-dry.

A wine rated (4) and above will be definitely sweet. The higher the number, the sweeter the wine. For example, ports and cream sherries will register between (10) and (14) on the sugar code.

Just to show you how sweet these wines can get, there is a fruit wine from Ontario made from blackcurrants that tips the sugar scale at (30)!

The difference in colour and in thickness of legs tells you what you'll experience on the palate. You predict that the Beaujolais will be lighter-bodied and less concentrated in flavour than the Aussie Shiraz.

When you swirl and "nose" the two wines, you detect the following:

- Beaujolais: Fresh and fruity with a cherry or plum bouquet and a touch of black pepper.
- Shiraz: Intense vanilla and blackberry with an earthy, smoky note and a peppery tone.

Taste both red wines beginning with the Beaujolais — which your nose has already told you will not be as concentrated and as rich as the Shiraz. You observe their distinctly different flavours:

- Beaujolais: Lively cherry fruit flavour. Fresh and easy-drinking with a peppery bite on the finish.
- Shiraz: *Unctuous* (rich and smooth) mouth feel. Full-bodied, jammy blackberry flavour with evident oak (vanilla) notes — a note of ground black pepper on the finish.

Some chilling advice

The act of cooling down a wine lowers the perception of sugar when you taste the wine and emphasizes the acidity. You chill white wines, sparkling wines, and especially dessert wines to take advantage of this phenomenon. When you chill a light red wine such as Beaujolais, the fruit flavours become more vibrant because of the heightened sensory awareness brought on by the acidity. Chilling makes the wine taste fresher.

If you really want to get adventurous, see what effect chilling has on a bottle of red wine. Take two identical bottles of Beaujolais. (There are several large, quality conscious producers of Beaujolais who ship to Canada including Duboeuf, Jaffelin, and Ferraud. Any of these is a good choice for your experiment.)

Chill one bottle for half an hour in the refrigerator and let the other stand at room temperature. Taste the room temperature wine first and then try the same wine chilled. You will find a marked difference in flavour.

The room temperature Beaujolais tastes rounder, with a greater perception of sweetness on the initial taste. The chilled Beaujolais seems leaner, fresher, and livelier. As to which you prefer — well, it's all a matter of taste.

Not all red wines accentuate their freshness when chilled. Highly tannic wines such as red Bordeaux or Barolo taste more austere and bitter if refrigerated, but light fruity reds, especially those that have been made by carbonic maceration (see Chapter 3) and are consequently low in tannin, are much livelier on the palate. Here are a few examples of chillable reds:

- Beaujolais from France
- Valpolicella from Italy's Veneto region
- Pinot Noir from France's Alsace region
- Pinot Noir (called Spätburgunder) from Germany
- Wines made by carbonic maceration, Beaujolais being the best known

Again, what would you pair these wines with, given their very different character? Check Chapter 14 for a complete food and wine-matching chart.

You and your friends (now a wine-tasting collective!) can repeat this experiment comparing the following wines in Table 6-1.

Table 6-1	Wines for Comparative Tastings
Compare This Wine	*With This Wine*
Whites	
Italian Pinot Grigio	British Columbia Pinot Gris
Riesling Kabinett (Rheingau, Germany)	Ontario or B.C. dry Riesling
Sancerre (Loire Valley)	New Zealand Sauvignon Blanc
Reds	
Californian red Zinfandel	Châteauneuf-du-Pape (Rhône)
Chilean Cabernet Sauvignon	Château-bottled red Bordeaux
Red Burgundy	Oregon Pinot Noir

Chapter 7

Judging the Good, the Bad, and the Ugly

*O*ne of the great pleasures of wine is to compare your reaction to a particular wine with those of friends, colleagues, and professional wine writers. It's also rewarding to record your changing reflections about a given wine at different stages in its development. Both you and the wine benefit from this.

Describing what a wine tastes like can be as basic or as sophisticated as you want it to be. It is merely a record of your experience of a wine at a point in time. You can give a wine a "thumbs up" or a "thumbs down," a simple "liked it" or "ugh." Or you can get more elaborate in your critique.

You need a basic template to record your verdict and a vocabulary that is consistent with each description you write. This chapter shows you how to score a wine just like the pros using a combined numerical and verbal rating system.

Describing How Wines Taste

There are three basic sensory elements when it comes to judging a wine: appearance, which you judge visually, bouquet, which you judge with your nose, and taste, which you judge by drinking the wine — the best part. See Chapters 5 and 6 for more on the important role your senses play in your enjoyment of wine.

A wine can have a terrific colour and appearance but taste unpleasant. A wine that smells bad will never taste good. Colour by itself is not an indication of quality although it *can* enhance your overall enjoyment of a wine. Confused? That's understandable. It's difficult at first to know what to focus on when evaluating a wine. You can fill out a standard *tasting sheet* a little later on in the chapter, the scorecard that is used to rate wines — even by those stuffy wine pros! But before you fill out the sheet, we suggest you sharpen your wine vocabulary and familiarize yourself with some descriptive terms.

There are certain basic adjectives that help you describe wines and communicate your tasting experiences to others.

- **Acidic:** Think of sucking on a lemon and the sharp, tart taste it produces. A wine that is highly acidic tastes very dry.

- **Aftertaste:** After you swallow, what kind of taste lingers on your palate? The longer the aftertaste lasts, the better the wine.

- **Alcoholic:** A hot sensation in the throat indicates a wine with high alcohol.

- **Bitter:** Too much tannin in the wine renders it austere and harsh.

- **Body:** The feel of the wine in your mouth indicates body. A light-bodied wine feels delicate on the tongue; a full-bodied wine fills the mouth.

- **Corky:** A wine tainted by cork smells like a mouldy, dank basement or worse: wet cardboard or rotting mushrooms.

- **Dry:** A wine whose grape sugars have been fermented out, usually high in acidity.

- **Finish:** The overall impression the wine leaves after tasting. A wine's finish is different from its aftertaste: aftertaste is a flavour consideration, whereas finish is also about the length and balance of a wine's different elements.

- **Flabby:** A fat wine that lacks acidity and structure. It is shapeless and fleshy.

- **Green:** The products of young grapevines or grapes picked before they are ripe taste green.

- **Hard:** Heavy tannins and acidity produce a hard effect.

- **Legs:** This is the liquid that runs down the side of your glass. The fatter and slower-moving the legs are, the higher the alcohol content of the wine.

- **Length:** The time a wine's flavour stays on your palate is its length.

- **Musty:** Rotting grapes or dirty barrels cause an off odour.

- **Oaky:** A wine tastes more of the barrel (vanilla) than of the fruit.

- ✔ **Oxidized:** A wine exposed to air results in a brownish tint in appearance and a flat, stewed bouquet.

- ✔ **Residual sugar:** Unfermented grape sugar in the wine renders it sweet-tasting.

- ✔ **Short:** A wine's flavour suddenly stops.

- ✔ **Sulphur:** The smell of burnt matchsticks or rubber in a wine that shows excessive use of sulphur as an antibacterial agent and an antioxidant.

- ✔ **Toasty:** Oak barrels impart a smoked or toasted note on wine, especially on the finish.

- ✔ **Varietal character:** A wine tastes of the grape from which it was fermented.

- ✔ **Well-balanced:** A wine's fruit, acidity, alcohol, oak, and tannins are harmonious without one element dominating the flavour.

Scoring Wine by Number

Now we get down to the actual scoring. Many wine professionals rate wines by number. That is, they taste the wines, write a description of them, and then accord each wine a number based on a set of criteria.

The most common rating system is the 100-point system, although many professional British tasters use a 20-point system and other tasters even use a 10-point system.

Some tasters, concerned that a wine's judgment is written in stone once it's given a number score, prefer a rating system using a series of five stars (sort of like the system your Grade 3 teacher used to mark that project you did on Kenya). The five-star system allows for the possibility of granting a half star. The argument is that this system allows room for recognition of a wine's more subtle qualities, presenting an alternative to the (what some tasters see as) rigid and arbitrary numerical rating system.

Your basic tasting sheet

For the entry-level wine lover, scoring a wine on a 10-point system is the easiest way to go. Figure 7-1 is a simple tasting sheet that will help you evaluate wine.

Tasting Sheet

Date: _____

Venue: _____

Wine	Appearance	Bouquet	Taste	Comments
1.				
2.				
3.				
4.				
5.				
6.				

Figure 7-1:
Wine-tasting sheet, 10-point system.

Use these scoring guidelines related to appearance, bouquet, and taste to help you fill out the sheet.

Appearance: 0–2 points

- **0:** A wine that is murky, has an unclean surface, or has particles of grape skin floating in it.
- **1 point:** A clean-looking wine, but lacking brilliance and depth of colour.
- **2 points:** A bright and lively looking wine, with good depth of colour.

Bouquet: 0–3 points

- **0:** Basically a bad-smelling wine. It might smell corked (damp, mouldy basement smells) or sulphury (burnt matchsticks or rubber).
- **1 point:** A wine with vague fruit smells but no immediate aroma of fruit.
- **2 points:** A fruity, clean-smelling wine with discernible oak aromas.
- **3 points:** A wine with a rich and complex bouquet with true varietal character, harmonious fruit, and oak undertones.

Taste: 0–5 points

- **0:** A wine that tastes flawed, oxidized, or tired, reminiscent of the taste of prune juice with alcohol.
- **1 point:** A wine that has a recognizable taste, but is insipid, lacking balance and fruit character.
- **2 points:** A ho-hum wine. It tastes enough like wine, but you don't care if you finish the glass or not.
- **3 points:** A decent glass of wine that you could drink every day.
- **4 points:** A rich, fully flavoured and complex wine. Terrific.
- **5 points:** A conversation stopper! Pour me the rest of the bottle!

The scores you give relate to the overall quality of the wine as you discern it:

0–3: Unacceptable, a good idea not to buy this again.

4–5: Average quality, nothing to write home about.

6–7: Good everyday quality, serve it to your guests.

8–9: Very good quality, serve it to those you want to impress.

10: The best. Keep for special occasions and cherish it.

The write words

In addition to scoring based on the three sensory aspects of wine, you want to add a few words to explain what the numbers mean. Remember that little "Comments" box on the right side of the tasting sheet? This section is about filling that box with words that say something about the wine and reflect your personal interpretation of it better than any number can. After all, how evocative is a number?

There's no need to get extravagant in this department and describe the bouquet, for example, as "the perfume of zephyr breezes from a Caribbean island, mingled with the aroma of a small fire in a hayloft." Give us a break! Just a few adjectives that spring spontaneously to mind when you sniff the bouquet (or look at the colour, or sample the taste) will suffice.

Appearance

Consider the descriptors in Table 7-1 when you comment on a wine's colour.

Table 7-1	Common Terms to Describe Wine's Appearance	
White Wines	*Red Wines*	*Pink Wines (Rosé)*
White gold	Cherry	Oeil-de-Perdrix (partridge's eye, literally translated, but indicates a pale peachy pink)
Straw	Strawberry	Pale pink
Golden	Ruby	Salmon
Yellow	Garnet	Yellow cherry
Green highlights	Purple	Blue highlights

Red wines have different intensities of colour. You can see through most red wines, but those with lots of fruit can be dense and opaque. To get a good sense of the depth of colour in a red wine, hold the glass up to a light source (a window, a candle flame, or a light) and place two fingers behind the glass. Look through the wine at your fingers. If you can't see them, the wine will be very concentrated and full-bodied.

Bouquet

Wines often smell of berries, other types of fruit, and/or spices. For example, you may smell raspberries, blackberries, blueberries, gooseberries, or mulberries. In terms of other fruit, look out for apples, lemons, bananas, grapefruit, cherries, apricots, or figs. Spices you may encounter include pepper, cinnamon, licorice, nutmeg, ginger, and grass.

Here are some common terms used to describe a wine's bouquet:

- Crisp (very dry)
- Floral
- Fresh (lively acidity)
- Fruity
- Honey
- Raisiny
- Smoky
- Spicy
- Toasty
- Vanilla

It's not that you'll bring your nose close to the rim and be overwhelmed by a particular smell, such as grapefruit. It's more subtle than that; more a suggestion of the smell. The more practised you become, the better you'll be able to discern this.

When describing the smell of a wine try to distinguish between how the fruit expresses itself and what effect the oak has on the bouquet. Oak imparts the smell of vanilla and some spicy notes. If the barrels have been charred, you may smell smoke and toast as well.

There are a surprising number of smells that you wouldn't associate with wine right off the bat. Wines can develop various organic smells as they age, not to mention other surprising odours — cigar, anyone? Then there are the send-it-back-at-all-costs smells. If you get a whiff of wet dog, garlic, or sour milk — we're not kidding — send that bottle back. So what do you do if "fruity" and "floral" just aren't cutting it, but you're not quite sure how to describe what you smell? Some of the terms in these lists will help.

Organic bouquets in wines:

- Asparagus
- Butter/butterscotch
- Grass
- Green bean
- Hay
- Mushroom
- Olive

- Sandalwood (American Oak)
- Tea leaf
- Tobacco

In older wines, you may smell:

- Balsamic
- Caramel
- Chemical
- Cigar box
- Coffee bean
- Leather
- Nuts
- Petrol (Riesling often smells this way)
- Tar
- Truffle

Some older wines elicit smells that are, well, just plain bad. Watch out for these:

- Acetone (nail polish)
- Cat pee
- Chemical
- Closed/dumb
- Garlic
- Green (underripe)
- Mouldy
- Musty
- Rubber
- Sour milk
- Stemmy (bitter)
- Sweaty (wet dog)
- Vegetative
- Vinegary
- Woody

Taste

You express how a wine tastes first by the spontaneous impression it creates in your mouth.

- ✔ Is it light, medium, or full-bodied?
- ✔ Is it dry, medium dry, or sweet?
- ✔ Is it soft and supple, or sharp and austere?

Think of taste not as a single sensation but as three progressive stages:

- ✔ **Stage 1: Initial taste.** One second after the wine hits your tongue, you can comment on the feel of it in your mouth. You can tell its weight and its degree of dryness or sweetness.

- ✔ **Stage 2: Secondary taste.** Five seconds after the wine has hit your tongue and spread to all parts of your palate, you experience all its elements — fruit, alcohol, acidity, tannin, and oak (if barrel-aged).

- ✔ **Stage 3: Aftertaste.** Five seconds after you swallow your first mouthful, you can determine the length of time the flavour remains in your mouth and comment on the finish. Is the wine well balanced, are all its elements in harmony? Are the tannins silky and supple or harsh and dusty?

Table 7-2 lists some descriptive terms associated with tasting wine.

Table 7-2	Common Terms to Describe Wine's Taste
Good Tastes	*Bad Tastes*
Balanced	Acidic (sharp, sour)
Complex	Austere (dry, without flavour)
Concentrated	Bitter
Firm	Dilute
Fleshy	Drying out
Fruity	Flabby (fat, lacking acidity)
Harmonious	Flawed
Length/lingering	Green
Lively	Harsh
Luscious	Hollow

(continued)

Table 7-2 (continued)

Good Tastes	Bad Tastes
Racy (we mean fresh and lively)	Hot (particularly alcoholic)
Rich	Oxidized
Round	Sharp
Sinewy	Short (fades on the palate)
Velvety	Stewed
Well-made	Tannic
	Tart
	Unbalanced

Chapter 8
Sharing Good Taste

• •

• •

*I*n Chapters 5 and 6, you read about how to taste wine. Now that you've got the idea, it might be fun to have some friends over to help you develop your newfound skill. It's a great excuse to get together, and who doesn't enjoy a little practise now and again? Perhaps you and your friends could form a tasting club. You can explore wine with a large or small group and in a variety of ways. There is a style of tasting to suit all occasions.

For the wine purist or taster who likes to emphasize the analytical side of wine, a tasting with no other distractions (such as food) is a good bet. Social butterflies, business professionals hosting clients, or people who just enjoy entertaining at home might prefer to combine a tasting with dinner. And when the local wine show comes to town, it provides an opportunity to step out with some of your wine-loving friends.

Organizing a Tasting

If you have never held a wine tasting before, the thought can be a bit daunting. It requires some forethought and a bit of extra effort, but when you get down to the nitty-gritty, it isn't difficult. Your first decision is what to taste. The simplest thing is to get two bottles of wine of any kind and compare them. See Chapters 5 and 6 for details on comparative tastings.

The whole point of a wine tasting is to learn something new about the wine. The best way to do this is to compare a wine you're already familiar with to one that's new to you. You can do this on a small scale at home alone: Go out and find a wine that tastes similar to a wine that you drink often, and take it from there. If you're going to the trouble of getting together with friends, anywhere from four to 10 different wines are enough to challenge the palate, but are still manageable in terms of organization. Barb's preferred number of wines for tastings at home is between six and eight. This allows for a good variety, and keeps more practical concerns, like the amount of glassware you have to have on hand, under control.

Planning a tasting is pretty much like planning a dinner party — you invite some friends, buy what you want to serve, turn the lights down low, and freshen the potpourri. Well, not quite. At a tasting, turn the lights up and forget about the potpourri.

Striking the right mood

Tasting wine is an intellectual challenge and a fun pastime that is enhanced by a suitable environment. Don't go out and buy a new house just because you want to taste wine, but set your dimmer switch to *high*, because a bright light is best to examine the wine and to see to write your notes (see Chapter 7 for a sample tasting sheet). Turn down the thermostat, as a cool room minimizes extraneous odours, prevents the wine from warming up too quickly, and makes it more comfortable for a group. The room will warm up anyway as conversation and enthusiasm escalate. If you like background music, by all means turn the stereo on softly, but Barb knows one wine journalist who finds even soothing classical music too distracting in a tasting. To be polite, you can ask your guests if they object.

When you invite your guests to the tasting, remind them not to wear perfume or any product that could interfere with the wine's bouquet or other guests' enjoyment of the experience. And don't put flowers on the table for the same reason. Their bouquet will compete with the wines'.

Setting the scene

You can hold your tasting in pretty much any room in your house — anywhere there's a table. Whether you usher your guests into your living room, dining room, kitchen, or some other inventive place, this list helps you spiff up your table and get down to some serious fun tasting.

> ✔ **White tablecloth(s).** You don't have to use your best linen — it's probably better that you don't, considering the potential for staining. You can buy a plastic-backed disposable tablecloth from the dollar store, the supermarket, or sometimes even the larger drugstores. They only cost $2 to $3 and they help protect your table as well as provide a white background for unbiased viewing. For more on the best ways to view wine, see Chapter 5.

- **Wineglasses.** Proper tasting glasses are best but not vital. Avoid those tiny, disposable plastic wineglasses — they're basically useless for tasting purposes. Try to find a glass that holds at least six ounces when filled to the brim. That way, when you pour in a two-ounce tasting portion, you've got plenty of space for swirling and studying the aromatics. A wineglass that is narrower at the rim than at the bowl helps keep the wine in the glass when you swirl and prevents the bouquet from escaping before you can get a good whiff. The glass should be clear, uncoloured/untinted, and smooth, not cut as in cut crystal. It should also have a stem so that you don't need to touch the bowl. Your hands can warm the wine too quickly and leave smudges that obscure your view of the colour and clarity. See Appendix C, "Coolers & Corkscrews" for information on where to buy tasting glasses.

- **Spittoons.** Yes, spittoons. Not the ornate kind, though. We suggest using either big, plastic disposable beer glasses, or large plastic yogurt containers. For aesthetic reasons, don't use transparent containers. It is proper etiquette to spit your tasting wine rather than swallow it. You may pour only two ounces into a glass but, if you taste 10 wines and drink them all, you've consumed almost a full bottle. That's just a bit too much of a good thing. If you have a problem spitting in public, practise in the bath. You'll soon get used to it, especially when you see everyone around you doing it — at the tasting, that is, not in your bathroom.

- **Tasting cards.** Use these to record your impressions of the various wines you taste. This way, you can remember the various wines better when you compare notes. You can use regular notepaper as well.

- **Fresh water.** Use this to cleanse your palate between wines or to rinse your glass if you are using it for more than one wine.

- **Crusty French bread.** Cut the loaf into bite-size cubes and nibble to cleanse your palate.

- **Paper bags.** Use these to hide the labels if you're having a *blind tasting*. A blind tasting is a great way to taste the wines without knowing which is which. It adds a dimension of guesswork to the tasting, which can be a lot of fun. If you, as host and tasting coordinator, would also like to taste them blind, you can always recruit a helper to organize the wines and pour them out.

Be sure to remove the entire *capsule* (the metal or plastic cap on top of the bottle) before you bring the wines out to your guests. The capsules on most bottles usually have some recognizable lettering or symbols that reveal the wine's identity.

Hopefully, no one will spill anything on your prize Persian rug. But just in case, it pays to be prepared. If someone spills red wine, quickly place a wad of paper towels over the spill to absorb as much of the wine as possible. Don't rub it into the carpet fibres. Pour some soda water on the stain and use a clean wad of paper towels to absorb that. Press hard into the carpet to squeeze the moisture into the towelling. Keep replacing the wet towels with dry ones until the fabric is almost dry. Take another dry wad of paper towels and weight it down over the stain with a book. Leave it overnight to dry. Soda water helps remove wine from clothing too, but it works best when the stain is very fresh.

Tasting in Private

Whether it's a small gathering of close friends or a bigger, more boisterous crew of business associates, holding a wine tasting in your home can be lots of fun for all involved. You might just want to have a tasting on its own, or maybe include it as part of a dinner party. In this section, we give you some guidelines to make your wine tasting an affair to remember.

Intimate encounters

Some styles of tastings are easier to manage if you are just a few people. As a rule of thumb, you can divide up a single bottle (750 ml) into at least 12 tasting portions. A steady hand and eye can squeeze out 16 servings. That's your guest limit if you want to keep it to one bottle per wine. If you have fewer people, you can always offer the rest of the wine with dinner or a snack after the tasting, or cork it up again with a wine preserving device (see Appendix C, "Coolers & Corkscrews").

If you have the space, seating everyone at the same table is the most congenial way to carry out the tasting, but smaller tables are fine also. Try to leave everyone enough room to have several glasses in front of them, as well as space to write notes. Put out a different glass for each wine in front of each guest.

If you don't have quite enough glasses to go around, you can divide the tasting into *flights* (sections), rinsing the glasses between each flight. When you are planning, try to make sure that the wines in each flight have something in common. You could serve the younger wines in the first flight, older or lighter-bodied ones in the second flight, and so on. (If you are not familiar with the wines, you might have to have a small preliminary taste prior to pouring them out.)

1. **Place the glasses in a row or semicircle in front of each taster.** Number the glasses in order from left to right (at least mentally) and make sure that you or your helper pours the same wine into the glass at the same position for all tasters (wine #1 in glass #1, etc.). If you don't want your guests to know what the wines are, cover the bottles with paper bags or pour out the wine and put the bottles away before your guests sit down. Don't forget to number the bottles to correspond to the glasses! Your guests will eventually want to know what they are tasting.

2. **Review tasting guidelines.** If your friends are completely new to tasting, it helps to provide them with some keywords for describing wines (see Chapter 7). You should also explain the basics of looking, smelling, and tasting as described in Chapters 5 and 6.

3. **Let everyone examine and taste the wines, noting their impressions on the tasting cards.** Estimate about three to five minutes a wine for this. Discourage conversation during this period to let each taster come to an unbiased opinion. (It is almost impossible to inhibit conversation completely in a recreational tasting, but you can ask your guests to respect those who wish to taste in relative quiet.)

4. **Deliver the verdict.** When people have completed their analysis and scored their wines, encourage them to express their views in an orderly fashion, and try to provoke some discussion. Ask them for their scores and tabulate them to see if there is a consensus in the room. Everybody likes to know whether their favourite wine got the top score.

Think about organizing your tasting around a particular wine-related theme, such as grape variety, geographic region, or even colour. Themed tastings are fun in an intimate setting and quite helpful, as they anchor the tasting around a particular wine characteristic and provide a focus for everyone. It's a really good idea if you and your friends are wine-tasting neophytes. These theme suggestions presume that you will taste the wines blind, but nobody says you have to!

- **Bordeaux blends from around the world.** Yes, it's an oxymoron, but everyone around the world wants to make great wines like Bordeaux's blends with some or all of Cabernet Sauvignon, Merlot, and Cabernet Franc. You can find these wines from Australia, California, and Canada, to name a few. The Californians have dubbed their Bordeaux-style blends *Meritage*.

- **Cool-climate Chardonnays.** The standard for this category is Burgundy, particularly Chablis, but Canadian Chardonnays fit right in. Other interesting cool-climate Chardonnays come from New Zealand's south island, Oregon, and the Carneros in California.

- **British Columbia Pinot Blanc.** This grape does very well in this province. It has much in common with Chardonnay, but a fresh character all its own, too. Try comparing the Pinot Blancs from several wineries, but try to get the same vintage, if possible. This makes it easier to pick up some of the wineries' individual style traits and terroirs. If you feel you need a traditional European standard for comparison, put an Alsatian Pinot Blanc in as a *ringer* (a wine with similar traits destined to confuse the tasters). A ringer only works in a blind tasting but you can still use it as a benchmark in a tasting where the wines are known.

- **A vertical of a Bordeaux château.** A *vertical tasting* is one in which you taste several vintages of the same wine, for example a Bordeaux château such as d'Angludet or Montalbert. For this type of tasting you need to collect the bottles over several years, as very few stores stock multiple vintages of any one wine. If you would like to organize a vertical tasting of a Canadian wine, look for a premium single vineyard red wine such as Hillebrand Glenlake Vineyard Cabernet Sauvignon from Niagara.

- **Dry white Bordeaux.** This generic type of tasting is a great way to familiarize yourself with the style of a particular wine-growing region. White Bordeaux is made from a blend of Sémillon and Sauvignon Blanc grapes. Wineries differ on which grape to emphasize. In this case, we recommend you pre-taste your wines and arrange the Sémillon-based wines in one flight and the Sauvignon Blanc in another.

- **Canadian Icewine versus German Eiswein.** The Germans invented it but Canadian winters are more reliably cold, providing suitable conditions for making Icewine just about every year. (Barb grudgingly admits that winter now has one redeeming feature.) Icewines, be they Canadian or German, usually come in half-bottles (375 ml) so you'll need to buy more bottles or invite fewer people to this tasting.

- **A comparison of red varietals.** You have a broad choice in this category. You can use obviously different grape types, like Pinot Noir, Nebbiolo, Gamay, and Zinfandel, or compare reds from one country or region, like Italy or California. If you prefer more of a challenge, taste the Bordeaux varietals side-by-side. To add still another twist, repeat one of the wines in a second glass and try to pick out the identical wine.

- **A comparison of Syrah from the Northern Rhône region and Shiraz from Australia.** The best Syrah-based wines from the Northern Rhône, Hermitage, and the best Australian Shiraz are expensive, but you can find excellent wines from the neighbouring appellations, Crozes-Hermitage and St. Joseph, to compare with some moderately priced Australian selections. Canada has a few, very young plantings of Syrah in both B.C. and Ontario. If you can find one, it's worth including in your tasting, but don't downgrade it for lack of intensity. Try to predict what the wine will be like as the vines mature.

- **British Columbia Riesling and Ontario Riesling.** Riesling has been a mainstay in the Canadian wine industry for a good many years now. You can find some interesting versions from several established vineyards. For a more specific comparison, limit the wines to B.C.'s Okanagan Valley and Ontario's Niagara Peninsula. You can even compare Rieslings from the north and south sections of the Okanagan or the Niagara Bench and the Niagara Plain.

- **Same wine, different glasses.** Pour the same wine into three or four different glasses. Try a standard tasting glass, an oversized balloon-shaped glass, even a tumbler. Each glass manufacturer claims to have designed the perfect glass for the various styles of wine. Is there really a difference?

> ✔ **A timed tasting.** Taste the same wine at different times to study the effect of aeration. Open several bottles of the same wine: one bottle just before the tasting begins, another one hour before, and another six hours before. Note if the wine changes. If it does, is it for better or worse?

Crowd scenes

If you intend to invite more people than you have chairs, you can arrange an ambulatory tasting where people walk around, glass in hand, stopping to taste the wines that interest them. Use several smaller tables instead of one large, communal one. Spread the tables (known as *tasting stations*) around the room and give each taster one glass. Place a large spittoon and some water for rinsing glasses at each tasting station. As the tasters go from table to table, they try one wine at a time, pour out any extra in the glass into the spittoon, rinse the glass, and taste the next wine. You may use up a little more wine this way, as it's more difficult to judge the amount. A measured pouring spout like those often used in bars can be very helpful. You can control the pouring better if you recruit some helpers to serve the wine.

As in a sit-down tasting, white cloths on the tables make it easier to look at the wine. Small pieces of bread or plain crackers are useful as palate cleansers. If you opt to serve snack food, keep it on a separate table so it doesn't interfere with the wines. Refer to the list earlier in the chapter to make sure your tables are properly outfitted.

Each tasting station can have one or several wines available. Try to group similar wines together — all whites, all Gewürztraminer, all Canadian, all reds under $10, and so on. At a larger table, you could have different categories of wine at each end. If it's a blind tasting, make a list of all the wines beforehand. You can either reveal the wines with great fanfare at the end of the tasting or distribute the list to your guests.

Most of the public wine shows and large trade tastings are organized as ambulatory tastings (separate tasting stations instead of one central tasting surface). You can get some ideas for your own event by spending some time at one of these affairs. Look for some tips on sampling a wine show later in this chapter.

Dinner parties

One of the easiest ways to add another dimension to your dinner parties or other gatherings at home is to incorporate a wine tasting. The only problem with this is that it's sometimes difficult to prevent cooking smells from interfering with the bouquet of the wines. One way around this is to use a barbecue or indoor grill and prepare your meal at the last minute. Roasted and stewed foods or particularly strong-smelling foods might be more of a problem, but some advance preparation and good ventilation will help.

There are no hard and fast rules for organizing a tasting around a dinner party. After all, the important thing is to enjoy the time with your friends. But, because food influences your perception of wine, it makes sense to hold the tasting before serving the meal.

As your guests arrive, you can offer them an apéritif, if you like — a light white wine without any powerful flavours that might interfere with the tasting to follow. Sparkling wine or champagne is ideal. *Still* (non-sparkling) whites could include a Canadian Vidal or Seyval Blanc, a Pinot Blanc, or light, unoaked Chardonnay. Any hors d'oeuvres served at this time should also be mild-flavoured. Once everyone has arrived, ask your guests to proceed to the tasting.

Tie your dinner to your wine-tasting theme if you think there will be wine left over from the tasting. Prolong the enjoyment — serve them with dinner.

Of course you want to serve quality wine at your tasting — but you need to consider what quantity you will need, too. As a rule of thumb, an individual can consume up to the equivalent of a full bottle of wine over the course of an evening where a variety of wines are served. This may seem like a lot, but if the wine is sipped slowly over several hours, and with food, it's not overly excessive. As a responsible host, however, you need to keep an eye on things. Encourage your guests to be moderate, provide spittoons for the tasting, and offer water to slow down consumption and prevent dehydration. Make sure you call a taxi for anyone you think might benefit.

Tasting in Public

Public wine tastings are more and more popular. Most city centres host a wine show every year at a convention centre. Non-profit organizations use tastings as fundraising vehicles, and wine-producing countries organize tastings to promote their wines both at home and around the world.

Cruising the best wines

Most of these "shows" are mega crowd scenes set up with booths, tables, or tasting stations around a large hall. In the case of a wine show, the booths showcase a number of products. The winery owner or a *wine agent* (a sales-person who represents the wines of a particular winery in a specific location) rents the booth on behalf of the owner. With any luck, the *winemaker*, who at a small winery might also be the owner, will be in the booth to talk to you about the wine. Often, a national trade organization rents a booth. You can usually find the Italian Trade Commission or the Australian Wine Council at the major shows, for example. Booths like theirs give you the chance to concentrate on the wines of one specific country. In other booths, wine agents showcase the wines they represent, which may come from several different countries.

When you arrive at the show, take a few minutes to study the program and locate a few key booths. As you wander around, you can always orient yourself by these locations. If the show extends into other halls, identify the booths that mark the entrances and exits. If you see some names that interest you, mark where they are on your plan. Find out if there are any seminars or demonstrations going on. Some of them require pre-registration or advance tickets, so do that as soon as you arrive and get it out of the way. Murphy's Law holds true: The seminar you want is invariably on the opposite side of the hall with the most popular speaker. Once you are all set, buy your tasting tickets if needed, and head out to taste.

Because these shows are often very large, it helps to have a plan of attack. The entrance fee for a public show scheduled over a weekend (Friday to Sunday) is often quite low, so you might consider going twice. If you are looking for wines to stock your cellar, you need to take time to choose. Don't forget to consider wines both for early drinking as well as for aging. Chapter 11 discusses storing wine at home.

You won't be able to taste every wine, so make a mental priority list. Some people like to start with whites, then move on to reds. Others like to run through all the wines that interest them at a particular booth. Fresh water for cleansing your palate is always available at these shows, so it's possible to change styles of wine without confusing your taste buds too much.

The best time to attend the show is as early as possible. Try to go when the show opens on the first day. The hordes descend after 5 p.m. and it gets harder to speak with the winemakers and agents.

All the right gear

Barb thinks going to a wine show is a bit like climbing a mountain and therefore equips herself accordingly. Instead of carrying a purse or briefcase, she wears a compact backpack. That way her hands are free to take notes. She carries a pen on a cord around her neck (did you ever have a teacher who did that?) and she even carries her tasting glass in a little harness slung around her neck. She found it at the Toronto Wine and Cheese Show and thinks it's indispensable. Keep your eyes open for them; they are very practical. It's so easy to put your glass down while you're writing your notes and then walk away (just ask Barb!).

Getting the right answers

You can walk away from a wine show with helpful information — if you know some of the right questions to ask. It can be intimidating talking to wine professionals at first if you're just getting to know the basics. These questions are designed to help you strike up a conversation with the winemakers and agents and find out if the wine you're tasting is really worth considering adding to your store.

- **Was it a good vintage?** Wine quality is compromised by bad weather, particularly frost or hail in the spring and rain just before harvest, but a sunny, warm summer can make up for some of those problems.

- **What was the yield in the vineyard?** Removing some bunches of grapes to reduce the yield results in more intense flavours. So the lower the yield, the better.

- **How was the wine fermented?** Winemakers can manipulate the fermentation process by controlling the temperature. Long cool fermentations contribute to elegance and balance. Hot turbulent fermentations, usually reserved for red wines, extract more colour and more intense flavours. Barrel fermentations, used more for whites than for reds, add oak flavours and richness. Because barrels are so expensive, this technique is reserved for the best grapes in the vineyard. You can expect a wine that receives this tender-loving care to be of high quality and likely to improve if you keep it in your cellar for a while.

- **How was the wine aged?** If barrels were used, were they small barrels that contribute lots of flavour, or large casks that add only subtle nuances if any at all. Were the barrels *new* (stronger flavoured) or *old* (milder flavoured)? Barrel-aged wines are more likely to improve in your cellar.

- **Is the wine ready to drink or does it need aging?** Wineries usually release their wines when they are ready to drink. Still, some wines may improve over time after they have been bottled. Your wine might taste great on the day that you buy it, but it might be even rounder and smoother to the taste if you wait six months, a year — even 10 years. Be forewarned, though, that many winemakers overestimate their wine's longevity because they base their predictions on ideal cellar conditions. Unless cooled, the average North American cellar is warmer than ideal and ages the wines more quickly.

- **What foods go well with the wine?** Other people's opinions on food matches can serve as good guidelines. Keep in mind, though, that they are often coloured by their own personal preferences.

Five important wine shows

Okanagan Wine Festivals
1527 Ellis Street, Kelowna, BC, V1Y 2A7
Tel: (250) 861-6654, Fax: (250) 861-3942
E-mail: info@owfs.com

Spring festival: A four-day event in May to coincide with the apple blossom season. Features about 30 events including tastings of new releases, luncheons, dinners, and tours of wineries.

Fall festival: The largest wine festival in the Okanagan Valley, held annually in September. Features close to 100 events — tastings, food, awards, and vineyard visits.

Icewine festival: Opportunities to taste award-winning Icewines, attend the winemakers' dinner, and visit a variety of seminars.

Vancouver Playhouse International Wine Festival
160 West 1st Avenue, Vancouver, BC, V5Y 1A4
Tel: (604) 872-6622, Fax: (604) 873-3714
E-mail: winefest@bc.sympatico.ca

A benefit tasting in support of the Vancouver Playhouse, this annual event centres on a specific international theme. In recent years, the wines of Spain, Italy, and Australia have been featured. It provides an opportunity to taste upwards of 500 wines, though few tasters have that much stamina. Approximately 150 wineries from 15 countries participate.

Niagara Grape and Wine Festivals
8 Church Street, Suite 100, St. Catharines, ON, L2R 3B3
Tel: (905) 688-0212, Fax: (905) 688-2570
E-mail: vidal@niagarafest.on.ca

Niagara New Vintage Release: A gala evening in early June. It showcases recent vintages that have not previously been released to the public. It gives an opportunity to talk with winemakers and winery owners about the recent vintage.

Niagara Grape and Wine Festival: Held over two weeks in September, the festival includes lots of opportunities to taste local wines and to visit area wineries.

Niagara Icewine Evening: A gala evening of food and wine held in January, during the period of the Icewine harvest. Tastings feature offerings from the most recent harvest, as well as other award-winning wines.

Grey Gables School Cuvée
1 Dexter Street, St. Catharines, ON, L2S 2L4
Tel: (905) 685-4577, Fax: (905) 685-5102
E-mail: office@greygablesschool.com

Grey Gables School offers Montessori and International Baccalaureate programs for children in preschool to grade 10. It holds a fundraiser that provides students with scholarships while showcasing Ontario's top wines. Wineries submit some of their finest wines to blind tasting competitions held in advance.

California Wine Fair
4145 North Service Road, Suite 200, Burlington, ON, L7L 6A3
Tel: 1-800-558-2675, Fax: (905) 319-4211

This series of consumer and trade tastings takes place in major city centres across Canada in the early spring. Representatives of many American wineries are on hand to pour wine and explain the conditions in which the wine was grown and made.

Watch your newspaper and local media for announcements about wine and food shows in your community. In some cities, these are annual events. These public shows provide good opportunities to taste many different wine styles from countries around the world. You can often find a range of wine accessories as well — from bottle stoppers to custom-built wine cellars. You might think you've seen it all, but you never know when you'll find something new and useful.

Part III
Enjoying Wine

The 5th Wave   By Rich Tennant

"I'M PRETTY SURE YOU'RE SUPPOSED TO JUST SMELL THE CORK."

In this part . . .

We dispense with the theory of wine tasting and get down to the fun, practical stuff: going out to restaurants and finding out if the waiter knows how to serve wine. We also explore reasons for sending wine back — and how to do it with aplomb. Then we provide a crash course on serving wine at home. That chapter covers everything from extracting the cork with style to choosing the right glass.

This part also takes you down to the basement to discover where to situate your cellar, how to make it a wine-friendly environment, and what to put in it. And for those celebrations to come, we check out some wines that will last longer than half the marriages you know.

If you'd like to buy some interesting wines for either immediate consumption or for aging in your cellar, you'll find out that there are more wine-buying options in Canada than you may have previously thought.

Chapter 9

Wine in Restaurants

• •

In This Chapter

▶ Getting out of the house and into your favourite bistro

▶ Dealing with wine lists

▶ Buying by the glass or bottle

▶ Sending wine back gracefully

▶ Choosing wine for vegetarians

• •

*L*et's face it, it can be a daunting experience to have a wine list thrust into your hands while the waiter hovers expectantly over you. What to do? You can always take the easy way out and ask for the *house wine* (usually bought in bulk by the restaurant and brought to the table in a glass or carafe rather than in a bottle with a label). But don't forget, there's another question you'll be asked: White or red? Or even, rosé?

Besides, why take the easy way out when you can have so much fun psyching out the waiter with your viticultural knowledge! Watch other restaurant patrons turn to you admiringly as you navigate the wine list, all with a great deal of style. This chapter shows you how. Did we forget to mention that this is also a great way to impress a date?

Getting to Know the House Wine

Ordering the house wine in a restaurant is for the most part a pretty safe bet — especially because you don't have to utter some unpronounceable European name (try saying Schloss von Schönborn Hattenheimer Pfaffenberg Riesling Spätlese 1999 Halbtrocken in a crowded restaurant!). At least the waiter can pronounce "house wine." Presto! Some kind of immediate communication has been established between you and your server, plus the house wine's sure to be in stock.

Almost every restaurant you patronize will have a house wine (both red and white, sometimes even rosé). These are wines usually offered by the glass or carafe and, unless you ask, you won't know what specific wine you're drinking. The waiter won't open the bottle at your table as it's probably already open in the back of the restaurant — it may have a screw top or even be "bag-in-a-box."

House wine is a good way to go if you only want a glass or two. You don't have to feel like you've wasted a whole bottle. It's also in the restaurant's best interest for you to have a glass of the house wine, as the mark-up is higher than it is on wines by the bottle — as well as on food. You might end up eating more too, as wine is an appetite stimulant.

Even though house wines appear to be the least expensive wine on a restaurant's wine list, and the diner assumes that the proprietor has carefully selected products that will not offend, the reality is that you pay a higher mark-up on house wines than you do on other wines. If you think you and your companion(s) will drink at least four glasses — almost a bottle — you're probably better off buying by the bottle rather than the glass. By spending five dollars more and choosing a wine with *provenance* (a named producer with a stated year and region) the discriminating diner gets better value.

Ordering wine by the glass can be deceptive in terms of the value of the glass relative to the cost of the full bottle. All restaurants are required to post the size of their *pour* (amount poured) by the glass. Usually this will be 6 ounces. The wait staff estimate that they get 4 pours from a 26-ounce bottle, allowing for spillage and heavy-handedness. Multiply the cost of a glass by four and compare it to the bottle price to see how much you are actually paying.

The idea of house wine

In Europe, the owners of restaurants would visit local wineries and try their wines out of the barrel. When they found one they liked, at the price they liked, they would buy the barrel and have it transported to their own cellar where they would bottle it, usually unlabelled, and sell it more cheaply than other wines.

The quality of these house wines invariably reflected the taste (or lack thereof) of the restaurant proprietor. European immigrants who opened their own restaurants in their newly adopted countries imported the concept. But you can understand why the practise lost its local flavour when there were no vineyards within an easy drive. Soon, restaurant owners had to purchase their house wines from the local store. These were usually screw-top *magnums* (1,500-ml bottles) at the cheapest price they could find.

Today, house wines are offered at the lowest price on the wine list. Restaurant owners are fully aware that the average diner has little or no knowledge about wine and doesn't know how to select wine off a wine list. They are content because the house wine is priced the lowest.

Most house wines, though inoffensive, are pretty bland. Now that you know a little more about wine, you can look for something with a bit more to offer in the flavour department.

Reading a Wine List

Wine lists come in all shapes and sizes. A wine list worth its salt describes the wines clearly — with no pretentious, overbearing adjectives that force you to read it three times. Besides being familiar with the different types of wine lists circulating out there, when ordering wine in a restaurant you also want to consider things like the wine's weight and acidity, and also how your food is being prepared. All of these factors help you choose a wine that elevates your meal to a whole new level.

Wine lists are laid out in seven basic styles:

1. **The Conventional List:** White and red wines on separate sheets, listed by country and region (invariably beginning with France — unless it's an Italian restaurant). This is the most common style and usually directs you to the wines you are most familiar with.

2. **The Varietal List:** Wines listed by grape variety. For example, listed under Cabernet Sauvignon is a list of wines made from the Cabernet Sauvignon grape, from several growing regions. This method allows you to experiment with grape varieties you enjoy. If you like the Chardonnay grape variety, you may enjoy a change from the growing region of California and try an example from Italy or New Zealand instead.

3. **The Trendy List:** Wines listed by style. You might see headings like "Full-Bodied," "Dry Reds," or "Dry Whites with Character." This method allows you to match your food with a wine more easily. For example, if your dish is light, you'll head for a light wine.

4. **The Old-Fashioned List:** Wines listed by labels. Usually leather-bound books found only in more up-market restaurants and clubs. This presentation has the advantage of showing you exactly what you're getting in a wine, but is time-consuming because of the number of pages you have to contend with.

5. **The No-Nonsense List:** Wines listed under two headings: Red and White, in ascending order of price with the country or region stated in brackets. What could be simpler?

6. **The Marketing-Minded List:** Wines listed next to specific dishes on the menu. Diners are taking more care these days about how they match food and wine. The canny restaurateur will suggest two or three wines in different price brackets with each item on the menu, or pair a dish with a specific glass of wine. This makes the choice easy for the unsure diner.

7. **The Price-Driven List:** Wines listed according to different price brackets.

We've all seen this before, and groaned in exasperation. Many wine lists describe the wines all right, but in such hyperbolic terms that whoever wrote it would have you believe each selection is fit for an emperor's table. Beware of such hucksterism, especially if the descriptions are as vague and contradictory as an astrologer's prediction. Descriptions such as, "Crisply dry, packed with sweet blackcurrant fruit, round and mellow on the palate with an elegant long finish" is meaningless unless you have experienced the wine before. What you want to know about a wine is:

- ✔ **Does it go with the dish I ordered?**
- ✔ **What is the grape variety or blend and the vintage?**
- ✔ **Is it full-bodied, medium-bodied, or light?**
- ✔ **Is it dry, off-dry, or sweet?**
- ✔ **Where does it come from and who made it?**
- ✔ **Is it ready for drinking?**
- ✔ **Is it being served to me at the right temperature?**
- ✔ **Will I have to take out a second mortgage to pay for it?**

If these important questions *aren't* answered in the wine's description, ask your server. She should know.

Pick the perfect wine

When it comes to matching the wine to the dish you've ordered, there are no hard and fast rules — only some basic principles to keep in mind. Forget those old clichés about pairing red wine with meat, white wine with fish, or white wine with white meat. These concepts are rules of thumb that have some validity — but if you follow them to the letter, you deny yourself a lot of wine possibility.

What happens if you don't like red wine or you react badly to it? Does this mean you can't enjoy a glass of wine with your steak? Certainly not. The only principle you have to keep in mind is *balance*.

Think of a boxing match when pairing wine and food. If you put two boxers in the ring and one is a heavyweight, the other a flyweight, there will be no contest. The heavier boxer will overpower the lighter one from the sound of the bell. The same is true of food. If you try a delicate red wine like an Ontario Gamay or Beaujolais with a spicy game dish in a rich sauce, you're not going to be able to taste the wine. By the same token, if you try an oaky California Chardonnay with a poached Dover sole, the wine will just about obliterate the taste of the fish. See Chapter 14 for matching wine and food.

Wines that work well with sole are Sauvignon Blanc from the Niagara region in Ontario and Pinot Blanc from B.C.'s Okanagan Valley.

Remember weight and acidity

A wine's colour is less important than its weight and acidity when it comes to pairing it with the appropriate food.

Weight

The weight of a wine is defined simply as how heavy it feels in your mouth. Wines with higher alcohol are full-bodied; they'll have a heavier feel on the palate than wines with lower alcohol. Try this experiment: Take a Gamay (Beaujolais) at 11.5 or 12 percent alcohol and compare it with a Châteauneuf-du-Pape at 13.5 percent alcohol. You'll notice a marked difference in the mouth feel. The Gamay will be light-bodied and fruity. The Châteauneuf will be full in your mouth and heavier on your palate.

Acidity

That freshness you taste in a wine, the zestiness that carries the flavour and cleans off the palate, is the effect of that wine's acidity. Acidity is more important than flavour in combination with food. Acid can clean the palate of strong food flavours such as butter, oil, salt, and smoke. A very dry wine, such as a Riesling or a crisp Chardonnay (Chablis, for example), works well with a strongly flavoured dish like smoked salmon, which is salty, smoky, fishy, *and* oily.

Try some smoked fish with a dry Riesling from Ontario or B.C. Then try the same fish with an off-dry Riesling, also from Ontario or B.C. The dry Riesling, with a high acid count, does an excellent job of cutting the fishiness, whereas the less acidic off-dry Riesling doesn't cut it at all, and leaves you tasting, well, fishy.

Consider how it's cooked

The way a dish is prepared alters the style of wine best suited to it. Take steak, for instance. A simple grilled steak will go with most medium-bodied red wines. But what happens when you add different condiments or spices to it? Or even a sauce? You'd be amazed at just how many wines — unique and exciting, all of them — you can pair with an unassuming steak.

✔ **Steak, simply grilled:** Medium-bodied reds (B.C. Pinot Noir, Burgundys, Chiantis, or red Rioja from Spain).

✔ **Steak with a spicy marinade:** Fuller-bodied reds with a sweeter fruit character (Southern Okanagan Cabernet Sauvignon, Chilean reds, Rhône reds, Australian Cabernets).

✔ **Pepper steak seared with brandy:** Heavyweight reds (Niagara Old Vines Foch, California Zinfandel, Australian Shiraz, Châteauneuf-du-Pape).

✔ **Steak with Béarnaise (or any cream) sauce:** Softer reds of medium weight with a touch of sweetness (Ontario Baco Noir, German reds, California Merlots, Oregon Pinot Noirs).

✔ **Steak tartar (raw steak):** Lighter, fruity reds with good acidity to clean the palate (Ontario and B.C Gamays, Beaujolais-Villages, Valpolicella).

How do you like your meat cooked? Do you like it mooing on the plate or cooked like shoe leather? You can enhance your dining pleasure by selecting the style of wine that goes best with the way your meat is "done." If you prefer your steak rare, choose a tannic wine. The blood of meat contains iron; tannic red wines cleanse the palate of that taste. For this type of rare fare, go for young red Bordeaux, Barabesco, Barolo, Chianti, and New World Cabernets. If you prefer your meat well done, select wines with as little tannins as possible — either mature reds in which the tannins have softened, or wines that have fewer tannins to begin with, such as Beaujolais.

Ordering Wine

Once you've selected your wine from the wine list, you initiate the time-honoured ritual between you and your server — a complicated dance that involves a lot of to-ing and fro-ing and finally results in you either accepting or rejecting the proffered bottle.

It is customary for the server to bring the unopened bottle to the table and show you the label. This is to ensure that the wine is exactly the one you ordered. If a particular vintage date is stated on the wine list, make sure it's the same one on the label. (Some restaurants don't update their lists with new vintages, and you may not want the younger wine.)

Now comes the test. Your server pours a sample of about two ounces into your glass. You pick it up, inspect the colour, swirl it, sniff it, and finally taste it. If it passes inspection, you accept it and the server pours for your guests and finally for you.

Your server should place the cork on the table beside you so that you can examine it. The end that has been in the bottle (referred to as the *business end*) should be swollen and wet. This tells you the wine has been stored on its side. A wet and swollen cork seals off the bottle more completely, leaving little room for air to get in and oxidize the wine. You should also sniff the

---

Going through the ritual

The pantomime between diner and server that is repeated every time a bottle of wine is ordered goes back to the days when wine was transported in wooden barrels by oxcart to the local inn.

After being filled at the winery, the wooden bungs used to seal the barrels were wrapped in burlap dipped in olive oil (it was thought to make them airtight). The winemaker would sample the wine from a hole in the barrel's side, which would then have to be sealed. Bungs were used for just this purpose. When the bung was hammered into the barrel, bits of burlap and drops of oil would often fall onto the surface of the wine. Later on, when the wine was racked off into jugs to be served at table, some of that debris would still be in the wine.

Therefore, it was the host who was poured the first taste of the wine, so that he (and not his guests) would be the one to encounter any bits of burlap or oil as he sipped. This was also a way of showing the guests that they wouldn't be poisoned!

The tradition continues to this day — albeit for different reasons!

---

cork to check for mouldy smells that indicate a bad bottle. See Chapter 10 for more details on corks and spoiled wine.

Sending Wine Back

What happens if the wine you order looks like bilge water, smells like your son's hockey bag, and you don't even want to bring it to your face let alone let it pass your lips? Your dinner companions will not thank you for foisting on them a wine that tastes like a flooded basement. Don't be bashful. Send it back. The waiter will not lose his job. The restaurant will not be forced to close. If the wine is patently bad then it should not have been served in the first place. Too many wines that are flawed are consumed in restaurants because patrons are nervous about returning them. Some of these spoiled bottles may just be mildly corked, but the experience is unpleasant enough and can ruin an evening out. Our Canadian politeness should not extend to bad bottles of wine. (See Chapter 5 for a description of corked wine.)

If you order wine by the glass, ask the waiter to bring the bottle over and pour it at your table. This ensures that the wine you get is the one advertised on the wine list. You can also see how much of the bottle has already been poured. If yours is the last glass poured from a bottle, there could be a problem. That bottle could have been sitting open for much of the day and slowly oxidizing. This exposure to air will age the wine and give it a flat or stewed flavour. If the end of the bottle is offered to you, politely ask your server to open a fresh one.

Deciding who tastes

It used to be that the man always ordered the wine — and paid the bill too! But dining etiquette has changed. Quite often, a woman chooses the wine and the cheque is split between diners. Usually, the server shows the wine and offers it for tasting to the person who ordered it, although that person may indicate someone else as taster. Some servers automatically offer the wine to the woman — perhaps in deference to equality of the sexes.

Many restaurants still present only one wine list to the table, in the belief that one person will take responsibility for ordering. This is a tradition that may soon change, however. Interest in wine is growing; most diners like to know what wines the restaurant has to offer, and to discuss the merits of several before deciding what to order.

Real-Life Wine Experiences

Experienced wait staff do not hesitate to take back a bottle you say is not up to scratch but, occasionally, you may run into a server who still has a few things to learn. By the same token, you need not feel intimidated by the waiter who brings you the wine or by the ritual of opening and pouring the first taste. Bad bottles are more common than you might think. Just take your time and taste the wine carefully. At first, you might be unsure of your ability to judge it accurately, but after a few times, it gets easier.

The wrong way

Once upon a time, a long, long time ago, when Barb was young, naive, and foolishly in love, she and her beloved went out for a very special celebratory dinner. The reason for the celebration has long since been forgotten but the memory of the dinner lingers on. Barb's beloved, who knew absolutely nothing about wine but who held with the time-honoured tradition of men being born with a capacity to choose wine, selected a half-bottle of something extremely expensive. Barb, who knew equally little about wine at the time, was impressed, as the situation dictated. The wine steward was dressed in a red jacket as this was a very elegant restaurant and he wore around his neck one of those tiny silver saucers known as tastevins. Of course, nobody uses those any more, but this was a long, long time ago.

The wine steward appeared at the table with the marvellous half-bottle and presented the label to whom else but the male, who, not knowing he was supposed to inspect the label for accuracy and vintage and having forgotten the foreign name of the expensive wine he had ordered anyway, indicated to the lordly major domo to open the bottle. The steward began to pour a small portion into the "gentleman's" glass. With a show of manly bravado, of which Barb had previously only seen glimmers, the gentleman instructed the waiter to dispatch with the tasting and pour immediately, serving the lady first. The waiter gasped, "You would not like to taste the wine first, M'sieur?"

"No," he replied. "That tradition is too old-fashioned, the wine will be good." The wine steward, being of the "Customer Is Always Right" school of service, poured as instructed, all the while peering down his nose in righteous indignation. Barb couldn't find any space under the table to crawl, so she just held her chin up and kept her peace.

Sure enough, the wine wasn't any good. Neither Barb nor her date (this was where he was demoted from "gentleman") knew why at the time, but the wine just didn't live up to expectations. It had a bit of a musty odour, too.

The moral of the story: Don't overdo the gentlemanly thing and don't second-guess the wine. A taste is all it takes.

The right way

Many years later, hardly more sophisticated but much more knowledgeable in wine, Barb and some friends went out for a cheap and cheery dinner at a tiny, small-town restaurant reputed to serve good food. The wine list was pretty basic and they chose an everyday Appellation Contrôlée Bordeaux known for its decent value. The waiter brought the bottle to the table and proceeded to open it, but without showing the label. The table deferred to Barb to taste the wine (she has accepted the fact that her reputation is put on the line every time she dines out). The wine was corked. The waiter, however, insisted that that type of wine was supposed to taste that way!

Barb was just as insistent, and the waiter took the wine into the back to confer with the cellar master, who doubled as the chef. The waiter returned shortly with a new bottle and stated, just as shortly, that the cellar master/chef/owner agreed that the wine was off. Fortunately, the food lived up to its reputation.

The moral? Anyone who can cook can open a restaurant and probably make a go of it — at least for a while. But there are many restaurants out there whose staff receives no training whatsoever in serving wine. You, as a diner, have the right to refuse a bottle of wine you feel is deficient. If the wait staff lacks training, be patient but be firm. Once you receive the replacement bottle, you might even offer the server a sample of the good wine to take back to the kitchen to compare with the bad one. Some restaurant staff might be uncomfortable with this, but others leap at the chance to learn.

It is your right to refuse a bad bottle of wine.

Wines for Vegetarians

Just because you don't eat meat doesn't mean you have to deny yourself the pleasure of wine. If your diet consists mainly of vegetables, fruits, and nuts, go for wines that have good acidity. The white grape variety that best suits most green vegetables (including such difficult veggies to match with wine as asparagus, avocado, and artichoke) is Sauvignon Blanc — especially from France's Loire Valley (Sancerre, Pouilly-Fumé) and New Zealand.

Your best red bets for vegetarian dishes are fresh, lighter-style, fruity wines, also with good acidity. Try a Beaujolais or any Gamay-based wine. Valpolicella, Alsace Pinot Noir, and light red Burgundies are good choices also. Pinot Noirs from Ontario and B.C. fit the bill as well.

White Wine as an Apéritif

If you sniff a dry wine, particularly a dry white wine, you'll find that you start to salivate. Literally, your mouth starts to water. The glands in your mouth begin to secrete saliva and you start to feel hungry. What you're experiencing is an involuntary response to the acidity in the wine. The same effect happens with dry *sherry* (a fortified wine that contains grape spirit and an alcohol percentage of up to 20 percent) and dry champagne.

When your mouth waters, your appetite is stimulated. That's why dry white wines, dry sherry, and dry champagne make first-rate apéritifs: They create a desire to eat. If you order a glass of Ontario dry Riesling or B.C. Pinot Blanc before dinner, we guarantee you'll look forward to the meal to come.

On the other hand, if you want to suppress your appetite, try a sweet wine before a meal — any late harvest or dessert wine, port, or sweet sherry. The residual sugar in the wine has the effect of momentarily satisfying any pangs of hunger.

If a crowd of friends suddenly descends on you and you have nothing in the house to feed them, serve them a glass of sweet wine!

Some of the best sweet wines come from Canada. B.C. and Ontario wineries offer a broad range of late harvest wines made from grapes picked in November, December, or even January.

Chapter 10

At Home with Wine

. . . .

. . . .

*F*our out of every five bottles of wine purchased by Canadians are consumed at home.

You might have your first experience of a particular wine at a restaurant, but statistics say the majority of your wine consumption occurs in your own or someone else's house. You probably don't have a *sommelier* (a trained wine steward) living under your roof, so this chapter is devoted to serving wine at your own table.

Wine Buyer Beware

You can bring a flawed wine back to the liquor or wine store and expect to have it replaced or your money refunded. That is, if you haven't consumed 90 percent of the contents and then decided it's off. But a bad bottle is a depressing experience when you're sitting at the table ready for a gastronomic treat. When it comes to flawed or spoiled wines, prevention, pre-emption, and avoidance are the watchwords.

Certain telltale signs warn you of spoilage. Next time you visit a liquor store for wine, look closely at prospective bottles for any of these "symptoms":

- ✔ **Check the capsule for signs of leaking.** If wine can get out, air can get in and oxidize the wine.
- ✔ **Check the *fill level* (the distance between the bottom of the cork and the *meniscus*, the top level, of the wine in the bottle).** If the distance is greater than one inch, too much air may be causing oxidation.

- ✔ **Check that the cork doesn't protrude above the lip of the bottle.** A swollen cork could indicate that the wine has been subjected to heat during transportation or warehousing. Or, equally bad, it has frozen and then thawed out again!

- ✔ **Check the label for scuffing and shredding.** A messy label suggests rough handling.

- ✔ **Check the colour of white and rosé wines.** If they have a brownish tint, they're probably oxidized.

Apart from inspecting the bottle itself, there are important environmental circumstances to be aware of:

- ✔ **Avoid wine that has been stored standing up for a long time.** The cork could dry out and break the *hermetic seal* (a completely airtight closure that runs the length of the cork), allowing air into the bottle.

- ✔ **Avoid wine that has been displayed in the store window or under bright lights.** Heat and light can prematurely age wine.

- ✔ **Avoid white wine whose vintage year stated on the bottle suggests that it's been hanging around for more than three years.** Unless you are looking specifically for an older wine of quality, most white wines should be consumed within two years of bottling.

Bringing Home the Wine

Once you have purchased your wine, pamper it. Wine is very sensitive. It doesn't like being shaken up when travelling or subjected to extremes of heat and cold.

If it's your intention to *hold* (not drink) the wine for a few weeks, *lay it down* somewhere cool and dark so that the cork remains wet at all times. A dry cork could mean that it no longer has an airtight seal. (For the whole story on cellaring wine, see Chapter 11.)

Handling reds

If you plan to open your bottle of red wine that evening, place it standing upright on the floor of the room in which you will be serving it, away from any heat source. Floor level is cooler than table level (remember your elementary physics: heat rises). Reds are best served just below room temperature.

Check the bottom of the bottle for sediment. Most red wines you buy will be free of sediment. Sediment only occurs in older wines that, over the years, have precipitated their tannins and colouring matter out into the bottle. If you see any sediment, decant the wine into another container so that the particles don't cloud the wine when it's poured into glasses. This is where you get to haul out granny's crystal decanter, but if she hasn't had the foresight to make you a gift of it yet, any container, preferably glass, will do.

If you have a magnificent older wine with sediment, stand the bottle upright for at least 12 hours before you want to decant it. This gives the sediment plenty of time to settle at the bottom of the bottle. When you start pouring into the decanter, hold the bottle up to a bright light so you can see when the sediment from the bottom begins to approach the lip of the bottle, threatening to spill over. Stop pouring at this point. Tradition dictates that you use a candle for your light source, but this is really not bright enough. Pour slowly and steadily. Once you start, *don't stop*. If you tip the bottle back and forth, you stir up all the sediment again.

If you're a waste-not-want-not kind of person, take the little bit of wine and the sediment left at the bottom of the bottle, strain it through some cheesecloth or a paper coffee filter, and use it in a sauce or soup. See Chapter 15 for all sorts of ways to cook with wine.

Handling whites and rosés

Place your bottle of either white or rosé in the refrigerator an hour before you intend to serve it or 20 minutes to half an hour in an ice bucket three-quarters full of ice cubes and water. Treat sparkling wines the same way.

Put salt in the ice bucket to *chill a wine down* more quickly. The ice cubes will melt in a shorter time. You can always stick the bottle in the freezer for ten minutes, but make sure you put the kitchen timer on so you don't forget it's there. Alcohol freezes at a lower temperature than water, but it *does* freeze. You don't want to end up with a wine popsicle!

Cork Procedures

The cork has spent most of its adult life in communion with the wine in a bottle. That's if the wine has been stored properly, on its side, so that the cork is kept wet at all times. This means the cork will pick up the character of the wine. If the wine is spoiled, you'll smell it on the cork.

The cork is your canary in the coalmine; the first indicator that something may be wrong with the wine it's been stoppering. Here are some warning signs that the wine might not be in prime condition:

- ✔ **If the cork is hard and wizened:** It has dried out and possibly broken its hermetic seal with the bottle. Air could have gotten in.

- ✔ **If the cork is spongy and the wine stains your fingers:** This is another sign that air could have gotten into the wine.

- ✔ **If the cork is stained with wine along its length:** Wine has been able to travel that distance, suggesting that air could do likewise.

- ✔ **If the business end of the cork, which has been in contact with the wine, smells like a sewer:** The wine will probably smell like that too. And if it smells like a sewer, well, you can imagine the taste implications.

This is why waiters in restaurants hand you the cork when they bring the wine to your table. It's not a souvenir; they expect you to feel it, look at it, and sniff it. A smelly cork does not necessarily mean that the wine is off. Older wines can develop what wine professionals call *bottle stink* — a fetid smell given off by the air trapped between the cork and the wine. This "stink" blows off within a few minutes, but it could make the cork smell pretty bad initially. There is much less of an excuse for bottle stink in younger wines. See Chapter 5 for more wine warning signs.

Choosing a corkscrew

There are many devices for removing a cork from a bottle; some are more efficient than others, some more difficult to use than others. It looks so easy when you see it done in restaurants, but you can end up with broken corks or

---

Champagne corks

A bottle of champagne has a unique cork. Because it has to withstand the pressure of the gas inside (up to 90 pounds per square inch, or 6 atmospheres), the stopper has to be wired on. This means it needs a tighter fit than a still table wine. If you study a champagne cork, you see that it's shaped like a mushroom with a stem that *flanges out* (expands) from its head.

Most of the champagne cork is an agglomeration of bits; only the business end is pure cork. In fact, a champagne cork is really two separate discs of cork glued together. It's too expensive to carve that shape out of one piece of cork bark, and the cork that's in contact with the wine has to be of the highest quality.

corks forced back into the bottle. Once you've mastered the technique though, there's no looking back. There are five commonly used types of corkscrews; these tools are illustrated in Figures 10-1 to 10-5.

The Waiter's Friend: This is the style of corkscrew used by wait staff in most restaurants (see Figure 10-1). It looks a lot like a Swiss Army Knife. It has a *helix* (also known as a "worm," this is the spiral part of the corkscrew that pulls the cork out of the bottle), a small knife blade, and a lever. When not in use, the helix tucks in and lies parallel to the handle as does the short, notched lever. This corkscrew works on something called the *lever principle*. Here's how it works: When you want to use the corkscrew, pull the helix out so it is perpendicular to the handle and twist the helix down deep into the cork. The lever is hinged so you can engage it against the lip of the bottle. The notch prevents it from slipping. With your other hand, you lever the handle upwards, causing the cork to rise. Because both hands are required, most people put the bottle between their knees to do this. The more refined models have a hinged lever with notches in two positions. Changing the position as you lever upwards ensures that the cork rises straight from the bottle without the possibility of breaking.

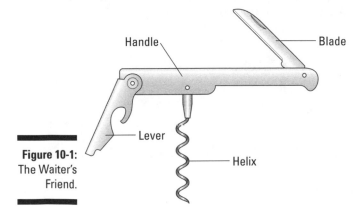

Handle   Blade

Lever

Figure 10-1:
The Waiter's
Friend.

Helix

The Screwpull: This is a two-piece gizmo (see Figure 10-2). One piece looks like a large plastic clothes peg. Place this over the neck of the bottle. The second piece is a plastic handle with a long, Teflon-coated helix that fits through a hole in the top of the "clothes peg." As the helix plunges into the cork, the "clothes peg" acts as an anchor and guides the helix to the centre of the cork. A continuous clockwise turning motion drives the helix into the cork. Once the helix meets resistance, it rises back out of the bottle, pulling the cork with it.

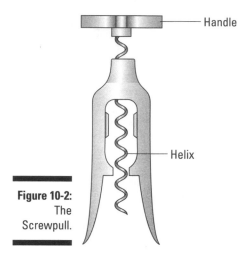

Handle

Helix

Figure 10-2:
The
Screwpull.

The Butterfly: This corkscrew has a *ratchet* (notched wheel) that causes two levers to rise in unison as you drill the helix into the cork (see Figure 10-3). When raised to *surrender level* (as far up as they can go) you press the levers down and the cork eases out of the bottle.

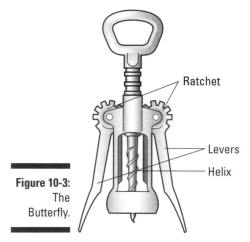

Ratchet

Levers

Helix

Figure 10-3:
The
Butterfly.

The Ah-So: This doesn't look like a corkscrew at all (see Figure 10-4). It's simply two thin metal prongs, one slightly longer than the other, with a handle grip. You slide the tip of the longer prong down between the cork and the glass neck. Then you engage the other prong on the other side of the cork. With a left–right rocking motion, you ease the two prongs downwards until they grip the length of the cork. Then you pull upwards with a twisting motion and extract the cork without damaging it. This device takes practise but is beautifully simple. You can even replace a cork in the bottle by reversing the procedure outlined above. In Barb's opinion, it is innate skill that is required, not practise. She has been practising with the Ah-So for years and has never failed to push the cork down into the bottle.

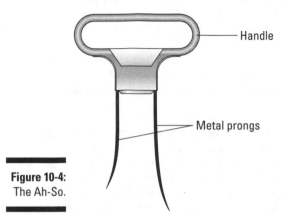

Handle

Metal prongs

Figure 10-4:
The Ah-So.

The T-Bar: This is the kind of corkscrew you find in hotel rooms (see Figure 10-5). It's basically a helix with a handle. The fancy kind have a handle made out of a lacquered piece of vine stalk, which, because it's basically a twisted and gnarled piece of wood, is not only difficult to hold, but badly balanced. With this model you have to work very hard to get the cork out. It's a tug of war between you and the cork with no assistance from any leverage.

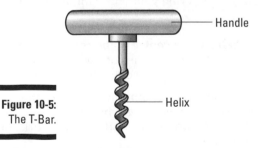

Handle

Helix

Figure 10-5:
The T-Bar.

When purchasing a corkscrew, have a look at the helix. It should be long enough to penetrate the longest cork (60 millimetres). The point should be sharp and centred in the middle of the helix. The helix should be coated with Teflon so that it passes easily through the cork. Avoid a corkscrew whose helix has a solid core or a sharp cutting edge. Also, steer clear of corkscrews with plastic helixes. The best helixes are long, slim, smooth, and graceful.

Uncorking the bottle

Whatever device you use to remove the cork from the bottle, the procedure is the same. First, remove the capsule that encases the top of the bottle. Some wineries have replaced the traditional capsule with a plastic disc that protects the head of the cork or the wax seal over the cork. If the bottle is a screw-top, then forget the corkscrew! All you need is a twist of the wrist.

Capsules are made from tin or plastic (they used to be made of lead or lead alloy, but this was viewed in the early 1990s as environmentally unfriendly). Some capsules have pull-tabs that allow you to remove the top part without having to resort to a knife.

If you do end up having to use the blade of a knife to cut the capsule, work the knife below the lip of the bottle. This way, the wine, when poured, won't come into contact with the capsule's upper edge. If you're preparing the wine for a blind tasting, remove the capsule in its entirety. You can cover up the label and the shape of the bottle with a paper bag, but the top of the bottle protrudes and, as many capsules are designed to promote the wine, they display telltale clues to the wine's identity. See Chapter 8 for more on organizing a wine tasting.

The wax seal is glued on top of the cork to protect it, and is about the size of a dime. Never open a bottle without removing this seal first. If you try to burrow through, it will ride up the helix of the corkscrew and be really difficult to remove.

The technique for opening a bottle with a corkscrew is pretty straight-forward, unless, as Barb can attest, you're trying your luck with the Ah-So (see Figure 10-4).

- ✔ **Always place the point of the helix at the centre of the cork before you drive in.** Make sure the helix enters the core of the cork and doesn't angle off to the side. A badly placed helix will cause the cork to tear and break up.

- ✔ **Keep turning until there is one complete revolution left before the helix disappears into the cork.** Less, and you might break the cork in two; more, and the point could come through the bottom of the cork and leave debris on the surface of the wine.

- ✔ **Presto! You're uncorked!**

The longest corks you'll have to deal with are usually found in vintage port bottles, although the Italian Barbaresco producer, Angelo Gaja, boasts the longest cork in a table wine — 60 millimetres.

The unspoken language of corks

The cork you have pulled from the bottle can tell you a lot about the wine even before you pour it into a glass.

There are various qualities of cork; the best are the longest and consequently the most expensive. Wine producers buy corks in the tens and hundreds of thousands, reserving the longer corks for their more expensive wines. Consequently, a short stubby cork tells you something about the quality of the wine.

Study the cork next time you draw one from a bottle. Some corks are made up of cork bits compacted and glued together. Others are in one piece but are made from different grades of cork, indicated by their length and quality (high-grade cork will have fewer indentations and irregularities than a lower-grade cork).

Increasingly, you'll find wines with *synthetic* (plastic) corks (especially wines for immediate consumption). These plastic corks come in a rainbow of colours including black and white.

Wine producers who have adopted the synthetic cork have found fewer incidences of flawed wines, although they've yet to prove that fine wines that need several years to mature in the bottle improve under plastic stoppers. Plastic corks don't "breathe" like natural cork, which allows minute amounts of air to come in contact with the wine. This ensures an even evolution of the wine. The quality of plastic used, incidentally, is extremely high-grade — the same surgical quality that goes into the manufacture of pace makers.

After you've opened the bottle

Once you've removed the cork from the bottle, wipe the lip of the bottle with a clean cloth to ensure that no residual dirt or cork particles fall into the wine when you pour it. If you're having a tasting, pour a two-ounce serving. This is all you need to assess a wine. It also allows you to swirl it easily in the glass without splashing your neighbour.

If you're serving the bottle at a meal or as an apéritif, pour a three- to four-ounce serving. Don't overpour. You may look like a generous host if you fill the glass to the brim, but your guest won't be able to sniff the wine, let alone swirl it to release the bouquet.

Make sure your wineglasses are clean. Residual soap marks or marks left from drying the glasses with a soiled cloth can impart flavours you don't want to taste.

The better the wine, the more information you find branded on the *barrel* (the body length) of the cork. The least expensive wines for the most part bear no defining information on their barrels. They might as well be anonymous. Better-quality wines have the producer's name on the barrel. Even-higher-quality wines have the producer's name and the vintage date. In Bordeaux, the top wines of the region bear the legend, *Mise en bouteille au château* (Bottled at the château) in addition to the producer and vintage. That's a lot of information in not a lot of space!

To air is divine

You should always open the bottle far enough in advance of your guests' arrival to allow yourself time to taste the wine beforehand — in case the bottle is corked or off in some other way. Opening a bottle of red wine in advance is good for it anyway. A little air will help develop the bouquet and the flavour.

To *aerate* (expose to air) a wine, pour it into a decanter or jug, or even into a glass. The tumbling effect is what introduces air into wine. For best results, do this for red wine half an hour to an hour before you serve it. The more tannic the wine, the longer you should aerate it. Red Bordeaux, Italian Barolo, and Babaresco, as well as Spanish Rioja (all very tannic) are notorious for needing a lot of air to show their paces.

White wines, because they are served chilled, don't require airing, so go ahead and pour them straight into your glass — or cork up the bottle and put it back in the fridge or cooler until you're ready to serve it.

What a Difference a Glass Makes

Shape dictates sensation. Believe it or not, the shape of the wineglass really affects the taste of the wine. Over the years, European wine regions have developed their own style of glass that they consider best suited to enjoy the style of their wine.

Contemporary research led by an Austrian glass manufacturer named Riedel has proven that the design of a wineglass greatly influences how you perceive the bouquet and flavour of a given wine. It all has to do with which part of the tongue the wine is directed to and how much air the wine is exposed to before you drink it. Chapter 6 explains in greater detail how we taste wine. Riedel has designed a range of glassware for specific wines for the most esoteric of collectors. (There is a Riedel glass for young red Bordeaux and one for well-aged red Bordeaux!). Check out Appendix C, "Coolers & Corkscrews," for information on where to purchase Riedel and other glasses.

You don't need a cabinet full of glasses dedicated uniquely to Chardonnay, Cabernet Sauvignon, Pinot Noir, dessert wines, and so on. But a well-chosen wineglass adds greatly to the pleasure of wine drinking. You wouldn't think of consuming champagne out of a tooth mug unless you were desperate, and a lovely Cabernet Sauvignon just wouldn't taste the same out of a champagne flute or martini glass.

A glass for red

Choose a wineglass with a round, full shape to allow more air to get at the wine. Red wines require a glass whose design still allows the bouquet of the wine to remain in the glass. It should be easy to swirl holding it by either the stem or the base. See Figure 10-6.

Those glasses the size of goldfish bowls may look sophisticated in Hollywood movies but the wine gets lost in them. And you take a terrible risk by either putting them in the dishwasher or washing them by hand.

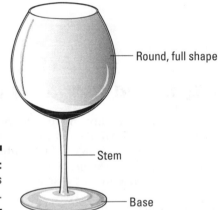

— Round, full shape

— Stem

Figure 10-6:
Wineglass
for red wine.

— Base

A glass for white

The ideal glass for white wine, shown in Figure 10-7, has the following attributes:

- ✔ Clear, plain, thin glass without any colour, etching, or engraving, so you can *see* the wine.
- ✔ A long stem, so that your fingers don't touch the bowl and warm up the wine.
- ✔ An elongated, tulip-shaped bowl whose belly is wider than its mouth, so that the bouquet is captured in the glass and not dissipated into the room.

When purchasing wineglasses, ensure that the rim is as thin and unobtrusive as possible. The less interference between your lip and the wine, the better the wine will taste.

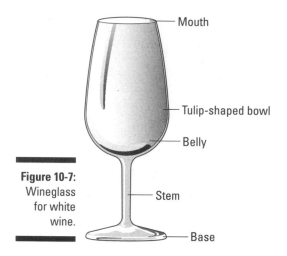

Figure 10-7:
Wineglass
for white
wine.

Mouth

Tulip-shaped bowl

Belly

Stem

Base

A glass for champagne and sparkling wines

The best glass for all sparkling wines — from champagne to Asti spumante — is a long, slender flute, shown in Figure 10-8. The tall narrow column keeps the wine chilled longer and allows you to enjoy the sight of the bubbles. The small aperture requires you to put your lips in the shape of a kiss to take a sip. This means you will take in less wine and consequently less gas.

A word to the wise: Champagne is the cruellest wine in terms of showing up your housekeeping. The tiniest bit of dirt in the glass will become immediately apparent when you pour the wine. Large, lazy bubbles will cling to the offending spot. Make sure your sparkling wine flutes are free from detergent residue by rinsing them thoroughly and drying them with a clean towel.

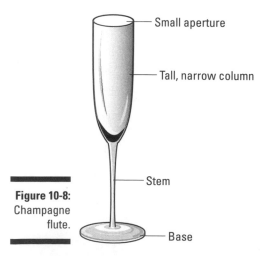

Figure 10-8:
Champagne
flute.

Small aperture

Tall, narrow column

Stem

Base

Ice cream, anyone?

Don't be fooled by the allure of the universal symbol for champagne: the saucer-shaped glass. This is the worst possible receptacle for one of the world's greatest beverages. Legend has it that the shape was invented for England's Queen Victoria, who reacted badly to the gas in champagne. The flat, lake-like surface of the bowl helps dissipate the bubbles that contain the gas — and doesn't pass it on to the imbiber!

Not only does this unfortunate design cause the wine to warm up quickly, but you're denied the pleasure of watching the bubbles rise; and when you take a sip, that large circumference means that you get a lot of wine in your mouth, and it foams on your palate. In addition, you give your nose a bath when you try to smell the bouquet. Apart from these drawbacks, the saucer-shaped glass is a perfect container for ice cream.

Chapter 11

Buying for Keeping

. . . .

. . . .

Most wines bought by consumers at liquor stores and supermarkets are opened within 24 hours of purchase. This is not necessarily a bad thing since most wines are made to be consumed as soon as they hit the shelves. But there are bottles that you really should not rush to drink, as the wine will only get better with time.

If you're going to keep wine for any length of time, you need a good place to store it. And, as your collection grows, you might even need an inventory system to keep track of what styles of wine you have and how long they should be kept.

You can collect an enviable cellar of Canadian wines, from a variety of interesting sources right across the country.

Storing Your Wines

Wine is not a commodity like baked beans or bottled water that will keep for years virtually anywhere without deteriorating. All the different elements in a wine are constantly interacting inside the bottle, causing the appearance, bouquet, and taste to change over time. Like all chemical processes, these changes occur more quickly and acutely when heat enters into the equation.

If you think about it, wine ages a lot like human beings do. A one-year-old Chardonnay will taste different from the same Chardonnay at three years old. The younger wine will be fresher, livelier, and fruitier; the older more mellow, softer, and more developed. Not to mention more worldly and mature!

The way you store your wines influences their development. If the conditions aren't right, wines can age prematurely, or worse, they can oxidize. Actually, all wines oxidize eventually. There's no getting around it. Air seeps through all corks at one time or another, speeding up the aging process and causing the wine to deteriorate. The trick is to maintain your wines at their peak condition so that you can enjoy them at their best. An oxidized red wine tastes like stewed prunes; an oxidized white wine like sherry.

If you hear the term *maderized* at a wine tasting, it refers to what happens when a white wine is subjected to oxidation over a long period of time. That's the way they make the fortified wine called Madeira, hence the name. Madeira is subjected to heat over a period of time (years, actually!). The barrels in which it's stored are sometimes heated by steam pipes to encourage oxidation. This fortified wine has a very particular taste that's definitely acquired. Deliberate oxidation is fine for Madeira, but not for your white wines that should taste fresh and lively.

The amount of time it takes for a wine to reach its peak of maturity differs by grape variety, production method, colour, and style. Table 11-1 shows you how long you can cellar a wine from the time you purchase the bottle.

Table 11-1	Guidelines for Aging Wine
Length of Time before Consuming	**Examples of Wine Types**
Immediate–3 months	Beaujolais Nouveau and all Nouveau or Primeur wines, Gamay Nouveau, Italian Novello wines
Immediate–1 year	Most fresh white wines made without recourse to oak aging: Muscadet, Soave, non-oaked whites from Canada, rosés
1–2 years	Oak-aged New World white wines (Chardonnay, Sauvignon Blanc), non-vintage champagne and sparkling wine, light non-oaked red wines (Beaujolais, Valpolicella), Rhône rosés (Tavel rosé)
2–5 years	White Burgundy (Puligny-Montrachet), Riesling (including Ontario Riesling), vintage champagne, New World reds (Chilean Cabernet Sauvignon), light Old World reds (Italian Dolcetto)
5–10 years	Château-bottled red Bordeaux (Château Palmer), domaine-bottled red Burgundy (Daniel Rion Vosne-Romanée), top Italian reds (Masi Amarone), sweet wines (Icewine, Sauternes); some Canadian reds are showing promise in this category
10 years plus	Vintage port (Grahams 1994), first growth red Bordeaux (Château Lafite 1998)

Burgundy does not have "châteaux" like in Bordeaux. A property that produces wine in Burgundy is called a "domaine."

Spirits such as whisky, brandy, rum, and so on do not improve with age. Once they are taken out of wood barrels and stored in glass bottles, their development ceases. Unlike wine, which should be laid down, bottles of spirits (35 to 40 percent alcohol by volume) should be stored standing upright so that the concentration of alcohol doesn't eat away at the cork over time.

Choosing the Best Cellar Site

The ideal cellar is dark, cool, and slightly damp. If that sounds like your basement, then go for it. Basements are ideal storage spaces — under the right circumstances: low traffic, rarely lit, generally cool, and constant in temperature.

Keep these tips in mind when planning your cellar:

- **Keep the corks wet at all times.** Lay the bottles flat so that the entire area at the bottom of the cork is in contact with the wine.

- **Maintain a consistent cool temperature.** Ideally, the temperature in your cellar should hover around 12°–13° Celsius (55° Fahrenheit). You can go up or down a few degrees, but any change has to be gradual. Your wines will oxidize sooner if you subject them to wildly fluctuating temperatures. These rapid changes encourage the effect of dissolved oxygen.

- **Keep moisture in the air.** If the air is too dry it could cause the corks to dry out at the top of the bottle, breaking the hermetic seal and allowing air in. If you find your cellar getting too dry, place a bucket of water on the floor. The evaporation should provide enough moisture for a small cellar. If not, you might have to resort to a small, cool-air vapourizer.

- **Set up your cellar well away from vibrating machinery.** This includes washing machines, spin dryers, compressors, and so on. Wines lying near appliances like this will be shaken, rattled, and rolled to a premature old age. Constant motion, like fluctuating temperatures, also increases the effect of oxidation.

- **Get rid of any strong-smelling solvents, paints, or cleaning agents.** The odour could affect the taste of the wine over the long term.

- **Turn out the lights!** Bright lights cause the wine to warm up, which also encourages oxidation.

If you intend to build a cellar in your basement and want to locate the coolest part, use a household thermometer and take readings over the course of several days — in the morning and at night — to see the fluctuation. The coolest part of your basement is a north-facing wall (as long as the furnace is not located there). The warmest part is a south-facing wall. Think of the passage of the sun, rising in the east, setting in the west. The hottest part of the day is mid-day. The closer to the ground, the cooler the temperature. (Think of your high school physics class: heat rises.)

No basement? No worries!

If you live in an apartment or a house that has no basement, what do you do? You *could* buy an expensive climate-controlled wine storage cabinet, but that's an investment for the collector who actually has wine to store. You're still figuring out where to put your cellar.

Ask yourself:

- ✔ Where is the coolest part of my home?
- ✔ What is the area of least traffic?
- ✔ What part of my home can remain in darkness most of the time?
- ✔ Is there easy access to the space?
- ✔ How much space can I afford to allocate to wine storage?

In an apartment or home with no basement, the best space to store wine is usually a closet in a bedroom. Most people keep their bedrooms at a cooler temperature than the other rooms anyway. There's less traffic in bedrooms than other living areas, and lights are only on at night for a short while. The back of the coat closet is another option, providing the hot water pipes don't run through it.

Some people have storage space under the staircase, which is ideal as long as the stairs are solidly built and the patter of little and not-so-little feet doesn't shake the foundation.

A cellar can be a cave that contains thousands of bottles or a stash of 12 bottles kept in a cardboard case under the stairs. Size doesn't matter. That's an ego thing. For all practical purposes, and your ultimate enjoyment of the wine, you only have to be concerned about the storage conditions.

Your home's worst cellaring spots

In your kitchen, particularly in a rack above the refrigerator.

Reason: The heat in kitchens fluctuates dramatically. The refrigerator's compressor will cause your wines to vibrate; the rising heat will "cook" them.

In clay tiles in the stone fireplace in your den.

Reason: The heat from the fire will pretty much "bake" your wines. Removing them from the tiles will scuff the labels.

In racks in a high-traffic hallway.

Reason: The vibrations will age your wines prematurely. You're asking for trouble in terms of breakage ("I wasn't swinging the bat *that* hard, Mom").

In a rack under the sink.

Reason: The proximity to cleaning fluids and other smells will ruin your wines.

In the closet where you keep your central vacuum.

Reason: Vibrations and dust will dry out your wines.

Setting up your cellar

You use a *racking system* to store your bottles in your cellar. A racking system is merely a cradle for your bottles. The wooden box or cardboard carton in which wines are shipped are examples of the most basic racking systems. Each bottle is contained in its own slot, protected from its neighbour, resting on its side.

You can store your wines in these boxes, but it's advisable not to stack them one on top of the other once they've been opened and bottles removed. They're just not strong enough. (You don't want to be awakened in the middle of the night to the sound of an avalanche of bottles.)

A more reliable racking system is a wooden, rubberized plastic or metal racking system that can be secured to the wall. These come in a variety of sizes beginning with enough space for a dozen bottles. Most are modular and can be added to as your collection (and enthusiasm) grows. Consult Appendix C, "Coolers & Corkscrews," for information on where to purchase racking systems.

If you are an organized person, you probably want your cellar to be organized, too. Group your wines in such a way that you can find what you want, when you want it. Buy some stickers or neck tags to identify the wine so you don't have to pull the bottle out of the rack each time to see what it is. More on these nifty little identifiers later in the chapter.

Why wines should sleep on their side

As many different styles of wine racks as there are, they're all constructed to perform one important function — keep the bottle lying on its side. This isn't just an aesthetic consideration. Lying the bottle on its side keeps the cork in contact with the wine (in other words, wet) and a wet cork fills the neck of the bottle better, preventing any gaps that could let in air and speed up oxidation.

You might be asking yourself, why not just keep the bottle upside-down? This is an option, believe it or not, but it has one drawback — sediment. If any sediment forms, it has a habit of sticking to the inside of the bottle as well as floating around in the wine. If the bottle is upside-down, the sediment will stick to the inside of the neck of the bottle and risks flaking off into the glass as you pour. When the bottle is lying down, the sediment collects at the fat end of the bottle near the bottom. It's out of the way and settles faster when you stand the bottle upright in preparation for decanting.

Some people like to group their wines by region or origin. Others put all their ready-to-drink wines together and their ageable wines in order of when they'll be ready to drink. Some people keep their white wines near the floor because it's cooler. You decide what sort of organization suits you best.

 The wines that you want to store for a long time should be placed at the lowest part of your cellar (nearest to the floor). Place them in the darkest part where there is the least movement of other bottles around them. Everyday house wines that you consume on a regular basis should be stored within easy reach.

Cataloguing Your Wines

Once you've chosen the site for your cellar and set up your racking system of choice, how do you keep track of all those bottles?

Buy yourself a notebook. When you purchase wine, enter the information according to the template shown in Figure 11-1.

By devoting a page to each wine, you can keep a sort of diary of its life. You can also enter such information as the dish you served it with and the names of the guests who enjoyed it with you. You want to achieve as comprehensive an entry as possible for each wine in your cellar.

You can also, of course, do the same thing on your computer. There is software that allows you to keep track of the wines in your cellar. Appendix C, "Coolers & Corkscrews," lists several of these wine-cataloguing programs. But keeping a *cellar book* near your wines allows you to make instant entries and gives you a tactile record of your wine cellar's contents and your response to individual bottles.

Wine: Inniskillin Chardonnay Founders' Show Reserve 1999

○

Region: *Ontario*

Cost: *$24.95*

Quantity: *3 bottles*

Date of Purchase: *March 9, 2000*

Notes: *Tasted this wine at the winery and bought three bottles. Winemaker says can be consumed now but will improve for at least two to three years.*

My Tasting Notes: *November 2, 2000*

Appearance: *good colour, bright, golden*

○ **Bouquet:** *vanilla, smoky, apple nose*

Taste: *full-bodied, apple and citrus flavours with a long, toasty finish*

○

Figure 1-11:
A page from
your cellar
book.

A good way to increase the number of bottles in your cellar without straining your budget too much is to use this formula: For every bottle you open, buy two more. It's amazing how quickly your inventory will grow!

Now, where did I put that Pinot Noir?

So, you bought this outstanding Pinot Noir eight months ago, carefully ferreted it away in your cellar, and now you want to unveil it to celebrate your friend's promotion. You walk down to the basement, flip on the light, and are confronted with a staggering array of bottles lying on their sides — and you can't tell one from the other to save your life. What do you do? Bottles in racks are difficult to identify, and you're bound to spend a fair amount of time down there pulling them out of their slots in order to read their labels. A simple way to tell what you've got at a glance, without even touching the bottles, is to purchase a set of plastic neck tags. (They look like small lobster bibs — a circle fits over the neck of the bottle with a flap on which to write the information.) We tell you where to find these handy little tags in Appendix C, "Coolers & Corkscrews." You can write the name of the wine, producer, and vintage in felt-tip pen on the label and hang it over the neck of the bottle. When you take out a bottle to celebrate with your friend, wash off the neck tag and use it again.

There's an old saying about giving yourself more time than you reasonably think you'll need to do something. The same holds true for the amount of space you allot in your wine cellar. Once you've got a number of bottles in your head — double it. You'll kick yourself for not allocating more space once you really get collecting.

Collecting a Canadian Cellar

Once you've organized your wine cellar, you're ready to start stocking it. Think of the possibilities: friends may drop in, you might have a romantic moment at home, or perhaps you just deserve a glass of pleasure at the end of a long day. These are the times when it's useful to have a few bottles on hand. Occasions vary widely, and even if you only have a small cellar, it's practical to have a variety of styles of wine at the ready.

Has it ever happened to you that friends drop over and all you have to serve them is that special bottle you were saving for your anniversary? Sorry honey! Or maybe you reach for a bottle and realize that it's the same wine you served last time they came over — because that's the wine you always buy.

It's too easy to get into a rut and serve the same wine again and again, but with all the different wines and styles to choose from, putting some variety into your cellar is a snap. You can build a good collection just concentrating on Canadian wines.

There is nothing wrong with buying on impulse. Some of the best wines are available in such small quantities that you need to snap them up as soon as you find them. With your varied cellar at home, you are bound to have a category into which your new bottle fits.

24 bottles of wine on your wall

Canadian wines have improved so dramatically over the past 10 years, it's worth accumulating a collection that encompasses as many different wineries and styles as is practical in your allotted space. Twenty-four bottles can fit snugly in your apartment cupboard as the basis of a small collection, or as the Canadian component of a larger acquisition. If you have more space, simply increase the number of bottles proportionately. The majority of wines should be for current consumption, split between white and red. Look at Table 11-2 for suggestions on how to build your proudly Canadian collection.

Table 11-2	A Quintessentially Canadian Wine Collection	
Quantity and Type of Wine	*Price Range*	*Suggested Varieties*
6 bottles of everyday white split between 4 dry and 2 semidry or slightly sweet	$8 – $15	Dry Riesling, demi-sec Riesling, Pinot Blanc, Vidal, Seyval Blanc, Auxerrois, Kerner, Ortega, unoaked or lightly oaked Chardonnay
6 bottles of everyday red	$8 – $15	Baco Noir, Maréchal Foch, Gamay Noir, Chancellor, Pinot Noir, unoaked blends of two or more of Cabernet Franc, Cabernet Sauvignon, and Merlot
4 bottles of fine white	Let your budget set the price range, but you should find a good choice from $20 – $40	Pinot Blanc, Pinot Gris, dry Riesling, Gewürztraminer, Sauvignon Blanc, barrel-fermented Chardonnay
4 bottles of fine red	$20 – $60	Cabernet Sauvignon, Merlot, Cabernet Franc or blends of any of those three; Pinot Noir, Syrah, barrel-aged Baco Noir
2 bottles of champagne-method sparkling wine	$20 – $30	Note that grape varietals are not stated on the labels of sparkling wines

(continued)

Table 11-2 *(continued)*

Quantity and Type of Wine	Price Range	Suggested Varieties
1 bottle (2 half-bottles) of late harvest dessert wines	$12 – $30	Vidal, Riesling
1 bottle (2 half-bottles) of Icewine	$45 – $90	Vidal, Riesling

Even for your everyday wines, look for the VQA symbol, particularly if you're buying wine produced in Ontario. Some B.C. wineries have opted not to join the VQA at this time, but state on the label that the grapes are B.C.-grown. Neither Québec nor Nova Scotia participates in the VQA system, although both may do so in the near future. If in doubt about the origin of the grapes, ask the vendor if the wine is 100 percent Canadian. Both large and small wineries produce wines in the "everyday" price range, but the wines of the larger wineries are more likely to turn up for sale outside the provinces of origin.

In Ontario, Pelee Island Winery has a good reputation for well-priced varietal wines and sells wines through the liquor boards in several provinces, not just Ontario. Jackson-Triggs also has a good selection of everyday wines both in and outside of Ontario and B.C. Take a tour of Canadian wineries starting with Ontario in Chapter 18.

Preparing for future consumption

Each time you enjoy one of your bottles, replace it with the same or similar wine to maintain your cellar size. If you want your cellar to grow, follow our advice and replace each bottle you consume with two others of the same style. You'll double up in no time. If you want to collect some wine to lay down, this is the best way. But at what point should you max out your cellar?

Suppose you consume an average of two bottles a week. You could replace each one with two other bottles, one to consume and one to age from three to 20 years. At the end of year one, you will have 104 bottles aging with the earliest ones coming into their prime in three years. At your rate of consumption, you'd have a year's worth of wine, except it isn't ready to drink.

Over the next three years, you should continue to collect so that you have wines to replace the ones that come of age. If space is a problem, slow down your accumulation until you start to draw on your mature cellar.

As you start to collect wine to age, you'll soon recognize the value in buying multiples of the same wine. This way, you can sample the wine several times over the course of its development and will know when it's at its best. If you're one of those people who once asked, "Who would ever need to buy a whole case of the same wine?" you might start to reconsider — if not a case of 12, then maybe a case of six.

When looking for finer wine or age-worthy wines, check the labels for single vineyard designations or the terms "reserve," "old vines," "special select," and in the case of white wine, Chardonnay in particular, "barrel fermented." The appearance of any of these on the label indicates special measures taken to increase the quality of the wine. In general, the more mature the vines, the more ageable they are. You're best to buy wine from wineries that source their grapes from the longest-established vineyards. In Ontario, some of these vineyards are owned by wineries like Inniskillin, Château des Charmes, Cave Spring Cellars, Henry of Pelham, Hillebrand, Marynissen Winery, Stoney Ridge, and Lakeview Cellars. Other wineries source grapes from long-established vineyards like Lailey, Lenko, and Sandstone. In B.C. look for Blue Mountain, Calona, CedarCreek, Gray Monk, Hainle, Hester Creek, Mission Hill, Nichol Vineyard, Quails' Gate, Hawthorne Mountain, and Sumac Ridge.

Buying Wine in Canada

Where do you buy your wine? Do you have a liquor board outlet in your neighbourhood? Do you ever wish you could find a shop that had a different selection? Canadians are brought up with the idea that alcohol of any kind is a controlled substance. Although many people feel that control is unnecessary, a small but united minority feels it should be more controlled. And the provincial governments see the control of alcohol as a tremendous tax opportunity. Whatever your viewpoint, the reality is that you have to go to a specially licensed store to buy your wine.

Some older wine lovers remember going to the liquor store, filling in a form to request products, and lining up to hand it in discreetly at a wicket. None of the wine or liquors were actually displayed. All were safely stowed behind a barrier. Today, the sale of wine is still being controlled, but products are boldly displayed and merchandising plays an important role — though information on specific wines is often lacking. Being an informed wine buyer means doing your own research: reading books such as this one as well as wine magazines and columns in newspapers. Published tasting notes and other informative material provide other guidelines for your purchasing.

Don't depend as much on the wine reviewer's rave remarks as on indicators of style and ageability. Decide how the particular wine will fit into the overall range of wines in your cellar and then decide if the reviewer's comments are enough to convince you to buy. Above all, does its description fit its price category?

In theory, the liquor boards have wine consultants to help you with your wine choices. Some of them are exceedingly well-informed and helpful, especially in large city centres. However, Barb encountered one branch manager/wine consultant in a smaller town who insisted that the Barbera grape was a variety of Nebbiolo. In fact, no two grapes could be less similar. This section reviews a variety of wine suppliers, from provincial liquor boards to on-line sources. But remember, always use your good judgment when making your final wine selection. In the end, *you* are the master of your own tastes.

The liquor monopolies

The liquor monopolies were established at the end of Prohibition as a sort of compromise, allowing for the sale of alcohol, albeit in a restrictive atmosphere. Prohibition had succeeded in encouraging people to go to great lengths to obtain whatever alcohol was available legally — and even illegally. At the time, alcohol was permitted as a base for many medications. Never have so many Canadians suffered from severe coughs and bronchial congestion as they did during Prohibition, and never have physicians been as liberal with prescriptions of cough remedies! For more insight into the history of wine and winemaking in Canada, turn to Chapter 17.

Provincial liquor boards (each province and territory has its own) continue to control the sale of wine in their jurisdictions. This means that wine lovers are limited to the choice offered by the liquor board in their province, and, in some provinces, the choice is, admittedly, very limited.

The Atlantic provinces have the most limited choice and some of the highest prices. Much of this has to do with economy of scale. They don't have the population numbers to support a better selection. At the other end of the spectrum, Alberta has privatized the sale of wine at the retail level so that the selection is broad and the prices the lowest in the country. Every province has put its own spin on the business.

In Québec, you can buy wine in grocery and corner stores, but only those products dictated by the Société des Alcools du Québec (SAQ), and most are wines bought in bulk and bottled by the SAQ itself. The quality of wine is generally mediocre, but the store hours are longer than at the liquor board outlets. Québec's policy of *Bring Your Own Bottle* in certain restaurants is a great way to enjoy wine without having to pay a hefty mark-up rate (though in a few of the BYOBs you do pay a *corkage fee*, charged by the restaurant for uncorking the bottle on its premises). This charge covers the waiter's service time and the cleaning of the glasses.

Ontario permits its wineries to sell their own wine on their premises and larger wineries to develop chains of boutiques across the province. In a most enlightened manner, British Columbia has recently licensed a number of independent specialty boutiques to sell VQA wines. About 10 of these establishments currently operate throughout the province.

Catalogue shopping

Some provinces offer an alternative to trekking from store to store to find the wine you want. The Québec and Ontario liquor boards distribute catalogues from which you can order both well-known and hard-to-find wines. They offer this service throughout the provinces and deliver the wine to the liquor board location that you request. Manitoba offers this type of service in Winnipeg, but will only deliver to your home or office.

Wine clubs also offer wines by catalogue with delivery to local liquor board outlets. Most of the clubs operate provincially, but the Opimian Society (www.opim.ca) offers wines across the country.

I have seen the future, and it is Bordeaux

Sometimes you can even buy *futures* (wine before it is bottled) from a catalogue. They are particularly hard to get through regular channels. Futures are more or less a Bordeaux (red wine) phenomenon. The château where the wine is produced releases futures shortly after the harvest, while the wine is still in the barrels and nowhere near ready to drink. The full quality of the wine cannot yet be ascertained, though an experienced buyer can judge fairly well. The newly bottled wine won't be ready to drink for two or three years, but the château is happy to take your money now and ship you the wine when it's bottled. The château gives you a preferential price for the privilege of paying them up front.

The famous Bordeaux châteaux don't take orders from individuals, but instead sell to *négotiants* (wine merchants) with whom the liquor boards must place their orders. By introducing this "middleman," you're paying two extra levels, but, believe it or not, you're *still* paying less than you would later on if you were to buy the wine once bottled.

Buying futures is particularly worthwhile in good vintages when the chances of prices escalating later on are high, and the worldwide demand for a fixed number of cases makes them difficult to find.

Wine agents, once limited to operating within provincial boundaries, are branching out to provide delivery of wines throughout Canada. Distillers, Vintners & Brewers Agencies (DVB), of Toronto, promotes itself as the one-stop shop for fine wines, spirits, and beer. They supply restaurants, caterers, and individual cellars from a list of available products.

Private orders

If you know of a wine that isn't carried by your provincial liquor board and you'd like to buy it, you can place a *private order* for that wine, in bulk. The minimum order is one case. This is a fairly lengthy, costly purchasing method, so you'd better be sure the wine in question is worth it. First of all, you fill out the requisite forms. Then, the liquor board contacts the supplier and establishes a price based on the price set by the supplier, taking into account transportation, taxes, and provincial mark-ups. The liquor board then notifies you. If you agree to the price, the liquor board orders it for you. You may have to wait several months until a shipment comes in from that particular supplier, but if you wish to pay the premium to have the case delivered air freight, most liquor boards will accommodate you. Be advised that some boards apply a surcharge to private orders.

Personal importation

If you're a Canadian citizen and travel outside the country, you're permitted to carry the equivalent of nine litres (a case of 12 standard bottles of 750 ml) of wine back into the country with your luggage. Some provinces permit more than one case. You can call your provincial Canada Customs office for details. You must declare your wine at the port of entry and pay the taxes, duties, and mark-up. These vary by province. It's a bit of a bureaucratic nuisance, but well worth it if the wine is one not available in Canada.

Privatized wine shops

The Alberta Liquor Board privatized the sale of wine in the mid-1980s. A number of private wine stores operate across the province and prices are very competitive. Manitoba and B.C. also have provision for private wine stores but there are fewer of them in those provinces. Prices are so reasonable because the privatized stores obtain their wine through the liquor boards at the wholesale level, and they are permitted to set their own retail prices.

Auctions

A few occasions to buy wine at an auction arise in various locations across the country. Wine auctions are only permitted for charitable purposes and must be licensed by the liquor licensing authority in the province in question.

The liquor licensing authority, a government office, operates separately from the liquor board. It is concerned with such issues as where alcohol can be legally served, whereas the focus of the liquor board is on selling wine.

Although wine auctions are held few and far between, they do sometimes offer some interesting selections. The two largest wine auctions in Canada are held in conjunction with fundraising events for the Toronto Symphony Orchestra and the Vancouver Playhouse. They follow an elegant black-tie dinner with all the trimmings and are part of an event that runs over several days.

Independent wine stores

Wine stores, as independent retailers, are limited to certain jurisdictions in Canada:

British Columbia

- Arrowsmith Wine Shoppe, Parksville, B.C.
- B.C. Wine Information Centre, Penticton, B.C.
- B.C. Wine Museum, Kelowna, B.C.
- Carol's Wines, Coquitlam, B.C.
- Cook Street Village Wines, Victoria, B.C.
- The Corkscrew, Surrey, B.C.
- Edgemont Village Wines, North Vancouver, B.C.
- Marquis Wine Cellars, Vancouver, B.C.
- Minter Garden's Wine Shop, Rosedale, B.C.
- VQA Wine Shop at Mattick's Farm, Victoria, B.C.
- The Wine Barrel, Victoria, B.C.

Alberta

- Andrew Hilton Wine and Spirits, Lethbridge, AB
- Banff Wine Store, Banff, AB
- Grape Vine Boutique, Grande Prairie, AB

- ✔ Kensington Wine Market, Calgary, AB
- ✔ Richmond Hill Wines, Calgary, AB
- ✔ Varsity Wine Merchants, Calgary, AB
- ✔ J. Webb Wine Merchant, Calgary, AB
- ✔ The Wine Cask, St. Albert/Edmonton, AB
- ✔ The Wine Cellar, Edmonton, AB
- ✔ The Wine Centre, Red Deer, AB

Manitoba

- ✔ Kenaston Wine Market, Winnipeg, MN

The Internet

Buying wine over the Internet is still in its infancy. Even in the United States, considered the leader in e-commerce, Internet wine buying is limited, mostly because of legislation that prevents alcoholic beverages from crossing some state lines.

In Canada, e-commerce in wines is conducted mostly within provincial boundaries, but inter-provincial shipping is becoming more commonplace. The Opimian Society (www.opim.ca) has the best Web site as far as facility in placing orders goes, but ordering is restricted to members (though you can become a member very easily: see Appendix C, "Coolers & Corkscrews"). Plus, the delay between ordering and delivery is long. Orders are placed through the provincial liquor board where the person placing the order lives. Minimum order is one case (of 6 or 12 bottles).

In Ontario, some of the wineries take advantage of the Internet to proffer their wines, as do wineries in B.C. In many cases, the initial contact is through the Web site, but the actual order is completed by e-mail, phone, or fax. Many other wineries have Web sites that provide information on their wine, but are not set up to take orders for delivery.

Wine agents who represent wineries from around the world concentrate their sales efforts on liquor boards and restaurants, but several have now established an Internet presence to take orders from individuals.

Purchasing wine on-line from Ontario wineries

These Ontario wineries' Web sites are set up for buying on-line:

- ✔ Hillebrand Winery/WineCountry at Home: www.winecountryathome.com
- ✔ Inniskillin Winery: www.winerack.com

- Pelee Island Winery: www.peleeisland.com
- Stoney Ridge Winery: www.stoneyridge.com
- Vineland Estates Winery: www.vineland.com

Purchasing wine on-line from B.C. wineries

Check out these wineries' sites to buy wine on-line in British Columbia:

- Gray Monk Winery: www.graymonk.com
- Hainle Winery: www.hainle.com

Purchasing wine on-line from wine agents

You can buy wine on-line from these wine agents. Go to www.canwine.com for an excellent Web site that links you to most of them.

- Alberta Wine Merchants (representing six stores): www.wep.ab.ca/albertawine
- Amethyst: www.telusplanet.net/public/methysta
- Boka Agencies: www.bokawines.com
- Churchill Cellars: www.churchhillcellars.com
- Distillers, Vintners & Brewers Agencies (DVB): www.interlog.com/~dvb
- Eurovintage: www.eurovintage.com/consignment.html
- Lifford Agencies: www.liffordwineagency.com
- Marquis Wine Cellars: www.marquis-wines.com

Purchasing wine on-line from your provincial liquor board

Three of the provincial liquor boards have an Internet presence with links to their specialty wine catalogues, but you must phone or fax your order. The excellent Web site, www.canwine.com, links you to them.

- Manitoba: www.mlcc.mb.ca Delivery within the city of Winnipeg only. Tel: (204) 987-8555
- Ontario: www.vintages.com/classics Delivery to specific liquor stores across the province. Tel: (416) 365-5767 or 1-800 266-4764
- Québec: www.saq.com Delivery to specific stores across the province. Tel: (514) 864-3253 or 1-800 317-9317

Part IV
Wine and Food

"No wonder the salesman said this was a dessert wine. I can hear the 'snickers' from my guests."

In this part . . .

Ultimately, this is what it's all about: The marriage of wine and food. Wine was made for food even though you can enjoy it on its own. But whatever the circumstance, wine is the beverage that most enhances the dining experience. A well-chosen bottle can turn a simple meal into a gastronomic delight. We're talking not only about wines *with* food (what goes best with your favourite dishes), but also wines *in* food (how to use wine in cooking).

Chapter 12

The Marriage of Wine and Food

....

....

*Y*ou may not hear wedding bells when you taste an Ontario Pinot Noir with a grilled Atlantic salmon steak, but it's a marriage made in gustatory heaven. Think of Barbara and Tony as marriage counsellors in this chapter as we do some matchmaking between the dining-room table and the cellar. (In Chapter 15 we hitch up the kitchen with the cellar when we uncork the wines to use in cooking.)

Food subtly alters the taste of wine and vice versa. Do you like white wines so dry that they make you pucker? Probably not (most people like some residual sugar in their wines). But if you swallow an oyster (and your mouth is suddenly awash with the taste of the sea), a really dry white wine like a Muscadet from the Loire Valley, a Chablis from Burgundy, or a Riesling Trocken from Germany's Mosel region, is just what you need to cut that salty taste and refresh your palate. And that's really what you want wine to do for you: cleanse your palate of one particular taste so you can enjoy another. If everything tasted like shellfish throughout a meal that started with oysters, well, you might as well stop eating.

Planning a Wine and Food Wedding

You probably know that old saying, "Red wine with meat, white wine with fish." The expression is one of those clichés that gets handed down. But if you stick to that advice you're missing out on some great taste sensations. For instance, if you react badly to red wine (the tannins in reds can cause headaches for those who are allergic to histamines) does this mean you have to forgo the

pH-balanced

A glass of wine with your meal helps you digest food. The pH (the measurement of concentration of acidity) in wine is expressed as a number: most wines are in the 3 to 3.5 range. The lower the pH, the drier the wine tastes (the pH of lemon juice, for instance, is 2.3). Actually, the acidity in wine is very similar in its pH value to the acidity in your stomach. That's pretty acidic! Stomach acids break down the food you eat into nutrients and waste products. Wine assists in this digestive process.

pleasure of a glass of wine with a grilled steak? No, you can drink white wine happily with red meat as long as the wine has enough body to stand up to the meat. (In Chapter 9 we tell you the best wine matches for different preparations of steak.) And why not red wine with fish if the wine has sufficient acidity to cut through the oiliness? One of the great marriages is grilled salmon with a lightly chilled young red Burgundy or Beaujolais.

When it comes to matching food and wine, throw away the rulebook. Well all right, not quite. Keep these suggestions in mind:

- ✔ **Match the weight of the food to the weight of the wine.** Delicate dishes are held up by light wines. Full-flavoured dishes can handle big, powerful wines.

- ✔ **Serve lighter wines before more full-bodied wines, younger wines before older wines, if you're serving more than one wine at a meal.**

- ✔ **Serve the wine at its optimum serving temperature.** Don't serve white wines too cold (you won't taste them properly) or red wines too warm (cellar temperature is best, around 20° Celsius [65° Fahrenheit]). If red wine is too warm, chill it for 5 to 10 minutes in an ice bucket.

- ✔ **Match the wine to the strongest flavour on the plate.** It may not be the meat. For example, turkey breast is not as assertive a taste as sweet potato or cranberry sauce. Your wine has to have a touch of sweet fruitiness to stand up to these flavours.

- ✔ **Serve wines that have good acidity with salty, smoky, oily, or buttery foods.** The wine cleanses and refreshes the palate. Try a crisp Chablis or a non-oaked Canadian Chardonnay.

- ✔ **Serve wines that have residual sweetness with hot or spicy foods.** Good bets are off-dry Riesling, semisweet Vouvray, and blush wines.

- ✔ **Dessert wines should always be sweeter than the dessert.** If the dessert is sweeter than the wine, it will accentuate the wine's acidity instead of its sweetness.

Reverse matching

In a restaurant, most people scan the menu first and choose the dish they want to eat. They then turn to the wine list and look for a wine to match it. Next time you dine out, reverse the procedure and select the wine first. The more familiar you become with certain wine styles, the better your taste memory will function in identifying a good food match for the wine you've selected. It will access the flavour of the wine and you will find it easier than trying to match the wine to the menu item you have chosen. You know what the wine tastes like, so you can select a dish from the menu that complements the wine. Give it a try. This is how Tony and Barb usually plan their meals — in a restaurant *and* at home. We've got our priorities straight!

Grape Expectations

Each of the major grape varieties has unique individual flavours that go well with certain types of food. You first select a particular grape to go with a dish, and then, depending on how you cook that dish, select a wine that matches it beautifully.

We match wine with specific food dishes in Chapter 14. But this section is a great primer of sorts, encouraging you to get to know different grapes and the foods they're best paired with. Read ahead and find out which flavours are pressed out of the most popular white and red grape varieties.

In this section, grape varieties are listed in alphabetical order, beginning with the white grapes and carrying on with the reds. Each entry describes the grape in terms of the wine and flavours it produces, and lists the regions where it's most commonly found. We also highlight the grape's *best expression* — particular wines that best exemplify the grape's flavour profile. We recommend you give them a try.

Chardonnay

Undoubtedly, Chardonnay is the world's most popular white wine grape. (So popular in fact that some people just won't order it anymore. They belong to the ABC movement: "Anything But Chardonnay.") Its range of flavours is very broad, depending on the soil and climate in which it is grown, and the treatment it's subjected to in the cellar. Flavours range from tart lemony, green apple in cool northern regions (Chablis and northern Italy) to pineapple and tropical fruits in warm climates (California and Australia). It can be rich, buttery, and nutty with overtones of vanilla, butterscotch, toast, and smoke from oak aging. Chardonnay develops caramel flavours and a deep golden colour as it matures.

Best expression:

- Montrachet, Corton-Charlemagne, Meursault (white Burgundy), top Californian, Australian Chardonnay
- Driest versions: Coteaux champenois (still wine [without bubbles] made in the Champagne region), unoaked Chablis (white Burgundy, not aged in oak barrels), Northern Italian Chardonnay
- Medium versions: Côte d'Or, Mâconnais (white Burgundy), Northern Italy, Ontario, British Columbia, New York, Washington, Oregon, New Zealand, South Africa
- Rich/full-bodied versions: California, Australia, Chile

Chardonnay-friendly foods:

- Driest versions: seafood
- Medium versions: chicken, white meat, tuna, runny cheeses
- Rich/full-bodied versions: meat in cream or fruit sauces, lobster with butter sauce

Chenin Blanc

An old, noble white grape variety, this has an astonishing flavour range, from tartly dry to honey sweet. This grape is capable of great age owing to its high acidity — 30 years and more is not uncommon. In cool-climate regions, like the Loire, the Chenin Blanc grape produces tart, full-flavoured wines that taste of quince and apple. In warm vintages, the wine takes on an off-dry, honeyed apricot note with a floral bouquet. When attacked (in a good way!) by *Botrytis cinerea* (a type of mould that dehydrates the grapes, increasing the ratio of sugar to fluid), the grapes become rich in sweetness, offering honeyed apricot and peach flavours. Grown in warm climates, such as California, this variety makes a rather neutral wine. Next to the Loire, South Africa makes the most representative style of Chenin, from dry to dessert wines.

Best expression:

- Driest versions: Vouvray, Saumur (Loire Valley)
- Off-dry versions: Vouvray, Coteaux du Layon (Loire Valley)
- Sweet versions: Bonnezeaux, Quarts de Chaume (Loire Valley), Edelkeur (South Africa)

Chenin Blanc-friendly foods:

- ✔ Driest versions: seafood
- ✔ Off-dry versions: fish in cream sauces, spicy Oriental dishes, pork with applesauce
- ✔ Sweet versions: fruit-based desserts

Gewürztraminer

The name says it all: *gewürz* in German means spicy; *traminer* is German for "of or from the town of Tramin." The town is located in the Süd Tirol/Alto Adige section of northern Italy, and it's where this highly perfumed grape was first propagated about 1,000 years ago. (This region was part of Austria until the First World War. Now, the Italian-speaking residents call Tramin Termeno).

At its most blatant, Gewürztraminer has a bouquet of lychee nuts and roses, with overtones of red pepper and cabbage leaf when over-ripe, giving it an oily mouth feel. It can range in taste from very dry (although its aromatic fruitiness gives the impression of sweetness on the nose) to off-dry and sweet when late harvested. If its pinkish berries are attacked by *Botrytis cinerea*, it becomes honeyed and can lose its distinctive flavour and be almost indistinguishable from the Riesling grape.

Best expression:

- ✔ Driest versions: Alto Adige (Italy), Austria, Ontario, British Columbia, New York State
- ✔ Medium-sweet versions: California, Australia, German Gewürztraminer Spätlese
- ✔ Sweet versions: Vendange Tardive and Sélection de Grains Nobles (Alsace), German Gewürztraminer Auslese (and higher sugar levels)

Gewürztraminer-friendly foods:

- ✔ Driest versions: smoked salmon and other smoked fish, spicy hors d'oeuvres, Münster cheese
- ✔ Medium-sweet versions: light chicken or beef curries; spicy, hot dishes; Thai and Mexican recipes
- ✔ Sweet versions: desserts that are less sweet than the wine (fruit-based desserts, light cakes)

Icewine

Any grape that can hang on the vine until the mercury drops to a sustained temperature of minus 8° Celsius (18° Fahrenheit) can make Icewine. Normally, you make it with white grapes because they withstand the cold better than red grapes but sometimes you see such anomalies as red Cabernet Franc Icewine.

In Canada, the preferred grapes for Icewine are Riesling and Vidal. Sometimes, Gewürztraminer and Chenin Blanc — varieties that have thick enough skins to withstand the rigours of the winter months, are also used. Canada is the world's largest producer of Icewine. You can find out why this is so in Chapter 16.

Although you can make Icewine from any grape that freezes, you must use only those grapes that are VQA-approved if you want your wine to be eligible for Canadian VQA status.

The classic Icewine has a bouquet of honey, peach, and apricot, with a caramel-like sweetness, tropical fruit flavours, and a sweet, citrusy finish. The best will have a finish that lingers long on your palate.

Best expression: Château des Charmes, Cave Spring, Inniskillin, Henry of Pelham, Vineland Estate, Stoney Ridge, Konzelmann (Canada)

Icewine-friendly foods: fruit-based desserts

Muscat

This is probably the oldest grape variety known, dating back to Greek times. Many of today's Muscat grapes were originally mutations from different *clones* (vines propagated from cuttings of other vines) of the variety. There are over 200 different types of Muscat grapes grown around the world — from palest white-yellow in colour to mourning black. Taken together, Muscat in its many forms is the most widely planted grape on the planet.

Equally delicious as table grapes, the wine produced from Muscat is the nearest to the taste of the actual grape as you will get. Generally sweet in flavour, Muscat leaves elements of carnation, cardamom, muskmelon, and orange blossom on the nose and the palate. Like the Gewürztraminer grape, its bouquet suggests sweetness, although it can be quite dry. The red grape version (Muscat Hamburg) has blackcurrant flavours. Its weight varies astonishingly — from the light and delicate low-alcohol still and sparkling wines of Moscato d'Asti in Piedmont, to the thick and lusciously sensuous Muscats of the Greek and Aeolian Islands.

Best expression:

- ✔ Driest versions: Alsace Muscat, Austrian Muscat
- ✔ Medium-sweet versions: Moscato d'Asti, Asti Spumante, Clairette de Die (France)
- ✔ Sweet versions: Beaumes de Venise, Frontignan, Banyuls, Rivesaltes (France), Samos and other Greek Muscats, Quady Elysium from California (a wonderful Black Muscat)

Muscat-friendly foods:

- ✔ Driest versions: spicy, hot finger foods (similar to Gewürztraminer)
- ✔ Medium-sweet versions: light curries, Mexican, Thai dishes, anything with hot peppers
- ✔ Sweet versions: light cake, biscuits

Pinot Blanc

Pinot Blanc lives in the shadow of its more glamorous sister Chardonnay, for whom it can be mistaken at a glance. What it lacks in popularity, however, it makes up for as a useful and generally less costly white grape variety. This is a wine to drink young and fresh as it has limited staying power — even at its best, in Alsace and California. With its high acidity, it's a good variety for the production of sparkling wines, especially in Alsace. Pinot Blanc grapes grown in this French region produce dry, fruity wine that usually exhibits white peach and apple flavours with high alcohol, giving the wine a full mouth feel. Pinot Blanc is not as complex as Chardonnay, but can resemble it with oak barrel treatment.

Best expression:

- ✔ Crémant d'Alsace (Alsace)
- ✔ Tiefenbrunner, Jermann, Ca'del Bosco (Northern Italy)
- ✔ Chalone, Au Bon Climat (California)
- ✔ Cameron (Oregon)
- ✔ Konzelmann (Ontario)
- ✔ Blue Mountain (British Columbia)
- ✔ Sweet versions: Austrian late harvest

Pinot Blanc-friendly foods: fish, Camembert cheese, brie cheese, chicken

Pinot Gris

The grey Pinot grape is a mutation of Pinot Noir, the grape that produces red Burgundy.

Pinot Gris has a skin colour that varies from blue to brownish pink. Depending on the soil conditions and climate, it can produce a light, *spritzy* (fizzy on the tongue), pale wine in Northern Italy when picked slightly underripe, as well as a rich, unctuous, honeyed, deeply coloured wine in Alsace, capable of late harvesting.

The wine has a dry, peachy-melon taste with a hint of spice and low acidity. It tends to be more acidic in cooler climates. When attacked by *Botrytis cinerea*, it produces deep golden wines with concentrated honeyed flavours.

Best expression:

- Alsace Pinot Gris
- Oregon Pinot Gris
- Driest versions: Pinot Grigio (Northern Italy)
- Sweet versions: Vendange Tardive and Sélection de Grains Nobles (Alsace), Grauburgunder or Ruländer Auslese (Germany), and styles with higher sugar levels

Pinot Gris-friendly foods:

- Dry versions: pork, chicken
- Sweet versions: fruit-based desserts

Riesling

As a grape variety, Riesling makes some of the best bone-dry wines on this planet, some of the finest dessert wines, and every shade of sweetness in between. With its fine spine of acidity and spicy complexity, Riesling is the most versatile of wines for matching with cuisines as diverse as French, Mexican, light curries, Thai, and Californian.

Wait, there's more praise yet to heap on this lovely white grape. No other dry white wine, with the possible exception of Chenin Blanc from the Loire, ages as long or as beautifully as Riesling. Riesling is uncompromising: What's in the grape is what you get in the wine, since it's seldom put into oak barrels that alter its taste. In cool climates such as Germany, Austria, Alsace, Ontario, and New York, Riesling has a racy acidity ameliorated either by the amount of sugar in the grapes at the time of harvest, or by the amount of residual sugar left in the wine after fermentation. Riesling is a highly aromatic wine. It offers floral notes with citrus flavours. The riper it gets, the more it exhibits peach and apricot flavours with a lemony-grapefruit finish. As it ages, it takes on a characteristic petrol or kerosene quality on the nose.

Best expression:

- ✔ Light-bodied versions: Mosel, Rheingau (Germany)
- ✔ Medium-bodied versions: Rheinhessen, Pfalz (Germany)
- ✔ Fuller-bodied versions: Alsace (France), Austria, New York, Ontario

Riesling-friendly foods:

- ✔ Dry versions: seafood, shellfish, fish
- ✔ Medium-dry versions: spicy, hot dishes, Oriental, Mexican dishes
- ✔ Sweet dessert wines: fruit-based desserts

Which Riesling is the sweetest? Ask a German or Austrian

German and Austrian label designations actually tell you the sweetness of the wine.

Qualitätswein bestimmer Anbaugebeite (mercifully, QbA for short): **the driest**

Kabinett: **dry but fruitier**

Spätlese (late harvest): **medium-sweet**

Auslese (selectively picked late harvest): **honeyed sweet**

Beerenauslese/Eiswein: **sweet and rich**

Trockenbeerenauslese: **unctuously sweet**

Austria has a unique designation of sweetness between Beerenauslese and Trockenbeerenauslese styles: It's called Ausbruch, a wine made from totally botrytised grapes (grapes that have been attacked by the *Botrytis cinerea* mould to bring out as much sweetness as possible).

Another wrinkle: Germany has three *further* classification levels within each sugar level category from QbA to Auslese: Trocken (dry), Halbtrocken (medium-dry), and Lieblich (sweet).

Riesling QbA Trocken and Kabinett Trocken are two of the driest wines you will find.

Sauvignon Blanc

Grown extensively in Bordeaux, where it is customarily blended with Sémillon (a similar white grape variety), Sauvignon Blanc has achieved more fame and fans either as the tart, refreshing wines from the villages of Sancerre and Pouilly-Fumé in the Loire Valley, or as more generous Sauvignons from New Zealand. The zingy freshness these regions extract from this variety is often lacking in Sauvignon Blanc grown in warmer regions — especially if the wine's fermented or aged in oak barrels. But California Sauvignon, sometimes styled as Fumé Blanc, can take on a richness and exhibit complex fruit aromas and flavours, similar to Chardonnay, albeit with an underlying herbaceous character. These dry wines are very versatile when it comes to matching with food because of their driving acidity.

Sauvignon Blanc's major flavour components are grassiness and green fruits, particularly gooseberries, elderberries, and figs. Other green fruits and vegetables are also detectable: pea pods, asparagus, green beans, and green peppers. In really ripe Sauvignon, particularly in New Zealand, you'll find nettles, passion fruit, papaya, and other tropical fruit flavours, but invariably with a firm acid base. This grape also has a tendency, when *overcropped* (too many bunches harvested from a single vine plant), to produce aromas reminiscent of your cat's litterbox.

Best expression:

- Dry versions: Sancerre, Pouilly-Fumé and the lesser Loire villages of Menetou-Salon, Quincy and Reuilly (France), Marlborough and Martinborough (New Zealand)
- Riper versions: Napa, Sonoma (USA) (often called Fumé Blanc)
- Sweet versions: California late harvest Sauvignon Blanc, Chile, Sauternes and Barsac (France)

Sauvignon Blanc-friendly foods:

- Dry versions: goat's cheese, green vegetables, fish
- Riper versions (California Fumé): chicken and white meats, soft cheeses
- Sweet versions: light cakes, fruit desserts

Robert Mondavi, one of the leading winemakers in California, coined the term Fumé Blanc for Sauvignon Blanc that he aged in oak, which gave it a smoky character. Many California wineries have followed his example. The allusion to Pouilly-Fumé, the well-known Sauvignon Blanc from the Loire Valley in France (which is not aged in oak, by the way), cannot be ignored.

Cabernet Franc

This lightly tannic red grape is usually blended with the Cabernet Sauvignon grape to enhance its flavour. It does well in cool climates, which is why it's such a good variety for Canadian regions. Cabernet Franc produces a medium-bodied wine with a flavour of blackberries and currants, not unlike Cabernet Sauvignon but less aggressive and herbaceous.

Best expression: Ontario Cabernet Franc, Chinon and Bourgueil from the Loire Valley

Cabernet Franc-friendly foods: lamb, beef, game, hard cheeses

Cabernet Sauvignon

Of all the red grapes, Cabernet Sauvignon has perhaps reached No. 1 on the consumer's hit parade more often than any other variety. While it enjoyed pre-eminence as the main constituent in Bordeaux wines of the Médoc and Graves regions, it was only when California got into the act with 100 percent Cabernet Sauvignon that adoration of this grape became a global phenomenon. The berries of its clusters are small — which means that the ratio of skin, pits, and stems to pulp is high. This affects the amount of tannin present. Since tannin occurs in the skin, pits, and stems of grapes, the tannic content of wines made from Cabernet Sauvignon is particularly high. The grapes taste harsh when young and take a long time to soften up, which is why they're usually blended with the fruitier Merlot grape (described later in this section) even when the label suggests a single varietal wine.

One of the easiest red wines to recognize blind, Cabernet Sauvignon has a bouquet of cedar and blackcurrant (cassis). In warm climates such as California, Australia, and Chile, the wines made from the Cabernet Sauvignon grape are *fruit-driven* (meaning they're made to be consumed young). Such wines are usually treated to French or American oak barrel-aging, which is noticeable as a vanilla or coconut aroma in the bouquet. In cool climates such as New Zealand and Ontario, where Cabernet Sauvignon grapes struggle to ripen, the wines take on herbaceous, green pepper flavours. Even in Bordeaux you'll find that in poor, wet years the wines are sinewy and lean. But at their best, there's no wine better for most meat dishes.

Cooler-climate Cabernet Sauvignon wines show more redcurrant, cranberry, and pomegranate flavours, while those from warm growing regions have notes of plum and blackberries, mint or eucalyptus, and smoke.

Best expression:

- Bordeaux (the *classified growths*, a hierarchy of quality established in 1855)
- Napa and Sonoma's top wineries
- Chilean Reserva wines
- Australia: top wineries
- South Africa: top wineries

Cabernet Sauvignon-friendly foods: same as Cabernet Franc

Gamay

The grape from the Beaujolais region that gives us the ever-popular Beaujolais Nouveau, Gamay produces an easy-drinking fruity wine with a characteristic flavour of cherries and pepper. Because it ripens early, the Gamay grape is ideal for fermenting into *vin nouveau* (wines that can be consumed a matter of weeks after the harvest). It's not a particularly challenging wine and certainly not one to lay down (age). It's at its best when consumed within a year or two of its vintage date. And for best results, Gamay-based wines and Beaujolais should be lightly chilled to bring out the freshness. I bet you thought we'd never suggest chilling a red wine!

The villages of Beaujolais

Beaujolais is divided into three areas according to soil type. The southern part of the region is flat with limestone soil. The wines grown here have the appellation "Beaujolais." In the northern part of the region, the landscape is more dramatic with granite hills. The wines grown here are more complex and go by the appellation "Beaujolais-Villages." The best wines of the region are those grown around the 10 named villages of Beaujolais known as the "Beaujolais *crus*" (the growths of Beaujolais).

Working from north to south, the 10 named villages are:

1. St. Amour
2. Juliénas
3. Chénas
4. Moulin-à-Vent
5. Fleurie
6. Chiroubles
7. Morgon
8. Régnié
9. Brouilly
10. Côte de Brouilly.

And if you've ever cycled up the *côte* (slope) of Brouilly, you could really use a chilled glass of Beaujolais to reward yourself.

Gamay has lively acidity, which makes it a very versatile food wine, especially when chilled. In Beaune, the capital of the Burgundy region, the restaurants serve poached eggs swimming in Beaujolais. While this may be the Breakfast of Champions for the Burgundians, we recommend you serve your Gamay wines with more traditional fare.

Best expression: Beaujolais-Villages and the 10 specified villages of Beaujolais

Gamay-friendly foods: chicken, turkey, cold cuts, white meat dishes, roasted chestnuts

Merlot

Although Merlot is the major grape of Bordeaux's St. Emilion and Pomerol regions — in fact, the entire right bank of the Gironde — it is also the most extensively planted variety throughout Bordeaux. It's grown extensively in southwest France and in the Midi, and also widely cultivated in northeastern Italy. The Merlot grape is usually blended with the more austere Cabernet Sauvignon grape to fill in the Cab Sauv's *middle palate* (the taste between immediate response to the wine and its aftertaste once you've swallowed it) and make it taste less tannic. There's less tannin in wine made from Merlot grapes because its berries are bigger than those of Cab Sauv, so the ratio of pulp to skin, pits, and stems is more even. Merlot ripens earlier and matures faster than Cabernet Sauvignon, and thus can be consumed with pleasure at a younger age.

Merlot has a distinctive plum and blueberry taste, though its structure is similar to Cabernet Sauvignon. It tends, however, to be less tannic and acidic than Cabernet Sauvignon.

California Meritages

Merlot is now as popular in California as the venerable Cabernet Sauvignon, where it's blended with Merlot and Cabernet Franc grapes to produce what the Californians call Meritage reds. It's also used in small amounts to soften varietally labelled Cabernet Sauvignon. (Legally, you can use up to 15 percent of another wine to blend in and still call the wine by the name of its major component. So, in the case of California Merlot and Cabernet Sauvignon, the resulting blend would still be labelled as Cabernet Sauvignon.) Merlot is, in fact, enjoying a vogue on its own as a varietal wine and commanding Cabernet Sauvignon prices. Some of the finest New World Merlots are coming out of Washington State.

Best expression:

- Château Pétrus, the greatest Pomerol, generally the better wines of St. Emilion and Pomerol, some Merlots from Friuli (Italy)
- Shafer and Arrowood (from the Napa Valley and Sonoma regions, respectively); Leonetti, Woodward Canyon, Andrew Will (Washington)

Merlot-friendly foods: red meat dishes, hard cheeses

Although a wine may be named for a single grape variety, it may actually contain a small amount of other varieties. For instance, in Canada, the VQA rules state that a wine named Cabernet Sauvignon (or other grape variety) may contain up to 15 percent of other varieties in its blend. Most wine-producing countries have a similar rule. This technique contributes complexity and other positive elements without influencing the flavour profile of the principal grape.

Nebbiolo

What Pinot Noir is to Burgundy, Nebbiolo is to the Piedmont region of north-eastern Italy. It is arguably that country's noblest red wine grape, despite its austere flavour. The grape itself has an ancient lineage and has been documented back to the 13th century. Wines made from the Nebbiolo grape are certainly the longest lived; but because of the high tannins and concentration of acids, they are rarely approachable until they have been tamed by several years in the bottle.

Nebbiolo is derived from the Italian word *nebbia*, meaning fog, which speaks to the climatic condition that occurs in the hills around Alba, in Piedmont, around harvest time. Acidic and tannic in its youth, Nebbiolo softens with age, developing a rich and complex bouquet of dried fruits, leather, black cherries, truffles, roses, herbs, and tar. It does not have the ready accessibility of Cabernet Sauvignon and exhibits a characteristic bitterness on the finish.

Best expression: Barolo (the king of Italian reds) and Barbaresco (the queen, more approachable)

Nebbiolo-friendly foods: game, Parmesan cheese

Pinot Noir

Any wine grower will tell you that Pinot Noir is the most difficult grape to grow. It is also the most difficult grape to capture at its peak of ripeness: picked too early its flavours are green; allowed to ripen fully it can turn into cooked raspberry jam. Imagine drinking that! Even in Burgundy, its spiritual home, Pinot Noir is a hit-and-miss affair that is very frustrating for consumers since the wines are generally on the expensive side. But at its finest, Pinot Noir is the greatest wine experience you'll ever have.

Few regions outside Burgundy can grow Pinot Noir successfully. Oregon has made the best wines from this variety and there are notable successes in the cooler regions of Australia, namely Tasmania. New Zealand also produces very fine Pinot Noir in Martinborough and Central Otago. Occasionally, Alsace and Germany can make commendable Pinot Noir as can Ontario, British Columbia, and New York — but it takes late fall sunshine and long dry spells leading up to harvest time. This grape's flavours include raspberries, violets, and sometimes strawberries. In grapes grown in warm climates, you'll taste more cherry to black cherry and a range of bouquets that can include rust, tomato, gamey animal smells, and what Burgundians refer to as "barnyard" aromas. Use your imagination.

Best expression:

- ✔ Top wines of Burgundy's Côte de Beaune region (medium-bodied) and Côte de Nuits region (fuller-bodied)

- ✔ Top Oregon wineries; Calera (California); Mondavi, Acacia, Saintsbury (Carneros region, California)

- ✔ Yarra Valley, Tasmania (Australia)

- ✔ Martinborough (New Zealand)

Pinot Noir-friendly foods:

- ✔ Red meats, fowl, light game, hard cheeses
- ✔ Drier, more acidic Pinot Noirs go well with fleshy fish, like salmon

Sangiovese

Literally translated as "blood of Jove," Sangiovese is the most recognizable grape of Italy, responsible for the wines of the Chianti, Brunello di Montalcino, and Vino Nobile di Montepulciano regions in Tuscany, and is planted extensively in other central and southern Italian provinces. It is, in fact, Italy's most widely planted red grape. Although Sangiovese is generally blended with other red wines, it makes fine varietal wine on its own (wine that is 100 percent made from Sangiovese grapes), as it does in Brunello di Montalcino as well as in some California vineyards. It reaches its peak of perfection when blended with up to 20 percent Cabernet Sauvignon, the recipe for many of the "Super Tuscan" blends.

The Sangiovese grape produces a firm, medium-bodied dry wine with a bouquet of chestnut, a floral note, and a bitter finish. You'll taste flavours of cherries, plums, and currants, but always with a healthy spine of acidity. This grape tends to brown with age, taking on leather, barnyard, and truffle notes.

Best Expression:

- ✔ Pure Sangiovese: La Pregole Torte di Monte Vertine, Badia a Coltibuono (Brunello di Montalcino)
- ✔ Blended: Chianti Classico Riservas, Vino Nobile di Montepulciano
- ✔ Super Tuscan wines, Rubesco Riserva (Super Umbrian)

Sangiovese-friendly foods: meat dishes with tomato-based sauces, smoked meats, hard cheeses

The Italians have created an intriguing category of wine outside the official appellation laws, known as "super wines." They contain quality grape types not sanctioned by the appellation, usually blended with local grapes such as Sangiovese. Most of the unsanctioned grapes are typical French varieties such as Cabernet Sauvignon. A movement is afoot to adapt the law to accommodate these premium wines.

Syrah/Shiraz

Syrah is an underappreciated grape in France, playing second fiddle to Cabernet Sauvignon, Merlot, and Pinot Noir. It makes the great wines of the Northern Rhône, Hermitage, and Côte Rôtie, which can age for many years. It is also a *constituent* (used in the blends) of the Southern Rhône reds like Châteauneuf-du-Pape. Don't confuse Syrah with Petite Sirah — a different variety grown in California.

The Australians and South Africans call the Syrah grape "Shiraz" and use it extensively as a blending wine with Cabernet Sauvignon, although some of Australia's finest wines are made exclusively from Shiraz.

Syrah makes a full-bodied wine that tends to be deeply coloured and has a bouquet of blackberry and smoke, tar, or iodine. The wine is fleshy with a good fruit flavour — you'll taste blackberries and freshly ground white or black pepper. Like Cabernet Sauvignon, the Syrah grape is highly tannic and requires a few years of bottle age to soften.

Australian Shiraz tends to be jammier and softer than the Syrah of the Northern Rhône.

Best Expression:

- ✔ Hermitage, Côte Rôtie, Cornas, St. Joseph, and Crozes-Hermitage (Northern Rhône region of France); look especially for producers Guigal, Vidal-Fleurie, Jaboulet, Chapoutier
- ✔ Grange, Eileen Hardy (Australia)
- ✔ Nichol Vineyards (British Columbia)

Syrah/Shiraz-friendly foods: game, spicy casseroles, marinated BBQ meats

Tempranillo

Temperano, the Spanish word from which the Tempranillo grape derives its name, means "early," and refers to the vine's early ripening abilities. The Tempranillo grape is the main variety in some of Spain's longest-lived and most elegant red wines, in spite of its low acidity and low alcohol. Although you do see it nowadays in the Rioja region as a varietal wine, it's usually blended with the Garnacha grape, as well as some Mazuelo and Graciano.

This grape produces a deeply coloured, light to medium-bodied wine when young, with a taste of strawberries, raspberries, or cherries. It can resemble red Bordeaux when young and Burgundy when aged in the bottle for several years. It is usually matured in American oak barrels, and takes on an exotic, spice bouquet rather like sandalwood.

Best expression: Vega Sicilia, Pesquera (Rioja, Navarra, Ribeira del Duero)

Tempranillo-friendly foods: red meats, fowl, light game

Zinfandel

The Zinfandel grape is unique to California, although there is some debate as to its ancestry since it is similar in style to the Primitivo grape grown in Apulia, at the heel of Italy. Beginning in the 1880s, Zinfandel became the workhorse grape of the California wine industry, but its popularity eventually became its downfall. In the early 1970s, when the American consuming public took to white wine with a vengeance, farmers with Zinfandel in the ground were forced either to grub up their vines and replant to Chardonnay or to graft across to Chardonnay with the vine still in the ground. (This is done by a processs called T-budding.) The only thing that spared Zinfandel from becoming a forgotten vine was the creation of white Zinfandel (a blush wine with a touch of sweetness). These days, the pendulum has swung back, and Zinfandel in its full lusty glory as a fruity red is now the signature wine of The Golden State. Old-Vine Zins from vineyards dating back three or four generations are all the rage.

T-budding in the vineyard

T-budding is a practise used by grape growers to convert one variety of grape vine over to another using an established rootstock that is still planted in the vineyard. The technique involves grafting buds from the desired variety onto an existing rootstock. A skilled grafter makes two T-shaped cuts in the bark of the rootstock. Peeling back the bark, he inserts a shield-shaped bud and wraps it tightly in place with budding tape. This procedure is time-consuming and expensive and can only be done during the summer months when the bark is loosest.

Depending on how it is *vinified* (fermented into wine), the Zinfandel grape can produce a range of wine styles — from fruity Beaujolais to late-harvest port-like wines. It generally produces medium- to full-bodied, *highly extracted* (concentrated fruit flavours) wines with a blackberry or black cherry flavour and a peppery finish, buttressed by smoky, vanilla oak.

Best expression: Ridge, Ravenswood, Rosenblum, Cline (California)

Zinfandel-friendly foods:

- ✔ Light versions (similar to Beaujolais): hamburger, pizza, ham, cold meats
- ✔ Full-bodied versions: game dishes, rich meats, hard cheeses
- ✔ Blush versions: spicy, hot dishes, Thai food, light curries

Don't Forget the Fortifieds

Fortified wines have a higher alcohol content than "regular" wines (generally between 15 and 22 percent). Sherry and port, two favourites, are usually served either as *apéritifs* at the beginning of a meal or as *digestifs* at the end of it. But this is incredibly restrictive. These fortified wines can also (believe it or not) be served *during* the meal in pretty creative, tasty ways.

Sherry: Any Palomino is a pal of mine

Sherry-producing Palomino grapes are grown in the hot Jerez de la Frontera region of southwest Spain. The resulting wine ranges from the delicate, bone-dry paleness of the fino and manzanilla styles, to the heavy, mahogany-coloured sweetness of cream sherry.

Sherry is fortified with brandy to bring it up to a minimum alcoholic strength of 15.5 percent. Generally speaking, the deeper the colour, the higher the alcohol content, which can rise to a permitted maximum of 20.9 percent.

Best expression:

- ✔ Dry versions: Fino or Manzanilla
- ✔ Off-dry versions: Palo Cortado, dry Oloroso
- ✔ Sweet versions: cream

Sherry-friendly foods:

- ✔ With Fino and Manzanilla: Use as apéritif wines to stimulate the appetite or as accompaniments for fish and seafood. These sherries are best served chilled.

- ✔ With Amontillado (a fino-style sherry that has been left to age): A nice accompaniment for soups served either in the bowl or the glass. This sherry is deeper in colour, higher in alcohol, and has a dry, nutty taste. Chill it lightly before serving.

- ✔ With Oloroso: This sherry can stand up to meat dishes and highly spiced foods. It's full-bodied and nutty, and can be dry or sweet as labelled.

- ✔ With pale cream: Light in colour and sweet, as the name suggests, pair this sherry with cake or fruit-based desserts. It's also a good complement to Christmas pudding.

Port: Overturning the tradition

Port is produced by stopping the fermentation of the *grape must* (the crushed grapes and their fermenting juice) with grape brandy so that residual sugar is left in the wine. Port's alcoholic strength varies from 20 to 22 percent. The well-worn tradition of drinking a glass of port after dinner has made us overlook its possibilities as a wine to accompany the meal or to be used in its preparation.

Grown in Portugal's hot and savagely beautiful Douro Valley, port is made from five preferred grape varieties — Touriga Nacional, Tinta Barroca, Touriga Francesa, Tinta Roriz (Spain's Tempranillo), and Tinta Cao.

The different designations of port can be confusing, but there are two basic types from which they all derive: ruby (bottle-aged) and tawny (cask-aged). A bottle-aged port is bottled two years after it's been fermented. The bottling allows for long maturation without the presence of air. A cask-aged port spends its life in wooden vats or barrels and is exposed to air that slowly oxidizes it.

Ruby ports (bottle-aged)

These deeply coloured ports have a distinct blackberry flavour, and are young and rugged. They are available in five designations:

- **Vintage Port:** The best wines of a declared vintage, bottled after two years and left for long aging. They have a rich, full-bodied, ripe blackberry and mulberry character, and are spicy and sweet.

- **LBV (Late Bottled Vintage):** A wine from a single year, bottled when it is between four and six years old. Not as rich and elegant as vintage but a less expensive and worthwhile substitute.

- **Single Quinta Vintage:** A wine of a declared year from a single farm, unblended. Usually not as intense and concentrated as a vintage port — which has been blended from several farms.

- **Crusted Port:** A wine from several vintages that throws a deposit in the bottle, behaving like a vintage port.

- **Vintage Character:** This ruby port is actually cask-aged (an anomaly!) and bottled after five years.

Tawny ports (cask-aged)

These ports are topaz in colour and taste of nuts and raisins, with a hint of oxidation.

- **Colheita:** Tawny ports from a single year. The vintage date appears on the bottle.

- **Aged Tawny:** Usually designated 10, 20, 30, or even 40 years old. Lighter in colour and drier, it has spicy dried fruit and nut flavours.

Best expression: Taylor, Fonseca, Graham, Dow, Warre, Quinta do Noval, Ramos Pinto, Sandeman, Niepoort

Port-friendly foods:

- Bottle-aged ports: chocolate, blue cheese
- Wood-aged ports (chillable): soups, cheeses, desserts

White port

White port is usually served as an apéritif either well chilled, on the rocks with a slice of lemon, or with soda water. These wines, produced from such grape varieties as Gouveio, Malvasia Fina, and Viosinho, are usually off-dry to medium sweet.

Chapter 13

Wine and Cheese

• •

In This Chapter

▶ Discovering why cheese is wine's perfect companion

▶ Determining cheese styles

▶ Selecting Canadian wines for Canadian cheeses

▶ Choosing international wines for international cheeses

• •

Cheese and wine. Wine and cheese. They go together like no other food pairing on this planet. It's humanity's attempt to make the perishable permanent. After all, wine and cheese last much longer than grapes and milk — and can you imagine eating grapes with milk!

The alchemy of fermentation renders both wine and cheese into long-lived and transportable products that are a delicious complement to one another. All the more so if they spring from the same soil (the grass that cows and sheep and goats eat has a direct effect on the taste of the cheese produced from their milk).

Whether you want a wine to drink at home with your old-style Cheddar cheese on a Friday night, or something to serve with that Danish blue at the dinner party you're hosting tonight, have a look at the wine and cheese matching charts in this chapter for inspiration. Who says you can't pair like with like? We've come up with some mouth-watering combinations of Canadian wines and cheeses. You can never have too much of a good thing, after all, and that's especially true when it comes to this gastronomic match made in heaven.

The Perfect Match

The most felicitous food combination you can experience is wine and cheese. Cheese is the perfect companion for wine because of its fat content, of all things. The fat in cheese coats the tongue, softening the tannic edge of red wines and mellowing the acidity in white wines.

Sell on cheese, buy on apples

Wine merchants in Bordeaux have a saying: "Sell on cheese and buy on apples." The reason is that a well-chosen wine flatters cheese and cheese brings out the best in wine. They're a natural pairing. Apples, because of their acidity, make a wine taste sour. However, if the wine has enough sweetness to overcome the effect of the apple on your palate, then it's certainly worth buying.

Canadian VQA wines are particularly suited to the cheeses we produce in this country because of their firm structure and lively acidity. The acid in wine cleanses and refreshes the palate, setting you up for the next mouthful.

There is such a diverse range of Canadian cheeses (from delicate cream to rich, aged Cheddar and savoury blue) that there's no single wine you can choose to match them all. And nobody seems to mind this embarrassment of riches.

Types of cheese

Half of the joy of wine and cheese is to discover the combination that appeals to your palate.

There are five categories of cheese:

- **Fresh:** Usually white cheeses: cottage, cream, ricotta
- **Soft:** Brie, Camembert
- **Semi-soft:** Bocconcini, mozzarella, havarti, Saint-Paulin
- **Firm:** Brick, Edam, Cheddar
- **Hard:** Parmesan, Romano

How cheese is made

With so many cheeses from which to choose, it helps to understand a bit about how they're made. The first step is to sour the milk (all cheese starts out as milk), either naturally — as happens in your fridge if you keep it too long — or by introducing a special bacteria. Once the milk is soured, the cheesemaker adds *rennin,* an enzyme that causes the milk to form *curds* (solid lumps). The curds contain and are surrounded by a white liquid called *whey.*

Here's where things get interesting. The amount of whey that remains in the curds affects the resulting style of cheese, so depending on what's desired, the cheesemaker uses one of a variety of methods to remove more or less of the whey. Cooking, pressing, and kneading not only reduces the liquid; each method results in a different texture of cheese.

Once the desired amount of whey is removed, the curds are shaped — by hand or in moulds — and salted, either by mixing salt into the curds or by rubbing a salt solution onto the surface of the curded cheese. The salt acts as a preservative while the cheese *ripens* (ages).

Different bacteria aimed at creating certain styles of cheese are added during the ripening stage. The bacteria used for Swiss cheese, for example, produce gas bubbles, which create the characteristic holes. A blue-green mould injected into the curd creates the greenish veins in blue cheeses and contributes to their creamy texture. These cheeses are termed *interior-ripened*. Bacteria rubbed on the outer surface of a cheese create a thick skin but also work their way inside to create a soft, pungent interior, as in brie and Camembert. Not surprisingly, these cheeses are referred to as *surface-ripened*.

Cheese is also categorized by its moisture content. Soft cheeses, such as cottage cheese, still contain a high proportion of whey. They remain *fresh* (not ripened). Hard cheese, like Cheddar, is pressed under the weight of its own curds to remove the whey, and Parmesan is cooked to achieve an even drier texture.

The stronger the cheese, the more robust a wine you need to serve with it. A quick rule of thumb: if it's a hard cheese, match it with red wine; white wine is best if it's a runny cheese (fresh and soft varieties).

Wine and cheese: A complex, yet comfortable pairing

The basis of all wine is grape juice, whatever the variety of the vine. The basis of all cheese is milk, whether it comes from the cow, sheep, goat, or water buffalo (the Italians use this animal's milk to make mozzarella). Both liquids are perishable, and only when fermented can they exist in a more long-lived state. Both take on qualities of the raw materials from which they're made, rendering them much more complex and satisfying to consume.

Wine, for example, exhibits a lot of the characteristics of the particular soil in which the grapevines are planted — taking on trace minerals from that soil. Similarly, cheese takes on flavour elements of the grass eaten by the animal from whose milk it was produced.

Keep these points in mind when you match wine and cheese:

- Determine the style of the cheese and the character of the wine.
- Decide between a complementary flavour match (a crisp, dry white wine with a buttery, nutty cheese) and a contrasting flavour match (a salty blue cheese with a sweet, round red wine).

White wine goes better with creamy cheeses (brie and Camembert) than does red.

Because blue cheese tends to be very salty, a sweeter wine will cut through that saltiness and refresh your taste buds. The stronger the flavour of the cheese, the sweeter and weightier the wine should be. For such powerful cheeses as Roquefort and Danish blue, go for equally powerful wines like port and sherry.

Classifying Cheeses

The classification we've done here is based on how the cheese in question is made and ripened. Within each category of cheese, we suggest the style of wine that best suits it.

- **Fresh Cheeses:** Usually white in colour, these cheeses are not fermented and are consumed unripened. Their flavour comes from curdling, which gives the cheese an acidic flavour. They can be salted or unsalted and have herb flavouring. Examples: Canadian cottage, cream cheese, mozzarella, quark, ricotta.

  Appropriate wine style: Dry sparkling or crisp, dry, light-bodied white wines.

- **Soft Cheeses:** These cheeses have a white, bloomy crust, with a soft spreadable butter-coloured paste. Examples: Canadian brie, Camembert, Canadian feta.

  Appropriate wine style: Dry white or fruity young reds.

- **Semi-soft Cheeses:** A large range of products and styles represents this category, somewhat firmer than its softer cousins. Examples, unripened: bocconcini, mozzarella; interior-ripened: havarti, Monterey Jack, Saint-Paulin; surface-ripened: Limburger, Oka; washed-rind cheeses (rubbed with salt and water during ripening): Münster.

  Appropriate wine style: Gamay, Cabernet blends, Pinot Noir (for highly aromatic cheeses like Reblochon).

The umami factor

Umami? Pronounce it "oo-mamee." The tongue perceives four tastes: sweet, sour, bitter, and salt. But Japanese researchers contend that there is a fifth taste: umami. Western scientists are beginning to agree.

Roughly translated from the Japanese, umami means "delicious," but that could reflect a difference in preferences between Oriental and Western cultures. Japanese taste analysts (and now, increasingly, Western ones) use this term to describe a taste found in a variety of foods including seafood, tomatoes, mushrooms, and fermented foods such as soy sauce and cheese.

Have you ever tasted a wine that leaves a metallic taste in your mouth? It could be that you ate a food with umami before drinking that wine.

You can experience this "fifth taste" with some blue cheese and a tannic red wine, like a young Cabernet Sauvignon or Cabernet Franc. The fat and the protein in the cheese should soften the perception of tannins in your mouth, but you'll probably find a bitter, metallic taste lingering on your tongue.

For a more palatable match, try a rounder, fruity wine or a wine with residual sugar (late harvest Riesling, for example).

✔ **Firm Cheeses:** You usually find these cheeses in large cylindrical shapes that have been pressed to remove a greater part of the whey. Examples (interior-ripened): brick, colby, Cheddar, Edam, Emmenthal, Gouda, Swiss, Friulano, provolone, raclette.

   Appropriate wine styles: Dry rosés; medium-bodied, fruity reds.

✔ **Hard Cheeses:** These are cooked and pressed to remove whey. They usually undergo a long ripening period. Examples: Parmesan, Romano.

   Appropriate wine styles: Young, acidic reds.

✔ **Blue Cheeses:** Example: Ermite blue, blue-veined Camembert.

   Appropriate wine styles: Sweet whites, robust sweet reds.

Matching Canadian Wines and Cheeses

The French may have invented the idea of wine and cheese, but today Canada takes its place not only among the wine-producing nations of the world but also among the cheese producers. From the Atlantic provinces to British Columbia, we make an amazing range and variety of cheeses (over 100 different styles!). And what better accompaniment than a well-chosen glass of Canadian wine? To help you find just the right cheese for your wine, we provide a useful matching guide in Table 13-1.

Table 13-1	Canadian Cheese and Wine Matching Chart
Canadian Cheese	*Canadian Wine Style*
Bocconcini	Gamay Noir, Zweigelt, Pinot Noir
Brick	Cabernet Franc, Merlot
Brie	Chardonnay Reserve, Pinot Blanc
Brie (double crème)	Very dry sparkling wine, Auxerrois
Brie (triple crème)	Unoaked Chardonnay, Aligoté, very dry sparkling wine
Camembert	Chardonnay (barrel-aged), Pinot Gris
Cantonnier	Chardonnay (medium-bodied), Gamay Noir
Cheddar (mild)	Chardonnay, Riesling Reserve
Cheddar (old)	Cabernet Sauvignon blends, Merlot
Colby	Pinot Noir, Gamay Noir, rosé or light un-oaked red
Crottin	Chardonnay, Sauvignon Blanc, Pinot Blanc
Emmenthal	Auxerrois, dry Riesling, Gamay Noir
Ermite bleu	Select late harvest Riesling, late harvest Vidal, port-style red
Farmers	Cabernet Franc, Merlot
Feta	Sauvignon Blanc, dry Riesling, dry sparkling
Friulano	Chardonnay, Reserve Riesling, Cabernet Sauvignon, Merlot
Gouda	Pinot Noir, Merlot, Cabernet blends
Gruyère	Riesling, lightly oaked Chardonnay; Cabernet/Merlot blend, Meritage
Havarti	Unoaked Chardonnay, Pinot Blanc, Pinot Gris
Lechevalier-Mailloux	Gewürztraminer, dry Muscat, off-dry Riesling
Marble	Chardonnay Reserve, Cabernet blends, Merlot
Monterey Jack	Oak-aged Chardonnay, Sauvignon Blanc
Mozzarella	Gamay, Zweigelt, Pinot Noir
Oka	Pinot Noir, Gamay Noir, light reds

Canadian Cheese	Canadian Wine Style
Provolone	Baco Noir, Maréchal Foch
Raclette	Dry Riesling, Gamay Noir
St. Benoit	Oak-aged Chardonnay, Gamay, Merlot
Saint-Paulin	Cabernet Sauvignon, Merlot, Cabernet Franc
Swiss	Chardonnay, Cabernet rosé, Gamay
Vacherin	Dry Riesling, young Cabernet Sauvignon

One of Barb's favourite wine and cheese combinations is blue cheese, digestive biscuits (they're a bit sweet) and Icewine — pure decadence.

Cheddar Cheese Fondue

If you thought the Swiss had the inside track on cheese fondue, just try making fondue with Canadian Cheddar. It gives this easy-to-make cheese dish a more intense and interesting flavour. Here is Barb's favourite fondue recipe. Believe it or not, a Swiss friend gave her the tip about cheddar!

Barb's Canadian Cheddar Cheese Fondue

1 garlic clove
¾ lb (350 g) Canadian Cheddar, grated
¼ lb (115 g) Swiss cheese (Emmental or Gruyère), grated
1½ tbsp flour
1½ cups (375 ml) dry white wine
2 tbsp (30 ml) Kirsch
Salt, white pepper, and nutmeg to taste
A loaf of French bread cut in cubes

Mix the grated cheese with the flour.

Smash the garlic clove with the flat side of a wide knife.

Pour the wine into a fondue pot and add the garlic clove and the cheese/flour mixture. Heat gently on the stove, stirring until smooth and creamy. Remove the garlic clove. Add the Kirsch, salt, pepper, and nutmeg. Transfer the pot to a fondue burner and place it in the middle of the table. To eat, spear a cube of bread on a fondue fork and dip it into the cheese mixture until coated.

Tony suggests you accompany this delicious dish with Canadian Gamay or a Beaujolais from France.

Matching International Wines and Cheeses

While we have an amazing selection of Canadian cheeses available to us as well as a formidable range of Canadian wines, we have to give credit where credit is due and admit that other countries produce some astounding cheeses, to say nothing of some wonderful wines. So, in the spirit of international brotherhood we offer Table 13-2, where we match cheeses from Europe with wine styles of the world.

Table 13-2	International Cheese and Wine Matching Chart
International Cheese	*International Wine*
Asiago	Barolo, Barbaresco, Nebbiolo d'Alba
Brick	Zinfandel, Côtes du Rhône, California Pinot Noir
Brie	Sancerre, Frascati/Beaujolais
Camembert	Burgundy, dry Riesling, Vouvray
Cheddar	Rhône, Bordeaux, Burgundy, Zinfandel
Cheshire	Beaujolais, Valpolicella, Gamay
Chèvre (goat's cheese)	Sancerre, Pouilly-Fumé
Coulommiers	Burgundy, Pinot Noir, Merlot
Crottin	Dry white Chablis, Sancerre
Danish blue	Oloroso sherry, Sauternes/late bottled vintage port
Edam	Beaujolais, Valpolicella, Gamay
Emmenthal	Mâcon Blanc, Riesling
Époisse	Marc de Bourgogne, grappa
Feta	Greek whites, Pouilly-Fumé, Fumé Blanc
Gorgonzola	Amarone, late harvest Zinfandel, ruby port
Gouda	Rioja, red Burgundy, Oregon Pinot Noir
Gruyère	Rhône white, Chilean Chardonnay/Chinon
Havarti	Frascati, Fendant, Muscadet
Mascarpone	German Riesling, Müller-Thurgau, dry Muscat
Monterey Jack	Chardonnay, white Rhône/red Burgundy
Mozzarella	Chianti, Barbera, Beaujolais

International Cheese	International Wine
Münster	Alsace Gewürztraminer, dry Muscat
Parmesan	Valpolicella, Bardolino, Chianti
Pont L'Evêque	Côtes de Roussillon, Zinfandel, Montepulciano d'Abruzzo
Port-Salut	Rhône white, New Zealand Sauvignon Blanc, Chardonnay
Reblochon	Chablis, Muscadet, Soave
Roquefort	Sauternes, Monbazillac/Recioto/port
Tête de Moine	Frascati, Fendant, Vernaccia di San Gimignano

Tony is especially partial to goat's cheese (chèvre) with a crisp Sauvignon Blanc (Sancerre from the Loire Valley is his favourite match). His favourite wine and cheese match of all time was part of a visit to Alsace. He was served Münster cheese warmed in layers of phylo pastry and sliced like birthday cake. With it he drank a chilled, dry Gewürztraminer. The marriage was made in culinary heaven and when he shuts his eyes he can still recall those remarkable flavour contrasts.

Stay away from citrus fruits as accompaniments to cheese. The citric acid in oranges and grapefruit is much stronger than the acids in wine. The sharper fruit acid will deaden your perception of the acidity in the wine and make it taste too sweet. Dried fruits also go well with cheese — figs, dates, raisins — but you'll need some sweetness in the wine to balance the fruit. In Spain and Portugal they make a wonderful marmalade from quince that works really well with the firm mountain cheeses of those countries.

The perfect cheese platter

If you want to serve cheese to a group of people, set out a selection of different cheeses with some wine (or a few different wines) and compare how they match up.

Try to include a range of flavours and textures, with a mild cheese like havarti, a creamy brie, an aged Cheddar, and a blue cheese. Serve them with a sliced baguette or some water wafers. Your crackers should be unsalted or only lightly salted, as cheese is already salty in flavour. If you would like to add some sweetness to the plate and some eye appeal as well, place a bit of fruit on the platter.

The all-time best fruit combination with cheese is pear. It's mildly flavoured and doesn't interfere with the flavours in the cheese. Better still, it's light in acid, so it won't make your wine taste flat. Other fruits that go well alongside cheese are strawberries, seedless grapes, and slices of kiwi. Arrange them around your cheese platter as finger food.

If you're serving fruit with cheese, Tony recommends that you go for a fortified wine, such as tawny or ruby port, Oloroso sherry, or Bual maderia.

TIP

If you're serving cheese as a course during a meal, follow the French example and offer it before the dessert. This allows you to finish the red wine from the main course with the cheese. Just as it's hard on the palate to go from a sweet wine to a dry wine (the dry wine tastes really sour), so your palate finds it difficult to appreciate the savoury taste of cheese after a sweet dessert.

Cheese-off — Canadian-style

Since 1999, the Dairy Farmers of Canada have held the Canadian Cheese Grand Prix. Tony was a judge in 2000 and tasted 160 entries in 15 categories over two days. A binding experience, he recalls, since you don't spit out cheese.

The judges assess the cheeses based on flavour (acidulous, nutty, creamy, fruity, sharp), colour (rind and centre uniformity), texture (unctuous, brittle, sticky, compact, creamy, regular, or irregular openings), and finish (overall appearance and saltiness). The best cheese in each category is then judged against its peers to select the Grand Champion Canadian Cheese. In the millennium year it was Bénédictin Blue Cheese from Abbaye Saint-Benoit in Québec. Nine of the winning cheeses came from *la belle province*, four from Ontario, two from British Columbia, and one from Alberta.

The judges also award a prize for the best retail packaging design.

Here are the winners:

- Fresh cheese: Délicrème/Plain, Agropur (QC)

- Soft cheese: Brie Double Crème, Fromagerie Cayer (QC)

- Semi-soft cheese: Monterey, Armstrong Cheese (BC)

- Washed-rind cheese: Cantonnier, Fromage Côté (QC)

- Firm cheese: Gouda, Sylvan Star Cheese (AB)

- Swiss-type cheese: Kingsberg, Fromage Côté (QC)

- Pasta Filata cheese (a texture that breaks up into string-like filaments): Provolone Sette Fette, National Cheese (ON)

- Mozzarella: Mozzarella, Saputo Food (QC)

- Blue cheese and Grand Champion: Bénédictin Blue Cheese, Abbaye Saint-Benoit (QC)

- Flavoured cheese (non-particulate flavouring): Anco Smoked Gouda, Agropur (QC)

- Flavoured cheese (particulate solids and flavouring): Brie Fine Herbs, Fromagerie Cayer (QC)

- Mild Cheddar cheese: Mild Cheddar, Village Cheese (BC)

- Medium Cheddar cheese: Medium Cheddar, Parmalat/Balderson Cheese (ON)

- Old, Extra Old Cheddar cheese: Balderson 6-Year Heritage, Parmalat/Balderson Cheese (ON)

- Cold Pack cheese: Old Sharpe, Ivanhoe Cheese (ON)

- Retail Packaging Design: Sir Laurier d'Arthabaska, Fromage Côté

Chapter 14

Planning Your Wine Matches

*T*his chapter gets down to the specifics of matching wine with virtually all the well-known dishes you may order in a restaurant or prepare in your own kitchen. There are guidelines only when it comes to choosing a wine to enhance your dining experience, no rulebook to go by. The wine-and-food-matching information in this chapter merely points you in the right direction; none of it's written in stone. You can choose whatever your palate fancies once you get beyond the "red with meat, white with fish" concept.

Wine and food are not disciplines; they are pleasures to be taken together. You can have endless enjoyment by experimenting to find what your palate likes best. You'll know you've done it right when the sum of the parts (the dish and the wine you select for it) tastes better than the parts taken separately.

In the following pages, we lead you through an entire meal — a banquet, if you prefer — from soup to nuts (including dessert), suggesting wine styles and specific wines to turn any meal into an occasion (that's when eating becomes dining). And if, like Tony, you're a confirmed chocoholic, we've included wines to complement *your* favourite "food."

Zeroing In On the Right Wine

Learning to match food and wine, as we've said, is not as intimidating as it might seem at first blush. It's not a riddle with only one right answer; there's no one perfect wine for a given dish, excluding all others. We can only repeat that there are no hard and fast rules when it comes to pairing wine and food.

After all, everyone's palate is different, and conditioned to different taste sensations. This is a good thing. How boring we'd be if we all gravitated to putting a Bordeaux with a filet mignon. Variety is the spice of life!

Take steak, for example. To say you must have a red Burgundy with steak begs several questions: How was the steak prepared? Was it marinated in olive oil and soy sauce? Was it grilled with pepper and flared with brandy? Is it to be served with a Béarnaise sauce or in a pastry shell? All these methods of preparation call for a different style of red wine.

In the next section, we outline some principles to help you choose wines for food, whether at home or in a restaurant. There's only one rule (we know we said there weren't any, but do keep this one in mind): You should never have to interrupt your conversation to stare at your wineglass and wonder what on earth possessed the host to pair the wine of his birth year with hot dogs.

Asking Two Easy Questions

There are only two issues you need to determine when matching a particular food with a wine. Once you've established these, the rest is just fine tuning.

1. **Are the food and the wine the same weight?** Match the weight of the food to the weight of the wine. A light dish demands a light wine. A hearty plate requires a full-bodied wine with lots of flavour.

    Determine whether the dish you want to serve is lightweight, medium weight, or heavyweight. Choose a wine style that corresponds.

    How do you determine the weight of a wine?

    Look on the label for the alcohol content:

    - Light-bodied wines contain 8 to 10 percent alcohol.
    - Medium-bodied wines contain 10.5 to 12 percent alcohol.
    - Full-bodied wines contain 12.5 to 16 percent alcohol.

2. **How acidic is the wine?** Acid cleanses the palate of various tastes, including salt (shellfish, pickles, etc.), smokiness (smoked fish or meat), and greasiness (animal fat, butter, oil). On the other hand, the fruit in the wine (its sweetness) reinforces the sweetness in the dish and works against saltiness, smokiness, and greasiness.

    Ask yourself how salty, smoky, or greasy is the dish? Consider the plate as a whole, not just the meat or fish. Vegetables can be highly acidic, as well as quite sweet if glazed with brown sugar or honey.

And where do you look for acidic wines?

Wines high in acid come from cool growing regions:

Austria: Krems, Wachau

France: Loire, Alsace, Champagne, Savoie, Jura

Germany: Mosel, Rheingau, Ahr, Franken

Italy: Trentino-Alto Adige, Friuli-Venezia Giulia, Veneto

British Columbia: Okanagan, Fraser Valley, Vancouver Island

Ontario: Niagara Peninsula, Lake Erie North Shore, Pelee Island

New York: Finger Lakes

New Zealand: South Island

Fruity wines with less acidity come from hot growing regions:

Australia: South Australia, Victoria, New South Wales

California: Napa, Sonoma, Mendocino, Central Valley

Chile: Maipo, Rapel, Aconcagua

Languedoc-Roussillon: Corbières, Minervois, St. Chinian

Mediterranean Islands: Corsica, Sardinia, Sicily

North Africa: Morocco, Algeria

Portugal: Douro, Dão, Bairrada

Rhône: Côtes-du-Rhône Villages, Cornas, Châteauneuf-du-Pape

Perhaps the saltiest, smokiest, oiliest dish out there is smoked salmon. Its rich, concentrated flavour puts it in a heavyweight class of its own. Imagine having a soft, delicate, sweet wine with smoked salmon: It's enough to make you gag. But match it with a full-bodied, dry white with lots of acidity and you have a marriage made in heaven. A dry Alsatian Gewürztraminer makes a wonderful partner. Try it also with a dry sparkling wine, preferably champagne. Bubbles have a wonderfully cleansing effect on the palate.

Matching Dish by Dish

Get comfortable and read on as we take you on a tour of your favourite foods, suggesting wines along the way. You might want to mark this section and come back to it the next time you're having a dinner party. Or, you might get inspired right away, throw the book down, and head out to the grocery store — followed by the liquor store. Either way, we hope this inspires you to get creative with wine and food.

Hot, spicy food and wine

Highly spiced dishes can throw off the balance of many wines. If you want to match wine to hot-tasting dishes, keep the following principles in mind:

✔ Choose wines with high acidity and some residual sugar (Vouvray, German Riesling, white Zinfandel) rather than wines with perceptible oak flavours, evident tannins, or high alcohol.

✔ For Mexican, Thai, or light curry dishes, select sweeter white wines, well chilled, such as Gewürztraminer or Riesling.

✔ For mildly spiced dishes, go with fruity reds with good acidity to refresh the palate (Beaujolais, Valpolicella). Serve chilled.

✔ For hot dishes that are also smoked, choose Zinfandel, Recioto della Valpolicella, or Châteauneuf-du-Pape.

Matching wine and soup

You may not have considered having wine with your soup course, but if you want to experiment with a new gastronomic sensation, we offer the recommendations in Table 14-1, first with a generic style of wine and then with our favourite choices.

Cold soups are easier to put together with wine because you're dealing with liquids of similar temperature. The combination makes for an interesting summer lunch. The most versatile wines for soup are sherry (in different degrees of dryness to sweetness depending on the recipe), white port, and madeira.

If the soup is hearty (beans or pasta) or contains chunks of meat, try matching it with a light red wine served at room temperature (well, just below room temperature, given the jungle temperatures many of us heat our homes to).

Table 14-1	Wine with Soup	
Soup	*Wine Style*	*Wine Recommendations*
Vegetable		
Borscht	Medium-bodied red	Cabernet Franc, Pinot Noir
Cream of vegetable	White fruity medium-bodied	Chardonnay
Gazpacho	Dry sherry, full-bodied dry white	Fino sherry, white Rhône

Soup	Wine Style	Wine Recommendations
Minestrone	Red medium-bodied	Chianti, Barbaresco
Onion	Light red, rosé	Beaujolais, Tavel rosé
Pasta & beans	Light-bodied red	Valpolicella, Beaujolais
Tomato	Light, acidic red	Valpolicella, Gamay
Vichyssoise	Fruity white/blush	Off-dry Vouvray, white Zinfandel
Fish		
Bouillabaisse	Light red/rosé	Beaujolais, Provence rosé
Clam chowder	Dry medium-bodied white, dry sherry	Chablis, fino sherry
Meat		
Chicken	Dry white	Chardonnay, Pinot Blanc
Consommé	Port, off-dry sherry, Madeira	White port, Amontillado sherry, Sercial madeira
Game	Port, sherry, Madeira	LBV port, Amontillado, Bual madeira
Mulligatawny	Aromatic white, sweet fortified	Gewürztraminer, Marsala
Sweet & sour	Aromatic white	Dry Muscat, Riesling Spätlese

Think of a particular dish's origin when you consider what wine you want to match it with. Regional cuisines develop alongside a country's wine industry; the most satisfying match is often a wine from that very region. For example, nothing works better with tomato-based dishes than the red wines of Tuscany and Piedmont — where the tomato is a kitchen staple.

Matching wine and fish

You may have seen a book with the provocative title, *Red Wine with Fish* — a concept that probably contradicts everything you've ever heard about matching wine and food. But, as you'll discover, there are opportunities to use red wine with fish (just as there are possibilities of using white wine with red meat).

Fish range in flavour and texture from light and delicate to rich and dense. Just think of the difference in taste between a poached Dover sole and a grilled tuna steak, and you soon realize the many options when it comes to wine selection. In Table 14-2 we suggest wine styles and specific recommendations to match a range of fish dishes.

Table 14-2	Wine with Fish	
Fish	*Wine Style*	*Wine Recommendations*
Bouillabaisse	Dry white/red/rosé	Entre-Deux-Mers/Beaujolais/Bandol
Fish & chips	Simple dry white	Soave, Alsace Pinot Blanc
Fish, raw	Acidic white	Mosel Riesling, Chasselas
Fish, cream sauce	Fruity dry white	New World Chardonnay or Sauvignon Blanc
Haddock, smoked	Dry white	Alsace Pinot Gris, Pouilly-Fumé, Viognier
Herring, pickled	Driest white/vodka	Muscadet, Franken Sylvaner
Sardines	Crisp white	Vinho Verde, Grüner Veltliner, Aligoté
Salmon, grilled	Oak-aged dry white	Graves, Rioja, Sancerre
Salmon, poached	Rich dry white/rosé	Burgundy, New World Chardonnay/Tavel
Salmon, smoked	Aromatic dry white/sparkling wine	Gewürztraminer, Riesling Trocken/Champagne Brut
Sole, poached	Dry white (no oak)	Chardonnay, Graves, Burgundy
Sole, grilled	Dry white	Alsace, Sauvignon Blanc
Trout, poached	Dry white/fruity dry red	Graves, Ontario Chardonnay/Beaujolais
Trout, smoked	Oak-aged dry white	New World Chardonnay, Pouilly-Fumé, Pinot Gris
Tuna	Rich whites/light acidic reds, dry rosé	Pouilly-Fumé/Beaujolais/Tavel rosé

Matching shellfish and seafood

Crustaceans are generally salty, tasting of brine with a faint iodine flavour from seaweed. To cleanse the palate of that saline taste, you need a white wine with lively acidity that cleans off your palate and sets you up for the next bite. When it comes to matching, again, think of the weight of the food: Lobster, crayfish, and crab have more powerful, meaty flavours than scallops, prawns, octopus, or calamari. Oysters and sea urchins are the most salty and individual in flavour.

So match weight for weight when it comes to choosing a wine. The wine for lobster should be richer and more full-bodied than the wine for oysters, especially if you're preparing the lobster in a cream sauce (Lobster Newburg) or serving it with dipping butter.

Avoid residual sweetness in wines for fish unless you're dealing with a highly spiced dish, such as curried shrimp. If you're preparing seafood in a tomato sauce (as in spaghetti vongole — baby clams) you have the option to go to a light, acidic red wine (like Valpolicella, Beaujolais, or an Ontario or BC Gamay).

Canadian wines, particularly the whites, are eminently suited to pairing with fish because of their fine spine of acidity. The acid in Ontario and British Columbia Chardonnay, Pinot Blanc, Pinot Gris, and especially dry Riesling cleanses and refreshes the palate of the fishy, oily, or salty taste of fish or seafood. A fruit-driven Chardonnay from California, Australia, or Chile (all warm growing regions) lacks acidity, in most cases, and tastes unstructured with fish dishes.

Your natural inclination is probably to serve a dry white wine with fish. For something different, consider serving a chilled rosé with fish or seafood dishes. You can select a dry pink wine from Ontario or British Columbia, which has the requisite acidity; or, for more flavourful, denser fish and seafood such as tuna, salmon, or lobster, a rosé from the Rhône Valley such as Tavel or Lirac. Pink wines look stunning in the glass, especially outdoors in summertime.

The best wine for oysters is a Brut champagne (the driest category), although the Irish swear that Guinness and oysters is a combination that brings tears to the eyes. Since one can't always afford champagne, Tony and Barb choose the driest wine they can find for oysters — Muscadet from the Loire Valley, Chablis from Burgundy, a Grüner Veltliner from Austria, or a very esoteric wine from the Jura region of France, called Abymes.

Matching wine and beef

Beef is an easy call when it comes to wine. Most reds that are medium-bodied will go with most cuts of beef. The principle in matching here has to do with the cut of beef: the better the cut, the better the wine. You wouldn't want to waste a Château Mouton-Rothschild 1961 on frankfurters and beans or a backyard barbecued burger. By the same token, an everyday red with filet mignon would be a bit of a letdown.

As you'll see in Table 14-3, your choice doesn't always have to be red. We've selected 12 popular beef dishes and suggested generic wine styles to match them — then specific wines — in order to give you as broad a selection as possible.

Table 14-3	Wine with Beef	
Beef	*Wine Style*	*Wine Recommendations*
Beef Bourgignon	Full-bodied red	Burgundy, Pinot Noir
Beef Wellington	Fine reds	Cabernet, Pinot Noir
Boiled beef	Full white/dry rosé	Chardonnay/Tavel
Brisket	Dry rosé/light red	Lirac/Grignolino, Gamay
Chili con carne	Young, acidic red	Shiraz, Zinfandel
Curried beef	Medium sweet white	Vouvray, Orvieto, Traminer
Hamburger	Light reds	Beaujolais, Dornfelder, Gamay
Roast beef (hot)	Full-bodied reds	Cabernet, Merlot
Shepherd's pie	Light reds	Beaujolais, Valpolicella
Steak (grilled)	Medium reds	Pinot Noir, Bordeaux
Steak tartar	Light tannic reds	Young Bordeaux, Barbera, Canadian Cabernet
Veal (roasted)	Medium-bodied red	Alsace Pinot Noir, Loire red

Matching wine and pork

Pork is a sweet meat, lighter in texture than beef and quite fatty. A wine with a touch of sweetness (residual sugar), but with good acidity, works best, especially if you're serving the pork dish with the traditional applesauce as an accompaniment. Again, we've selected 12 of the most popular pork dishes in Table 14-4 and matched them first with generic wine styles, then with actual wines.

Wine enthusiasts enjoy tasting different wines throughout the course of a fine dinner: a white wine with the starter course, a red wine with the main course, maybe another red with the cheese, and a dessert wine to finish the meal. But if you don't want to serve more than one wine throughout, what should you choose? What single wine goes with just about anything you put on the table? The answer is champagne. You can even have it for breakfast, with orange juice (a Mimosa)!

Table 14-4	Wine with Pork	
Pork	*Wine Style*	*Wine Recommendations*
Bacon & eggs	Fruity red/dry rosé	Beaujolais, Gamay/Tavel Rosé
Baked ham	Dry red	Oregon Pinot Noir, Canadian Pinot Noir, Californian Merlot
Boiled ham	Light red	Beaujolais, Gamay, German red, Alsace Pinot Noir
Curried pork	Off-dry white	Vouvray, Riesling Spätlese
Pork chops	Light reds	Merlot, Cabernet Franc, Gamay
Pork sausages	Fruity dry red	Beaujolais, Gamay, Valpolicella
Prosciutto & melon	Sweet white or red	Pineau des Charentes/white or ruby port
Roast pork & applesauce	Off-dry white	Vouvray, Chenin Blanc, Riesling Spätlese
Roast suckling pig	Dry red/dry white	St. Julien, Beaune/Pinot Gris
Salami	Dry red/rosé	Chianti, Barbera/Bandol
Sweet & sour pork	Fruity white	Silvaner, Muscat, Gewürztraminer
Veal & ham pie	Dry red	Beaujolais *crus*, Sangiovese, Pinot Noir

Don't waste your most expensive wines on barbecued food. If you're eating outdoors, the complex bouquet of your wine has to compete with all the smells of your backyard, including the smoke from the barbecue. All the subtleties and nuances of a fine wine will be lost in carbon, wood smoke, and that spice-driven marinade. Go for gutsy, fruit-driven, inexpensive wines that you can drink out of plastic glasses (a real affront to an expensive wine). And if you're in the sun, pop the bottles in the ice bucket or cooler to bring down their temperature.

Wine and your barbecue

A number of factors affect the flavour of food that's prepared on the barbecue:

Most barbecues are held outdoors. So all those outdoor smells are brought to bear on the preparation and eating of food.

The food you barbecue is highly spiced and marinated. (The sugar in most marinades caramelizes when subjected to direct heat. That's what gives you those yummy, crispy, burnt bits.)

The result? Food prepared on the barbecue is strongly flavourful. You need wines with personality to stand up to the taste of spicy marinades, carbon, smoke, and any condiments such as mustards or ketchups.

Wimpy wines just won't cut the mustard, as the saying goes, so when you fire up the barbecue, choose wines that have lots of fruit and low tannins. This means heading for the New World or warm-weather regions in Europe (if meat's on the menu).

Recommended BBQ wines for beef/lamb/pork:

Australian Shiraz
California Zinfandel
Chilean Merlot
Rhône reds

When it comes to fish and seafood, on the other hand, acidity is the key. Wines that work well with grilled tuna and salmon are fresh young reds from cool climates — Pinot Noir (red Burgundy) and Gamay (Beaujolais).

For shellfish (lobster, shrimp), go with full-bodied dry whites from cool climates (white Burgundy, Ontario/BC Chardonnay) and dry rosés.

Matching wine and lamb

Lamb and mutton are highly flavoured meats. They cry out for wines with lots of character. If you had to choose one grape to go with lamb, choose Cabernet Sauvignon, either as a red Bordeaux or a New World Cabernet. In Table 14-5, we've chosen 12 of the most-often-served lamb dishes and suggested the style of wine best suited to it, followed by our personal recommendations.

Table 14-5	Wine with Lamb	
Lamb	*Wine Style*	*Wine Recommendations*
Barbecued lamb	Young New World Cabernets	Chile, California
Chops (grilled)	Medium-bodied red	Médoc, Ontario Cabernet
Curried lamb	Full-bodied red/rosé	Châteauneuf, Zinfandel/Tavel rosé
Irish stew	Full-bodied white	Pouilly-Fumé, California Chardonnay
Lancashire hotpot	Medium-bodied white/medium-bodied red	Australian Chardonnay, Rhine white/Beaujolais

Lamb	*Wine Style*	*Wine Recommendations*
Leg of lamb	Medium-bodied red	Bordeaux, Burgundy, California Cabernet
Moussaka	Full-bodied red	Rhône red, Amarone, Shiraz
Rack of lamb	Good Bordeaux, Rhône	Pauillac, Margaux, Côte Rotie
Roast mutton	Soft red	California Merlot, Chilean Cabernet
Saddle of lamb	Cabernet, Pinot Noir	St. Émilion, California Cabernet, Beaune
Shishkebab	Fruity red	Beaujolais named village wines, Recioto della Valpolicella
Tomato-based stews	Acidic red	Barbaresco, Chianti, Loire reds

Life Is Short: Start with Dessert

You don't need to have wine with your dessert, but then again you don't need to take pleasure in being alive either. A glass of sweet wine at the end of a meal can round it off with style. Very impressive, too, if you're entertaining. And if you haven't had time to prepare a dessert, a small glass of sweet wine — such as a late harvest Riesling or an Icewine — will make your guests forget that you didn't make that floating island or strawberry shortcake.

As with soups and bisques, if a dessert has been prepared with a particular wine or liqueur, or flambéd in alcohol, whatever was used in its preparation is the ideal match to accompany it.

When it comes to choosing a wine for dessert, keep the following principles in mind:

- ✔ **The sweetness of the dessert dictates the sweetness of the wine.** Sweet food makes wine taste drier. Too sweet a dessert can make even a sweet wine taste sharp and sour.

- ✔ **The texture of the dessert suggests the weight of the wine required.** A rich dessert made with butter, eggs, and cream needs a luscious, full-bodied wine to stand up to it. Fresh berries, on the other hand, because of their lightness and acidity, take a lighter wine with sweetness and acidity.

- ✔ **When in doubt, select an off-dry sparkling wine.** One of our favourites is an Asti Spumante, from Piedmont in Italy. These sparklers can hold their own against custards and creams — and they refresh the palate.

Getting sticky

Australian winemakers refer to their dessert wines as "stickies" for the very good reason that if you spill some on your fingers that's how it feels. When Aussie wines are made in really sweet style, they call them "ultra stickies."

Sugar tends to dull your palate and make you feel full. If you complement a sweet dessert with a sparkling wine with lively acidity, it will cleanse your palate and enliven your taste buds. One of the best sparkling dessert wines we've found comes from Austria and it's produced not from grapes but from apricots. The trade name is Mariandl. Always serve this, and other sweet wines, chilled. Chilling lowers the perception of sugar and brings out the freshness in the wine.

The best matches are the simplest: a fresh peach or pear with Sauternes from Bordeaux; strawberries and champagne; almond biscuits (biscotti) with Vin Santo from Tuscany; cake with Madeira. Fifteen of the best dessert and wine matches are in Table 14-6.

Table 14-6	Wine with Dessert
Dessert	*Wine Recommendations*
Apple pie/strüdel	White, sweet, light-bodied (late harvest Riesling)
Cake	Madeira, tawny port
Cheesecake	White, sweet, medium-bodied
Christmas pudding	White, sweet, sparkling (Asti Spumante)
Crème Brûlé	White, sweet, full-bodied
Crêpes	White, sweet, medium-bodied/sweet sparkling
Fresh fruit	White, sweet, medium-bodied
Fruit in alcohol	White, sweet, full-bodied; robust reds (Recioto della Valpolicella, Zinfandel)
Fruit tart	White, sweet, medium-bodied/sweet sparkling
Lemon meringue	Icewine
Pastries	Off-dry, sparkling
Pumpkin pie	Cream sherry, tawny port

Dessert	Wine Recommendations
Strawberries and cream	Sauternes/off-dry sparkling
Strawberry shortcake	White, sweet, full-bodied
Summer pudding	White, sweet, medium-bodied

Canada is justly famous for one of the world's great dessert wines — Icewine. This wine is so significant to the local industry and has been so acclaimed by connoisseurs around the world that we have devoted an entire chapter to it (see Chapter 16).

Facing Up to the Big No-No: Wine and Chocolate

If you looked closely at Table 14-6, you probably said to yourself: "Tony and Barb left out the chocolate!" We did, for a very good reason. Chocolate is one of the most difficult foods (and all chocolate lovers consider it a food!) to match with wine. The sweetness and unctuous mouth feel of chocolate make it a difficult partner for most wines. But don't despair. The marriage can be "arranged," and it can work.

Virtually every wine book out there admonishes readers never to — under any circumstance — put wine and chocolate together. This pairing supposedly results in instant divorce in matrimonial terms. But, like all truisms, this one needs to be (deserves to be!) tested from time to time.

Was Dante a chocoholic, too?

Tony recalls the time when, as a young (younger!) wine writer, he visited an ancient wine estate in Italy's Veneto region. His host, Conte Pieralvise Serègo Alighieri (who can trace his ancestry back 13 generations to Italy's most famous poet, Dante Alighieri) delighted in perplexing visitors by offering them After Eight mints with his Amarone. Tony, perhaps thinking of all those books that say never to pair chocolate and wine, didn't know whether to take the proffered chocolate mint or refuse it. Being Canadian, he accepted it and debated whether to secret it into his pocket. The count waited until Tony had actually eaten the chocolate and then taken a sip of his wine. It was an epiphany: the chocolate mint went beautifully with the powerful, sweet red wine.

There is, of course, a difference between a slab of chocolate (chocoholics never say "piece" or "square") and a chocolate-flavoured dessert. Raw chocolate is always more intense (and satisfying for the true believer). Just as chocolate cake has a different flavour response on the palate than chocolate mousse or chocolate pâté, so do the wines that you need to match. Table 14-7 is the chocoholic's quick fix, offering wines to pair with white, milk, and dark chocolate.

Table 14-7	Wine with Chocolate
Chocolate	*Wine Recommendations*
White Chocolate	Ruby port
	Recioto della Valpolicella
	Late Harvest Zinfandel
	Banyuls
	Cream sherry
	Tawny port
Milk Chocolate	Black Muscat
	Orange Muscat
	Samos Muscat
	Ruby/LBV port
Dark Chocolate	Sauternes
	Icewine
	Merlot
	Zinfandel
	Petite Sirah
Best All-Round Solution	Brut champagne
	Cognac/armagnac
	Coffee liqueur
	Orange liqueur
	Fruit eaux-de-vie

What about Nuts?

One of life's great pleasures is to sit down at the end of a hard day with a glass of wine and a bowl of nuts. Nuts, like other foods, have their own character and taste that can be enhanced by your wine selection. Because of the oils in nuts, you should pick substantial wines with higher alcohol (including fortified wines) or with some sweetness. If you prefer salty nuts, look for wines with good acidity. Table 14-8 lists good wine matches for a variety of nuts. We know there are "nutaholics" out there, too!

Table 14-8	Wine with Nuts
Nut	*Wine Recommendations*
Almonds	Red: Chianti Classico Riserva, Amarone White: Orvieto Abocatto, off-dry Vouvray
Brazil nuts	Pineau des Charentes/mature Barolo
Cashews	Ontario off-dry Riesling, German Müller-Thurgau
Chestnuts (roast)	Recioto della Valpolicella, Beaujolais, Gamay
Chestnuts (puréed)	Sauternes, Asti Spumante
Hazelnuts	White Burgundy, vintage port
Macadamia	Tokaji Aszu, Setúbal, champagne
Mixed nuts	Medium sherry, Bual (madeira)
Nuts & raisins	Amarone, dry Muscat
Pecans	Madeira, ruby port, Pineau des Charentes
Pistachio	Soave, off-dry Vouvray
Smoked nuts	Zinfandel, Australian Shiraz
Spiced nuts	Traminer, red Rhône
Walnuts	Beaujolais, port, sweet sherry, sweet madeira

Advice from Bernard Callebaut: Master chocolatier

Bernard Callebaut began making his Belgian chocolates in Calgary in the mid-1980s. In 1998, Callebaut won the top prize at the International Festival of Chocolate in Roanne, France — the first North American to do so.

We asked Bernard Callebaut for his thoughts in general on putting wine and chocolate together.

"There's not much difference from choosing wines for food," he contends. "You have to see which chocolate you're going to serve. If you go for white chocolate, you should choose a sweeter wine than one for milk or dark chocolate. For dark, bittersweet chocolate, you should go to a Sauternes-type wine. With white chocolate, I would suggest a red wine with some tannin in it.

"The best and easiest all-round solution for chocolate is champagne or liqueurs. With Brut champagne, you can serve any style of chocolate. With a champagne that has residual sugar, you're putting sweet with sweet and that doesn't work well. When it comes to liqueurs, the drier types work best, like pear eau-de-vie, armagnac and cognac. Coffee-based liqueurs go very well and so do orange-based liqueurs such as Grand Marnier — as long as you serve a non-sweet chocolate. I would avoid white or milk [chocolate] with that."

What red wines would he recommend with chocolate? "Merlot. Zinfandel would be my choice for bittersweet chocolate, although my preference is Icewine. . . . [I've taken] Ontario Icewine to France twice now and served it with my dark chocolate. The people loved it."

And is there any difference between having wine with chocolate by itself and wine with a chocolate-based dessert? "The principles stay the same. Port — late bottled vintage or ruby — goes very well with milk chocolate and definitely with dark chocolate but don't waste a fine vintage port. It deserves to be consumed alone."

Chapter 15

Cooking with Wine

*W*ine is a highly versatile beverage. Apart from its well-documented health benefits, if taken in moderation, it can be consumed between meals, before a meal as an *apéritif*, throughout the meal to enhance the flavours of the food and aid digestion, and after the meal as a *digestif* — or in the meal itself.

Cooking with wine can mean different things. You can have a glass of wine at your elbow as you go about the business of putting together a meal. You can also use wine in the preparation of food. While we wholeheartedly endorse the first proposition, it is the latter that we investigate here. You could call this chapter, "The Wooden Spoon Meets the Corkscrew," because our intention is to explore the relationship of wine and food in the kitchen.

Why Cook with Wine?

Just what does wine do to food when you cook with it? The answer is, a lot! Wine brings out food's natural flavours and stimulates your taste buds. The tannin in wine aids digestion, particularly of fat. If you use wine in a sauce, the glycerine in the wine helps bind the sauce. But what about the alcohol content? All but a very small amount evaporates during cooking. If we had to boil it down, we'd say that wine simply encourages a dish to be its best. Plus, it gives the cook a real morale boost. And we all need a morale booster now and again!

You've probably seen those celebrity chefs on TV who can't resist shaking the wine bottle into virtually every dish they prepare. They never measure the amount and invariably return to the dish and, with a theatrical flourish, give it another dose, as if more is better. Well, we recommend you be a little more circumspect and follow our suggestions.

- Use wine in the preparation of stocks, the base for sauces and soups.

- Use wine as a marinade for meat. The meat will be ever so tender.

- Use wine to moisten turkey stuffing.

- Use white wine to briefly marinate fish. Don't do it for more than 15 to 20 minutes, though, or the more delicate fish might break up.

- Use wine to make gravy or other sauces made in a roasting pan. *Deglazing* (making a sauce of the meat juices and bits) with wine gives great flavour (and makes cleaning up easier!).

- Use wine to cut the oily richness of cheese sauces.

- Use wine (we suggest a Riesling) as a substitute for vinegar or lemon juice in mayonnaise.

- Use wine (reduced to half its volume) as a substitute for vinegar in salad dressings.

- Use wine as a dessert marinade. One of our favourites is pears poached slowly in red wine. Amarone or Recioto della Valpolicella works best.

- Use wine (Gewürztraminer and lemon juice, actually) as a substitute for champagne.

What happens to wine when you heat it? The boiling point of alcohol is 78° Celsius (172° Fahrenheit), much lower than the boiling point of water. This means that when you heat wine (without bringing it to a rolling boil) you're driving off the alcohol and leaving only the flavour components behind. Continuous heating reduces the amount of wine and concentrates the acidity and residual sugar in the wine that's left. If you reduce the wine too much, however, the acidity will predominate and add bitterness to the sauce.

Here are some more pointers for using wine in your kitchen:

- Cook with wines that you are equally comfortable drinking. Why introduce flavours to a dish that you don't like on the palate? Oxidized wine or a corked bottle will taint the flavour of the food. Don't cook with cheap wine.

- Use gutsy, full-flavoured wines in the kitchen, instead of delicate, subtle ones. Demure wines get lost in the battle of flavours.

- Add wine near the end of the preparation of a meal. The acidity in wine can curdle milk, cream, butter, and eggs if left in contact with them for too long. It can also ruin green vegetables — it discolours them and makes them tough.

- Reduce wine you cook with by heating it. Heating wine causes the alcohol to evaporate, leaving only the flavour behind, which is what you want. Reducing wine by half concentrates residual sugar and acidity. Don't reduce more than 75 percent, however, or the acidity will predominate. Reduce wine over low heat so that it doesn't burn the pan.

> ✔ Make sauces using one part of wine to four parts of the other liquid or cream. The same goes for casseroles, stews, and soups.
>
> ✔ Add ⅛ of an inch of olive oil to the heel of a bottle of wine you want to store for cooking. The oil forms an airtight seal. (When you're ready to use the wine in the kitchen, it will naturally separate from the oil as you pour.)

You'd be surprised what a splash of wine in the pan will do for an ordinary everyday dish. And think of the applause you'll get as the chef!

If you're using the heel of a fine bottle of wine that you enjoyed the evening before, don't expect to get the same ravishing flavours in the dish you prepare the next day. Some flavour elements are lost during heating, which alters the balance of the wine.

What Wine to Use in the Kitchen

Just as you wouldn't open a bottle of expensive Burgundy to accompany a hot dog (unless you just won the lottery or founded a dot-com company), you don't want to pull the cork on a really great wine just to pour it into a saucepan. Heating wine destroys the complex nuances of the bouquet, leaving behind only broad flavours. While you never want to use cheap wine to cook with, save your really fine bottles for drinking. Cook with "weekday wines" — wines you enjoy drinking on an everyday basis.

Where to start

That heel of wine at the end of the bottle you didn't finish last night is now ideal for cooking. If you've kept the bottle in the fridge overnight, take it out and let it warm up to room temperature before you add the wine to a hot pan. It's a good idea to warm the measure of wine in a microwave before you add it to meat or fish dishes. It's fine to pour it into a pan for deglazing, but a sauce could curdle if the wine is too cold.

If you want to use the "dregs" of a fine wine that you've decanted and don't want to waste, make sure you separate the liquid from the sediment. Sediment in old wine is made up of tannin and colouring matter, and is very bitter. Pour the wine through a paper coffee filter. That should do the trick.

Some dishes call for fortified wines (port, sherry, madeira, or vermouth). Keep in mind that the alcohol content in these products is almost twice as high as that in regular table wines: Two tablespoons of fortified wine are equal to about half a cup of red, white, rosé, or sparkling wine, in terms of alcohol.

Blame it on the Romans

The legendary Roman gourmet and chef, Marcus Gabius Apicius, who lived at the time of the emperors Augustus and Tiberius, created a vast number of recipes to titillate the palates of his well-heeled contemporaries. Apicius was famous for using wine in his sauces, a practise that has been followed by chefs throughout the ages.

But Apicius's extravagant lifestyle caught up with him eventually: Deeply in debt, he ended his life by poison. We're pretty sure he didn't do it with one of his sauces.

The wine you use in cooking will alter the colour of the sauce or gravy you prepare. If the dish looks better with a light sauce (fish, seafood, and white meats) choose a white wine. Most red meat dishes look better dressed in a sauce or gravy made with red wine. Rosé, when used in cooking, tends to lose its pink hue and turn light brown. There are, of course, exceptions to every rule. The French prepare their classic coq au vin using wine from the region in which they live. So in Burgundy, it's red, whereas in Alsace, it's white (Riesling). Both are equally delicious.

The wines of Canada are first-rate for use in the kitchen. Their natural acidity and lively fruit flavours make them ideal ingredients for food preparation, whether as marinades or as flavouring agents for sauces, stews, and casseroles.

How much wine to use

A standard wine bottle that you purchase in the liquor store contains 26 ounces of wine — which is 750 ml (or in Europe, 75 centilitres).

- 1 cup of wine = 8 fluid ounces = 16 tablespoons = just under ⅓ of a bottle
- ½ cup of wine = 4 fluid ounces = 8 tablespoons = just under ⅙ of a bottle
- 1 tablespoon of wine = ½ fluid ounce = ¹⁄₁₆ cup
- 1 liquid quart = 1 litre (actually 3 tablespoons shy of a litre)

Never add too much wine to a dish (in spite of what you see those TV chefs do!). An overabundance of wine simply overpowers the flavour of the food. Make sure the amount of wine you add is within the called-for amount of liquid ingredients for that particular dish. Think of wine in cooking as a condiment — like salt and pepper, or herbs and spices. Only add as much as will flavour the dish without overshadowing the essential taste of the primary ingredient. If the recipe calls for a glass of wine, you're not doing your guests any favours by adding a bottle.

Leftover champagne? No problem

You can prepare a terrific chicken dish with just a cup of champagne.

Drunken Chicken

2 chickens (1 kilo each) cut in pieces
½ cup butter
¼ cup flour
2 tsp seasoned salt
⅛ tsp pepper
½ tsp ground ginger
2 tsp brown sugar
½ cup dry white wine
1 cup orange juice
½ cup chicken broth
2 oranges, sliced in circles
1 cup champagne

Wash the chicken pieces and dry with paper towelling. In a heavy skillet melt the butter over low heat. Brown chicken on all sides, slowly. Remove from pan. In a bowl, mix seasoned salt, pepper, ginger, and brown sugar and then stir into pan drippings. In a pouring cup, mix white wine, orange juice, and broth and add slowly to pan drippings, stirring constantly until the sauce thickens. Remove pan from heat, add chicken pieces, cover and allow to cool. Refrigerate until one hour before serving time. Reheat on low until the sauce begins to simmer. Cover pan and cook until chicken is tender (25–30 minutes). Add slices of orange and the champagne. Spoon sauce over each serving and decorate with more orange slices.

Serves 8 (or 2 if you're really hungry).

Going Back to (Cooking) School

It's a pretty simple progression: Where there's grapes, there's wine; where there's wine, there's food; and where there's wine and food, there are schools to teach you how to enjoy both. There are some outstanding international cooking schools that offer extensive (and expensive) courses geared to cooking with wine. But Canada has two exceptional schools of its own.

The Wine Country Cooking School at Strewn

The Wine Country Cooking School is affiliated with Strewn Winery, in the Niagara Peninsula (turn to Chapter 18 to read about other Ontario wineries), and is dedicated to promoting regional cuisine and the relationship between food and wine. The focus is on locally grown and raised products. Recipes change with the seasons. How about this for a menu: Chardonnay Chicken with Leeks and Wild Mushrooms, Roast Harvest Vegetables with Grilled Rosemary Polenta, and Cabernet Poached Pears with Chocolate Sauce and Crème Anglaise?

Wine in dessert

You can use wine in fruit salad or over berries. If the flavour is lacking in either sweetness or acidity, you can always add sugar, or lemon/ lime juice. If you're preparing a fruit salad, say, for the whole family, and you want the taste of wine but not the alcohol, heat the wine first and allow it to cool before pouring it over the fruit.

Tony and Barb are very partial to strawberries in red wine (with just a touch of pepper to bring out the flavour) and to cantaloupe melon with ruby port.

Facilities include two separate teaching areas: a hands-on teaching kitchen and a demonstration classroom. Aspiring cooks can take course packages that range from one-, two- or three-hour classes, two-day weekend sessions, or week-long sessions.

The Cooking School at Hainle Vineyards

In British Columbia, the Cooking School at Hainle Vineyards is the place for inspirational cuisine. You can observe visiting or celebrity chefs prepare mouth-watering dishes in the studio kitchen. Many of the demonstrations are followed by dinner in the Amphora Bistro, also at the winery.

To contact these schools:

The Wine Country Cooking School at Strewn
General Delivery, 1339 Lakeshore Road,
Niagara-on-the-Lake, ON, L0S 1J0
Tel: (905) 468-8304, Fax: (905) 468-8305
E-mail: info@winecountrycooking.com
Web site: www.winecountrycooking.com

The Cooking School at Hainle Vineyards
Box 650, 5355 Trepanier Bench Road,
Peachland, BC, V0H 1X0
Tel: (250) 767-2525, Toll Free: 1-800-767-3109, Fax: (250) 767-2543
E-mail: tilman@hainle.com
Web site: www.hainle.com

Chapter 16

Icewine: Canada's Icing on the Cake

C anada is the land of ice and snow. So it should be easy to make Icewine, right? Wrong. It's winemaker against winter to make tiny quantities of this luscious dessert wine that sells for about $50 a half-bottle (375 ml). Icewine is a dessert unto itself or can be served as an accompaniment to a fruit tart or other fruit-based dessert. It is wonderful too with pâté de foie gras or creamy cheeses.

To make Icewine, you can't just put an unopened bottle of regular wine in the freezer or add ice cubes to a glass of your favourite white. Icewine has to be made from grapes frozen on the vine. Canada has recently emerged as a prime producer of this icy delicacy — and we're proud of it! This chapter introduces you to this unique variety of wine, with tips on what foods to match it with, and how to store it (it's a great cellaring wine). Go ahead, add Icewine to your list the next time you're at the liquor store.

What Exactly Is Icewine?

Icewine is very sweet and very high in acid. Without the acidity, the wine would be just too sweet to taste, and without the sweetness the acid would taste as if it could take the paint off a car. But together the balance of sugar and acid makes Icewine the nectar of the gods!

Icewine is made from grapes frozen on the vine. Because of this, the harvest period for Icewine is later than for other varieties. Grapes for Icewine can't be harvested until the temperature falls to at least –8 or –10° Celsius. Harvesters collect the frozen fruit and maintain it in that condition until it reaches the winery and is pressed to get juice that can be fermented into Icewine.

The flavours you taste in Icewine range from dried apricot and peach to tropical fruits, honey, and caramel. Some tasters detect sweet grapefruit, tangerine, brown sugar, butterscotch, green tea, and other exotic tastes, depending on the producer and the grape variety used.

Icewine is usually sold in half-bottle format (375-ml bottles). It is never inexpensive, ranging from $25 to $65 depending on the producer. Some wineries sell Icewine in a 200-ml size, and Inniskillin Winery makes miniatures (50 ml).

Where Icewine comes from

As the story goes, Icewine's discovery was the result of a natural disaster. In 1794, in Franconia, Germany, the wine producers were getting ready to harvest the grapes (on which their livelihood depended) when an unexpected, early cold snap swept through the vineyards, freezing the grapes where they hung. The loss of an entire harvest was unthinkable, so the wine producers brought in the rock-hard bunches and tried to press them. They were relieved to see a thick juice trickle out of the grapes from which they made a small quantity of sweeter-than-expected wine. *Eiswein* has been pretty much a German or Austrian thing ever since — until Canada got in on the act.

In 1991, Ontario's Inniskillin Winery entered their 1989 Vidal Icewine in a competition held at *Vinexpo* in Bordeaux, France. Vinexpo is *the* big trade show for wine; buyers from all around the world go there to taste the latest vintages and check out the award-winning wines. Guess who won the Grand Prix *d'honneur* in the Icewine category? That's right, little ol' Inniskillin. The wine trade was stunned. All of a sudden, the whole world knew that Canada could make wine. Everybody wanted the Icewine — even at $50 or more a half-bottle.

How Icewine is made

In the fall, before all the grapes are harvested, the winery decides how many vines or rows of vines will be reserved for Icewine and separated from the rest of the crop, which will be harvested normally. The Icewine rows are then covered with netting so the birds can't get at them. Gradually, some of the grapes start to shrivel up like raisins and fall off the vine. They are now lost to the harvest. Some of the grapes actually rot, and if they don't fall off on their own the bad grapes are removed before any of the grapes are pressed.

Late harvest wines

Late harvest wines are similar to Icewine but much less intense in flavour because the juice is more dilute. In the usual course of events, late harvest grapes are picked before Icewine grapes. If a winemaker finds herself with a poor batch of Icewine one year — maybe the weather conditions weren't right, or the sugar content isn't high enough for Icewine standards — she might *declassify* it (downgrade it) to the level of late harvest wine.

For this reason, late harvest wines sell for much less: between $15 and $30 a bottle. They are packaged in half-bottles (375 ml), like Icewine.

Sometime around the end of December or beginning of January, when the temperature outdoors drops to about –8° Celsius, the water left in the grapes freezes. As this point, it's time to make Icewine. Just to be safe, winemakers usually wait until the temperature drops even further. The harder the grapes are frozen, the less likely they are to thaw before they are pressed.

As soon as the temperature conditions are met, the winemaker calls in the harvesters. They start harvesting the frozen grapes after dark and work through the night. They work in the dark because, even if it stays cold, the sun can have just enough warmth to melt the grapes.

It all sounds pretty romantic. Well, it's not.

The harvesters pick through the frozen grapes and discard the bad ones. The rest go into the press. When squeezed, the frozen grapes produce a concentrated syrup, heavy with sugar, which then gets dumped into stainless steel vats (or, if the winemaker wants to put a twist on the flavour, wooden barrels) for fermentation.

You can't drink large amounts of Icewine, for a variety of reasons. For one, the yield is very low. The volume of Icewine a winery produces may amount to only five percent of what it produces with regularly harvested grapes. So, of course, the price for Icewine is very high. Also, the wine is very sweet and intensely flavoured; your taste buds can't take too much of it — which is maybe just as well.

Canadian Content: Icewine in Canada

Most Icewines in Canada are made from thick-skinned white grape varieties such as Riesling, Gewürztraminer or Vidal; although Pinot Blanc, Chenin Blanc, and even red varieties such as Cabernet Franc have been turned into Icewine.

The Vidal grape

The hybrid grape Vidal is the mainstay of Canada's Icewine production and it's perfectly suited to the job. Its thick skin protects it against mould and rot throughout the damp autumn months, its high sugar content and soft fruity flavours are mouth-filling and appealing, and its high acids balance the sugar and prevent the wine from being too cloyingly sweet. Because it results in such a high-class wine, Vidal is one of the few non-vinifera grapes to receive VQA approval. The VQA rules stipulate that only vinifera grapes or a few stipulated, high-quality hybrid grapes can be used in wine that qualifies for VQA status. For more information on vinifera and hybrid grapes, turn to Chapter 4.

The Riesling grape

As hugely suited to Icewine as the Vidal grape is, another grape can outshine it: That grape is Riesling. Unfortunately, this grape is a bit more susceptible to loss during the period between the normal harvest and the Icewine harvest. It's also in high demand as a dry wine. Therefore, while Riesling forms the basis of most German *Eiswein*, it makes up only a small amount of Canada's output. Nevertheless, it has the sugar, it has the acid, and it has something more — that certain *je ne sais quoi* — a quality that is hard to describe but that translates into an impression of elegance and refinement.

A transcendent Icewine experience

Barb was at an all-Icewine tasting — the first she had ever attended — in January, 2000. Among the first wines she tried was the Cave Spring Riesling Icewine 1998. She felt as though she had been transported into another realm. For the rest of the evening she tried to find another Icewine to equal it, but, as excellent as they all were, none, in her opinion, compared to that particular Riesling. The 1998 vintage was ideal right through the growing season with lots of summer sun, so the sugars had built up in the grapes. This wine was dark gold in colour and had a sophisticated nose of peaches and dried apricots. The taste was full of succulent tropical fruit, yet was deliciously refreshing. The flavour lingered on and left an overall impression of elegance.

Tiny bubbles

Some Ontario wineries are beginning to make *sparkling* Icewine (carbon dioxide gas produces bubbles in the wine). Magnotta came up with the idea and Inniskillin followed suit. Peller Estates adds Icewine to one of their sparkling wines, while Kittling Ridge produces an Icewine *grappa* (a type of *eau de vie* made from the leftover skins and solids of the Icewine grapes). Barb contends that sparkling Icewine is no more than a gimmick. She says that the effervescent effect detracts from Icewine's inherent opulence and dilutes the concentrated flavours.

On the other hand, sparkling Icewine does combine the qualities of the two most luxurious wines in the world — champagne and dessert wine. It would certainly add an original touch to any special celebration.

The parade of awards

Canada is recognized as the world's leading producer of Icewine in terms of volume. Virtually every winery in Ontario produces an Icewine consistently every year and most of the British Columbia wineries do too. Canada is, in fact, the largest Icewine producer in the world. Canadian Icewines regularly win trophies and gold medals in national and international competitions. Table 16-1 lists award-winning Canadian Icewines and the distinctions they received.

Table 16-1	Award-Winning Canadian Icewines
Name of Wine	*Award*
Hester Creek Estate Reserve Pinot Blanc Icewine 1998 $49.95	Okanagan Wine Festival 2nd Gold
Inniskillin Vidal Icewine 1997 $53	Challenge International du Vin (France) Prix d'excellence
Jackson-Triggs Proprietors' Grand Reserve Riesling Icewine 1998 $70	Okanagan Wine Festival Walter Hainle Award for Best Icewine & 1st Gold
Konzelmann Vidal Icewine 1997 $45	Concours Mondiale (Belgium) Grande Médaille d'Or
Magnotta Sparkling Vidal Icewine Limited Edition (NV) $50	Intervin (North America) Gold
Stoney Ridge Cellars Gewürztraminer Icewine 1997 $50	Challenge International du Vin (France) Civart Trophy
Strewn Vidal Icewine 1997 $45	VinItaly (Italy) Grand Gold

Here come the Icewine police

Another type of police as Canadian as the Mounties has emerged in the wake of Icewine's great success in this country. The "Icewine Police" are not police in the usual sense of the word — they're inspectors who travel from vineyard to vineyard during the Icewine harvest to ensure that all VQA (Vintners Quality Alliance) criteria are being met. They are armed — not with guns, but with probes and hydrometers — to verify that the grapes remain frozen, that the sugar levels are high enough, and that all other procedures are strictly by the book. Winemakers are obliged to notify the VQA four to six hours before sending the harvesters out into the vineyard.

The need for this form of "policing" arose after a client in Taiwan bought some counterfeit Icewine. It's not all that difficult to throw some grapes in a freezer, add some grape concentrate and sugar, make a sweet-tasting wine, and stick a reasonable facsimile of a label on the bottle. But that's all it is — a sweet wine with a fake label — without character or quality. You won't find any legitimate producers of VQA wine making this sort of plonk, so always look for the VQA logo on the capsule on top of the bottle.

Savouring Icewine

Icewine is such a sweet delicacy that it is best enjoyed on its own or with dessert. You would find it too sugary to serve with a meat or fish course. Any time you taste anything really sweet, it makes what you put in your mouth afterwards taste sour. You need a food that is already sweet, so that the wine flavour complements the sweetness in the food rather than contrasts with it. High-fat, salty foods are the exception, as described below. But generally speaking, you're better off serving a dry table wine with your main course, instead of Icewine.

Matching Icewine with food

You can serve foie gras as an hors d'oeuvres with Icewine as an apéritif but remember, a little bit goes a long way. If you prefer foie gras as an appetizer course, you might add a bit of fruit chutney, which blends in with the fruitiness of the Icewine. It's difficult to follow that combination with a dry wine for your next course, but by serving a salad with some sparkling water between courses you refresh the mouth and prepare it for the drier wine.

To serve Icewine after a meal, you can end off with some creamy cheese, perhaps some nice runny Brie or a creamy blue cheese like St. Agur. Decorate your cheese plate with some strawberries and pears, which will contribute a fresh touch of sweetness.

North Americans tend to like very sweet desserts, but these aren't the best match for Icewine. Cakes with icing and puddings with syrup can overwhelm the sugar in the wine and make it appear too acidic. A simple hazelnut torte or fruit compote makes a much better accompaniment. Of course, you can always forget about cakes and the like and just savour the Icewine on its own.

Laying down Icewine

We would all like to think that we can age gracefully, but there's never any guarantee. As with people, nobody knows exactly why some wines age well and others don't, but it has been noted that wines with certain characteristics last longer. Notable characteristics in long-lived wines are acid, sugar, and concentrated fruit. And acid. Did we say acid? As you may have guessed by now, acid is important in aging wines — or at least in our being able to appreciate older wines. Acid is what gives wine a refreshing, palate-cleansing appeal. Without it wine appears dull, flat, and cloying.

During the aging process, the sugar flavour dries out and the fruitiness fades. We would find the result of these changes unappealing if the acid didn't continue to impart a crispness to the wine.

Because of its high sugar content, Icewine is an ideal wine to *lay down* (age in your cellar) for several years. The wine tastes good at all stages of its development, but some varieties keep longer than others because of the quality of their acidity. Vidal Icewine has a rounder, more mouth-filling taste than Riesling; but Riesling Icewine has better acidity and will last longer. You can keep most Icewine for 10 years or more. See Chapter 11 for information on starting your own wine collection and on keeping your cellared wine in tip-top condition.

In Ontario, try Icewines made from Riesling, Gewürztraminer, Vidal, or the red Cabernet Franc grape. In British Columbia, try the Riesling, Vidal, Pinot Blanc, Chenin Blanc, or Ehrenfelser grape.

Part V
Wineries across Canada

The 5th Wave   By Rich Tennant

"Well, I'm enough of a wine expert to know that if the boat were sinking, there'd be several cases of this Icewine that would go into a lifeboat before you would."

In this part . . .

Now that you've got the basics of wine appreciation down (how wine is made, how to taste wine, how to serve and match wine with food), you might like to visit some Canadian wineries. In this part, you can find out just what makes each winery individual and unique. There are over 120 wineries across Canada, and by the time you read this, there will be more.

Chapter 17

The Origins of Canadian Wine

Canada doesn't have a wine tradition of long standing like you find in France or Italy; nor is wine a major economic influence here as it is in Australia, or even California. Only four tiny pockets across the country produce wine. It's very much a modern-day phenomenon. There are no family dynasties of Canadian wine, like Europe's Bouchards or Antinoris. It's really only since the 1970s that Canadian growers and winemakers have figured out what grapes to plant where — and how to work with them in the winery.

As short as the history of Canadian wine is, it is not without its stories of both hardship and triumph. This chapter takes you back in time to trace the sometimes erratic evolution of Canada's wine industry. It is a story of ups and downs, frustrations and false starts — even some questionable philosophies. Canada's wine may have come of age, but not without some growing pains along the way.

The First 700 Years: 1000 to 1700

Was Canadian wine uncorked by a Viking? The story goes that the Viking Leif Ericsson discovered North America in the year 1001, and named the place where he landed Vinland (Land of Wine). By most accounts, it's more than likely that Ericsson landed on what is now Newfoundland. It's a little challenging to imagine wine-producing grapes growing there. Most Canadians would probably agree to call Newfoundland the Land of Screech, after its famous alcoholic beverage, or even the Land of the Moosehead, after its famous beer. But, Land of Wine? Who's kidding whom?

The great debate

Over 1000 years have passed since Leif Ericsson's great voyage to North America, but no one can say definitely where he landed. Despite the discovery of L'Anse aux Meadows, the massive Viking settlement in Newfoundland, there is still disagreement over where exactly Leif and his crew first set foot.

A Swedish archaeologist, Mats Larsson, pinpoints the Vikings' landing at Chegoggin, Nova Scotia, just north of Yarmouth, on the province's south shore.

A Canadian archaelogist, Brigitta Wallace, has put forth a different theory. She thinks that the Nova Scotia location is too far south and too distant from the Viking settlements in Newfoundland and Greenland. She puts their landing in the Miramichi area of northern New Brunswick.

It will take years of research and digging to prove or disprove either of these theories. Until then, Canadian wine lovers will have to endure the uncertainty over where the first Canadian vines were found.

In the reports of Ericsson's exploits, specifically those recorded by chronicler Adam of Bremen in about 1075, it is said that Ericsson discovered a land in which "vines yielding the best of wine grow there wild." Nowadays, wine lovers, knowing what wine from indigenous Canadian grapes tastes like, wonder what sort of taste these people had. (Or were they so happy to have found a restorative beverage in their isolation, that the finer points of flavour and bouquet just didn't matter?) Certainly, if the stories of stupendous wine were designed to attract settlers to the new Vinland, they failed dismally. In all probability, this early libation was valued more for its sustaining powers on a long, cold ocean voyage than for its subtle nuances.

Archaeological digs have revealed remnants of the Vikings' arduous life in Newfoundland, but concrete evidence of the existence of grapes at that time has eluded researchers. Archaeologists look for seeds and grains in the hope of identifying what Ericsson and his ancient compatriots ate (and drank), but those fabled grape seeds have yet to be found.

Early health implications

Modern medical science has shown that moderate consumption of wine can be a contributory factor to heart health. In the days of the Vikings, however, the explorers may have been more concerned with the quality of their drinking water and how wine was effective in making it safe to consume. Naming the new land Vinland implies that grapes and wine were extremely important to these worldly wanderers.

Settlers and the sacrament

Following Jacques Cartier's revelations of the new land in 1535, waves of French settlers braved the gruelling journey looking for new opportunities overseas.

With them came Jesuit missionaries to spread the Catholic word. Several written accounts of the Jesuits' early days in the new land survive — much to our benefit. Though they brought plenty of French wine with them for sacramental purposes, they eventually ran out and had to resort to producing it locally. Although they chronicled that grapes were plentiful, they had little to say about the quality of the wine they produced. It served its purpose at mass, but few found it palatable enough to drink as a secular beverage.

Jacques Cartier and the French tradition: 1535

Following Leif Ericsson's early exploits, the next explorer to stumble upon grapes growing in Canada was Jacques Cartier. In 1535, during his second voyage to Canada, Cartier found wild grapes on an island near what is now Québec City. Historians say his immediate reaction was to name this island Île de Bacchus, after the Greek god of wine, but he must have suddenly remembered that he was in the service of the King of France. Cartier ended up naming the island after the son of his royal patron (Île d'Orleans, after the Duc d'Orleans).

In the roughly 500-year span between Ericsson's and Cartier's trips to Canada, other visitor traffic wasn't particularly heavy. Christopher Columbus and John Cabot were likely the only other explorers who graced our shores during that period. So it's quite remarkable that two of the four explorers were impressed by the presence of vines in the vast new land they discovered. Their mandate may have been to find gold, but they seemed to have been well satisfied to find grapes instead.

Crossbred resistance and the American influence: 1619

The early inhabitants south of the border were just as eager to find a replacement for one of the most important liquid comforts of home. As early as 1619, British settlers in the colonies of Virginia and Carolina tried to transplant vines from Europe. Their efforts met with dismal failure: Every single one of the transplanted vines died. For over 100 years, viticulturists

17th-century wine milestones

1648: Jacques Boisdon opens the first tavern in Québec City. The Council of New France supplies him with eight barrels of French wine to get him started.

1668: Jesuit Father Jacques Bruyas encourages settlers to become wine growers. In a letter he writes, "If one were to take the trouble to plant some vines and trees they would yield as well as they do in France . . . and (properly pruned) the grapes would be as good as those of France."

tried in vain to create an environment in which the imported vines would grow. Eventually, they recognized that the vines suffered not so much from the harsh winters, but from disease and infestation against which they hadn't built up a resistance.

This dismal situation would soon change, however. During the American Revolution, a determined Governor John Penn of North Carolina kept his gardener, John Alexander, busy in his vineyard experimenting with European grape varieties. While Alexander had no luck at first, he was destined to go down in the annals of the North American wine industry. One day, he discovered a vine on the governor's property that he didn't recognize. After some investigation, he deduced that the vine was derived from the cross-pollination of one of the European vines with which he had been struggling and a wild local variety growing nearby. He took cuttings from the new vine and propagated them successfully in the governor's vineyard. The new *hybrid grape* (the result of crossing vines of different species) was called the Alexander grape, after the gardener who'd made it grow.

President Thomas Jefferson, a well-known *oenophile* (wine lover), was extremely fond of the Alexander grape, and planted it in his Virginia garden. But new, more successful hybrids soon replaced it in popularity. The Isabella

Bureaucratic controls of the 17th century

Regulations regarding the consumption of alcohol played a role in the 17th century. In 1648, when the French settler Jacques Boisdon wanted to open Québec City's first tavern, he had to apply to the Council of New France for a licence. The Council had no argument with Boisdon's plan, presumably understanding the social need for such an establishment. They even supplied the new tavern with its first eight barrels of French wine, free of charge. The only hitch? The community would tolerate neither unseemly behaviour nor gambling, so the tavern had to be located in a public square within full view of the church.

and the Catawba grapes, developed in 1816 and 1823, respectively, exhibited more desirable characteristics and enjoyed a long history and leading role in many northern North American vineyards.

Potential in Ontario: 1800 to 1866

Up until the early 1800s, there was no grape-growing activity of note in Canada. The first grower of any importance (and considered the father of the Canadian wine industry) was a retired German soldier named Johann Schiller. Schiller served in the British Army in Québec, and, as was common practise at the time, received a grant of land on his discharge. He farmed on 400 acres near Montréal for eight years before moving to Ontario, where he applied for and received a grant of equal size in what is now Mississauga. Schiller planted cuttings of wild Labrusca vines, as well as some American hybrids, with which he made wine for his family's consumption and for sale to the neighbouring farmers. He was a success.

First international recognition

Upon Schiller's death five years later, his sons partitioned and sold the property. One of the purchasers was Count Justin M. de Courtenay, an outspoken and determined personality, who ended up being the first person to bring Canadian wine to the attention of the rest of the world.

In 1867, in celebration of Confederation, de Courtenay exhibited his Clair House wine in Paris at the French Exposition. It was a resounding success. Some even compared it to the renowned French Beaujolais.

Canadian wine at the French Expo

This is what a Toronto newspaper of the day had to say about the wine brought to the 1867 French Exposition in Paris by Count Justin de Courtenay:

"The French exposition has established the character of our Canadian wines. The jury on wines, which would naturally be composed of the best judges to be found in Europe, speak[s] in very high terms of the wines sent from the Clair House Vineyards, Cooksville. They find in them a resemblance to the Beaujolais wine, which is known to be the best produced in France. They say of those wines that they resemble more the great French table wines than any other foreign wines they have examined, and that the fact of the wine being so *solide* as to bear the sea voyage, and the variations of heat and cold without losing anything of either its quality or limpidity, should be a question of great consideration even to our own producers."

Counting on the Concord

In 1854, an enterprising grower in Concord, Massachusetts, named Ephraim Wales Bull, developed a grape that would revolutionize the grape-growing industry in North America. It would also make waves in the wine industry, though in a much less positive way. The grape in question is the Concord.

Bull's ambition was to grow a grape that would mature quickly and be winter-hardy. The Concord was extremely successful in those regards. It's a prolific producer, grows anywhere in heat or cold, is resistant to infestation and is extremely winter hardy. It's such a successful grape, in fact, that it's still widely used as the basis for grape juice, jellies, flavourings, and sweeteners. Some of our earliest memories are of peanut butter and jam sandwiches, with grape jelly made from the Concord.

Although the Concord had a good deal more sugar than a lot of the hybrid grapes around at the time (that were causing winemakers such headaches), when you get right down to it, the Concord is actually pretty pathetic as a wine grape. Not that that made anybody stop using it, though! It epitomizes a characteristic found in all Labrusca grapes — an unpleasant odour called "foxy." Nobody seems to know who coined this term, nor has anyone ever described it adequately. You need to experience it once, and then you'll know what all the stink is about.

Despite its unsuitability, the Concord actually became the mainstay of the Canadian wine industry for many years — right up until the early 1970s. Disguised in the sweet alcoholic wines that were Canada's idea of vinous splendour throughout the first half of the 20th century, the Concord's "foxiness" was less offensive.

The Concord's most striking characteristic is its sweetness, but the end of its creator's story is rather bitter. Bull never obtained the rights to his discovery, which other nurseries started to propagate for themselves. He died in penury in 1895.

De Courtenay's good fortune was highly publicized. Unfortunately, from a financial viewpoint, he enjoyed much less success. He depended on government grants to keep his business going and, in 1878, this monetary support was withdrawn. He was forced to close down the winery, and his illustrious winemaking career came to an end.

Except for de Courtenay's brief moment of glory, the grape-growing and winemaking industries in Canada during the 19th century gave no cause for excitement. The fact that the wine that *was* being produced was in high demand as the basis of a number of medications speaks to its quality. On a positive note, however, the Niagara Peninsula was gradually making a name for itself in the area of grape production.

Niagara developments

Nineteenth-century grape growers in the Niagara region were beginning to gain some notoriety for the quality of their fruit and for their wine. Porter

Adams, who had a farm in Queenston, near Niagara Falls, managed to sell his grapes into the Toronto market. John Kilborn, with a farm in Beamsville, was growing grapes and making wine that was in great demand locally. In 1862, he even won a prize at the Provincial Exhibition in Toronto for the "best bottles of wine made from the grape." He took home a prize of a resounding $3. A contemporary of Kilborn's, W.W. Kitchen, made wine in the neighbouring town of Grimsby. He sold his wine primarily to churches for sacramental purposes and to druggists for use in medicines.

Winemaking condoned practises back then that are virtually outlawed today. Though growers were working with hybrid grapes by the mid-19th century, which were certainly better than the local varieties, they still had their limitations — most noticeably, a lack of sugar and high acid levels. To compensate, winemakers added sugar to the wine during fermentation, which raised the alcohol levels. To make matters worse, they also added water or syrup to the grape skins and pressed them a second time. Winemakers now know that the best wines are made from the juice of *very lightly* pressed grapes. Hard pressing and second pressings add bitterness to the wine. Unfortunately, such practises persisted in the industry until well into the middle of the 20th century. You can bet that the VQA prohibits them today, however.

Ontario's Potential Realized: 1866 to 1900

The sweet, highly acidic beverages that were Ontario's first attempts at making wine held the fancy of the populace for the first half of the 19th century. But that was about to change. As Canada came into its own as a country, so did Ontario as its wine-producing capital. These new developments started with a trio of Americans, funnily enough. D.J. Williams, Thomas Williams, and Thaddeus Smith came north from Kentucky in 1866, looking for winemaking opportunities. They found them on Pelee Island, just off the shore of Lake Erie. They named Canada's first commercial winery Vin Villa. It featured an elaborate underground cellar. Soon after the two Williamses and one Smith set up shop — a matter of months, in fact — Pelee Island attracted another wine venture; this time in the shape of two brothers from England, Edward and John Wardoper. The Wardoper brothers founded the Pelee Island Wine and Vineyard Company. It didn't take long before both companies found a market for their product. All this foreign interest in wine from the soon-to-be Canada makes you wonder why people living here were so slow off the mark!

The market for the wines of Vin Villa and the Pelee Island Wine and Vineyard Company was about to get bigger, however — much bigger, thanks to one Major J.S. Hamilton, a grocer in Brantford, Ontario, who had an enterprising eye towards the south. In 1874, Hamilton formed an agreement with both wineries to sell their wines into the eastern United States. The endeavour proved extremely successful.

Wine milestones of the 19th century

1811: Johann Schiller, a retired corporal, plants the first commercial vineyard in Cooksville, Ontario (now Mississauga). Schiller, considered the father of Canadian wine, brought his winemaking experience over from Germany's Rhine Valley. He domesticated wild grapes he found growing along the banks of the Credit River.

1861: Farmer John Kilborn, of Beamsville, Ontario, wins a $3 prize at the Provincial Exhibition in Toronto for "best bottles of wine made from the grape."

1864: Count Justin M. de Courtenay buys Johann Schiller's property in Ontario and names it Clair House and increases the vineyard acreage to 40 acres.

1866: Three gentlemen farmers from Kentucky buy land on Pelee Island to create the Vin Villa winery. They are soon followed by two English brothers, Edward and John Wardoper, who plant a competing vineyard.

1867: Count Justin M. de Courtenay wins praise from judges at the Paris Exposition for his wine from Clair House that resembles the famous French Beaujolais style.

1873: George Barnes creates the Ontario Grape Growing and Wine Manufacturing Co. Ltd. in St. Catharines, Ontario.

1874: Major J.S. Hamilton, a Brantford, Ontario, businessman, joins forces with Vin Villa and the Pelee Island Wine and Vineyard Company. The winemaking operations are transferred from Pelee Island to Brantford.

Thomas Bright and F.A. Shirriff open a winery in Toronto called the Niagara Falls Wine Company (16 years later it would move to the outskirts of that town).

Two other mainstays of the Canadian wine industry also got their start in the late 19th century. The Ontario Grape Growing and Wine Manufacturing Co. Ltd., opened in St. Catharines, Ontario, in 1873, operated for over 100 years until its closing in 1988.

In 1874, two partners, Thomas Bright and F.A. Shirriff, opened the Niagara Falls Wine Company in Toronto, moving it to Niagara Falls proper in 1890. In 1911, its name changed to T.G. Bright and Company — a name that would become synonymous with the Canadian wine industry for many years.

Temperance in a teacup

The fledgling Canadian wine industry was in for some rough times as the 20th century began. The Temperance Movement (the populist support movement behind Prohibition) was gaining ground. An ultra-conservative movement, it cited "demon alcohol" as the cause of the world's great ills. A large segment of society was ready to embrace abstinence. A handful of grape growers even refused to sell to the wineries.

The demand for industrial alcohol to make explosives during the First World War advanced the ambitions of the anti-alcohol movement. In 1916, the Ontario government, under Sir William Hearst, an outspoken supporter of Prohibition, passed the Ontario Temperance Act. It stipulated that no one could sell alcohol unless permitted to do so by the province. The government established the Board of Licence Commissioners — a legal body that could issue permits to produce alcohol for personal consumption, medicinal purposes, or religious rites. The distilleries, which had been making hard liquor, mostly from grains, converted their premises to supply the war effort with industrial alcohol, but the grape growers' lobby went into high gear.

Grape-growing was a major industry in Ontario at the time, and the growers had a fair amount of political clout. They needed a network of wineries to whom they could sell their produce. Their pressure tactics resulted in the Conservative government exempting from the Temperance Act wines made from Ontario-grown grapes and produced by manufacturers who held permits from the provincial Board of Licence Commissioners. Booze was out, wine was in — but there was a catch.

The 10 wineries operating in the province at the time the Ontario Temperance Act came into effect continued to produce wine — but they had to find new ways of making it available to customers. The law allowed the wineries to establish one retail outlet on their premises. Even though it limited the amount a consumer could buy to five gallons (about two cases), this loophole inspired almost anyone with some talent in making wine to open a winery. Far from curtailing the wine industry, Prohibition actually spurred its growth.

During Prohibition, ironically enough, the wineries in Ontario grew in number from 10 to 67, centred in three different areas:

- In Toronto, to take advantage of the urban market
- In Niagara, to take advantage of nearby vineyards
- In Windsor, to take advantage of cross-border traffic

Getting around the problem of Prohibition

If alcohol was not readily available to the consumer, it *was* to religious establishments, as well as to industry and medical practitioners.

As humourist Stephen Leacock wrote, "To get a drink during Prohibition it is necessary to go to the drug store . . . and lean up against the counter making a gurgling sigh like apoplexy. One often sees there apoplexy cases lined up four deep."

Understandably, illness increased to epidemic proportions around the Christmas holiday season.

New wineries also cropped up in a few surprising locations:

- ✔ In Port Arthur and Fort William, two towns that later amalgamated to become Thunder Bay
- ✔ In Kitchener, operating out of the basement of a private home
- ✔ In Belleville, a winery that was eventually absorbed by the larger Belleville Wine Company
- ✔ In Sudbury, servicing the mining towns in that part of the province

The distance the wine had to travel from where it was produced to where it would be sold was another factor that affected its overall quality. Without the benefit of refrigeration, the wine oxidized in transit and the grapes started to rot, although in the sweet, high-alcohol wines that were the flavour of the day these faults were less obvious.

Quality control for these new wineries was minimal, if not non-existent. The government had no inspectors, nor any apparent interest in inspecting. Winemakers were self-taught and not necessarily talented or informed.

The large wineries weren't the only culprits in the bad wine category. Home winemakers everywhere got in on the act. All they needed was a home winemaking licence, which was easy to obtain. With little risk of prosecution considering the somewhat lax legislation at the time, home winemakers sold their amateur concoctions right out their back doors.

The birth of the liquor boards

By the time Prohibition was repealed across the country (between 1920 and 1927, depending on the province), Canadians had become accustomed to drinking Canadian wine. As awful as it was, it had been the only thing readily available. Not only was Prohibition seen as a failure in attempting to stem the tide of alcohol consumption, it had also done its fair share to promote the Canadian wine industry.

In 1927, Ontario replaced its Temperance Act with the Liquor Control Act and established a network of government-run stores. One by one the other provinces followed suit, setting up their own "liquor boards," as they are known today, to control the sale of alcoholic beverages. The liquor boards served not only to regulate the sale of alcohol, but also to control the pricing and the quality of the products. Each province developed its own system of retail distribution, pricing, and taxation. In Ontario, the wineries had to have a licence from the board to operate a retail outlet on their premises, but these had already been issued during Prohibition. (No new permits were issued until 1974, when Donald Ziraldo and Karl Kaiser applied to open Ontario's first modern, boutique-style winery, Inniskillin. At the same time, Karl Podamer

An attempt at quality control

Ontario's newly formed liquor board developed a set of standards related to domestic wines that they purchased for sale in their stores. They seem laughable today, but reflect the depths to which quality control had sunk during Prohibition.

The liquor board stipulated:

That a maximum of 250 gallons of wine be produced per tonne of grape.

That the addition of water to the wine be strictly limited.

That production facilities meet certain standards of cleanliness.

That the amount of *volatile acid* in the wine (acid that can change due to evaporation or exposure to air) be limited to four percent (though this wasn't actually low enough to prevent the wine from tasting like vinegar).

These standards helped improve the quality of the wine to a certain degree, but political and social realities — particularly the onset of the Great Depression — prevented them from becoming any stricter. Introducing quality controls at this time would cost money, money that a lot of growers just didn't have. The risk that wineries would close rather than refit their equipment was high. This would have resulted in a smaller market for grapes, and the ever-powerful grape growers' lobby was already vocal about falling prices.

received a licence to create a sparkling wine facility, which he called the Podamer Champagne Company.)

The permit system is still in full force today. New wineries must first obtain a manufacturing licence to make wine, then a retail licence to sell wine on their premises in their winery shops.

Provincial governments had suddenly become the arbiters of good taste. It was they, not the consumer, who decided which products could be sold, including which wines and from which countries. The only place where the consumer really had any influence was in quality control: Wine drinkers in droves started bringing back inferior products. Want some examples of the kind of stuff that was out there? Wines that tasted like vinegar, wines in bottles half-filled with sediment, wine bottles that contained flies, spiders, and other questionable foreign matter. Customers sometimes complained that bottles had exploded, but more complaints of this nature actually came from liquor board employees, who were in constant danger of flying glass as stray yeast cells caused secondary fermentation in the bottle. Remember the formula: When fermentation occurs, sugar is converted into alcohol and carbonic gas in almost equal proportions. If this happens in a corked bottle, well, you might as well be holding a hand grenade.

Different strains of yeast consume the grape sugars at different rates. If the winemaker is not careful about how the yeast is applied, some airborne yeast of unknown origins can insinuate itself into the wine and cause unexpected, secondary fermentation.

Preventative measures

The liquor boards controlled the commercial sale of alcohol, but any number of medications containing alcohol were still readily available at the pharmacy. By legislating that producers of these medications had to blend an *emetic* (an ingredient that causes vomiting) into the potion, a "patient" who consumed more than the recommended dose would quickly lose the desire to drink. The strategy worked like a charm, bringing the consumption of these "medications" under control.

The new standards introduced just before the Great Depression improved the quality of the wines to a certain degree, but the wines were still Labrusca- and hybrid-based, full of sugar, and high in alcohol (almost twice that of the European norm).

Post-Prohibition days

While the provincial government supported the wine industry, it also had to deal with the forces of the anti-drinkers. At the same time, the Great Depression had the country in its grip. For several years, the wine industry had to weather its ups and downs.

- **In 1929:** The Ontario government removed the 50-cent-a-gallon tax on wines that had previously been a much-needed subsidy for the wine industry and growers.

- **In 1930:** The industry received permission from the provincial government to sell fortified wines. This proved a benefit during those lean times, as it solved the problem of having to throw away wine that didn't make the grade, and was therefore more cost-effective. The wineries distilled any sub-standard wine and added port or sherry to it. The public embraced these fortified wines with enthusiasm and continued to favour them above all others until the late 1960s.

- **In 1931:** The government disallowed any importation of grapes from outside the province and fixed a minimum levy of $40 per tonne on grapes that were brought in this way.

- **In 1932:** The government realized that the sales of the new fortified wines had skyrocketed and started questioning their own policies, remembering the still-influential teetotallers. It established a maximum of 20 percent alcohol volume for wine and instituted a public relations campaign promoting the benefits of lower-alcohol table wine. It expected that the wine industry, in response, would begin making lighter wines with lower alcohol content to conform to the new policies. The only problem was the consumer. The average wine buyer stuck loyally to the fortified wines.

Although on the one hand the wineries had some support from the province, their other hand was tied squarely behind their backs. The Prohibitionist mentality was still very much alive, and the advertising of alcoholic beverages was restricted by law. So the wineries struggled, but at least the government offered some support by refusing to issue new licences. This action — or lack of action — prevented any new wineries from opening, preventing further dilution of the market.

In all the doom and gloom of Prohibition, followed by the Depression, combined with the collective bad taste of the Canadian public, one small light glimmered in the seemingly endless tunnel of bad wine. A handful of determined growers and wine professionals, recognizing the limitations of the grape types they were growing, tried to find better alternatives. They made no explosive discoveries; grape breeding is a slow and laborious occupation. But they persevered. It takes a minimum of three years before you can take a true measure of a particular grape's suitability for wine. Many of the grapes failed the test of winter and trials had to begin all over again.

Eventually, a few hybrid vines emerged from the pack as being winter-hardy and, equally important, capable of creating a palatable wine.

A Brights spot during the Depression

By the 1930s, Brights, still the leader in wine production, had a new and dynamic owner, Harry Hatch. He recognized the talent of a young chemist and winemaker working at Brights' Montréal plant — actually a French viscount

Wine styles of the Depression

Fortified wines in the style of sherry and port were all the rage during the Depression. The two best-selling products of the time were Brights' Catawba Sherry and Jordan's Bran-Vin. The fact that the former was referred to as Brights' Disease didn't decrease its popularity at all. It was as though Canadians didn't expect to find anything better. This was perhaps a reaction to Prohibition, when anything was better than nothing. Or perhaps the fortified wines appealed to the public because times were tough and wine was cheaper than hard liquor. Few consumers had any point of reference anyway, as they had little exposure to the better wines of Europe.

who had immigrated to Canada — and transferred him to the Brights winery in Niagara Falls. His name was Adhemar de Chaunac, and he would make some discoveries crucial to the furthering of the wine industry in Canada. It's somewhat ironic, because de Chaunac made no bones about expressing his distaste for Canadian wines compared to those of his French homeland. For our part, we're glad he felt inspired.

Although Brights' Niagara vineyard contained mostly Concord grapes, the French chemist (now a bit of a celebrity) located some small plots of Catawba and Delaware grapes on the property. From these he made batches of experimental dry wine that impressed Hatch very much. Hatch enlarged the Catawba and Delaware plantings with vines purchased from nurseries in New York and urged the chemist to continue experimenting. He later sent him back to France, where researchers had had some success with hybrid grapes, to carry out further experiments.

Changing styles in the postwar years

The wineries limped through the war into a new era of Canadian wine. The postwar years were critical in the industry's development. Adhemar de Chaunac returned to France in 1946, where he purchased and brought back 40 European grape varieties for experimentation at Brights. Among them were a variety of hybrids, along with some noble vinifera varieties, including Chardonnay and Pinot Noir, the famous grapes of the Burgundy region.

Of the 40 types he brought back, de Chaunac had success with 10 of them (not bad!), including the Chardonnay and Pinot Noir varieties — although the Pinot Noir didn't produce sufficient quantities of grapes to be commercially successful. Nine years later, Brights produced their first 100-percent Chardonnay.

Today, Chardonnay is the leader among the many wines produced by Canadian wineries.

Wine restricted by war

Research into winemaking in Canada stopped abruptly at the outbreak of the Second World War. Servicemen left the country in droves and exchange of personnel and agricultural products (such as grapes) with Europe ceased. Brights was no longer able to send their star winemaker, Adhemar de Chaunac, on voyages of discovery to the vineyards in France.

The wineries struggled to stay open, but as part of a non-essential industry they had difficulty obtaining even the most basic materials — like bottles. The federal government rationed the wineries' production, and a shortage of product developed. People lined up as early as 7:00 a.m. outside the liquor stores (they didn't open until 10:00 a.m.).

Hybrids hit a high point

One of the most important hybrids Adhemar de Chaunac brought back from France for planting at Brights was a variety known as Seibel 9549. It was later renamed de Chaunac, honouring the man whose contributions changed the face of the Canadian wine industry. It became the red grape of choice during the 1960s and 1970s, and is still grown in limited quantity in Québec, where its winter-hardiness is well appreciated.

Another success story grew out of a red hybrid called Maréchal Foch, a grape developed in Alsace and named for a famous French general. In the late 1950s, Brights made a wine from it called Canadian Burgundy.

The tradition of Maréchal Foch has endured in the Ontario wine scene, where it has earned a well-deserved reputation for quality. Several wineries produce an old vines Foch. These mature plantings (usually at least 25 years old) produce intense grapes with well-defined acids and tannins.

The daffy world of Baby Duck

By the early 1960s, most of the wineries in Ontario were producing wines from the Seibel, Maréchal Foch, and Verdelet varieties, as well as from a limited number of vinifera varieties. Their efforts met with increasing success in the marketplace as wine drinkers discovered the pleasures of European-style dry wines with lower alcohol levels (between 9 and 13 percent).

It would be a while, however, before this style of wine gained universal acceptance. A postwar generation raised on soda pop wasn't going to embrace drier wines without some sort of transitional phase. This appeared in the form of a tavern owner in Detroit, Michigan, who, with his finger exactly on the pulse of his customers, commissioned the blending of a sweet, sparkling wine, from Labrusca grapes, made the "old-fashioned" way with sugar and water added. He called his low-alcohol (12 percent) creation Cold Duck — and started a craze.

In Canada, Brights went one better — developing a sweet, sparkling wine with only seven percent alcohol, named (rather unfortunately) Winette. Today, the name sounds like "wetnap," but it was a winner at the time. Brights even convinced the Ontario government to lower the tax levied on sparkling wine of this type because of its low alcohol content.

Winette was a moneymaker for Brights. Not only did they make it from Labrusca grapes, the cheapest on the market, but they added water and sugar to increase the quantities produced. The addition of a sister product, Du Barry Sparkling Vin Rosé, gave Brights control of the Canadian market for several years. Competition finally came from a British Columbia winery that created a line of sparkling wine called Chanté — designed to evoke an "enchanted"

French character. From these wines evolved a product called Baby Duck, launched by Andrés in 1971. By 1973, it accounted for almost 25 percent of all wine sold in Canada. The Baby had a number of imitators with imaginative names like Fuddle Duck and Gimli Goose, but none enjoyed the same success as the original. More on the evolution of winemaking in British Columbia later in this chapter.

Other trends were developing independently of the Duck craze. Gradually, the demand for non-sparkling dry wines increased — to the extent that the liquor boards almost tripled the number of wines they imported from other countries. The public gained a taste for French, German, Italian, Spanish, and Portuguese wines. They appealed to the Baby Duck crowd, plus had the added advantage of being "sophisticated imports."

The invasion of the imports

The Canadian marketplace was saturated with inexpensive, imported wine, and Ontario grape growers and winemakers began to see the writing on the wall. They presented their problem to the provincial government, which took their concerns seriously and, in 1976, introduced the Ontario Wine Industry Assistance Program. The program was two-pronged. The Ontario liquor board was made to *de-list* (not re-order) any imported products that weren't meeting sales quotas and replace them with Canadian wine. And, liquor store managers and wine consultants were instructed to promote Ontario products whenever possible.

The assistance program extended to the vineyards as well. It provided interest-free loans for five years to growers who would replace their Labrusca vines with vinifera varieties — a closer match to the grapes being grown in Europe. The goal was to produce wines that would compete directly with the European imports.

The fabulous four

Four large Ontario wineries dominated the Canadian wine industry in the 1960s and 1970s: Brights, Andrés (although founded in British Columbia, it centred its activities in Ontario), Château-Gai, and Jordan. To increase their presence in provinces where grapes were not grown, they opened bottling plants across the country. By providing jobs, the wineries ingratiated themselves with the various provincial governments, who responded by accepting their products for sale in the liquor boards. The companies benefited financially from fewer regulations than they had to deal with in Ontario.

The dawn of a new era

In the 1970s, economic optimism prevailed. Quality hybrids and some vinifera vines were growing successfully in Canadian vineyards, and the large wineries were doing well. One young, wine-loving nurseryman, Donald Ziraldo, wanted to start his own small winery with his winemaking partner, Karl Kaiser.

Up until this time, the large wineries that had survived Prohibition, the Depression, and the Second World War ruled the roost. The issuing of new winery licences had been curtailed during the Depression to help the existing wineries survive. Those wineries had bought up any existing licences for their retail outlets. No new licences had been issued since.

Ziraldo and Kaiser faced opposition at first, but found an ally in the Ontario liquor board chairman, Major General George Kitching. He granted them the first licence since Prohibition in 1974. In 1975, Ziraldo and Kaiser opened Inniskillin Winery, the first of Canada's boutique wineries, along with the Podamer Champagne Company, founded by Karl Podamer.

Never one to rest on his laurels, Ziraldo later spearheaded the drive to establish a system of identifying wines according to criteria already in use in Europe. The Vintners Quality Alliance (VQA) is an *appellation system* (a method of naming wines so that the geographic origins are identified) that was introduced in Ontario in 1988 and in British Columbia in 1990.

The European competition was embodied in several best-selling blends: Black Tower, Blue Nun, Colli Albani, and Donini. Market trends indicated that consumers were leaning towards white wines rather than reds.

The first winery to meet the European competition head-on was Calona Wines, in British Columbia. The Capozzi family, who owned the winery, were great fans of Ernest and Julio Gallo, who had founded their California winery in 1933. They watched the Gallos climb to success with great interest, putting some of the same strategies to work in their own business. They had everything right when they released Schloss Laderheim, a blended white wine made from white hybrids designed to compete with Black Tower, the best-selling of all the imported blends. The Capozzis dressed their wine up to look like its rival, using a dark bottle and a Germanic-style label.

Two years later, in 1978, Ontario's Château-Gai winery entered the fray with a product called Alpenweiss. It had the same look as Schloss Laderheim, but its blend contained California grapes and the Ontario white hybrid Seyval. Canadian consumers, still leaning toward European products, had little knowledge about Canadian wine. These were the days of, "I know what I like, but I don't know why." But they knew the style of the wine by its packaging. It was pleasant, easy drinking, cheap, and flew off the shelves. Backed by heavy advertising, these wines sold gratifyingly well for the large commercial wineries.

Beginnings in British Columbia: 1920

The wine industry in British Columbia got a somewhat later start than in Ontario, coming into its own after Prohibition and the Depression. Until then, there was little interest in growing wine grapes, though the Roman Catholic Church had planted some vines near Kelowna in the mid-1800s. (This is considered the first planting of grapes in the province.) The first commercial vineyards in British Columbia yielded only grapes for eating. Two pioneers in this area were W.J. Wilcox, who planted a vineyard at Salmon Arm in the northern part of the Okanagan Valley, and Jim Creighton, whose Penticton vineyard was and is still in a location much more conducive to grape growing.

Tried, tested, and true

The real history of grape growing and winemaking in British Columbia dates to the mid-1920s, when Jesse Willard Hughes planted grapes at the Roman Catholic site near Kelowna, using vines that had been propagated locally, in B.C. vineyards. The grapes were not vinified where they were grown, however, but were instead shipped all the way to Victoria to the Growers' Wine Company, a farming cooperative that until that time had specialized in producing loganberry wine. This dark red berry is a cross between a raspberry and a blackberry (first produced in 1881 by an American horticulturist and lawyer named J.H. Logan). It grows abundantly at the south end of Vancouver Island. It made a wine that at the time was highly appreciated by residents of Victoria and the surrounding area.

The wine industry in B.C. got another kick-start in the early 1930s. Apple farmers in the province found themselves in a bit of a tight spot when a succession of good apple harvests produced an overabundance of fruit, which resulted in prices bottoming out and the market collapsing. The Growers' Wine Company was increasing wine production at the time, however, and needed more grapes. They paid desperate apple farmers handsomely for them.

Pointing the way

British Columbia's first trained wine professionals were brothers from Hungary: Eugene Rittich, an oenologist, and Virgil Rittich, a viticulturist. They undertook a series of experiments to uncover the best varietals for growing grapes for wine. They tried 44 different vine types, including some vinifera vines that had grown successfully in Europe. They published the results of their work in 1934, in a book titled *European Grape Growing*. They recommended a number of varieties suitable for regions in which winter protection was necessary. Yet it would be nearly 50 years before these European varietals were successfully grown in the province.

An apple a day couldn't keep creditors at bay

Giuseppe Ghezzi, an enterprising Italian winemaker, moved to Kelowna to take advantage of the apple market — to produce wine! He joined forces with Pasquale "Cap" Capozzi, a grocer also of Italian descent, and with then-hardware store owner and future premier of the province, William Andrew Cecil Bennett. Their apple-wine-producing winery was called Domestic Wines and By-Products — a name that would be laughed out of existence by today's marketing professionals. Ghezzi stayed with the company only briefly; he soon moved on to new ventures in California.

Bennett and Capozzi were plagued with problems of quality control and consumer resistance to their products for the first three years they were in business. Not only did their wines have a habit of refermenting in the bottle, but they also couldn't compete with the wines put out by the Growers' Wine Company, which had been in business since 1922. Even the colourful names of their apple wines — Okay Red, Okay Clear, Okay Port, and Okay Champagne — made no difference.

Facing ruin, Bennett and Capozzi decided to join 'em rather than be beat. They switched over to grapes, and renamed their winery Calona Wines Limited. One of their new products under this venture was called Calona Clear Grape Wine — a sweet wine with a whopping alcohol content of 20 percent.

In 1941, W.A.C. Bennett was elected to the provincial legislature of British Columbia — just as Calona Wines Limited was beginning to make its mark. Bennett sold out to Capozzi, but never forgot his roots. Throughout his time in government, Bennett did what he could to encourage the wine industry in B.C. In 1960, as premier, he supported a new law stating that wine made in the province had to contain a minimum amount of B.C. fruit. The logic behind this was that if government-run liquor stores were benefitting from the sale of wine — and they were the only outlet where wine could be purchased — then the government should support the wine industry and encourage the use of locally grown fruit. Ideally, the law would have required that B.C. wine contain 100 percent B.C. grapes. But, at the time, the local vineyards couldn't supply the whole of the industry, so the minimum was held to 25 percent for the first two years. It rose to 50 percent in 1962 and 65 percent in 1965.

Winds of change

The 1960s and 1970s represented a period of serious growth for the B.C. wine industry, fostered by provincial government support. Grape growers planted vines fast and furiously, concentrating on French and American hybrids like De Chaunac, Maréchal Foch, Rougeon, Chelois, and Baco Noir. Vineyard land

Uncle Ben's gourmet wine

In 1969, the Mission Hill Winery, which later became one of British Columbia's leading wineries, changed hands and was renamed Uncle Ben's Gourmet Winery by new owner and construction magnate Ben Ginter. He named his wines in an equally charming manner, dubbing them the likes of Fuddle Duck and Hot Goose. Ginter owned the winery until 1981, when the accumulation of a poor reputation from wines of questionable virtue, union problems at his Red Deer Brewery, and the threat of bank foreclosure forced him to sell the winery. He found a buyer in Anthony von Mandl, a successful wine importer. Von Mandl modernized the facility considerably. Today, with its bell tower and imposing underground cellars, it is the most stunning property in the Okanagan Valley.

Von Mandl reinstated the winery's original name: Mission Hill. He also put the winery on the industry map.

in B.C. quadrupled in four years. Large wineries were in their element: Andrés opened a new facility just outside of Vancouver; Southern Okanagan Wines, of Penticton, opened a few years later; and Mission Hill Winery opened at Westbank, high on a ridge overlooking Lake Okanagan. See Chapter 19 for profiles of British Columbia wineries.

In the vineyards, the winds of change were blowing, as growers started importing vinifera vines from California and Washington. They tried a broad selection of both white and red vinifera varieties, including Chenin Blanc, Gewürztraminer, Sémillon, Cabernet Sauvignon, and Merlot.

In 1975, George Heiss, a grower who would later open his own winery, Gray Monk Cellars, planted vines imported from France — Auxerrois, Pinot Gris, and Gewürztraminer — varieties that he still grows successfully.

With a little help from the legislature

In 1977, the provincial government launched a new support program in response to strong lobbying by B.C. grape growers and wineries. The mark-up on domestic wines was reduced from 66 percent to 46 percent. The mark-up on imported wines, though less important to the B.C. industry, was also reduced, from 117 percent to 100 percent. The government also created legislation permitting wineries to open retail stores on site, at which they could sell their own products.

At the same time, the Ministry of Agriculture introduced a five-year grape-growing program designed to upgrade the quality of grapes being grown in B.C. The ministry commissioned a German viticulturist, the late Dr. Helmut Becker, who suggested 27 European grape varieties for testing in B.C.

Of these 27 varieties planted, the best grapes turned out to be Auxerrois, Ehrenfelser, Pinot Blanc, Bacchus, Gewürztraminer, Müller-Thurgau, Schönberger, and Scheurebe.

The government was considerably slower in moving on another aspect of the wine industry's potential. Finally, after several years of bouncing the idea around, it introduced measures to encourage tourism in the Okanagan Valley by permitting the creation of *farm wineries*. These were smaller, self-contained facilities where tourists could learn about local wines, as well as taste and buy the product. The first of these farm wineries was Claremont Winery, founded in 1979.

At the time, different licences were required for "farm," "estate," and "major" wineries, best explained as "small," "medium," and "large." In 1998, the B.C. government simplified the system by creating one licence for all. Occasionally, you hear people still using the outdated terms to describe the wineries.

The first medium-size winery, then called an "estate" winery, also opened in 1979, at Sumac Ridge. This winery is particularly noteworthy because it was founded by Harry McWatters, the driving force behind B.C.'s modern-day wine industry.

The turning point

At the end of the 1980s, the spectre of the U.S.–Canada Free Trade Agreement struck little less than terror into the hearts of the B.C. wine industry. Winemakers who depended on hybrid vines would never be able to compete with American wines based on the higher-quality vinifera varietals that were now flooding the market. The federal government responded, providing funds that enabled winemakers to replace their inferior vines. The 1988–89 Pullout Program enabled the industry to retrench itself in time for Free Trade, and it's never looked back.

It took several years for production to reach pre-Free Trade levels, since about two-thirds of the acreage was uprooted. But when it did reach those levels, consumers were ready and predisposed to try the new wines. Sales grew and so did the quality of wine. In 1990, the province adopted the VQA guidelines.

Ontario, too, was affected by the Free Trade Agreement. Undesirable grape varieties were torn out, reducing vineyard acreage from 24,000 acres to 17,000 acres.

Québec's Story begins in 1870

In the 1870s, at the same time that the Roman Catholic fathers were producing sacramental wine in the Okanagan Valley, and Major Hamilton was selling wine made from Pelee Island vineyards, a Mr. Menzies, of Pointe-Claire, Québec, established the Beaconsfield Vineyard. Despite the unforgiving winters, Menzies persevered, taking on a partner two years later. But the two men obviously disagreed on the direction the business should take, for not long after, Menzies' partner began selling imported American wine — also under the Beaconsfield Vineyard name!

This and other attempts at winemaking in Québec eventually fell victim to the harsh winters. There is no record of any commercial wineries operating in Québec until 1980. It took an oenologist from the south of France to prove that it could be done. Hervé Durand had learned the technique of *hilling* grapevines in Russia and China. This procedure involves cutting the vines down in the fall and piling earth up over the stumps to provide added protection over the winter — very much the same way gardeners cover their rosebushes. Other keen winemakers have emulated Durand's efforts in Québec, and today there is a vibrant (if small) community of wineries southeast of Montréal.

These winemakers are modern-day pioneers who must devise original ways of defeating the cruel devastation of winter. In their own way, they are as courageous as the first settlers who came to Québec at the beginning of the 17th century. Their experience will be passed on to the next generation of winemakers in the province — much to their benefit.

Buying Canadian

Although wine is available for purchase in all provinces and territories, buying Canadian wine is a challenge. Unless you live in a wine-producing province, availability of Canadian wine is limited. Some of this has to do with the fact that so many Canadian wineries produce small quantities of wine. This is particularly true in British Columbia, where many wineries sell their entire production on site. Québec and Nova Scotia wineries also sell just about everything from their own premises. Gradually, the wineries with larger productions are finding ways to have their products listed in different provinces and the increase in opportunities to order by mail (or e-mail) is helping matters, also.

Experimentation in Nova Scotia: 1913

Perhaps Nova Scotia will prove to be Leif Ericsson's true Vinland — or maybe the location where the Vikings landed all those years ago will remain a mystery forever. But historical records dating from the time of the French explorer Samuel Champlain recount that, in 1611, an apothecary accompanying Champlain brought grapevines to the new land from France. He transported the vines by canoe, up the Bear River from the Annapolis Basin, with the intention of starting a vineyard. Knowing what we do about the success rate for European vines in North America, it's likely this apothecary didn't have much luck. Perhaps he was able to find other fruits from which to create his potions.

Vineyards had no profile in the history of Nova Scotia until about 1913, when horticulturists at the Agriculture Canada Research Station at Kentville in the Annapolis Valley started planting some experimental plots. Grape-growing in Nova Scotia is limited by a short, cool growing season. By 1971, having tried to grow over 100 different grapevines, the researchers concluded that not even the hardy Concord grape ripened sufficiently, but that some other early-ripening *table grapes* (grapes for eating, not suitable for wine) could survive.

It took a professor of political science to prove wine grapes could be grown in Nova Scotia, and that wine could be made from them. Roger Dial, a Californian, was a partner in a small winery in the Napa Valley. When he assumed a teaching post at Dalhousie University in Halifax, he met a colleague in the department of economics, Norman Morse, who grew table grapes on a property at Grand Pré in the Annapolis Valley. Dial, who was a keen home winemaker, persuaded his friend to plant some wine grapes.

In 1978, Dial and Morse planted two hardy Russian varieties, Michurinetz and Severnyi, on three acres. In 1979, they tried some Chardonnay and Gewürztraminer, but lost almost all of it during the particularly harsh winter of that year. Grand Pré's subsequent success was based on the enduring Russian grapes.

For the love of wine

In 1980, Roger Dial's red, Michurinetz-based wine romantically named Cuvée d'Amur (after the Amur Valley on the border of Russia and China where the grapes are grown) won a gold medal at the International Wine and Spirit Competition in New York — and a silver at a competition in Bristol, England.

In 1981, encouraged by the success of his wine in international competitions, Dial bought Morse's vineyard and opened a small winery that he named Grand Pré Estate Winery. In 1982, Dial became chairman of the newly formed Wine Growers' Association of Nova Scotia. He received yet another accolade for his wine in that same year: His Cuvée d'Amur was chosen as the official wine served at Canadian embassies around the world.

In 1983, Dial planted 22 more acres of vines a short distance from Grand Pré. His wines were in great demand at the local provincial liquor store, the only outlet, at the time, where he could sell them. It wasn't until 1986 that the Nova Scotia Farm Winery Act allowed wineries to sell wine directly from their boutiques.

Wine milestones of the 20th century

1900: The Niagara Peninsula boasts some 5,000 acres of vines.

1908: J.S. Hamilton's company takes over the Pelee Island Wine and Vineyard Company.

1911: The Niagara Falls Wine Company changes its name to T.G. Bright and Company.

1916: Prohibition is introduced. Within a year, all provinces (with the exception of Québec) proscribe the sale of alcoholic beverages. Wine is exempt.

1927: Prohibition is repealed. During its 11 years of enforcement, 57 new winery licences are issued in Ontario.

The provincial liquor board system is instituted.

1932: Guiseppe Ghezzi, a winemaker from Italy, together with W.A.C. Bennett and Pasquale "Cap" Capozzi, form a company called Domestic Wines and By-products, which would eventually become Calona Wines Limited.

Ontario government restricts the alcoholic strength of sherry and port to 20 percent by volume.

1937: Brights sends its winemaker Adhemar de Chaunac to France to learn about hybrids.

1946: De Chaunac returns to France to purchase hybrid cuttings to be planted at the Horticultural Research Institute at Vineland, Ontario.

1949: J.S. Hamilton's company is sold to the London Winery.

1955: Brights produces the first Chardonnay from cuttings brought back from France by de Chaunac.

1971: Baby Duck, the first pop sparkling wine, is introduced by Andrés.

1974: The first winery licence since Prohibition is issued to Inniskillin.

1979: Claremont, the first estate winery in British Columbia, opens its doors.

1988: Introduction of the Vintners Quality Alliance (VQA) in Ontario.

1990: British Columbia introduces VQA regulations.

1997: Canada's first wine school is founded at Brock University, Ontario.

1999: VQA becomes Canada's national appellation.

2000: Canada signs treaty with Germany and Austria setting international Icewine production standards.

Chapter 18

Ontario Wineries

- -

In This Chapter

▶ Understanding the great lake effect

▶ Exploring the Niagara Escarpment

▶ Finding the plain facts in Niagara-on-the-Lake

▶ Discovering that Toronto-area wineries are closer than you think

- -

*P*eople like to say that Canada's vineyards are on the same latitude as the vineyards in France and Italy. This statement implies that the climates are similar, and that similar wines can therefore be produced. But think about it: You just don't hear of anyone shovelling the driveway in Tuscany, and you can't make Icewine in Rioja.

The Canadian and Western European climates aren't really comparable. But, in the summer, there are some important similarities. The extra hours of daylight help to ripen the grapes. Also, average summer temperatures are about the same in Ontario's Niagara region as they are in Bordeaux and Burgundy.

This chapter and the two that follow describe each one of Canada's wine-making regions and give thumbnail sketches of the wineries. We hope this information inspires you to visit at least one of our country's wine-producing areas. In Appendix B, "Directory of Canadian Wineries," you'll find a comprehensive list of winery addresses, telephone numbers, and Web site addresses. To help whittle it down for you, at the end of this chapter and the chapter on British Columbia wineries (Chapter 19), we give you our top 10 wineries in each region worth a visit. A word of advice: It's always best to call ahead to find out when the wineries are open to the public. The larger ones may be open year-round, but their hours may change, depending on the season. The smaller wineries don't always have the staff to keep their hospitality areas open every day of the year, but they're usually open on weekends.

Between a Rock and a Wet Place

Figure 18-1 is a map of Ontario's wine-growing regions. Most of the vineyards in Ontario are close to either Lake Ontario or Lake Erie. This is critical because these huge bodies of water act like great heat sinks. All the warmth they soak up from the summer sun flows onto the shore during winter and helps keep the temperatures mild. It rarely gets too cold for vines planted close to the lakes. The water surface also reflects summer sunlight onto vineyards near the water.

Grapevines can't take extreme cold but they love it when it's cool. A long, cool growing season encourages the production of natural acids, which gives the wines body, elegance, and aging capability. In this sense, Ontario is as ideal as any northern European wine region for wine production.

The proximity to Lake Ontario and Lake Erie has a bit of a downside, though: unpredictable weather. One day can be glorious, the next damp, dismal, and punctuated by thundershowers — not all that different from many grape-

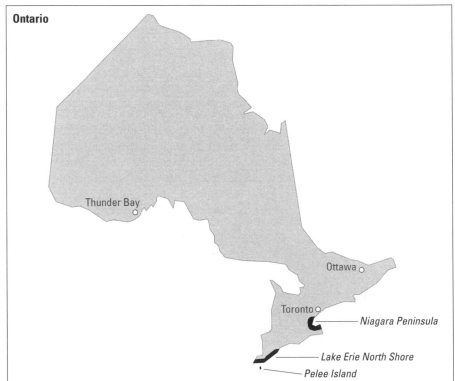

Figure 18-1:
Ontario
wine
regions.

Ontario

Thunder Bay

Ottawa

Toronto

Niagara Peninsula

Lake Erie North Shore

Pelee Island

The uncertainty of it all

In 1997 and 1998, southern Ontario was the driest it's been in many years and the wines were spectacular. The hot, sun-filled summer days caused the vineyards to dry out, resulting in highly concentrated flavours in the grapes. Winemakers extolled the quality of their wine. But the spring and summer of 2000 brought them back down to earth. It rained, rained, and rained again. The lake levels, which had dropped to record lows after two dry years, started to come back to normal; but in the vineyards, the vines put out excess green growth and workers struggled to cut them back to direct the plants' energy into the fruit. There wasn't much extolling done.

growing areas in France. Because the weather is so random, winemaking in Ontario is always a challenge. Sometimes, there just isn't enough sunshine.

Wine grapes grow along the northern edge of the Niagara Peninsula between the city of Hamilton, in the west, and Niagara Falls, in the east. The importance of geography is especially apparent in this region.

The Niagara Escarpment is a high ridge of land that stretches the length of the Niagara Peninsula. A number of vineyards have been planted between the Escarpment and the Lake Ontario shore. The air over the lake is always a different temperature than that over the land: cooler in the summer months, warmer in the winter. The air rises off the lake and draws the different-temperature air (cooler or warmer, depending) up behind it. It hits the Escarpment and is forced up and back out over the lake. This circulating motion of air creates a constant breeze during summer, which cools and dries the vineyards. In the winter and spring, when the grapevines start to grow, it keeps the air over the vineyards warm, preventing cold air from settling on the ground (which can cause frost damage). When you stand in an Escarpment vineyard, you can feel this wind on your face. The vine leaves tremble gently, in response.

The degree of the lake effect varies in different parts of the Peninsula, depending on how close the Escarpment (and the vineyards on it) is to the lakeshore.

The section of the Escarpment between Hamilton and St. Catharines is fairly close to the lake. Along the base of this part of the Escarpment is a moderately sloped piece of land called the Niagara Bench. The wineries clustered around the town of Beamsville like to refer to this land as the "Beamsville Bench," but they're just being possessive. It extends from Hamilton to St. Catharines, and is rightfully called the Niagara Bench.

The goût de terroir

The topic of soil enters into many discussions about wine. Winemakers believe that soil composition is a major influence on the flavour of their wine. Certainly, there is no doubt that well-drained soil is critical to a healthy vine, as it encourages deep rooting and a well-distributed root system adapted to reaching underground water when needed.

What is debatable is whether the minerals in different soils impart distinctive flavours. Experienced tasters will tell you that they do, but there are no scientific findings to back this up. However, winemakers are taking the idea seriously enough that the soil and the taste it imparts to the wine is being included in the development of many appellation systems. Often, scientists only serve to confirm what lay observers have said all along — but at this point you'll just have to wait and see.

Winemakers on the Niagara Bench, and in other areas of the Peninsula, talk about *terroir* — how

their wines reflect the characteristics of the soil in which the vines were grown. Cave Spring Vineyards, on the Beamsville Bench, plants vines at a density of 4,500 vines per hectare — twice the density at which most of the other vineyards plant. By doing this, they force the vines to compete for nutrients, driving the roots deeper and deeper into the soil. The closer they come to the bedrock, which is mostly limestone in that area, the more trace elements they absorb. The wine's flavour is more complex as a result.

But there are other elements in force as well. For example, Cave Spring pays special attention when pruning the vines in winter and removes fruit in the summer to reduce the yields (reduced yields mean more intense flavour). Cave Spring's location on the Bench, its mature vineyards, and other incidentals all contribute to the particular terroir reflected in its wine.

Niagara Bench Wineries

The effect of the airflow is most pronounced in this area. Because of the sloping land, the vineyards on the Niagara Bench experience refreshing breezes during the summer and enough air movement in the winter to stop cold air from settling on the ground as frost. These cool summer conditions result in a slow, steady maturation that results in wine of finesse and elegance. Many grapes produce outstanding results here: particularly Riesling, Chardonnay, and Cabernet Franc.

13th Street Wine Company

Thirteenth Street is a collaborative partnership of dedicated amateur-turned-professionals and top-rated growers. Officially opened in November 1999, the group operates out of small premises on the Jordan plain in the lee of the Niagara Escarpment. Owned by grower Gunther Funk, this locale houses Funk Wine Supplies, the winery, and a recently refurbished tasting room. The Funk vineyard supplies Pinot Noir, Riesling, and Gewürztraminer. Working with Gunther as winemaking collaborator is Herb Jacobson, a mechanical technologist with a large steel company. A second vineyard, located in Niagara-on-the-Lake and owned by Erwin Willms, is recognized for its rich Gamay fruit and some Chardonnay. Lawyer Ken Douglas supplies the winemaking talent. Consultant winemaker Deborah Paskus is another partner who specializes in Chardonnay and buys fruit from selected Niagara Bench vineyards. All members of the group have the same philosophy — to make ultra-premium wines in small quantities with a maximum production of approximately 10,000 litres.

Andrés Wines Ltd.

Andrés has a large bottling facility that you can visit in the town of Grimsby, just east of Hamilton. Here they bottle both VQA wines as well as blended table wines. They have no vines growing at this location but you can see vineyards at their affiliate wineries, Hillebrand and Peller Estates in Niagara-on-the-Lake.

Birchwood Estates Wines

Birchwood Estates, despite its small size, is one of the easiest wineries in Niagara to find — it is just off the Queen Elizabeth Way in Beamsville. Birchwood is the new name for Vine Court Winery, formerly owned by grape grower Joseph Zimmermann and partners. For a while, Ron Speranzini leased the property for his Willow Heights, which is now located up higher on the Bench.

The new owners, as of March 2000, are a mother and son team, Elizabeth and Andrew Green. Andrew is an agent for imported wines and spirits in Toronto and Elizabeth, whose family is originally from Niagara, brings retail experience to the operation. Joseph Zimmermann is winemaking consultant and also a major supplier of fruit, specifically Chardonnay, Gewürztraminer, and Cabernet Franc, for the new enterprise. He aims for lighter-style, fruit-driven wines.

The Birchwood home vineyards comprise three acres of Riesling and 5.5 acres of Seyval Blanc, soon to be replanted to Riesling and Cabernet Franc. Andrew plans to add a small amount of other fruit types to the production lineup. He released some cherry wine from stock already at the winery when he and his mother purchased it.

Cave Spring Cellars

A beautiful, grey stone building that dates to 1870 and houses the winery is the focal point of Main Street, Jordan, one of Niagara's most appealing attractions for visitors. You can stroll along a flower-lined stone walkway and window shop or drop into the intriguing boutiques adjacent to the winery. You could even have a meal at On the Twenty, one of the top restaurants on the Peninsula. Across the street is the On the Twenty Inn (formerly called The Vintner's Inn), a top-notch wine country hotel with fireplaces in every room.

Cave Spring was one of the first wineries on the Niagara Bench to take the plunge and plant vinifera vines. Their original six acres of Riesling and Chardonnay planted in 1978 are now some of the most mature in the area and reserved for use in their ultra-premium labels identified by the initials CSV, standing for Cave Spring Vineyard.

The winery has since accumulated over 100 acres of vineyards that include a variety of both red and white grapes, although almost half of Cave Spring's production is Riesling.

Cave Spring's Riesling Icewine is probably the most elegantly styled of any produced in the area. Under the direction of owner Len Pennachetti and winemaker/partner Angelo Pavan, Cave Spring has set many of the standards to which more recent arrivals on the scene aspire.

Angelo received the Winemaker of the Year Award in 1999 at the Air Ontario Wine Awards.

- Cave Spring Cellars Cabernet/Merlot
- Cave Spring Cellars Chardonnay Reserve
- Cave Spring Cellars CSV Chardonnay
- Cave Spring Cellars Estate Bottled Gewürztraminer
- Cave Spring Cellars Estate Bottled Reserve Riesling
- Cave Spring Cellars Off-Dry Riesling
- Cave Spring Cellars Riesling Icewine

Creekside Estate Winery

Creekside is the Ontario arm of Peter Jensen and Laura McCain Jensen's winery business, the Nova Scotia arm being Habitant Vineyards. Before taking the giant step into boutique winery ownership, Peter was involved in the business of designing and building wineries for bulk production. Now, he gets literally blown away by his own wines — he was standing in front of a grape crusher full of Pinot Noir one day when it blocked up, then suddenly unblocked itself releasing a powerful jet of purple pulp straight at him.

The Jensens bought the small property formerly owned by VP Cellars in Jordan Station on the Niagara Bench in 1998 and then purchased a 50-acre plot of land in Niagara-on-the-Lake. Starting out with a production of 5,000 cases at Creekside, they produced 20,000 in 1999. At the same time they decided to enlarge the winery to 30,000 square feet and to increase the hospitality area. The emphasis at Creekside is on white wine while the Niagara-on-the-Lake property, called Paragon, will specialize in premium red Bordeaux varieties beginning in 2001 — although about 500 cases of very promising wine was initially vinified at the Creekside location. The Jensens intend to limit the Paragon production to about 5,000 cases.

Since the crush in 1999, wine production is under the control of Marcus Ansems, a talented, young Australian winemaker. Despite his youth (he is 25), Marcus already has 10 years' experience. Starting at an uncle's winery in Australia, Marcus went on to work at other Australian wineries as well as in Italy and South Africa. Contrary to what most people expect from an Australian-trained winemaker, Marcus's wines show a light, elegant character. He leans away from the intense, big-fruit style of wine, concentrating on true varietal expression and superb balance.

Besides his responsibilities at Creekside and Paragon, Marcus also oversees the winemaking at the Jensens' Nova Scotia location.

- ✔ Creekside Laura (a Bordeaux blend)
- ✔ Creekside Pinot Noir
- ✔ Creekside Sauvignon Blanc
- ✔ Paragon Chardonnay

Crown Bench Estates

Peter Kocsis grew up on the land. He left it briefly to put his master's degree in international law to good use in Ottawa, but his heart was always on the Beamsville Bench. Peter's father, who had been deputy minister of agriculture in Hungary before immigrating to Canada, had taught him to recognize the inherent quality of the Bench fruit. He purchased his own 15-acre vineyard in the mid-1970s, planting mostly Chardonnay. These vines have become well known as the source of the premium Kocsis Vineyard Chardonnay, which is produced by the Thirty Bench winery and vinified by Deborah Paskus, who is now also consulting winemaker for Crown Bench. An additional eight acres of vines have recently been planted and Peter's current varietal mix includes Vidal, the Bordeaux red varietals, and Pinot Noir. He would also like to try something a bit off the wall and is thinking about planting some Furmint vines from Hungary.

Daniel Lenko Estate Winery

This is a new winery, but it's one to watch. Daniel Lenko's father was planting vinifera varieties as early as 1959 and today, the Lenko vineyard boasts the oldest Chardonnay vines in Ontario with an average age of 25 years. In recent years, the grapes have been in great demand by Niagara winemakers. They form the basis of some impressive Chardonnay wines at several highly reputed wineries in the region. Although Daniel will now make his own wine with the help of Jim Warren, founder of Stoney Ridge winery, who has branched out into consulting, he will continue to sell some of the grapes to wineries with whom he has long-standing contracts.

Over the years, the maintenance of the vineyard has been a family affair and the conversion to winery has been no different. Even his father, although officially retired, is enthusiastically involved. Daniel speaks with pride as he describes how they constructed the winery buildings themselves, refurbished equipment, and converted steel tanks for winemaking. He named the winery the Daniel Lenko Estate Winery to reflect the importance of family and its traditions. He will concentrate on Chardonnay and red varietals, primarily Pinot Noir, Cabernet Franc, Cabernet Sauvignon, and Merlot.

Jim Warren has a reputation, not only for excellence in winemaking, but also for variety, and he brought that tendency to this new enterprise. In their first year of production, Jim and Daniel made 15 different products for a total of only 4,500 cases. As an example, they made three versions of Chardonnay — one is unoaked, one went into French oak, and the other into American oak. They also made a wine from the Viognier grape, which is the signature white grape of the Northern Rhône. Very little of it is grown in Ontario but plantings are increasing and the wines show great promise. In red wine, Jim and Daniel made some blends and some single varietal wines showing, once more, that a few basic varietals can result in a diverse range of wine. Initial tastings of these wines have people talking. They won six gold medals in their first year of production at the 2000 All-Canadian Wine Championships.

- Daniel Lenko Estate Winery Cabernet Franc
- Daniel Lenko Estate Winery Cabernet Rosé
- Daniel Lenko Estate Winery Dry Riesling
- Daniel Lenko Estate Winery Select Late Harvest Vidal
- Daniel Lenko Estate Winery Vidal Blanc
- Daniel Lenko Estate Winery Viognier

EastDell's Bench Bistro

EastDell's rustic setting and magnificent view is an added draw for visiting wine lovers. The aim of Susan O'Dell, one of the owners, is to develop a winery destination to attract people not only for the wine, but also for an opportunity to enjoy the country setting with woods, a pond, and hiking trails.

For "foodies," the Bench Bistro restaurant rounds out the attractions. Surrounded on three sides by picture windows, the restaurant overlooks the gently sloping EastDell vineyards, while in the kitchen, chef Norman Riel turns out a menu featuring regional cuisine with ethnic flair.

EastDell Estates

EastDell is a small winery that grew out of an amateur winemaker's passion and growing talents. Michael East teamed up with partner Susan O'Dell to buy a 15-acre vineyard on the Beamsville Bench in 1996. For three years they sold their grapes to local wineries until they bought a small, existing winery next door to their home. Their recently appointed winemaker is Tatjana Cuk, from Yugoslavia, who worked with Stoney Ridge's Jim Warren, one of Niagara's leading talents. Tatjana, whose roots are in war-torn Bosnia, came to Canada with her husband, who is trained in animal husbandry, and her two young children.

Carving out a new life for herself and her family, Tatjana has the inner track to put EastDell on the map. Her first vintage was 1999 in which she tried her hand at a Baco Noir Nouveau in the style of Beaujolais Nouveau, using the technique of carbonic maceration to create a fresh, light-bodied red. Her philosophy is to work in small batches and create wine that is crisp, clean, and truly representative of the grape type. In 2000, the winery produced about 6,000 cases with plans to increase the volume to 10,000 cases.

Harbour Estates Winery Limited

Harbour Estates Winery takes its name from the small harbour at Jordan Station on the shore of Lake Ontario. This eye-catching 30-acre estate is one of the newest to be licenced in Ontario. The first harvest was crushed at nearby Vineland Estate Winery under the watchful eye of winemaker Brian Schmidt. The planned new facility will include winery and barrel cellar with an elaborate hospitality area complete with two-storey waterfall, restaurant, scenic patio, wine bar, and nature trails along the waterfront. Owner Fraser Mowat, currently a credit advisor with the Farm Credit Corporation, will concentrate on premium red wines from Bordeaux varietals.

Henry of Pelham Family Estate Winery

Owners of Henry of Pelham, the Speck family are direct descendants of the original owner, Nicolas Smith, who received a grant of Crown land as a United Empire Loyalist. This adventurous young patriot was a 15-year-old bugle boy in Butler's Rangers during the American Revolutionary War. He went on to have 14 children. One of them, Henry, built an inn and tollgate on the property and became known as Henry of Pelham after Pelham Road, which followed the path of an old Iroquois trail.

Present generation Paul, Matthew, and Daniel Speck took over management of the winery on the premature death of their father from cancer. Paul Sr. had planted vinifera grapes in the early 1980s when most people still thought that only indigenous grapes and hybrids could survive. Along with such leaders in the industry as Donald Ziraldo and Karl Kaiser, he proved his point and transformed his passion into one of the country's top producers of premium VQA wines. His vision continues under the youthful direction of his sons and talented winemaker Ron Giesbrecht. A medium-size winery in terms of production, it concentrates on Chardonnay, Riesling, Cabernet Sauvignon, Baco Noir, and Riesling Icewine. They have a proven talent for bringing out the best in the hybrid Baco Noir.

- ✔ Henry of Pelham Family Estate Winery Barrel Fermented Chardonnay
- ✔ Henry of Pelham Family Estate Winery Cabernet/Merlot
- ✔ Henry of Pelham Family Estate Winery Reserve Baco Noir
- ✔ Henry of Pelham Family Estate Winery Reserve Chardonnay
- ✔ Henry of Pelham Family Estate Winery Reserve Riesling

Hernder Estates Winery

For several generations, the members of the Hernder family have been respected grape growers and juice producers. Fred Hernder had long thought that a historical cattle barn located on the Niagara Bench would be the perfect location for processing juice. When it finally came on the market, he snapped it up and started renovating the huge structure, although he was careful not to sacrifice the integrity of the Victorian style. Before long, tourists, thinking the picturesque building had to be a winery, started stopping in. This was when Fred took the only logical next step. In 1991, he hired Ray Cornell, formerly with Stoney Ridge, as part-time winemaker. Later, as production grew, Ray took on full-time responsibilities. Hernder produces a variety of wines, led by an ultra-crisp Riesling and some age-worthy Cabernet Sauvignon. They also produce a couple of fruit wines.

✔ Hernder Estate Wines Barrel Fermented Chardonnay

✔ Hernder Estate Wines Cabernet Franc

✔ Hernder Estate Wines Icewine

✔ Hernder Estate Wines Riesling

✔ Hernder Estate Wines Select Late Harvest Vidal

Kittling Ridge Estate Wines & Spirits

Founded in 1971 as a distillery by Swiss stillmaster Otto Rieder, Kittling Ridge is now one of the few winery/distillery combinations in Ontario. They branched out into winemaking in 1993 and only two years later became the sixth largest winery in the province. Under the ownership of winemaker John K. Hall, Kittling Ridge purchases grapes from growers both on the Bench and Niagara-on-the-Lake for processing at their Grimsby location. With about 10 percent of their production VQA, the majority of their business is blended wine for which they buy grapes from France, Italy, Chile, and California. Their full range is available from their own retail wine shops throughout the province.

✔ Kittling Ridge Estate Wines Maréchal Foch

Lakeview Cellars Estate Winery

In 1991, having grown grapes for many years and making wine as a hobby, Eddy Gurinskas and his wife, Lorraine, decided to open their own winery. In 1996 and 1997 respectively, they were joined by neighbouring grape growers Larry and Debbie Hipple and Stu and Ginnie Morgan. They have enlarged their shop and added space for tasting but remain, by choice, one of the smallest wineries in the area. The excellent drainage and clay/loam soil in the vineyard adjacent to the winery contributes to the intensity of Eddy's remarkable Cabernet Sauvignon.

Kittling Ridge Winery Inn

In the spring of 2000, Kittling Ridge opened the 79-room Kittling Ridge Winery Inn and Suites. The inn boasts three restaurants: Vintages, a fine dining room; Forty Creek Grill, for more casual fare; and Distillations, a rooftop bar with panoramic views of Lake Ontario on one side (with Toronto in the distance, if the weather is clear) and the Niagara Escarpment on the other.

- ✔ Lakeview Cellars Estate Winery Baco Noir
- ✔ Lakeview Cellars Estate Winery Cabernet/Merlot
- ✔ Lakeview Cellars Estate Winery Chardonnay Musqué
- ✔ Lakeview Cellars Estate Winery Vidal Icewine
- ✔ Lakeview Cellars Estate Winery Vinc Vineyard Reserve Chardonnay

Malivoire Wine Company

As winery architecture goes, Malivoire tends towards the functional. Two attached Quonset huts cling to the side of a slope. But Martin Malivoire is a motion picture special effects producer and his creativity shines through this deceptively simple architectural concept. In the first place, when you drive up to the winery, you have no sense of the plain, utilitarian building behind. The entranceway is brilliantly contrived with natural stone pillars and rock gardens that blend into the hillside.

The building itself is constructed to take advantage of a 30-foot drop in the hillside that allows Martin to operate the winery on a gravity feed system. The winery's procedures are carried out on seven levels so that the wine can be made without any need for pumping, a harsh procedure that Martin believes reduces quality. His philosophy is to preserve everything that nature contributes to the wine with as little human interference as possible.

The same philosophy governs vineyard activities. Insecticides and herbicides are avoided. Wooden posts support the trellises. Martin feels that the metal stakes, more commonly used because they facilitate mechanical harvesting, may have a negative effect on the microclimate of each vine. This means the grapes must be picked by hand, but that is all part of the plan as it allows more control over the quality of the grapes. As soon as they are picked, the grapes are carried to the winery so there is no chance of deterioration.

The winery concentrates on premium labels under managing winemaker Ann Sperling's watchful eye. Her wines are complex yet delicate enough to make you believe that all the TLC must work.

- ✔ Malivoire Winery Chardonnay
- ✔ Malivoire Winery Dry Late Harvest Gewürztraminer
- ✔ Malivoire Winery Gewürztraminer Icewine
- ✔ Malivoire Winery Ladybug Rosé
- ✔ Malivoire Winery Old Vines Foch

Techno corks

The Malivoire Wine Company uses synthetic corks in the hopes of eliminating any risk of the cork tainting the wine — a good idea, considering that current studies done by the cork industry suggest that one bottle in 12 may be "corked." The Malivoire corks are made from high-grade thermoplastic elastomer that meets all food safety standards in Canada and the U.S. This material is also used to make replacement heart valves. This plastic cork behaves almost the same as natural cork and isn't subject to the same taints and irregularities.

Peninsula Ridge Estates Winery

Norman Beal left the Niagara of his childhood to pursue a career in oil, a vocation that took him first to Alberta and then to the United States. The Ontario wine industry he had left behind was hardly worth remembering, and for many years he dreamed of buying a vineyard in Napa, California. His sister, Theresa MacNeil, a vineyardist, tried for the longest time to get him to come back to Niagara just to see how it had developed. Finally, discouraged by the prices in Napa, he did go to visit his sister and was astounded to discover "an unknown jewel." He was impressed not only by the wines, but also by the obvious quality of life the area offered. He bought a property on the Bench to concentrate on premium red wine.

To achieve the highest level of quality, yields are reduced to under three tonnes an acre and 90 percent of the wine is aged in oak. Theresa is now vineyard manager and Norman has hired a very high-profile winemaker, Jean-Pierre Colas, who was formerly with a well-known Chablis *négociant* company in Burgundy.

Royal deMaria Wines Co. Ltd.

Joseph deMaria supports his fledgling winery by pursuing his career as a hairstylist in Toronto three days a week. He likes both aspects of his life and appreciates being able to leave one behind as he concentrates on the other. For about three years, pending construction of a retail storefront, he exported his wine to the U.S. He now makes small quantities of various varietals for local distribution, increasing in volume each year. Joseph has a passion for Icewine and bills his winery as the "Icewine Specialist." He has made Icewine from as many as seven grape varieties including a red Cabernet Franc.

Stoney Ridge Cellars Ltd.

In 1998, the Cuesta Corporation, a group of investors from Ottawa, bought Stoney Ridge from founder Jim Warren and partner Murray Puddicombe.

Irrefutably one of the best winemakers in the region, Jim, a former Air Ontario Winemaker of the Year, started his commercial wine career with 500 cases produced in a small tin shed from purchased grapes. In 15 years the business grew a thousand-fold. Jim loves variety and produced some 51 different wines, including a line of fruit wines. He turned a vibrant winery over to Cuesta, who increased the vineyard holdings with a 73-acre property that was planted in 1999. It will dedicate this vineyard exclusively to premium wines and plans to build a large, new winery to house production.

- ✔ Stoney Ridge Cellars Barrel Fermented Gewürztraminer Icewine
- ✔ Stoney Ridge Cellars Bench Riesling
- ✔ Stoney Ridge Cellars Butler's Grant Vineyard Reserve Pinot Noir
- ✔ Stoney Ridge Cellars Cuesta Old Vines Chardonnay
- ✔ Stoney Ridge Cellars Full Oak Chardonnay
- ✔ Stoney Ridge Cellars Lenko Vineyard Old Vines Chardonnay
- ✔ Stoney Ridge Cellars Reserve Chardonnay
- ✔ Stoney Ridge Cellars Riesling Reserve
- ✔ Stoney Ridge Cellars Wismer Vineyard Cabernet Franc

Thirty Bench Vineyard & Winery

Four partners operate this tiny winery that boasts "the driest vineyard on the (Beamsville) Bench." Tom Muckle, a physician specializing in pain management, is CEO. Other partners are Yorgos Papageorgiou, Frank Zeritsch, and Deborah Paskus. Riesling is the cornerstone grape at this winery. It's made into a variety of Icewine styles ranging from dry to sweet. Rounding out the portfolio in steadily increasing quantities are Vidal, Chardonnay, and a range of red vinifera.

Wine in the legislature

Stoney Ridge became the official supplier of the Ontario legislature's red and white wine for the year 2000. It's the first time in 30 years that the same winery was chosen to provide both white and red. The wines are selected from about 50 submissions. The tasting panel includes the premier, cabinet ministers, members of provincial parliament and Queen's Park staff.

What's in a number?

With 13th Street Wine Company, it's obvious — it's located on 13th Street in Jordan. But what about Thirty Bench, On the Twenty Restaurant, or Forty Creek Grill? Until you've visited the Niagara Bench region, the use of numbers in names seems quite obtuse; but believe it or not, there is a logic behind it. Thirty Bench is situated near Thirty Road and is located on the Niagara Bench. On the Twenty Restaurant, in the town of Jordan — and one of the best places to eat in the region — overlooks Twenty Mile Creek. Forty Creek Grill is part of the Kittling Ridge Inn, which is itself located — where else? — at the mouth of Forty Mile Creek! Does it make more sense now?

The winery's philosophy is to reduce yields for concentrated flavours and to age the wine in barrels as long as possible.

- ✔ Thirty Bench Winery Reserve Cabernet Sauvignon
- ✔ Thirty Bench Winery Reserve Chardonnay

Thomas & Vaughan Vintners

Following the lead of many of his contemporaries, Thomas Kocsis transformed an established family vineyard into a winery. With 20 years' growing experience, he has done much in the past to improve the quality of his fruit. Situated in a prime location on the Niagara Escarpment, between the towns of Beamsville and Vineland, the property has all the qualities that Thomas and partner Barbara Vaughan need to produce premium wine. Like some of the other newly established small wineries, theirs will concentrate on red grape types.

Vineland Estates Wines Ltd.

John Howard purchased Vineland Estates in 1992 from German horticulturist Herman Weis, who returned to Germany to concentrate on his nursery business. Herman left a legacy in the form of a Riesling vineyard that is the cornerstone of Vineland Estates' production. He had chosen a location on the Niagara Bench where the terroir and soil particularly suits the cultivation of this noble grape.

Industry leader: John Howard

Owner of Vineland Estates Winery on the Niagara Bench, John Howard grew up in Montréal and completed a Bachelor of Arts degree at the University of Western Ontario. After a brief stint in construction, he worked for O.E. Canon Canada, where he became a vice-president and member of the board of directors.

John's is a story of corporate success coupled with love of the land. The Niagara Peninsula and its wine are his passions. In 1992, he purchased Vineland Estates Winery. John developed the land and enlarged the winery building, opening a restaurant with a magnificent view of Lake Ontario, and incorporating a tastefully decorated retail boutique and banquet hall in a historical farm homestead. All the new construction is in keeping with the turn-of-the-century stone building. As large as it is, the winery complex fits snugly and unobtrusively into the hillside.

John has plans for a new winery and a state-of-the-art gourmet centre. He was also on the frontlines in the planning and financing of the Cool Climate Oenology and Viticulture Institute (CCOVI) at Brock University.

Since he has owned the property, John has overseen an expansion and created a winery that is one of the most stylish in the region while still retaining all the charm of the century-old farmhouse that now houses the retail shop. Overlooking Lake Ontario, with Toronto in the distance, Vineland Estates boasts the most picturesque location and rounds out its attractions with a superb restaurant and tiny bed and breakfast cottage.

Brian Schmidt succeeded his brother Allan, who is now Vineland's general manager, as winemaker. About 80 percent of the grapes used are estate grown on about 300 acres of vineyard land. Besides Riesling, they grow and produce excellent examples of Chardonnay, Vidal, Sauvignon Blanc, Cabernet Sauvignon, Cabernet Franc, Merlot, and Pinot Noir.

- Vineland Estates Gewürztraminer
- Vineland Estates Reserve Riesling
- Vineland Estates Riesling Icewine
- Vineland Estates Semi-Dry Riesling
- Vineland Estates Seyval Blanc

Willow Heights Estate Winery

Ron Speranzini, a confirmed Pinot Noir addict, is another graduate of the school of amateur winemaking. He and his wife, Avis, opened a small winery in a rented property just off the main highway. In 1998 they purchased a larger property on the Niagara Bench in Vineland. A recently planted vineyard of Pinot Noir is just coming on stream and Ron rounds out his repertoire with Chardonnay, Auxerrois, Gewürztraminer, Riesling, Vidal, and Gamay. The new winery, built in the California mission style, features a stunning interior decor and a charming patio where visitors can sip their wine.

- ✔ Willow Heights Chardonnay Reserve
- ✔ Willow Heights Gamay Noir
- ✔ Willow Heights Pinot Noir

Mainly on the Plain

There's a broad plain that stretches east from St. Catharines to the Niagara River that feeds Niagara Falls. Most of the wineries here are spread around the central section, in Niagara-on-the-Lake. In this part of the Niagara Peninsula, the Niagara Escarpment is set well back from Lake Ontario, so the air movement is less pronounced than on the Niagara Bench. The plain warms up quickly in spring and summer, which gives the vineyards a slightly earlier growing start, with plenty of time to bask in the hot summer sun. On the downside, there are some areas that fall victim to spring frost, as the lake effect airflow is not strong enough to move the cold air away.

The grapes in this area are capable of rich, concentrated flavors thanks to the summer heat and their early start in the spring. Because of the variation in climate conditions, stylistic differences have been noted in the wines of the Niagara Bench and Niagara-on-the-Lake and its surrounding grape-growing areas. Researchers at the Cool Climate Oenological and Viticultural Institute (CCOVI) at Brock University are evaluating these characteristics by means of analytical tastings. They hope to identify a set of reliable criteria on which to form the basis of an official regional appellation. At the present time, the only VQA designation for this region is "Niagara Peninsula." The ultimate goal is to develop more specific appellation areas, starting with Niagara Bench and Niagara-on-the-Lake, and eventually getting down to the names of specific vineyards, similar to the French appellation system.

Niagara-on-the-Lake Wineries

Niagara-on-the-Lake is home to Inniskillin Winery, founded in 1974, and Château des Charmes, founded in 1978, among many others, as you'll see. These two wineries were pioneers in Niagara-on-the-Lake, proving that vinifera grapes could grow in Niagara and that world-class wine could be made from them.

Château des Charmes Wines Ltd.

In 1978, Paul Bosc was one of the first to plant vinifera vines in Ontario. Having studied the Niagara Peninsula for 15 years and worked for a time at Château-Gai, one of the largest wine producers in the 1970s, Paul was convinced that the area could produce excellent wine. Since then he has been committed to developing top-notch vineyard sites and to producing wine that has helped guide the Canadian wine industry on the path of quality.

With family origins in Alsace and training at the University of Burgundy at Dijon, Paul knew that vinifera grapes were necessary to make the best wine. He ignored anyone who said those vines would not survive the winter and was instrumental in convincing other growers that vinifera was the wave of Ontario's future.

Industry leader: Paul Michel Bosc

Paul Bosc represents the fifth generation of a winemaking family that immigrated to Algeria from France in the 1840s. Bosc was the first member of his family to return to France (in 1954) to study formally the art of winemaking, obtaining a diploma at the University of Burgundy, in Dijon. When he returned to French Algeria a year later, he became general manager of the Société Civile de Vinification, one of the country's largest cooperatives (a large crushing and fermenting facility where growers can have their grapes made into wine).

Paul immigrated to Canada in 1963, and found work at Château-Gai Wines in Niagara Falls as winemaker. He would enjoy a fruitful 15-year career there. At that time, Labrusca grapes, notably the Concord, formed the basis of most Canadian wines, and Bosc couldn't help but feel that the industry had to make the move to better grapes. He began to experiment with classic vinifera varieties, and by the early 1970s, earned a reputation for producing fine wine.

In 1978, Bosc, in partnership with lawyer Rodger Gordon, founded Château des Charmes in Niagara-on-the-Lake and planted Canada's first vineyard dedicated exclusively to vinifera grapes.

Over the years, Bosc has continued to experiment with techniques to improve the quality of wine. He has affiliated himself and Château des Charmes with the National Research Council (NRC) to test such techniques as carbonic maceration, clonal selection, reverse osmosis, and canopy management. He is currently involved with the University of Guelph and the NRC to examine transgenic grapevines. These "supervines" contain a gene from a wild broccoli plant that should provide them with extra protection against the cold. Since planting the vines in 1997, a series of mild winters unfortunately have failed to provide the right conditions to test this hypothesis.

Bosc has won over 200 awards in national and international wine competitions, including the first-ever gold medals for Canadian red and white table wines (as opposed to fortified wines) at Vinexpo, in Bordeaux. He was also awarded an honorary doctorate from Brock University in 1996, for "impressive contributions to Canada's modern grape industry," and was appointed to the Order of Ontario in 1999.

Giving frost the chop

Although the Château des Charmes vineyard (the largest winery-owned vineyard in the region) benefits from 190 frost-free days in a good year, frost is always a threat at certain intervals. The vineyard has, on occasion, hired a helicopter — at a mere $3,000 an hour — to hover over the ground and create enough wind to prevent frost from settling on the vines.

Paul's wife, Andrée, is very involved in the winery, as are his sons, Paul Jr. and Pierre-Jean, who followed in his father's footsteps and studied in Dijon. The Burgundian training comes through in Château des Charmes' style. They also have a special touch when it comes to making Champagne-method sparkling wine.

As much as tradition rules in the production of their wine, the Boscs have embraced technological advances. They are testing the first "supervine," a vine that has been genetically altered to withstand cold.

- ✔ Château des Charmes Aligoté
- ✔ Château des Charmes Auxerrois
- ✔ Château des Charmes Late Harvest Riesling
- ✔ Château des Charmes Paul Bosc Riesling Icewine
- ✔ Château des Charmes Sec Méthode Traditionelle
- ✔ Château des Charmes St. David's Bench Vineyard Cabernet Franc
- ✔ Château des Charmes St. David's Bench Vineyard Chardonnay
- ✔ Château des Charmes Viognier

Domaine Vagners

Five acres is the sum total of Martin Vagners' holdings and from that he makes only about 1,000 cases. This labour of love will be increased gradually but only as the vines mature. When he started his tiny operation, Martin's driving ambition was to make good red wine. His emphasis is on Merlot with smaller amounts of Cabernet Franc and Cabernet Sauvignon. He grows some whites but, contrary to current trends, he avoids Chardonnay. In time, he aims to make champagne-method sparklers.

- ✔ Domaine Vagners Creek Road Red
- ✔ Domaine Vagners Merlot

Hillebrand Estates Winery

Before there was Hillebrand, there was a tiny vineyard and winery called Newark, founded in 1979 by Joseph Pohorly. Joseph sold the property to a Swiss company, Underberg, who renamed it Hillebrand Estates. Underberg provided the capital and marketing savvy to turn Hillebrand into the prestigious estate it is today. They then sold it to Andrés Wines, so the ownership is once more 100-percent Canadian.

Hillebrand draws on its own vineyards and those of contracted growers for a full range of products, from everyday wines to top of the line premium whites and reds. Winemaking activities are under the direction of its French winemaker J.L. Groux (a former Air Ontario Winemaker of the Year) and labels include varietals such as Chardonnay, Riesling, Cabernet Sauvignon, and Cabernet Franc and Gamay. Their Trius Red is a premium blend of Bordeaux grapes and the Trius line includes Riesling Dry, Chardonnay (Niagara-on-the-Lake), Chardonnay (Lakeshore), Brut Sparkling Wine, and Icewine. Hillebrand has a beautiful facility with a first-class restaurant, the Vineyard Café, and a charming deck overlooking the vineyards. Every hour, on the hour, they conduct tours, which provide an excellent overview for the first-time visitor.

Industry leader: Donald Ziraldo

Co-founder and president of Inniskillin Wines, Donald Ziraldo, a native of St. Catharines, Ontario, knew from a young age that he wanted to produce world-class wines from grapes grown in the Niagara Peninsula.

After obtaining a degree in agriculture from the University of Guelph, in 1972, Ziraldo took an active role in managing his family's nursery that specialized in fruit trees and grapevines. He became friends with Karl Kaiser, an Austrian newly arrived in Canada, who had some wine-making experience. The more they talked, the more they realized they shared the same dream. They applied for and received a winery licence in 1974, and Inniskillin Wines was born. Ziraldo was only 27 at the time. Ziraldo transformed Inniskillin Wines from a rudimentary winemaking facility in a disused packing shed into a landmark winery in Niagara-on-the-Lake.

Ziraldo has always left the winemaking to Kaiser, devoting himself to sales and marketing, first of his wine, and more recently of the entire Niagara region. Energetic and outspoken, he founded the Vintners Quality Alliance (VQA), and was a driving force in developing the Cool Climate Oenology and Viticulture Institute (CCOVI) at Brock University, as well as the creation of the Niagara wine route. His success as an innovator and entrepreneur in the Canadian wine industry has earned Ziraldo many honours over the years. He was appointed to the Order of Ontario in 1993, and, in 1998, to the Order of Canada.

> ✔ Hillebrand Estates Winery Glenlake Showcase Unfiltered Cabernet
>
> ✔ Hillebrand Estates Winery Harvest Riesling
>
> ✔ Hillebrand Estates Winery Muscat
>
> ✔ Hillebrand Estates Winery Trius Chardonnay

Inniskillin Wines Inc.

Donald Ziraldo and Karl Kaiser of Inniskillin Wines started it all. Donald, as a young vineyardist, and Karl, as his winemaking partner, saw the potential for vinifera grapes in the Niagara region and approached the Liquor Control Board of Ontario in 1974 with the request for a licence to operate a cottage winery. As no new winery licences had been granted since 1930, their endeavours initially met with some resistance. But in the end, reason prevailed and Inniskillin was born. The then-tiny winery went out to prove its worth among the giant companies who were flooding the wine market with such concoctions as Baby Duck and Gimli Goose.

Year after year, Karl Kaiser turns out increasingly successful renditions of Chardonnay, Pinot Noir, Cabernet Sauvignon, and Vidal Icewine. A seemingly inexhaustible Donald Ziraldo spearheaded the Vintners Quality Alliance, Canada's appellation system, lobbied the Ontario government to create a "wine route" through the Peninsula, and provided the impetus to establish the Cool Climate Oenology and Viticulture Institute at Brock University. Through all this, he strives to bring the Canadian wine industry to the attention of the outside world. A great step forward was taken when Inniskillin's Vidal Icewine 1989 took a gold award in 1991 at the world's largest wine show, Vinexpo, held in Bordeaux.

In 1992, Inniskillin merged with Cartier Wines, which was almost immediately bought by Brights, making it Canada's largest wine company. It was then renamed Vincor International. Although Inniskillin operates independently, it benefits from the financial clout of the parent company, which made it easier to set up an operation out west in British Columbia — Inniskillin Okanagan.

Inniskillin is on track to increase its vineyard acreage and build a wine education centre that will focus on the culinary arts. At present, the winery retains the services of a resident chef to prepare representative regional cuisine matched to Inniskillin wines for special events and demonstrations.

Industry leader: Karl Kaiser

Co-founder and winemaker at Inniskillin Wines, Karl Kaiser was born and raised in Austria. He attended a private monastery school, where he was exposed to the time-honoured traditions of viticulture and winemaking.

Kaiser came to Canada and did an honours degree in chemistry and biochemistry at Brock University. He rounded out his education by visiting international wine regions and attending lectures and symposia.

He first met his partner and co-founder of Inniskillin, Donald Ziraldo, at Ziraldo's family's nursery. They entered into partnership in 1974.

Kaiser's dedication and craftsmanship have made Inniskillin the leader in the evolution of quality wine in Canada. In 1991, Inniskillin's 1989 Icewine received Vinexpo's highest accolade, the Grand Prix d'Honneur.

Kaiser is a professional member of the Canadian Society of Oenology and Viticulture, and is also a committee member of the Canadian General Standards Board for wine standards. In 1995, his fellow Canadian winemakers elected Kaiser "Winemaker of the Year."

- ✔ Inniskillin Cabernet Franc
- ✔ Inniskillin Culp Vineyard Chardonnay
- ✔ Inniskillin Pinot Noir Reserve
- ✔ Inniskillin Reserve Chardonnay
- ✔ Inniskillin Riesling Icewine
- ✔ Inniskillin Sparkling Vidal Icewine
- ✔ Inniskillin Vidal Icewine
- ✔ Inniskillin Viognier

Jackson-Triggs Estate Winery

The Jackson-Triggs label was created by Vincor CEO Don Triggs and winemaker Allan Jackson to adorn the bottles of moderately priced wine blended from both imported and Canadian grapes. The market embraced the price/quality ratio and these products became the first Canadian-produced varietally named wines that were generally available in all provinces. As acreage increased in Ontario and British Columbia, the Jackson-Triggs label changed to the all-Canadian VQA designation and plans are to move it steadily up-market.

Until recently, Jackson-Triggs wines did not have their own dedicated winery but were produced at Vincor's large facilities in Niagara Falls, Ontario, and North Oliver, B.C. In 1999, Vincor broke ground in Niagara-on-the-Lake for the construction of a distinctive winery to showcase the full range of Jackson-Triggs products. The winery is due to open to the public in 2001.

Jackson-Triggs has also entered into a joint venture with the giant Burgundy shipper, Boisset, to build a winery called Le Clos Jordan that will produce Burgundian-style Chardonnay and Pinot Noir in a newly planted vineyard. The consulting winemaker on the project is a talented young Québecois, Pascal Marchand, who used to make wine in Pommard, Burgundy, at Clos des Épineaux. These wines are projected for release in 2005.

Joseph's Estate Wines

Joseph Pohorly was the original owner of Newark Winery that later became Hillebrand Estates. He sold his property to the Swiss bitters giant Underberg in 1983 to devote himself to his hotel business, but in 1992 relaunched himself into wine, buying a 20-acre estate just down the road from his original vineyard. Joseph's Estate produces about 15,000 cases of vinifera and hybrid wines as well as a small amount of fruit wine.

- ✔ Joseph's Estate Wines Cabernet Franc
- ✔ Joseph's Estate Wines Petite Sirah
- ✔ Joseph's Estate Wines Pinot Gris
- ✔ Joseph's Estate Wines Vidal Icewine

Konzelmann Estate Winery

German Herbert Konzelmann (the first winner of the Air Ontario Winemaker of the Year Award in 1996) came to Canada for the first time in 1980 on a hunting trip. He was so impressed by the potential for making wine in Niagara that he actually took soil samples back to Germany for analysis. Within four years he moved himself and his family to Niagara-on-the-Lake. With 25 years' experience running the family winery in Germany, Konzelmann had a head start on many Canadian winemakers. Most of his wines are distinctly German in style and he really knows how to bring out the delicate nuances of the fruit.

Konzelmann introduced vertical vine training to the region — a form of canopy management that enables the sun and wind to extract some of the moisture from the grapes and concentrate the flavour without compromising the acid balance.

He regularly makes about 30 different wines and experiments with other grape varieties and winemaking techniques.

    ✔ Konzelmann Estate Winery Late Harvest Riesling

    ✔ Konzelmann Estate Winery Pinot Blanc

    ✔ Konzelmann Estate Winery Pinot Noir

    ✔ Konzelmann Estate Winery Riesling/Traminer Icewine

    ✔ Konzelmann Estate Winery Select Late Harvest Vidal

    ✔ Konzelmann Estate Winery Vidal Icewine

Marynissen Estates Limited

John Marynissen burst onto the wine scene in 1990 as a grower with a long history of awards for homemade wine. With encouragement from his family and some backing from Tony Doyle, former owner of Willowbank winery, John made the transition from amateur to professional by opening a small winemaking operation. He has been growing grapes for over 40 years and planted Chardonnay in the mid-1970s, followed by Cabernet in 1978. He is able to extract great concentration from this mature fruit.

Towards the end of the 1990s, John's daughter Sandra and her husband, Glenn Muir, became involved in the winemaking. They continue the Marynissen winemaking tradition, which is characterized by low yields to increase concentrated flavours and the use of oak for both fermentation and aging.

    ✔ Marynissen Estate Winery Cabernet Lot 65

    ✔ Marynissen Estate Winery Cabernet/Merlot

    ✔ Marynissen Estate Winery Riesling

    ✔ Marynissen Estate Winery Vidal Icewine

Peller Estates

Andrés Wines, founded in 1961 by Andrew Peller, enjoyed enormous success as producers of that rather dubious wine-like product called "Baby Duck." A sweet, lightly sparkling, pink grape-based product, the "Baby" was all the rage during the 1960s and 1970s but started to flounder once the shift to vinifera-based wines took hold. As the public demanded better quality and European-style, dry wines, the Baby Duck days drew to a close. But, when Andrés tried to catch the vinifera wave, they found their name had been tarred with Duck's feathers. The solution was to create the Peller Estates label, after the company's founder.

Winemaker Jamie Macfarlane studied in Burgundy and at Montpellier in France, and brings education and experience to the Peller line. Many of its wines sell in the more moderately priced range, but the Oakridge Premium labels respond to the demand for a more upscale line. Peller Estate wines are available from the LCBO and from the Andrés chain of The Wine Shoppes.

- ✔ Peller Estates Chardonnay Sur Lie
- ✔ Peller Estates Founder's Series Chardonnay

Pillitteri Estates Winery

Gary Pillitteri came to Niagara-on-the-Lake from Sicily following the Second World War. He established himself in the community with his vineyard and a talent for amateur winemaking. Over the years he became involved with the Ontario Grape Growers' Marketing Board and the Ontario Federation of Agriculture. On the home and business front, he and his family operated Gary's Farm Market and Cheryl's Authentic Home Baked Goods.

In 1993, he opened his winery. That same year, as a member of parliament, he joined the Liberal caucus. He has served on the Standing Committee on Finance and the Prime Minister's Task Force on Youth Entrepreneurship. "Back on the farm," so to speak, winery operations are in the hands of Gary's son Charles, his daughter-in-law Lili, and son-in-law Jamie Slingerland, who takes care of the Pillitteri vineyard as well as his own. Daughters Lucy and Connie and Connie's husband Helmut Friesen are also involved. Winemaker is Sue-Ann Staff, who trained at Roseworthy College in Australia.

Most of the wine is made with grapes from Pillitteri family vineyards in Niagara-on-the-Lake. It is a matter of pride as well as an assurance of quality control. The style of each wine is closely linked to the grape types used and the vineyard in which they were grown, resulting in the fullest expression of "terroir."

To your health: Good news for Ontario wine lovers

A study completed at Cornell University, in New York, has some interesting implications for anyone drinking red wines from Ontario. A team of researchers found that wines from New York had much higher concentrations of resveratrol (the fungicide that occurs naturally in grapes and other plants that has been shown to reduce the risk of heart disease and cancer) than wines from any other state — or country.

The researchers concluded that resveratrol develops in response to the cool, humid climate prevalent in New York (its effects being in greater demand by the vine in humid conditions). Because Ontario's climate is similar to that of northern New York's, it stands to reason that Ontario grapes also contain quite high amounts of resveratrol — particularly in wet years.

- Pillitteri Estates Winery Baco Noir
- Pillitteri Estates Winery Family Reserve Merlot
- Pillitteri Estates Winery Riesling Icewine
- Pillitteri Estates Winery Trevalante

Reif Estate Winery

Opened in 1983, Reif was one of the first wave of new Niagara wineries. Ewald Reif moved to Canada from Germany in 1977 and spent the first years replacing native Labrusca vines with European vinifera varieties. With 13 generations of family winemaking tradition behind him, he was confident in the potential of the Peninsula for making quality wine. The Reif property is located on the scenic Niagara Parkway and features a historical stagecoach house, now the site of the retail shop and tour centre. Some of the large, German wine casks brought over from the family domaine add to the historic ambience. Winemaker is Ewald's nephew Klaus Reif, who joined the Canadian enterprise in 1987. One of his first accomplishments was to tickle the palate of the high-profile wine writer Robert Parker, who included Reif's Vidal Icewine 1987 in his list of 10 best wines of the year.

- Reif Estate Winery Off-Dry Riesling
- Reif Estate Winery Reserve Chardonnay
- Reif Estate Winery Riesling Icewine
- Reif Estate Winery Tesoro

Stonechurch Vineyards

It has been said of the Hunse family vineyards that they are the tidiest in the region. This is quite a feat, considering that Stonechurch is one of the larger estate wineries. The Hunse family has been growing grapes since 1972 and opened their winery in 1990 partly as a consequence of increased quantities of fruit from their vineyards. They hired German winemaker Jens Gemmrich, trained not only in grape growing and winemaking, but in barrel making as well. In 1999, he experimented with a barrel-fermented old vines Vidal. This is rather extraordinary treatment for what is considered a somewhat simple varietal, but the results are encouraging.

Although Lambert and Grace Hunse retired from the family business, handing the operations over to their son Rick and his wife, Fran, Lambert still stays active in the vineyards. A visit to Stonechurch provides some interesting insight into how grapes are grown and wine made. Informative signs are set up at 100-metre intervals throughout parts of the vineyards.

The Hunses also offer an interesting evening activity for anyone who enjoys stargazing. From time to time, they set up telescopes on the lawn outside the winery so that visitors can study the skies.

- ✔ Stonechurch Vineyards Late Harvest Vidal
- ✔ Stonechurch Vineyards Pinot Noir
- ✔ Stonechurch Vineyards Vidal Icewine

Strewn Inc.

The Strewn winery is a perfect example of what to do with an old cannery. Joe Will and his wife, Jane Langdon, have worked magic with the renovations that encompass not only the winery, but also Jane's cooking school and their own home.

The winery is owned by chairman Newman Smith, who worked for many years in the business end of a large Canadian winery, and Joe, who trained in wine-making at Roseworthy, in Australia, and worked at Pillitteri as winemaker before striking out on his own. The distinct oaky character of his wines reflects his Australian experience. He has won a number of awards for his dessert wines and is developing an interesting line of age-worthy reds based on the Bordeaux varietals.

Strewn now has its own restaurant on site called Terroir La Cachette, with a 30-seat wine bar and 65-seat dining room. The specialty is "Niagara Provençal" cuisine.

- ✔ Strewn Pinot Blanc
- ✔ Strewn Select Late Harvest Vidal
- ✔ Strewn Vidal Icewine

Vincor International Inc.

Enter Canada's wine giant, the offspring of buyouts and mergers. T.G. Bright and Cartier, two of Canada's most influential wineries, merged in 1993 with leading boutique winery Inniskillin. The resulting corporate entity, now publicly traded on the Toronto Stock Exchange, was christened Vincor. It went on to consolidate all the wine stores of Brights and Cartier into one chain of Wine Rack stores and it acquired Dumont Vins et Spiriteux in Québec and Okanagan Vineyards in British Columbia. It also bought R.J. Grape Products and Spagnols, thereby diversifying into the home winemaking market. But its greatest coup must be a joint venture with the Burgundy-based Boisset Group, the largest shipper in France.

Canada's Deep South

There are four wineries located in the "deep southwest" of Ontario, between Leamington and Amherstburg, directly south of Windsor. Pelee Island, which is just off the Lake Erie shore at Kingsville, is the southernmost territory in Canada. The lake effect from Lake Erie combined with the southern latitude gives this region the second longest growing season in Canada after Victoria, British Columbia. Pelee Island's growing season is almost 30 days longer than on the mainland.

Lake Erie North Shore Wineries

Because Lake Erie is quite shallow, it warms up quickly, giving the growing season a kick-start. Summer temperatures can be very hot as well. In winter, however, the shallower water cools quickly, and it's possible for Lake Erie to freeze over. Although this doesn't happen often, it does put the vines at risk.

Colio Estate Wines

With production of close to 200,000 cases, Colio is one of Ontario's largest wine producers. The combination of winning climatic conditions and winemaker Carlo Negri's talent have provided the edge. In the beginning, they deliberately went contrary to the trend and planted vinifera vines while others were still producing the sparkling "pop" wines that were all the rage. But they had studied the area before establishing their winery and were convinced that the soils and microclimate would support the fine European varietals.

They own 180 acres in Harrow and Colchester that benefit from a southern exposure to Lake Erie. With their long sun hours and extended growing season, they have little problem ripening some of the later grapes like Cabernet Sauvignon.

Their products are divided between four brands:

- The Colio Estate Vineyards (CEV) label represents estate-grown, prestige VQA labels. These wines came on line with the 1997 vintage and are made from hand-selected grapes that undergo a gentle pressing and oak aging. Limited bottlings are made and include Merlot Reserve, Pinot Noir Reserve, Cabernet Franc Reserve, Gamay Noir, Chardonnay Reserve, Chardonnay (no oak), and Sauvignon Blanc.

- The Harrow Estate Selection comprises all VQA wines sourced from the Colchester vineyard.

✔ The Oak Aged Classics are international blends of premium vinifera.

✔ Colio Estate Wines are popular house blends.

Colio wines are available in most other provinces and in some countries in Europe, the Orient, the Caribbean, and Greenland. They have a number of retail shops across Ontario.

✔ Colio Estate Merlot CEV Reserve

✔ Colio Harrow Estate Cabernet Franc

✔ Colio Harrow Estate Late Harvest Vidal

D'Angelo Estate Winery

Salvatore (Sal) D'Angelo was a talented amateur winemaker when he planted his Lake Erie North Shore vineyard in 1983. His long-term goal was attained in 1990 when he opened his own winery. Procedures are carefully monitored but never detract from the emphasis placed on the vineyard. Sal uses only estate-grown grapes, which are divided between vinifera and high-quality hybirds.

Sal trains his grapes on a variety of different trellising systems to encourage ripeness and air circulation.

✔ D'Angelo Estate Cabernet Franc

✔ D'Angelo Estate Maréchal Foch

✔ D'Angelo Estate Select Late Harvest Vidal

✔ D'Angelo Estate Vidal Icewine

LeBlanc Estate Winery

LeBlanc is the smallest of the Lake Erie North Shore wineries, with a production of only 3,500 cases. Alphonse and Monique LeBlanc planted the vineyard in 1984, but it was their son Pierre and his wife, Lyse, who carried out its transformation to winery, in 1993. Pierre and Lyse eventually bought the operation from their parents; both the vineyard and winery are now run by Lyse herself. She concentrates on white varieties but has started to plant some Cabernet Sauvignon and Merlot.

✔ LeBlanc Estate Winery Cabernet Franc

✔ LeBlanc Estate Winery Vidal Icewine

Pelee Island Winery

All of the Pelee Island vineyards are located on the island, but this winery, located on-shore at Kingsville, poses a logistics problem not faced by any other winery in the region. But it is admirably dealt with: The grapes are harvested in the cool of the night and loaded onto the first ferry in the morning. The winery is located only a short distance from the dock on shore, so the grapes are quickly transported before they have any chance to deteriorate in the heat. For the time being, the grapes are transported on the regularly scheduled morning ferry but winemaker Walter Schmoranz predicts that, at some point in the future, a dedicated ferry will be needed.

If Colio operates under an Italian influence, Pelee Island Winery has a decidedly German bent. The winery is owned by German/Canadian lawyer and business-man Wolf Teichmann, and Walter Schmoranz has overseen the winemaking since he arrived from Germany just in time for the 1985 harvest. Pelee is always trying out new grape varieties, but they concentrate on Chardonnay in particular. They also grow Riesling, Gewürztraminer, Zweigelt, Vidal, Gamay, and Pinot Noir. Their products are available at the winery and throughout the LCBO system. They are known for their solid quality/price ratio.

    ✔ Pelee Island Winery Cabernet Franc

    ✔ Pelee Island Winery Gamay/Zweigelt

Urban Corkfitters

There are several wineries located in urban industrial parks, mostly to the north of Toronto, but there are no adjacent vineyards. These wineries bring

---

Quai du Vin

Quai du Vin Estate Winery is off the beaten track as far as Ontario wineries go; it's located about two hours west of the Niagara region, in St. Thomas, well on the road to Windsor. This is verdant agricultural land, however, and wine-maker Redi Quai took advantage of it, planting a vineyard there in the mid-1970s.

Quai's son, Roberto, opened Quai du Vin in 1988, with the intention of keeping it a small, one-man operation.

Roberto's approach to winemaking is un-fussy and hands-off. He interferes as little as possible in the winemaking process. By charging a deposit on his bottles, he fosters ecological principles while adding an incentive for his customers to keep coming back for their refunds.

their grapes in from the Niagara Peninsula or import wine for blending and bottling. One of them, Southbrook Farms, vinifies a variety of other fruits with increasing success.

Toronto (GTA) and North of Toronto Wineries

Visiting a winery in an urban setting may not be quite as romantic as touring an actual vineyard, but it *is* a lot more convenient, especially for city dwellers. In the end analysis, you still get to taste some great wines and get a feel for the dedication of the people who make the wine, wherever their location.

Cilento Wines

Grace Locilento's dream of owning a winery was inspired by her grandmother's vineyard in Italy. When she came to Canada with her family in 1952, Grace and her husband, Angelo, bought a juice company, supplying quality juice and accessories to home winemakers, but she never lost sight of her goal. In 1995, the Locilentos established their own winery in temporary quarters located just outside of Toronto and bought grapes from Niagara growers. Their own 55-acre vineyard in Niagara-on-the-Lake was planted in 1996 and came on stream in 2000. They have since purchased and planted further land and hired full-time winemaker Terence van Rooyen, who brought with him 25 years' experience in South Africa. A new building, in Woodbridge, Ontario, just north of Toronto, comprises 36,000 square feet. This California mission-style building houses state-of-the-art equipment and one of the largest barrel-aging cellars in Ontario.

- ✔ Cilento Barrel Fermented Reserve Chardonnay
- ✔ Cilento Late Harvest Riesling
- ✔ Cilento Vidal Icewine

De Sousa Wine Cellars

The De Sousas have the unique distinction of owning the only winery in downtown Toronto. This facility, which opened in 1998, is intended as a hospitable oasis in the heart of an urban setting. Used not only for the production and sale of wine, the second storey features an atmospheric Portuguese restaurant.

The vineyards are located about an hour-and-a-half away, high on the Beamsville Bench in Niagara, where the De Sousas originally founded their winery. The De Sousas' Portuguese heritage is evident in both the vineyards and the winery. Their red and white table wines with the Dois Amigos label are aimed at the Portuguese community and the red is even aged in oak in the traditional Portuguese manner.

Magnotta Winery Estates

Gabe Magnotta claims to have won the most medals of any winery in Canada, and there's no reason to doubt him, as his wines win time and again in competitions. He and his wife, Rosanna, built their successful business on the basis of imported wines blended with local produce. Their main winery is located in north Toronto, where Gabe and Rosanna had developed a highly successful juice business, catering to home winemakers. They have since opened four other locations. Based on the success of their operation, they purchased 72 acres of land in the Niagara Peninsula to develop a line of VQA wines. They also operate a distillery, and own a 375-acre vineyard in Chile.

- Magnotta Barrel Fermented Chardonnay
- Magnotta Limited Edition Cabernet Franc Icewine
- Magnotta Limited Edition Riesling Icewine
- Magnotta Limited Edition Sparkling Vidal Icewine
- Magnotta Select Late Harvest Vidal
- Magnotta Vidal Icewine

Milan Wineries

Located within the city confines of Toronto, Milan bottles wine from both imported and Ontario grapes. Although trained as an oenologist in the University of Conegliano, in Italy, Alberto Milan ran a large imported juice company for many years before buying the 3,000-square-foot facility in this urban milieu. The company philosophy is to create "wines of interest at reasonable prices." Alberto plans to enlarge the winery and increase the product line to include different grape types and develop some oak-aged riservas.

Southbrook Farms & Winery

There are no vineyards attached to this award-winning winery located north of Toronto, but grapes are purchased from some of the most highly respected growers in Niagara.

The grapes are crushed on the spot and the juice transported in refrigerated trucks. Vinification is overseen by Winemaker Derek Barnett, who won the Winemaker of the Year Award at the 2000 Air Ontario Wine Awards. Derek ferments in stainless steel or oak barrels, as appropriate to the variety. About half of the winery's production is dedicated to fruit wines. More on fruit wines in Chapter 21.

Southbrook Farm's fortified "Framboise" was the first Ontario wine ever carried by Harrods, in London.

- ✔ Southbrook Farms Lailey Vineyard Cabernet Sauvignon
- ✔ Southbrook Farms Pinot Gris
- ✔ Southbrook Farms Reserve Chardonnay
- ✔ Southbrook Farms Sauvignon Blanc
- ✔ Southbrook Farms Select Late Harvest Vidal
- ✔ Southbrook Farms 'Triomphe' Pinot Noir

Vinoteca

In 1992 Giovanni and Rosanna Follegot acquired a small winery property at the foot of the Niagara Escarpment, in Beamsville. Up until that time they had been making wine from imported juice and Niagara grapes at their facility in an industrial park in Woodbridge, a community just north of Toronto.

Vineyard region-in-waiting

The Bay of Quinte, in Prince Edward County, between Toronto and Kingston, has some 150 acres of grapevines already in the ground.

Spurred on by a handful of growers excited by the soil variation in the area, the Bay of Quinte is destined to become Ontario's fourth designated viticultural area, after the Niagara Peninsula, the Lake Erie North Shore, and Pelee Island. Although the region is more northerly than the Niagara Peninsula and has colder winters by an average of seven degrees, its growing season is just as long. More significantly, its vineyard plantings face south and east, exactly the exposure enjoyed by all the great vineyards of Europe.

There's a collegial feeling among these pioneer growers reminiscent of Oregon in the 1960s, when a few intrepid vintners left California to create a new wine region — against all accepted wisdom. With the clearing of a few bureaucratic hurdles, the Bay of Quinte growers should be able to do the same.

By choice, their Niagara location remains small, growing only as quickly as the maturity of their vineyards allow. At this location, they limit their production to 100 percent Ontario wines, concentrating on red varieties. The bulk of their production is still handled in Woodbridge.

- ✔ Vinoteca Cabernet Sauvignon
- ✔ Vinoteca Chardonnay

Table 18-1	Top 10 Ontario Wineries to Visit
Winery	*What to Look For*
Cave Spring Cellars	Some of the best Riesling in the province and the most attractive location in terms of visitor appeal.
Château des Charmes	One of the first boutique wineries, it has the largest holdings of vinifera vineyards, and a great ambiance. Try the sparkling wines.
Daniel Lenko Estate Winery	The new winery to watch, but they're small, so best to call first.
Henry of Pelham Family Estate Winery	A picturesque location, lots of history, and a full range of great wines.
Hillebrand Estates Winery	One of the bigger wineries, well organized for visitors. A well-thought-out introductory tour. There's an elegant restaurant, too.
Inniskillin Wines	The first boutique winery — the one that started the quality revolution in Canada. Don't miss this little bit of history. Broad range of excellent wines. Something for everyone.
Malivoire Wine Company	A very small, but interesting, range of wines. If you want to find out how a gravity-fed system of winemaking works, this is the place to go. Call ahead.
Marynissen Estates	Consistently good red wines from some of the oldest vinifera plantings in Ontario.
Thirty Bench Vineyard and Winery	Tiny production dedicated to low yields, but the result is intensely flavoured wines.
Vineland Estates Wines	A leader in the industry, with a spectacular view and a superb restaurant.

Chapter 19

British Columbia Wineries

Most of the wineries in British Columbia are small, family businesses. More often than not, they sell all of their wine in their own shops or to local restaurants — which makes it difficult for anyone living in Prince Edward Island or anywhere else east of B.C. to taste it. So, take a trip to the spectacular Okanagan Valley or to the green, green shores of Vancouver Island. See Figure 19-1 for a map of the province's wine-growing regions. Don't forget to check out our top 10 picks in Table 19-1, at the end of the chapter. Overall production may be much less than in Ontario, but the vintner's quest for quality is just as passionate. If you have a chance to taste wine from each of the regions, you don't have to be an expert to notice the difference in style. Ever been to see a Gray Monk or a Wild Goose? How about a Burrowing Owl? British Columbia wineries have pretty cool names, too.

North of the Border, Down Okanagan Way

The Okanagan is a long, skinny valley, stretching from north to south, flanked by sloping land that provides great exposure to the sun in many areas. But did you know that about 25 percent of the Okanagan Valley is a desert? When we think of desert landscapes, images of dry, parched wastelands, like we see in movies, come to mind. But the southern end of the Okanagan Valley receives a mere 15 centimetres of rain per year! The area's salvation is at the bottom of the valley: Even if there's no water from the sky, there is water on the ground, in the shape of the 100-kilometre-long Lake Okanagan. The Okanagan River, as well as several smaller lakes in the area that extend south through the desert area to the American border, are other water sources. The water's primary use is irrigation, though it also has the same mitigating effect on the growing vines as do Lakes Ontario and Erie, back east: cooler air in the summer, warmer air in the winter. This benefits the growing season.

The southern Okanagan Valley has typical desert-like conditions: The summer days are very hot, while the nights are positively chilly. This is good for grapes. The dramatic difference in temperature between day and night makes the grapes accumulate extra acid, which adds elegance to the wine and gives it aging potential.

Highly acidic wines are also the best for making champagne-method sparkling wines.

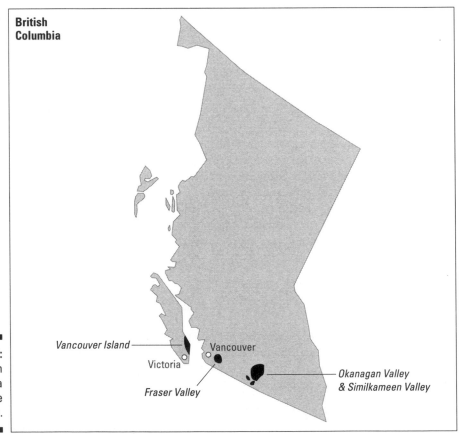

Figure 19-1: British Columbia wine regions.

British Columbia

Vancouver Island

Victoria

Vancouver

Fraser Valley

Okanagan Valley & Similkameen Valley

Because of the amazing variation in climate in the Okanagan Valley, a wide variety of grapes are successfully grown there. The town of Osoyoos, right on the border of the good old U.S. of A., experiences the warmest temperatures. The area is particularly suited to red grapes, so just about everybody is planting Cabernet Franc, Merlot, and Cabernet Sauvignon, the grapes used in great Bordeaux wines.

The stretch of the Okanagan Valley between the towns of Oliver and Okanagan Falls is almost as hot as the area around Osoyoos, but as you move farther north — to Penticton and Naramata, at the south end of Lake Okanagan, temperatures start to cool down. Even here, though, there are microclimates where heat-seeking grapes can thrive. From this point north, it gets progressively cooler. Up around Salmon Arm, most of the wines are made from Germanic grape types that like a cooler climate. White grapes like Siegerrebe, Madeleine Angevine, Madeleine Sylvaner, Optima, and Ortega are good bets there.

Okanagan Valley Wineries

There are close to 40 wineries in the Okanagan Valley, producing a great variety of wines. Any keen skiers should note that the dry Okanagan climate means great powder-like conditions in winter. That's just one more reason to attend the Okanagan Icewine Festival in January. See Chapter 8 for information on this and other wine festivals across the country.

Bella Vista Vineyards

Bella Vista is one of the wineries in the cooler, northern end of the Okanagan and its vista is "molto bella." Three levels of balconies on the imposing colonial-style winery offer a spectacular view of the lake, the surrounding farmland, and mountain ranges. The facilities are fully equipped for any form of special event from BBQs to formal weddings. There is even a helipad for quick getaways. Owner Larry Passmore, once an avid home winemaker, now works with consultant winemaker Gary Strachan to craft his wines from Chardonnay, Gewürztraminer, Pinot Auxerrois, Maréchal Foch, and Pinot Noir. Plans are in place to upgrade the equipment. At this time, most primary fermenting is done outside in a covered work area but, if need be, the cellar has enough space to bring the wine in for cold curing or for heating if the fermentation sticks. Until the new, mechanized bottling line is installed, bottling is done by hand and visitors are encouraged to help out. If there's a little sampling done before the cork goes in, that's okay.

Black Hills Estate Winery

Black Hills is an extremely focused new winery in Oliver, near the southern tip of the Valley. Owned by a partnership of two couples, the winery will produce only two wines — a red Bordeaux blend named Nota Bene, from Cabernet Sauvignon, Merlot, and Cabernet Franc, and a late harvest Sauvignon Blanc named Black Hills Gold.

Partners Bob and Senka Tennant and Peter and Susan McCarrell bought the 34-acre vineyard, located on Black Sage Road, in 1996. Although Bob has a BSc in agriculture, the partners were nevertheless grateful for advice from neighbour Dick Cleave on which clones and rootstocks to plant. The land is on a southwest sloping bench, just north of Osoyoos Lake, and the heat and sunlight in the summer are intense.

They found early on that their grapes were in great demand — they sell about 50 percent of their yield to CedarCreek Estate Winery — and decided to take the plunge and develop their own winery too. Their first crush was in 1999, when they produced the red blend. They added the late harvest wine in 2000.

Consulting winemaker is Berle (Rusty) Figgins, from the Walla Walla region of Washington State, who trained in Waga Waga, Australia. (Seriously, that's the truth — there can't be too many winemakers who can say that.) On-site, hands-on winemaker is Senka Tennant, who has a diploma in winemaking.

Winemaking techniques include hand-harvesting, minimal crushing before fermenting in small batches, and pressing. Fermentation continues after the must has been transferred to French and American oak barrels and the wine goes through a malolactic fermentation to soften the acids. Intervention is kept to a minimum — no other techniques are used to adjust acidity and none of the wine is chaptalized.

Blue Mountain Vineyard & Cellars

Ian and Jane Mavety didn't waste a minute in making their mark once their winery opened in 1991. They had been growing grapes in their Okanagan Falls vineyard for more than 20 years, so they had high-quality, mature fruit with which to start. In their location, towards the south of the Valley, summer temperatures are similar to those in Burgundy, so they decided to go with Chardonnay and Pinot Noir grapes. This was leading edge at the time — just about everybody else was stuck on Riesling. But, it paid off. With their very first commercial harvest, they made a terrific Pinot Noir that made everybody else sit up and take note. With their Chardonnay, they launched right into barrel fermenting, which was also a resounding success. Then, they hired consultant winemaker Raphael Brisbois, who was working at Iron Horse in Sonoma, California. With his help, they made some amazing champagne-method sparkling wines. The Mavetys' son, Mark, got his degree in agricultural economics at UBC, and went off to New Zealand for a while to study oenology. He is taking on more of the responsibility for winemaking at Blue Mountain.

- ✔ Blue Mountain Brut
- ✔ Blue Mountain Chardonnay
- ✔ Blue Mountain Gamay
- ✔ Blue Mountain Pinot Blanc
- ✔ Blue Mountain Pinot Gris
- ✔ Blue Mountain Pinot Noir

Burrowing Owl Vineyards

Merlot is the sit-up-and-take-note grape for this southern Okanagan winery. Vancouver businessman Jim Wyse and partners swept up to the Valley in the early 1990s, bought about 200 acres of land, and hired winemaker Bill Dyer, who had made a name for himself at Sterling Vineyards, in Napa, California. Jim and Bill then visited a number of wineries in the Okanagan, Washington, and Oregon before constructing a gravity-feed winery with temperature-controlled cellars for fermentation and barrel aging.

Originally owned by Albert LeComte, who earlier founded LeComte Winery, the property includes a 20-acre block of vines, some of which were planted in 1985. The terrain consists of a sandy plateau on the east side of the Okanagan Valley, which slopes off gently to the southwest. Late afternoon heat units in the summer are very high, providing good conditions that encourage the ripening of the reds. Although there are 16 different vinifera varieties growing, Burrowing Owl is concentrating on four — Chardonnay, Pinot Gris, Cabernet Sauvignon, and Merlot.

The Merlot 1995, bottled off premises before the winery was built, won a gold medal in the 1997 International Wine and Spirit Competition in England. Merlot is a consistent winner here.

Calona Vineyards

Calona has its place in B.C. history. Founded in 1932, their early successes were apple-based products with catchy names like "Apple Jack." Over the years they broadened their scope to a mix of fruit wines and their very successful blended, grape-based wines Schloss Laderheim and Sommet Rouge. In 1998, Calona made a strong commitment to VQA wines. Winemaker Howard Soon oversees a total production of about 30,000 cases — quite large by B.C. standards — and has turned out a number of medal-winning wines. The best are bottled under the Private Reserve and Artist Series labels. A range of lower-priced imported wines are bottled under the Heritage Collection label.

Founded and still owned by the Capozzi family, much of the company's success rests on sound business principles. The Capozzis are open about the fact that they admire the strategies of Ernest and Julio Gallo in California. At one point, they even entered into discussions with the Gallos about merging the two companies.

✔ Calona Vineyards Artist Series Chardonnay

✔ Calona Vineyards Artist Series Pinot Blanc

✔ Calona Vineyards Private Reserve Cabernet Sauvignon

✔ Calona Vineyards Private Reserve Fumé Blanc

✔ Calona Vineyards Private Reserve Late Harvest Ehrenfelser

✔ Calona Vineyards Private Reserve Merlot

✔ Calona Vineyards Sandhill Pinot Blanc

Carriage House Wines

This tiny winery in Oliver bases its success on reduced yields in the vineyard and the exclusive use of French oak barrels in the cellar. Their goal is to make small quantities of high-quality wines. Best known for their Kerner, owners Dave and Karen Wagner also make an excellent Pinot Blanc, one of the grapes that shows particular promise in B.C. They added Pinot Noir, Merlot, and Cabernet Sauvignon to their line-up in 1995. With the advantage of a southwest exposure, they can coax the best from their vineyard.

CedarCreek Estate Winery

CedarCreek was created in 1986 when senator Ross Fitzpatrick purchased the property formerly known as Uniacke. At that time production was at 2,500 cases. Through expanding vinifera plantings over the years, production rose to 30,000 cases. In 1996, the senator's son, Gordon, joined the winery as president.

CedarCreek hired winemaker Kevin Willenborg in 1998. With 10 years' experience at Louis Martini Winery in California, he dramatically improved the quality of CedarCreek's wine and turned over a thriving premium program to his successor Thomas di Bello, formerly of Washington State. Thomas has added two new lines — Estate Select and Platinum Reserve, both of which include a Chardonnay and Pinot Noir. The Estate Select line also includes Merlot and a Cabernet Merlot blend.

Kevin's technique for improving the wines started in the vineyard, where he left the grapes on the vine until he felt the flavours were right. In the winery, he used oak but never to the point where it overwhelmed the fruit. Winery president Gordon Fitzpatrick also brought in a viticultural consultant who recommended controlling foliage, reducing crop quantities, and adjusting the soil content by adding gypsum. The results were quickly seen in more intense flavours, complexity, and elegance.

- ✔ CedarCreek Estate Select Pinot Noir
- ✔ CedarCreek Estate Merlot
- ✔ CedarCreek Estate Reserve Chardonnay Icewine

Domaine Combret

Robert Combret, his wife, Maité, and son, Olivier, emigrated from Provence, France, in 1992. Robert's family has been in winemaking for 10 generations. He established Domaine Combret overlooking Lake Osoyoos and the town of Oliver, building a gravity-fed winery and installing all the bells and whistles needed to make the operation run efficiently.

Olivier, who trained in winemaking at Montpellier in the south of France, won a medal for one of his first wines, Domaine Combret Riesling, 1993, at an international competition in Bordeaux. Only one year later, his Chardonnay 1993 was included in "Best Chardonnay of the World" at the annual Chardonnay challenge in Burgundy. Domaine Combret has won an award at every Chardonnay du Monde competition since, one of only six wineries in the world to do so.

Fairview Cellars

Bill Eggert's small production is devoted exclusively to red wine from Cabernet Sauvignon, Merlot, Cabernet Franc, Syrah, and Gamay Noir. In production only a few years, Fairview has a hot advantage. They are located in the "Golden Mile" of the southern Okanagan. Here the red varieties get all the heat units they need to coax even the later varieties to ripeness.

- ✔ Fairview Cellars Merlot/Cabernet

The proliferation of B.C. wineries

In 1991, there were 24 active wineries in British Columbia. The Pullout Program, put in place by the federal government with the advent of Free Trade, with the idea being to plant better grape varieties on fewer acres, had nevertheless left the industry demoralized. Received wisdom at the time was that the industry couldn't compete with the economies of scale enjoyed by winemakers south of the border in California, Washington, and Oregon. Vineyard acreage was reduced by a full two-thirds.

But that was then, and this is now. Realizing they had to make better wine to compete with imported products, the wineries and the growers got down to the business of planting better varieites and concentrating on quality wines. At the time of writing, there are no less than 60 wineries in four designated viticultural areas of the province. A lot of these wineries are boutique (small volume) wineries operating off a few acres of vines, however, which partly explains why B.C. currently produces about 25 percent of the amount of wine that Ontario does, even though it has more wineries.

These B.C. wineries have just opened or are waiting in the wings:

Benchland Vineyard (Penticton)

Bonaparte Bend (fruit wine, Kamloops)

Elephant Island Orchard (fruit wines) (Elephant Island)

Glenterrra Vineyards (Duncan)

Godfrey-Brownell Vineyards (Duncan)

Inkameep Cellars (Osoyoos)

Salt Spring Island Vineyards (Salt Spring Island)

Silver Sage Winery (Oliver)

Thornhaven Vineyards (Giant's Head Mountain)

Victoria Estate Winery (Vancouver Island)

Yellow Point Vineyards (Ladysmith)

Gehringer Brothers Estate Winery

Walter and Gordon Gehringer planned their winery every step of the way before opening in 1985. Resolute in what they wanted to do as early as high school, both brothers, upon graduating, went off to study in Germany. Walter went to the University of Geisenheim, where he obtained an engineering degree in viticulture, and Gordon got a degree from oenology school at Weinsberg. Each summer, when they returned home for the holidays, they brought back some new equipment for the winery. Before they made the decision to buy their vineyard, they studied its micro-climate for seven years. It is located out of the frost zone on a bench, at the southern end of the Okanagan. A south-facing slope gives it good exposure. They produced their first vintage in 1985. As you would think from their training, their style leans to the Germanic.

They made their reputation on wines that were made without oak but with reserve unfermented juice for blending into the wine before bottling. For the 1999 vintage, they have introduced a new series of wines under the Dry Rock Vineyard label, all of which have had contact with oak.

- Gehringer Brothers Estate Winery Minus 9 Ehrenfelser Icewine
- Gehringer Brothers Estate Winery Optimum Pinot Noir
- Gehringer Brothers Estate Winery Pinot Auxerrois

Gersighel Wineberg

Dirk de Gussen and Gerda Torck came up with the striking name for their winery, not from the family history as might be suspected, but from blending parts of their three children's names: Gerd, Sigrid, and Helgi. Wineberg is a reference to the nearby Mount Baldy, but the family felt that "berg," the German word for mountain, was more evocative. The reference is further strengthened by the use of the bald eagle on their labels. They are one of the southernmost wineries in the Okanagan, and make mostly white wines. The Pinot Blanc and Sauvignon Blanc are particularly recommended. Dirk has no illusions about this being an overnight venture. He recognizes that it may require more than one generation before the best-suited varieties are found.

Golden Mile Cellars

The Golden Mile reference relates to the southern stretch of the Okanagan Valley where good drainage and high heat units contribute to the intensity of flavours. Peter and Helga Serwo's vineyard dates back to the 1970s, but they didn't open their farm winery until 1998. Constructed out of cement blocks, the winery building is reminiscent of a medieval castle, complete with turret. Winemaker Ross Mirko takes advantage of the varying soil structure to impart individuality to the soft and fruity property style.

B.C.'s direction — Wine-wise

According to the latest grape census conducted by the Grape Growers Association of British Columbia (yes, they actually count the grapevines!) There are currently 4,200 acres *under vine* (devoted to growing grapevines). This is a staggering 73 percent increase in only two years — 96 percent of these are red and white vinifera vines. The heavy plantings done by major players such as Vincor International, Andrés Wines (B.C.) Ltd., and Mission Hill Winery, explain this sharp increase.

Gray Monk Estate Winery

In the 1960s it was an orchard. Then came George and Trudy Heiss, of Austrian descent, who wanted to grow grapes like those of their heritage. They grubbed out the trees and planted the hybrids recommended by the Canadian government. Well, the grapes might have been guaranteed to grow but they didn't make great wine. Gradually, George and Trudy regrafted their vines to European vinifera vines. By the late 1970s, they were ready, but they had to get a licence to make wine commercially. They were among the first of the vineyardists to apply for the newly created "estate winery" licence. They called the winery Gray Monk, which is the Austrian nickname for the Pinot Gris grape. In 1990, it was time to upgrade the labels and packaging and introduce a premium "proprietor's cuvée." Sons George Jr. and Steven got in on the act, with George Jr. as winemaker and Steven looking after the Heiss family vineyard nursery. The winery has prospered and production is up to about 40,000 cases.

- ✔ Gray Monk Estate Winery Baco Noir
- ✔ Gray Monk Estate Winery Chardonnay Unwooded
- ✔ Gray Monk Estate Winery Ehrenfelser Select Late Harvest
- ✔ Gray Monk Estate Winery Gewürztraminer
- ✔ Gray Monk Estate Winery Kerner Late Harvest
- ✔ Gray Monk Estate Winery Pinot Auxerrois
- ✔ Gray Monk Estate Winery Riesling

Hainle Vineyards Estate Winery

This is the Canadian birthplace of Icewine. Walter Hainle, with 10 generations of winemaking tradition in Germany behind him, was familiar with the concept and made the first Canadian Icewine in 1973, but not for commercial sale. Only lucky family and friends were privy to the new wine. Walter was joined by his son, Tilman, and they received their winery licence in 1988. The winery remains small, with a production of about 5,500 cases.

In 1993, the winery was renovated and a restaurant added. In 1995, Walter passed away in a tragic hiking accident, but his legacy lives on in a collection of wines going back to 1978, and in Tilman's dedication to quality production. For information about the cooking school at Hainle, see Chapter 15.

To increase the plants' resistance to pests, yields are kept very low.

- ✔ Hainle Vineyards Pinot Noir
- ✔ Hainle Vineyards Riesling-Traminer

Hawthorne Mountain Vineyards

The Hawthorne brothers, homesteaders who farmed the land for 10 years, first settled this property in 1909. In 1983, Albert and Dixie LeComte bought the land from Major Hugh McKenzie (who buried his pet collies in a dog cemetery on the property) and created LeComte Winery. Harry McWatters, of Sumac Ridge, bought the property from the LeComtes in 1995 and renamed it Hawthorne Mountain Vineyards in recognition of its history. He renovated the original Hawthorne brothers' homestead carefully to retain its English country cottage charm. English-style flower and herb gardens have been planted around the cottage and the retail wine shop inside has been refurbished.

The original vineyard, planted in the early 1960s, retains some of the original vines, but grape types like Buffalo and Bath have been replaced with vinifera varieties. Acreage has been increased under the McWatters regime and now numbers 170. Production is up to 25,000 cases. Harry sold his Sumac Ridge property to Vincor in April 2000 and Hawthorne Mountain Vineyards became part of the package in June. Harry and his partner, Bob Wareham, will continue to manage the property.

- Hawthorne Mountain Vineyards Chardonnay
- Hawthorne Mountain Vineyards Chardonnay/Sémillon
- Hawthorne Mountain Vineyards Ehrenfelser Icewine
- Hawthorne Mountain Vineyards Gamay Noir
- Hawthorne Mountain Vineyards Gewürztraminer
- Hawthorne Mountain Vineyards Lemberger
- Hawthorne Mountain Vineyards Merlot
- Hawthorne Mountain Vineyards Riesling

Hester Creek Estate Winery

Some of B.C.'s oldest vinifera *cultivars* (a plant variety produced by cultivation) are planted on this property, as this is where Joe Busnardo first located his Divino Estate about 30 years ago. In 1996 he sold the property to Hans Lochbichler, Henry Rathje, and Frank Supernak, and relocated to Vancouver Island. The present owners are continuing his tradition of quality while upgrading the physical plant. Intense flavours are drawn out of the grapes by the hot days and cool nights of the "Golden Mile" in the southern Okanagan.

Winemaker Supernak, who used to work for Vincor, uses both French and American oak for fermenting and aging, and produces only VQA wines.

✔ Hester Creek Estate Winery Blanc de Noirs

 ✔ Hester Creek Estate Winery Grand Reserve Pinot Blanc

 ✔ Hester Creek Estate Winery Late Harvest Trebbiano

 ✔ Hester Creek Estate Winery Reserve Pinot Blanc Icewine

Hillside Estate Winery

Founders Vera and Bohumir Klokocka produced 25 cases in Hillside Estate's first year of operation — 1990. Their first commercial release was awarded a VQA gold medal. Six years later, they produced 1,200 cases. They sold the winery in 1996, as Bohumir's health had declined. The new owners, a group of Alberta and B.C. investors, rebuilt and enlarged the winery, hiring Eric von Krosigk as winemaker. Eric studied oenology in Germany in the 1980s and, since returning to Canada, has earned a number of awards both nationally and internationally.

 ✔ Hillside Estate Winery Late Harvest Vidal

 ✔ Hillside Estate Winery Sémillon

House of Rose Vineyards

Vern Rose's predominantly hybrid vineyard sits high above Lake Okanagan, in Kelowna. When he bought the property in 1982, there were vines already planted, and he began to make wine as a hobby. With a teaching career behind him, it's logical that he followed an academic route to commercial winemaking. He took courses in winemaking at UC Davis in California and Okanagan College and travelled to Germany and New Zealand to attend symposia. In 1992, he opened the doors to his commercial winery, and, because of the altitude at which he is located, can almost guarantee an Icewine every year.

Inniskillin Okanagan Vineyards Inc.

The Okanagan Valley was a natural progression for Ontario industry leaders Donald Ziraldo and Karl Kaiser. When T.G. Bright merged with Cartier and Inniskillin, Donald and Karl moved temporarily to the Brights' winery facility in Oliver. They entered into a partnership with the Inkameep Indian Band to obtain grapes from the Inkameep vineyard and produced their first vintage in 1994, with 3,000 cases. The success of this project led them to acquire the winery known as Okanagan Vineyards, along with the 22-acre Dark Horse Vineyard. Current production is about 20,000 cases, but plans are underway to construct a new facility with the capacity for 100,000 cases. In 1998, Sandor Mayer, a Hungarian-trained oenologist who has worked with Inniskillin

Okanagan since 1990, was appointed general manager and winemaker. Inniskillin Okanagan Vineyards is owned by Vincor International.

- ✔ Inniskillin Okanagan Ehrenfelser Icewine
- ✔ Inniskillin Okanagan Meritage
- ✔ Inniskillin Okanagan Pinot Noir
- ✔ Inniskillin Okanagan Riesling Icewine
- ✔ Inniskillin Okanagan Vidal Icewine

Kettle Valley Winery

Owners Tim Watts and his brother-in-law Bob Ferguson must have had a childhood passion for railways, as they named their winery Kettle Valley, after the railroad that used to chug up the east side of Lake Okanagan through Naramata. As adults, Tim and Bob's interests seem to have shifted to red wine, as they grow mostly red grapes on their property — not trains. They started with Pinot Noir in the mid-1980s, and a few years later put in Cabernet Sauvignon, Cabernet Franc, and Merlot. Their latest choice of variety was Shiraz, a grape that needs lots of heat. Although the climate around Naramata is somewhat cooler than farther down the Valley, there are some warmer micro-climates where Shiraz does well. Construction of a new winery is scheduled to start in 2000.

- ✔ Kettle Valley Cabernet/Merlot
- ✔ Kettle Valley Cabernet Sauvignon
- ✔ Kettle Valley Merlot
- ✔ Kettle Valley Pinot Noir

Lake Breeze Vineyards

Lake Breeze is the first Canadian winery to vinify South Africa's signature varietal, Pinotage. Winemaker Garron Elmes came from South Africa with Lake Breeze's previous owners, the Mosers. Current owners Wayne and Joan Finn have identified different soil types on their Naramata property and are careful to plant their vines in the soils most suited to the grape variety. Pinot Blanc, for instance, is made from vines grown in sandy clay soils, while Chardonnay and Ehrenfelser are planted in heavier soils. The Lake Breeze winemaking philosophy is to manipulate the wine as little as possible during winemaking and to concentrate on vineyard management and selected vinifera varietals.

- ✔ Lake Breeze Vineyards Pinot Blanc

Lang Vineyard

Founded by Guenther and Kristina Lang, who moved to Canada from Germany in 1980, Lang Vineyard was the first "farm winery" established in Canada.

It didn't happen overnight — it took years of lobbying the government, which finally established criteria under which farm wineries could operate. Farm wineries were required to own a minimum of four acres and produce a maximum of 10,000 gallons of wine from B.C. grapes. The wine could only be sold at the winery or through restaurants. The Langs' persistence paid off; they now produce about 5,000 cases, mostly from vinifera varieties.

▌ ✔ Lang Vineyard Limited Edition Riesling

Larch Hills Winery

This tiny winery was carved out of the bush, literally. It took about 11 years to clear the land, plant some experimental vines and, finally, select the best varietals for their location. Settling on Ortega, Madeleine Angevine and Siegerrebe, Hans, and Hazel Nevrkla opened their farm winery in 1996. They continue to try out new varieties, however, and hope to vinify at least one red in the near future. Larch Hills Winery is the northernmost winery in the Okanagan, located on some bench land near Salmon Arm. Their steeply sloped vineyards look to the sunny south. Hans, an award-winning winemaker as an amateur, favours a German, cool-climate style of wine, although his drier wines are more reminiscent of Austria.

Mission Hill Winery

Mission Hill is one of the largest B.C. wineries, with a production of over 200,000 cases. Founded by Anthony von Mandl in 1980, the winery has a definite California look and feel to it and, in fact, Anthony draws much of his inspiration from Robert Mondavi's influence in the Napa Valley. Situated on top of Boucherie Mountain with a magnificent view of the Okanagan Valley, Mission Hill has vineyard holdings in several locations in the southern Valley, including Black Sage Road Vineyard in Oliver and Osoyoos Estate in Osoyoos. Despite its size, Mission Hill remains a family-owned enterprise and Anthony stays hands-on.

Although state of the art technology has already been installed in the winery, rebuilding is underway. A $30-million visitors' centre will include a cellar for 6,000 barrels and a wine and food centre with test kitchen, reception hall, and audiovisual theatre. A 75-foot bell tower will provide visitors with a spectacular 360-degree view of the surrounding mountains and vineyards.

John Simes is Mission Hill's Winemaker. John hails from New Zealand, and wins numerous awards in international circles for his wines, the most prestigious being the Avery Trophy for best Chardonnay worldwide for the 1992 vintage, his first with Mission Hill.

- ✔ Mission Hill Winery Estate Red
- ✔ Mission Hill Winery Estate Shiraz
- ✔ Mission Hill Winery Grand Reserve Cabernet Sauvignon
- ✔ Mission Hill Winery Grand Reserve Chardonnay
- ✔ Mission Hill Winery Grand Reserve Merlot/Cabernet
- ✔ Mission Hill Winery Grand Reserve Pinot Gris
- ✔ Mission Hill Winery Private Reserve Merlot

Nichol Vineyard & Farm Winery

Alex Nichol's first career was as a double bassist in a symphony orchestra, but he had always loved wine. He followed the development of the wine industry in the Okanagan Valley very carefully and wrote articles for a variety of publications. He even wrote a book called *Wine and Vines of British Columbia*, which was the first to record the development of B.C. wines. In 1989, Alex and his wife, Kathleen, bought a property in Naramata. Over the course of three years they transformed an alfalfa field into what could almost be called a self-heating vineyard. Situated under a granite cliff, the land is warmed not only by the sun reflecting off the rock, but also by the heat retained in the stone face. Alex is making some of the most intensely flavoured and powerful wines in the region and is even able to grow Syrah, normally at home in southern climates. He makes only premium wines by barrel-fermenting the whites and aging them on the lees and by oak-aging the reds. He allows the wines to clear naturally so they don't require filtering. Production maxes out at 1,200 cases and is only available at the winery and selected restaurants.

- ✔ Nichol Vineyard Cabernet Franc
- ✔ Nichol Vineyard Pinot Gris
- ✔ Nichol Vineyard Syrah

Pinot Reach Cellars

Susan Dulik grew up in a grape-growing family and established her winery on property in Kelowna acquired by her grandfather. As suggested by the label, Susan has a thing for the Pinot family of grapes, especially the reds. Besides

Pinot Blanc, Pinot Noir, and Pinot Meunier, she grows a variety of white grapes — mostly Germanic varieties — and some Cabernet Sauvignon. As winemaker, she has enlisted the services of the talented consultant Eric von Krosigk.

- ↙ Pinot Reach Cellars Pinot Noir
- ↙ Pinot Reach Cellars Riesling
- ↙ Pinot Reach Cellars Riesling Brut Sparkling Wine

Poplar Grove Farm Winery

Ian Sutherland and his wife Gitta bought an eight-acre property in Penticton in 1992 with the express purpose of making Bordeaux-style reds — and to heck with the whites that everyone else was planting. They planted mostly Merlot and Cabernet Franc, with a small concession to whites in the form of some Chardonnay and Pinot Gris. Although their goal is to stay small, they still had to pull out an orchard of apple trees to make room for their vines. They found that the soil is clay loam and not unlike that of St. Émilion in France, where Merlot and Cabernet Franc form the basis of the wines. Ian had an opportunity to work for one harvest at a winery in New Zealand and translated that experience into an exceptionally successful 1997 Chardonnay from Poplar Grove. Gitta and Ian also collaborate with former Quails' Gate winemaker Jeff Martin to produce Jeff's La Frenz label (Cabernet Sauvignon, Merlot, Gamay, Semillon, Pinot Gris, Riesling, and Sauvignon Blanc).

- ↙ Poplar Grove Cabernet Franc
- ↙ Poplar Grove Merlot

Prpich Hills

Dan Prpich (pronounced pur-pitch) moved his amateur winemaking career out of the basement when he relocated, with his family, from Hamilton, Ontario, to Okanagan Falls. He bought a 60-acre farm property in 1973 and started to replace the orchards with vineyards. The first grapes he planted were Okanagan Riesling and Maréchal Foch, along with some Chardonnay, Cabernet Sauvignon, and Verdelet. He decreased his hybrid acreage during the federally sponsored Pullout Program, replacing them with vinifera, and has plans to continue replanting with an emphasis on Cabernet Franc, Cabernet Sauvignon, Ehrenfelser, and Lemberger.

Quails' Gate Estate Winery

In just over 10 years, Quails' Gate has gone from producing 4,000 cases to 60,000 cases without ever losing sight of the quest for increasing quality. Dick Stewart and his son Ben started the business fully prepared. They were soon joined by another son, Tony, and together they built the winery to its present stature. They planted and experimented for years before turning their dream into reality. Their ultimate goal was to grow Pinot Noir, even though those who supposedly knew better said it was impossible. The vineyard is located in Kelowna, on a south-facing slope at the foot of Mount Boucherie, an extinct volcano. The soil is a mix of volcanic rock and clay. The Stewarts believe this terrain contributes greatly to the particular character of their wines. Besides Pinot Noir, which is their flagship wine, they produce a broad range of varieties in styles from dry to late harvest and Icewine.

In 1997 they demolished their entire production facility with the exception of their finished goods warehouse and started construction on a new 18,000-square-foot building that incorporates modern technology and design but respects the heritage of the property. Winemaker Ashley Hooper, an Australian, succeeded compatriot Peter Draper, who died very suddenly during the 1999 harvest, of heart failure, at the age of 39.

- ✔ Quails' Gate Estate Winery Late Harvest Optima Botrytis Affected
- ✔ Quails' Gate Estate Winery Limited Release Chardonnay
- ✔ Quails' Gate Estate Winery Limited Release Chenin Blanc
- ✔ Quails' Gate Estate Winery Limited Release Dry Riesling
- ✔ Quails' Gate Estate Winery Limited Release Meritage
- ✔ Quails' Gate Estate Winery Limited Release Old Vines Foch

If you can get them, the Quails' Gate Family Reserve Pinot Noir and Chardonnay are some of the best wines produced in B.C., but very little is made.

Recline Ridge Vineyards & Winery Ltd.

What started as a hobby over 25 years ago has turned into a successful winery at the northern tip of the Okanagan Valley. Over the years, Mike and Sue Smith experimented with such varietals as Ortega, Optima, Siegerrebe, and Madeleine Angevine and learned as much as they could about growing conditions before actually launching their winery.

They concentrate on Germanic whites in an off-dry style and full-bodied reds put through malolactic fermentation and oak aging. Expansion of the winery started in 1998 and resulted in a natural log construction building with 3,300 square feet on three levels and a magnificent view of the Tappen Mountains and Tappen and Skimikin Valleys.

Red Rooster Winery

Beat and Prudence Mahrer moved to the Okanagan Valley from Switzerland a little over 10 years ago. They opened a winery near Naramata in 1997 in time to release their first vintage. They produce Gewürztraminer, Pinot Gris, Riesling, Chardonnay, Pinot Noir, Merlot, a sparkling wine, late harvest, and Icewine. To assure the success of their sparkling wine, Red Rooster Brut, they called on Eric von Krosigk, who has made a specialty of sparkling wine at other wineries including Summerhill, Pinot Reach, and Saturna Island. The Mahrers manage their own vineyard as well as others nearby.

St. Hubertus Estate Winery

There's a little bit of Switzerland in Kelowna at St. Hubertus, which is the name of the Gebert brothers' family lodge in Switzerland. Two vineyards, side by side — St. Hubertus and Oak Bay — are owned by Leo and Andy Gebert respectively, and are among some of the oldest in the Okanagan. A few of the original hybrid vines (planted in the 1920s) remain, but the rest have been replaced by vinifera and premium hybrids. Each property represents a different style of wine. Those under the Oak Bay label are barrel-fermented and/or aged in oak, while the St. Hubertus label indicates unoaked wines.

The Geberts use no chemicals to keep the vineyards in top condition and have maintained some of the original buildings dating from the 1930s to house the winery and retail shop. A charming little cottage now houses the "Stampers Paradise," which caters to collectors of rubber stamps. Several antique farm machines, still in working condition, complete the period decor. St. Hubertus rounds out its winemaking activities with a number of events over the course of the year. Visitors can lunch or dine in the vineyard in the summer or harvest Icewine in the winter. There are the spring and fall festivals and even the occasional Swiss Yodeller Club concert, held right in the vineyard.

- ✔ St. Hubertus Estate Winery Oak Bay Chardonnay/Pinot Blanc
- ✔ St. Hubertus Estate Winery Oak Bay Pinot Meunier
- ✔ St. Hubertus Estate Winery Pinot Blanc/Riesling Icewine
- ✔ St. Hubertus Estate Winery Rosé Gamay
- ✔ St. Hubertus Estate Winery Summer Symphony

Scherzinger Vineyards

The timing was not quite as good as hoped when Edgar and Elizabeth Scherzinger bought their cherry orchard in Summerland in 1974. As soon as they acquired the property, the cherry market went downhill. As a way out of a bad situation, they decided to replant the orchard with Labrusca grape varieties. Edgar vinified the grapes, but found the wine so uninspiring he was reluctant to sell it at all. He then took a gamble that paid off: At a time when everybody was saying that vinifera varieties were not suited to the Canadian climate, he planted Gewürztraminer that he sold to the Sumac Ridge winery. Later, he planted some Chardonnay and Pinot Noir. In 1994, with a mature producing vineyard, he obtained his winery licence. The production is small but Edgar is intent on quality. In his spare time he makes woodcarvings, some of which are on display in the winery tasting room.

Slamka Cellars Winery

The Slamka family opened their winery in the fall of 1996, but their vineyard had been planted 25 years previously, giving them mature vines with which they could immediately start making wine. Among the vines that flourish in the volcanic ash and sandy, gravel mixture of the southeast slope of Boucherie Mountain are Pinot Noir, Auxerrois, Lemberger, Merlot, and Siegerrebe. They start with great raw material and use modern winemaking techniques with either oak or stainless steel aging to bring out the best in each grape type.

▮ ✔ Slamka Cellars Pinot Noir

Stag's Hollow Winery & Vineyard

From 1992 to 1996, Larry Gerelus, an actuary, and his wife, Linda Pruegger, an accountant, commuted from Calgary, Alberta, to tend their Okanagan Falls vineyard, as they worked towards their dream. Their winery building went up in 1995 but not in time for the crush. That year, they made their wine at Sumac Ridge but opened their shop in time to sell three of their whites on their own property. The following summer, Larry and Linda moved to their new home and christened their winery with the 1996 harvest. In the following years they shifted their emphasis from whites to reds. They grow Merlot, Pinot Noir, some Chardonnay, and Vidal.

▮ ✔ Stag's Hollow Vidal

Sumac Ridge Estate Winery Ltd.

Harry McWatters established Sumac Ridge in Summerland in 1979 with partner Lloyd Schmidt, who has since sold his interest in the winery. Bob Wareham then came in as a co-owner. McWatters and Wareham retained ownership of Sumac Ridge for over 20 years until its sale to Vincor International in early 2000. The winery undoubtedly benefitted from being in the hands of a single owner for such a stretch — the longest period of ownership by a founder in the entire Okanagan region. Located on a bench overlooking Lake Okanagan, the vineyards were developed in 1981 on what were once fairways #1 and # 2 of the Sumac Ridge Golf and Country Club. They are planted to Riesling and Gewürztraminer used for the award-winning Private Reserve, and Pinot Noir used in Blanc de Noirs sparkling wine. All these grapes are hand-picked and moved quickly into the winery for crushing.

About 50 percent of the grapes used by Sumac Ridge come from growers in the South Okanagan with whom the winery has long-term contracts. In 1991, Harry and Bob developed Black Sage Vineyard, 115 acres of premium land. Grape varieties planted here are predominantly red and are the ones best known in France — Cabernet Sauvignon, Cabernet Franc, Merlot, Pinot Noir, Malbec. Whites are Chardonnay and Pinot Blanc. Production runs about 50,000 cases and tourism attracts some 55,000 visitors a year. In 1995, Sumac Ridge acquired Hawthorne Mountain Vineyards, which was first planted in 1961. Both properties produce only VQA wines. In 2000, Vincor International acquired both Sumac Ridge and Hawthorne Mountain.

Of all the winery owners, Harry has been the most active within the wine community. He founded the British Columbia Wine Institute and was founding chair of both the Okanagan Wine Festival board and VQA Canada. He and Bob will remain with the wineries as president and vice-president respectively, and will manage what has become the Sumac Ridge Wine Group.

✔ Sumac Ridge Estate Winery Blanc de Noirs

✔ Sumac Ridge Estate Winery Cabernet Sauvignon

✔ Sumac Ridge Estate Winery Meritage

✔ Sumac Ridge Estate Winery Meritage White

✔ Sumac Ridge Estate Winery Merlot

✔ Sumac Ridge Estate Winery Okanagan Blush

✔ Sumac Ridge Estate Winery Pinnacle (Bordeaux blend)

✔ Sumac Ridge Estate Winery Pinot Blanc Icewine

✔ Sumac Ridge Estate Winery Private Reserve Gewürztraminer

✔ Sumac Ridge Estate Winery Private Reserve Pinot Blanc

✔ Sumac Ridge Estate Winery Steller's Jay

Industry leader: Harry McWatters

Harry McWatters has led the British Columbia wine industry into the 21st century. Born in Toronto, he moved as a child to Vancouver with his family and completed his education there. He became interested in wine and winemaking as a young man and, in 1968, began his career with Casabello Wines, a newly formed winery in Penticton.

McWatters worked in sales in the Vancouver area. He excelled, and in 1978 was promoted to marketing manager for the entire Okanagan Valley.

McWatters founded Sumac Ridge Estate Winery with a partner in 1979, creating the first estate winery in the province (a small operation using its own grapes). He has long believed that B.C. could produce premium quality wines, and has worked relentlessly, helping direct the evolution of the wine industry there.

In 1990, the province of British Columbia appointed McWatters chair of the newly established British Columbia Wine Institute. This association of winery owners and grape growers guided the industry through the challenges brought on by the Free Trade Agreement with the U.S. (the dropping of trade barriers that exposed the local industry to the heat of competition from California and the Pacific Northwest wineries). McWatters also implemented the Vintners Quality Alliance (VQA) in British Columbia.

McWatters served as co-chair of the Cool Climate Oenology and Viticulture Institute (CCOVI) at Brock University, in St. Catharines, Ontario, which has an exchange agreement with the University of British Columbia. He's also a member of UBC's Wine Research Advisory Board. In 1999, McWatters' Sumac Ridge Estate Winery received the Top Winery of the Year award from the *Globe and Mail*.

Summerhill Estate Winery

Summerhill's owner, Stephen Cipes, has an original theory. He believes that wines age better when they are stored in a pyramid, so he built one. It is a small replica of the Great Pyramid at Cheops in Egypt and was constructed with the aid of a surveyor and an astronomer to line it up with the exact True North and the North Star. The ground below the foundation was compacted to floor strength and it was checked for interfering energies such as underground streams, electrical currents, or gas lines. The pyramid is used for the storage and aging of sparkling wine, which is almost half of the Summerhill production. Taste comparisons made over the course of three years of wines aged in the pyramid and in a traditional cellar show that people prefer the pyramid-aged wines.

The decision to concentrate on sparkling wines was made at the outset, as Steve was convinced that the characteristics of the grapes grown in the near desert-like conditions of the Okanagan were perfect for making champagne-method wines. He seems to have made the right decision, as his wines have outsold French champagne in the B.C. market.

Summerhill also makes a variety of still wines including Pinot Blanc, Chardonnay, Gewürztraminer, Pinot Noir, and Merlot.

- Summerhill Estate Winery Cabernet Sauvignon Platinum Series
- Summerhill Estate Winery Cipes Aurora Blanc de Blancs
- Summerhill Estate Winery Cipes Gabriel Chardonnay (champagne method)
- Summerhill Estate Winery Ehrenfelser
- Summerhill Estate Winery Gewürztraminer Reserve
- Summerhill Estate Winery Late Harvest Riesling
- Summerhill Estate Winery Pinot Blanc
- Summerhill Estate Winery Platinum Series Pinot Noir
- Summerhill Estate Winery Riesling Icewine

Tinhorn Creek Vineyards

A limited number of grape varieties, reduced yields in the vineyards, and American oak barrels in the winery form the fundamentals of winemaking at Tinhorn Creek, and the California influence is unmistakable. Partners Kenn and Sandra Oldfield met while they were both studying at the University of California at Davis. Kenn, a chemical engineer from Ontario, trained in viticulture, Sandra in winemaking. In the early 1990s, they teamed with two other partners, Robert and Barbara Shaunessy, from Calgary, who were buying up planted vineyards at a time when local growers were feeling the downside of the Free Trade Agreement.

The partners have wasted no time in replanting to premium varietals and building an impressive winemaking facility. They impressed the critics within a very short period of time with their roster of wines. Beyond the wine, they have created a fascinating environment for visitors. There are panoramic views, educational self-guided tours, walking trails, even a water fountain and rock garden resembling nearby Tinhorn Creek, now depleted of all the gold that once attracted prospectors.

- Tinhorn Creek Vineyards Cabernet Franc
- Tinhorn Creek Vineyards Chardonnay
- Tinhorn Creek Vineyards Gewürztraminer
- Tinhorn Creek Vineyards Kerner Icewine
- Tinhorn Creek Vineyards Merlot
- Tinhorn Creek Vineyards Pinot Gris

Vincor/Jackson-Triggs Vintners

Vincor's recent agreement with the Osoyoos Indian Band to lease 2,000 acres of land will eventually double the supply of high-quality wine grapes in B.C. The area around Osoyoos Lake in the southern end of the Okanagan Valley is known for its high heat units during the day and cool nights. This is what is needed to ripen grapes like Cabernet Sauvignon and Merlot and develop the best acid balance. These and other varieties will be used to develop a line of ultra-premium wines under the Jackson-Triggs label.

Winemaker Bruce Nicholson's talent has led to a number of awards in recent years. Some pundits predict he will soon become known as Canada's best winemaker.

Vincor also owns Inniskillin Okanagan, Sumac Ridge, and Hawthorne Mountain. Its latest venture is a joint project with the Bordeaux shippers Groupe Taillan, to produce a Bordeaux-style claret using all five Bordeaux varieties. The wine will be called Osoyoos Larose, after Lake Osoyoos and the Groupe Taillan's flagship Bordeaux property, Château Gruaud-Larose. Renowned French wine-maker Michel Rolland is the consulting winemaker on the joint venture. The first wine from the newly planted vineyard is expected to be 2005.

- Jackson-Triggs Vintners Proprietors' Grand Reserve Chardonnay
- Jackson-Triggs Vintners Proprietors' Grand Reserve Merlot
- Jackson-Triggs Vintners Proprietors' Grand Reserve Riesling Icewine
- Jackson-Triggs Vintners Proprietors' Reserve Cabernet Sauvignon
- Jackson-Triggs Vintners Proprietors' Reserve Chardonnay
- Jackson-Triggs Vintners Proprietors' Reserve Chenin Blanc Icewine
- Jackson-Triggs Vintners Proprietors' Reserve Merlot
- Jackson-Triggs Vintners Proprietors' Reserve Pinot Blanc
- Jackson-Triggs Vintners Proprietors' Reserve Riesling Dry
- Jackson-Triggs Vintners Proprietors' Reserve Riesling Icewine

Wild Goose Vineyards

This Okanagan Falls winery was another leader in the early 1990s movement to allow farm wineries to operate in the Okanagan region. Founder Adolf Kruger joined the Langs, of Lang Vineyards, and the Klokockas, of Hillside Estate, in lobbying the government to allow sales of wine from their vineyards. Adolf, an electrical engineer, found jobs scarce in the economic doldrums of the late 1980s; his sons Roland and Hagen helped him turn his winemaking hobby into a business. A 10-acre vineyard had been planted in 1984, but the Krugers contracted a further 10 acres to produce about 5,000 cases a year. The home vineyard faces south. Its rocky soil absorbs heat during the day and warms the vineyard at night.

- ✔ Wild Goose Vineyards Late Harvest Riesling
- ✔ Wild Goose Vineyards Maréchal Foch
- ✔ Wild Goose Vineyards Merlot
- ✔ Wild Goose Vineyards Pinot Blanc

Over the Hill, Not Too Far Away

Just over a ridge of mountains to the west of the Okanagan Valley, running almost parallel to it, is the Similkameen Valley. Its climatic conditions are similar to those of the southern Okanagan. The Similkameen River supplies water and some mitigating influence in the winter.

Similkameen Valley Wineries

To date only two wineries have been established here, but there are likely to be more in the future. The Similkameen is an undiscovered byway compared to the Okanagan, boasting two very small towns and a highway free of traffic. For many tourists it's seen as too far off the beaten track but that may well be its appeal for future winemakers who find the Okanagan just too crowded.

When Crowsnest Vineyards received its licence to serve food on its patio in the summer of 2000, visitors were attracted to the area in greater numbers. This in turn may encourage other growers to take the leap.

Crowsnest Vineyards

When Andrea and Hugh McDonald married, they brought together skills and experience to create a successful winery. Andrea's career as a lab technician at Okanagan Vineyards and then at Brights blended well with Hugh's experience on the land as a fruit farmer. Their first planting, in 1990, featured a mere two acres of Pinot Auxerrois. Their first commercial crush was four years later, and they followed that up by adding a number of varieties to their sandy loam soils in the Similkameen Valley. The high heat units from their western exposure encourage ripeness in the fruit and richness in the resulting wines.

In 1999, Olaf and Sabine Heinecke bought the property with their winemaker daughter Anna and son Sascha, who is sales and marketing manager. They have since added a patio featuring wines by the glass and German delicacies.

St. Laszlo Vineyards

Joe Ritlop and his family bring a little bit of the former Yugoslavia to the B.C. mountains. Joe was born in St. Laszlo and some of his wines are typical of eastern Europe, including Riesling and Tokaji Aszu. The Ritlops planted their vineyards in Keremos in the early 1970s and have been making wine since 1978. Joe has experimented with a number of different hybrids and viniferas over the years. By his own admission, he can only create wine in his own particular fashion and has earned a reputation as a bit of a maverick because of that. He makes organic wines, adds no chemicals to the vineyard and no sulphites to the wine. He also allows the grapes to ferment on their own yeasts. The result is a range of full-bodied wines with the late harvest wines leading the bunch, augmented by a growing range of fruit wines.

A Gentle Style of Wine

Two wineries and one fruit winery have established themselves in the Fraser Valley, not far from greater Vancouver. The Fraser Valley does have a number of other growers — apart from these established winemaking facilities — but none yet large enough to establish a winery. The newest additions are Corey and Gwen Coleman, who worked at several Okanagan wineries before going out on their own with the Campbell Valley Winery (not far from Domaine de Chaberton). They made their first crush in the fall of 2000.

The climate in the Fraser Valley is more temperate than the Okanagan; so the wines are very different in character. They don't have the high acidity of the Okanagan; they're soft, round, and smooth.

Greater Vancouver and Fraser Valley Wineries

Two wineries are within an easy drive from Vancouver, but don't expect to see vineyards at Andrés, which is located in an urban district. They bring all their grapes in from the Okanagan Valley. Columbia Valley, a fruit winery, is a little further out — an hour-and-a-half drive east of Vancouver. Domaine de Chaberton is, currently, the only grape winery with vineyards in the appellation.

Andrés Wines (B.C.) Ltd.

It all started in Port Moody, a suburb of Vancouver; then, on the wings of their success, Andrés Wines opened operations in Nova Scotia, Alberta, Québec, Manitoba, and Ontario.

When Andrew Peller started the company, he was making wines from California grapes. At that point in time (1961) they were probably not much different from wines from B.C. grapes, but they were extremely popular and the company grew like crazy. Over the years, momentum has been sustained by bottling imported wines under a variety of labels.

In the 1970s, the government-contracted consultant from Germany, Helmut Becker, was recommending that vintners plant hybrid and vinifera vines. Andrés developed 300 acres of these vines on land leased from the Inkameep Indian Band near Oliver and, in keeping up with the times, has since made a serious commitment to VQA wines, which are sold under the Peller Estates and Bighorn Vineyards labels.

With production totalling 500,000 cases, Andrés' main operation is now in Ontario, but there is a great loyalty to the B.C. location as shown by a $1-million investment in new equipment.

- ✔ Peller Estates Wines Limited Edition Pinot Gris
- ✔ Peller Estates Wines Trinity Icewine

Domaine de Chaberton Estates Limited

Domaine de Chaberton is the only winery to actually grow grapes in the Fraser Valley, and the vineyard in South Langley is the most southerly on the B.C. mainland. The vineyard was planted by Claude Violet when he and his wife, Inge, settled in B.C. after emigrating from France in 1981. Although a Parisian, Claude owned land in the south of France and his family had made wine for more than 300 years. He and Inge travelled throughout the United States and Canada before deciding to settle in the Fraser Valley. In 1991, he converted his vineyard into a winery, where he and his winemaker Elias Phiniotis (a veteran of Calona Wines, Okanagan Vineyards, and Quails' Gate) produce mostly hybrid-based wines that have won numerous awards. Gradually over the years production has increased, and much of it is exported to France, Taiwan, China, Hong Kong, and Japan. Domaine de Chaberton is still very much a family business with Claude and Elias making the wine as Inge oversees sales, marketing, exports, and the on-site retail shop.

✔ Domaine de Chaberton Estates Bacchus

✔ Domaine de Chaberton Estates Gewürztraminer

✔ Domaine de Chaberton Estates Madeleine Angevine

✔ Domaine de Chaberton Estates Rouge

New Kids on the Block

Vancouver Island is a more recent discovery in terms of wine but is already showing interesting results. Most of the wineries here are located in the Cowichan Valley, on the east coast between Victoria and Duncan. Included in this group of wineries are two tiny operations located on smaller islands a short ferry ride from either Vancouver or Victoria.

Vancouver Island Wineries

The climate on Vancouver Island and surrounding islands is temperate and maritime. The wine produced here has more in common with wines from the Niagara Peninsula than wines from the Okanagan Valley.

Alderlea Vineyards

Alderlea's vineyards benefit not only from their southern exposure but also from the proximity of a large lake. This charming, rural setting, nestled in the Cowichan Valley at the southern end of Vancouver Island, and not far from the town of Duncan, has been called home since 1992 by ex-Vancouverites Roger and Nancy Dosman. The winery's first crush, in 1996, produced an Auxerrois and a Bacchus. Subsequent vintages included a notable Pinot Gris, a blended white, some Pinot Noir, Maréchal Foch, and a port-style fortified red. The Dosmans source all grapes from their own property to create hand-crafted wines designed to reflect their Cowichan Valley origins. In 1998 they opened a new winery that houses stainless steel tanks for the fermentation and aging of whites and a mix of French and American barrels for aging the reds. This is a winery to watch.

Blue Grouse Vineyards & Winery

This Vancouver Island winery is among the first to have been founded off the mainland. It fulfilled a dream for Hans Kiltz, who was a veterinarian before coming to Canada from Germany. Hans tested over 100 grape varieties before narrowing down the selection that produces the best results in the cool Cowichan Valley. It includes Pinot Gris, Pinot Noir, Müller-Thurgau, and Bacchus. Blue Grouse Vineyards benefits from their location in the warmest micro-climate on the island. In 1996, all elements conspired to permit production of the first botrytis-affected late harvest wine in the Vancouver Island designation, the Ortega Special Selection 1996. Leaning towards a Germanic style of wine, Hans, his wife, Evangeline, and their children, Sandrina and Richard, are all committed to the success of the winery, managing the vineyard, the winery, and the wine shop between them. Bavarian food specialties are served on the patio.

- Blue Grouse Vineyards Bacchus
- Blue Grouse Vineyards Siegerrebe

Chateau Wolff

From Latvia, a young Harry von Wolff travelled to Switzerland and hotel school. One of his principal accomplishments there was to acquire a love of wine. When he first arrived in B.C., he worked in the hotel business, and then switched to shoemaking, founding the successful Island Boot and Saddle Shop. Throughout all this, however, his love affair with the grape endured. A few backyard vines sufficed for a time, but eventually, Harry bought an eight-acre farm with a woodlot. Sale of the wood enabled him to create a small vineyard with Pinot Noir and Chardonnay in one section and Müller-Thurgau, Bacchus, Siegerrebe, and Viognier in another. He has plans to burrow under the side of the hill to construct a new cellar.

Cherry Point Vineyards

Wayne and Helena Ulrich blend sheep husbandry with grape production to maintain an ecological balance on their property (26 acres of vines, the largest of the Duncan area wineries). The sheep provided some income while they planted their vineyard and got it up and running. Their Cowichan Valley property is underlain with a gravelly glacial deposit that they compare to terroir in Alsace and Chablis, and they keep one acre aside to test different varieties. In a few short years they have had quite a bit of success with varietals as well as with branded blends.

- ✔ Cherry Point Vineyards Gewürztraminer
- ✔ Cherry Point Vineyards Ortega
- ✔ Cherry Point Vineyards Pinot Gris
- ✔ Cherry Point Vineyards Pinot Noir

Divino Estate Winery

Divino Estate is a transplant from the Okanagan. Founder Joe Busnardo started growing grapes about 30 years ago in Oliver, on a property now called Hester Creek Vineyards. Over the years he experimented with more than 100 different grape types, many of which came, like Joe himself, from the Veneto, in Italy. He emphasizes that to have good wine, you must have good grapes. In his new location on Vancouver Island, he continues to experiment on his 40-acre vineyard. Among the varieties he has planted are Merlot, Cabernet Franc, Trebbiano, Tocai, Pinot Grigio, Malvasia, and Pinot Nero. He was planning to be close to full production by 2000. He is also growing a variety of other fruits including kiwis, figs, and apples.

An independent thinker, Joe prefers to operate on his own, rather than participate in the B.C. Wine Institute. Just the same, he uses traditional methods of winemaking, with stainless steel tanks for fermentation and "whole berry fermentation" to extract soft fruity flavours.

Saturna Vineyard

Saturna Vineyard was the first farm winery established in B.C.'s Gulf Islands. Owners of the Saturna Lodge & Restaurant, Lawrence and Robyn Page started to prepare the grounds for the vineyard in the spring of 1995, with six acres of vines planted to Pinot Noir and Gewürztraminer. The Rebecca Vineyard was named after their daughter. A further eight acres planted to Chardonnay, Merlot, and Pinot Noir was christened the Robyn Vineyard. The Pages vinified their first harvest in 1999 with assistance from winemakers Eric von Krosigk and Steve Cozine and released the wines in the spring of 2000. They are building a 3,000-square-foot building to house the winery and the tasting room.

Venturi-Schulze Vineyards

The dynamic husband and wife team of Giordano Venturi from Italy and Marilyn Schulze from Australia are making their mark on the Vancouver Island winery scene. Their production is under 1,000 cases and every bottle receives personal attention including a mini-pamphlet that describes how the wine was made.

Giordano was an electronics instructor in Italy and Marilyn a microbiologist and French teacher. They chose Vancouver Island primarily for its tranquility, buying a 100-year-old farm in 1988. They have experimented with about 25 grape varieties and chosen 12 with which to work, including Pinot Noir, Pinot Auxerrois, and Pinot Gris. They have a good, south-facing location that is cooled by ocean breezes. They vary their winemaking techniques according to the varieties and conditions. All the reds are destemmed manually to avoid bitter tannins.

Giordano has an interesting sideline — making balsamic vinegar — but his production is kept well away from the winery to avoid contamination.

Vigneti Zanatta Winery and Vineyards

Dennis and Claudia Zanatta were planting vines on Vancouver Island as early as 1959, transforming an acquired dairy farm into a vineyard. In 1983, they took part in the government-sponsored program to help select grape varieties best suited to their location. Among the grapes planted at that time were Ortega and Cayuga. Today their vineyard is planted to Ortega, Auxerrois, Pinot Grigio, Pinot Nero, and Muscat. They vinify only grapes from their own vineyards and try to bring out as much of the regional character of their wines as they can.

▮ ✔ Vigneti Zanatta Glenora Fantasia

The Vineyard at Bowen Island

Bowen Island is one of many islands that pepper the Strait of Georgia and serve as cottage country for city-worn Vancouverites. This vineyard is tiny, practically an adjunct to the guest house run by Lary and Elena Waldman, who planted Pinot Blanc and Pinot Noir in 1994. Their inaugural vintage (1998) was bottled in 1999 and sold at their on-site wine shop. The Waldmans have a great deal of faith in their mild, maritime climate to produce quality wine.

Table 19-1	Top 10 B.C. Wineries to Visit
Winery	**What to Look For**
Blue Mountain Vineyard and Cellars	A small but elegant winery making top-class wines, especially from the Pinot family of grapes, as well as sparkling wines.
Calona Vineyards	Calona has a long and interesting history. Taste the award-winning Artist Series and Private Reserve wines.

Winery	What to Look For
Domaine de Chaberton Estates	Find out about the French influence on the wines of the Fraser Valley. Taste the difference in style from the Okanagan.
Gehringer Brothers Estate Winery	Walter and Gordon Gehringer have been winning awards for their wines for many years. Enjoy their fresh, Germanic style.
Hillside Estate Winery	One of the first vineyards to convert to a farm winery, in 1989.
Mission Hill Winery	An established winery with a history of award-winning wines, not to mention a magnificent view of the Okanagan Valley.
Nichol Vineyard & Farm Winery	Find out how the micro-climate of a sheltered vineyard affects the quality of the wine. This is a small winery; best to call first.
Sumac Ridge Estate Winery	Founded by Harry McWatters, who shepherded it and the entire B.C. wine industry towards quality wine production using vinifera grape types.
Summerhill Estate Winery	A specialist in marketing wine, Summerhill also introduces wine lovers to the concept of pyramid aging. Worth a visit.
Tinhorn Creek Vineyards	Newcomer to the wine scene in B.C. produces intense, California-style wines.

Chapter 20

Québec and Atlantic Province Wineries

Québec winters are brutal, and winter in the Atlantic region is no picnic either — typically Canadian. You might well ask how any wine could come from two of the country's least forgiving regions, weather-wise. The answer is that some people thrive on challenge. They love wine, and they'll defy all odds to make it. They adapt their methods to a short growing season by finding sheltered locations and sunny exposures, and by using just the right grape types.

This chapter takes you to these unlikely grape-growing regions and shows you that it can in fact be done. Most of the wineries are tiny, as is their production — there are very few with any wines listed at the liquor board, so you really have to visit the wineries themselves to find out what it's all about. Check out our map of Québec wine regions in Figure 20-1 and of Atlantic regions in Figure 20-2. In Québec, in particular, you'll find that many wineries sell honey, jam, maple syrup, T-shirts, and crafts in addition to their wine, just to make a go of it. What you'll also find, though, is a passion and dedication to overcome winter and make good wine.

If you plan to visit any of these wineries, though, it pays to call ahead. While they enjoy receiving visitors, they also have to work out in the vineyards, so there might not always be someone in the shop. Check out Appendix B, "Directory of Canadian Wineries," for details on how to get in touch.

Québec Wineries: And They Said It Couldn't Be Done!

You can't just go out and plant vines in a climate like Québec's. Temperatures drop regularly to –25° Celsius, so you have to think about how to keep your vines from freezing their little buds off. There are a couple of things you can do. Firstly, select your vines very carefully. You need hardy stock. Most of those vinifera varieties that make all the great wines in Europe don't cut it in Québec. It's safer to stick with some of the hybrids. They make good wine, just not as complex or full-bodied as wine from the "noble" grapes.

Québec

Québec ○

Montréal ○

Montérégie and Estrie (Eastern Townships)

Figure 20-1: Québec wine regions.

Québec's best hybrid grapes

One of the most successful hybrids in Québec is Seyval, which makes a crisp, refreshing white wine. Because of its success, just about every Québec vineyard jumped on the bandwagon and started growing it — bo-ring! Fortunately, winemakers like to experiment, too. Several are doing good things with Geisenheim clones that resemble the white varieties Riesling and Cayuga. For reds, De Chaunac and Maréchal Foch are good bets; but as you don't often see single varietal wines (made only from one grape type) in Québec (except for Seyval), you need to look at the back label or ask at the shop to find out which grapes are in the blend — and which have the most influence on the flavour.

Secondly, your vines need a winter coat to protect them from the elements as they "hibernate" — a good layer of earth will do. After the harvest, growers cut down the vines and "hill up" the earth around them. Because this "hilling" is hard work and expensive, some growers go to great lengths to get around it. Some are experimenting with specific clones that they buy from various nurseries around the world to find more winter-hardy varieties. Others are training their vines on trellises high off the ground to give the leaves and berries better exposure to the sun in the hopes of strengthening the vines. Planting vines on a sheltered slope is another way to outsmart Old Man Winter. Grape selection is important, too: the white Cliche-Vandal and red Ste-Croix varieties are cold-hardy enough to stand up straight in winter.

Eastern Townships Wineries

There are no VQA appellations in Québec, but two distinct regions are recognized south and southwest of Montréal. A large glacial plain, stretching down to the U.S. border, supports mixed farming, including a number of apple orchards that supply an active cider industry. On the eastern side of this plain are the Eastern Townships (Estrie). Several wineries have sprung up in the areas around Farnum and Dunham.

Domaine Félibre

While appearing quite hostile to the cultivation of vines, the land owned by Gilles Desjardins and Catherine Hébert nevertheless yields up a wine that is quickly sold off in the winery boutique. They make two styles, a still dry wine and an off-dry *perlant* (lightly sparkling), using the hardy American cross, Éona, that can survive the frigid winters and produce in the short growing season. Even if it's not the perfect spot for grape-growing, the vineyard, high on a hill at an altitude of 425 metres above sea level, offers a magnificent panorama of the surrounding mountains. The view extends from Mount Orford, one of the Eastern Townships' better-known ski hills, to the Green and Appalachian mountain ranges south of the U.S. border.

Vignoble de l'Aurore Boréale

If the thought of the aurora borealis makes you shiver, check out this Eastern Townships property. The vineyards thrive in a nice, warm micro-climate (just keep in mind this is still Québec). Owner Guy Desrochers is entertainment editor of the French-language daily *La Presse*, a job he maintains to help support the winery until its income catches up with expenses. His partner, Eugène Robitaille, a horticulturist by training, runs the vineyards and winery operations.

Vignoble de la Sablière

One of the newest guys on the block, Vignoble de la Sablière started out making an 8.5 percent alcohol Vinho Verde style wine. Reds are on the agenda, but not till later. Owners Irénée Belley and Sandra Moreau are concerned about the environment and use neither pesticides nor herbicides in the vineyards. They have planted Seyval, Geisenheim, Maréchal Foch, Vidal, and St. Croix.

Vignoble Domaine de l'Ardennais

Owner/winemaker François Samray planted his vineyard just west of Dunham, in the heart of Québec's "wine belt." His winemaking philosophy is simple — just let the grapes do their thing and the wine practically makes itself.

François Samray lets the fermentation run its course and allows the wine to complete a malolactic fermentation. He makes a white based on Seyval, a red based on Chancellor, and a very pleasant rosé. Both whites and reds are aged in large oak vats.

Vignoble Domaine des Côtes d'Ardoise

This is "numero uno," the first vineyard planted in Québec. The original owner, Christian Barthomeuf, chose the location very carefully. In 1980, he planted vines in this sheltered, horseshoe-shaped terrain. The micro-climate is just warm enough to support some of the hardier vinifera vines. Riesling and Gamay are planted alongside a selection of hybrids. Some slate in the soil, as implied in the name "Ardoise," helps with drainage and retains some heat from the sun. In 1984 the property was sold to Jacques Papillon, who hired winemakers Vera Klokocka and John Fletcher, formerly of Hillside Estate Winery in British Columbia. Their wine portfolio is now one of the most diversified of the Québec wineries.

Vignoble l'Orpailleur

L'Opailleur's Seyval has consistently led the way for Québec wines and, as the vines have matured, the wine has become more complex. The winery is one of the province's largest in terms of production, with 6,500 cases, but Hervé Durand limits the varieties of grapes, preferring to concentrate on Seyval and Vidal.

Ownership is shared with three other partners: Charles-Henri de Coussergues, a Frenchman from the south of France who is vineyard manager, Frank Furtado, an impresario specializing in fireworks productions, and Pierre Rodrigue, a lawyer and businessman. Winemaker since 1991 is Marc Grau, who hails from the south of France and who trained at the school of oenology at Montpellier.

- ✔ L'Orpailleur Mousse d'Or
- ✔ L'Orpailleur Seyval Blanc

Vignoble la Bauge

And now for something completely different. If hunting with bow and arrow is your thing, this is the place to be. After 40 years as a dairy farmer, the late Alcide Naud diversified into raising wild boar, deer, wild sheep, stags, wild pheasant, and exotic fowl. You can pay a fee to hunt the game or just buy some delicious wild boar terrine, ready-made. The vineyard is yet another interest. Alcide's son, Simon, is winemaker and produces about five labels with original names like "La Bête Rousse," a rosé, and "Sélection Camille," a late harvest dessert wine.

Searching for gold

Folk singer Gilles Vigneault (French Canada's answer to Bob Dylan) once said that, "Making wine in Québec is like panning for gold." That is why Hervé Durand called his winery "l'Orpailleur" — someone who pans for gold. But Hervé has proven he had the Midas touch all along; he created one of Québec's best wines.

The wildlife at la Bauge

If you're looking for something different on a winery tour, you should drop in at la Bauge. Hop on their trolley that takes you through the vineyards. Most of the vines here are over 10 years old. The tour winds into the woods, where you are met by a motley crew of exotic animals (fenced in!). You might see the likes of Texas Long Horn cattle (now an endangered species), Australian emus, European deer, reas from South America, Japanese Sika deer, and two types of boar. The Naud family has been breeding wild boar for over 20 years.

If hunting is your game, you can rent a cross-bow from la Bauge and try your hand in a nearby protected terrain. If your hunt is fruitful, la Bauge personnel will help you prepare and transport your meat.

Vignoble le Cep d'Argent

François Scieur and his brother Jean-Paul came to Québec from the Champagne region of France and were the first winemakers in Québec to make a champagne-method sparkling wine from local grapes. After a thorough search, partner Jacques Daniel and his son chose a sloped vineyard site — the most easterly in the province. With third partner Denis Drouhin, all are in agreement that they should "ignore the ideas of people who say that the vines can't produce wines of quality in Québec."

Vignoble les Arpents de Neige

Les Arpents de Neige translates as "acres of snow." These few acres, 12 to be precise, have had their ups and downs, but current owner Gilles Séguin and his winemaker, Jean-Paul Martin, have had good success with their Seyval.

Jacques Breault, who worked at l'Orpailleur, founded Les Arpents de Neige. He planted the vineyard to a number of hybrids — most of which are used in blended cuvées. Only the Seyval is bottled as a single varietal. The property changed hands after going bankrupt in 1992.

Vignoble les Blancs Coteaux

This Dunham location is warmed by air currents off Lake Champlain in the late spring and early fall that help fend off severe frost. Owner Pierre Genesse learned winemaking in Burgundy as a grape picker.

To promote ripeness, Pierre removes leaves from the vine so that bunches are exposed to the sun. He is experimenting with French and American oak but, for most varieties, uses stainless steel to maximize the fruity perfume.

▐ ↙ Vignoble les Blancs Coteaux Seyval

Vignoble les Chants de Vignes

Only a few years old, les Chants de Vignes has already earned a medal in a national wine championship. Although production is small, the owners have a very professional attitude towards their business, supplementing the wine revenues by renting a reception hall and restaurant to groups.

Winemaker Marc Daniel's successful philosophy is to intervene as little as possible in the vinification and just let the wine express itself. He works with two grape varieties, Seyval Blanc and Seyval Noir.

Vignoble les Pervenches

Bread and butter production for this winery is a nicely balanced Seyval Blanc, but owner Michael Marler is bound and determined to grow vinifera vines. He has planted Pinot Gris, Chardonnay, and the red Maréchal Foch close to a wooded area that provides protection from the wind and keeps the area two to three degrees warmer all year round. Michael is considering planting some winter-hardy hybrid grapes as well.

During the winter, the vulnerable vines are bent low to the ground and buried. The hardier varieties are hilled up. During the growing season, vines are trained high on their trellises for maximum exposure to the sun.

Vignoble les Trois Clochers

First planted in 1986, this Dunham vineyard changed hands in 1997, with Robert Brisebois and Nadège Mariam taking possession. Production remains small and is split between a Seyval-based white and a strawberry wine. They have established Seyval, Chancellor, and Maréchal Foch vines and young plantings of Vidal and Cliche. This winery is closely situated to Domaine des Côtes d'Ardoise, on the Dunham road.

Montérégie Wineries

The Montérégie region, on the western section of the glacial plain, is just a degree or two warmer, on average, than the Eastern Townships, and therefore supports a slightly broader range of grape types.

Clos Saint-Denis, Verger-Vignoble

Practise makes perfect. Winemaker Christian Donaldson, who trained in Burgundy, is constantly looking for ways to improve the wines and he seems to make them better each year. This lovely property on the banks of the Richelieu River is divided between orchards and vineyard. Owner Guy Tardif works the land with his son, François, a trained agronomist and experienced vineyardist. By using hardy varieties they get around having to hill the vines up in the winter.

Keep an eye out for wines from this talented winemaker.

Vignoble Angell

Vignoble Angell is in the deep south of Québec, right on the border with the U.S. at St. Bernard de Lacolle. Their growing season is actually about three weeks longer than most of the other Québec wineries. Believing he had more than a fighting chance, Jean-Guy Angell, who owns a chain of karate schools across Canada, was one of the first enthusiasts to plant vines and open a winery. It is now one of the largest family-owned wineries in the province. They started in 1978 with about 200 vines in the ground. They now have close to 40,000. Jean-Guy's son, Guy, is the winemaker. They work mostly with Seyval Blanc, Vidal, Chardonnay, and De Chaunac, but they have planted some experimental Merlot and Pinot Noir, also.

Vignoble Cappabianca

As the name suggests, there is an Italian influence at work here. The Lapenna family lost their vineyard in Italy to the ravages of the Second World War and it was something Francesco Lapenna found hard to forget. Working in the nursery business in Montréal, Francesco heard about hybrid vines that could survive a Canadian winter and decided to try them out in a small vineyard just outside of Montréal. Taking the name Cappabianca from his mother's family, he planted Seyval Blanc, Maréchal Foch, and Lucie Kuhlmann.

Vignoble Clos de la Montagne

Only about 20 minutes farther from Montréal than Vignoble Cappabianca, Vignoble Clos de la Montagne offers something for everyone. Besides wine, you can sample some cider, pick apples, browse through a stained glass studio, watch the llamas and exotic birds, or check on the hens' productivity. It's a fact of life that most Québec wineries have to use this multi-faceted approach to attract enough people. They have planted both red and white hybrids and are also trying some Gamay.

Vignoble des Négondos

The newest winery in the Montérégie, Vignoble des Négondos is located on rue Saint-Vincent in Saint-Benoit de Mirabel — Saint-Vincent is the patron saint of grape growers!

Owners Carole Desrochers and Mario Plante had to clear their land before they could plant their vines. They removed 100 truckloads of rocks before putting in 8,000 vines of hybrids that include Seyval, Cayuga, Geisenheim, and De Chaunac. They felt it worth the effort as it gave them a sloped terrain with natural drainage and limestone soils. They practise organic farming and are the first vineyard to be certified organic in Québec.

Vignoble des Pins

By keeping it small, Gilles Benoit can manage his winery operation and still have time to experiment in the vineyard. He hills up his vines in the winter and heaps straw on the vinifera vines for extra protection. Along with a selection of hardy hybrids, he has planted reds — Gamay, Cabernet Franc, and Lemberger. He looks for a light, fruity style with an emphasis on reds, a daring move in this part of the world. He also makes a Champagne-method sparkler using Seyval.

Calling on Old-World traditions

Victor Dietrich and Christiane Jooss maintain an experimental plot in their vineyard with about 30 different grape varieties from as far afield as Australia, the U.S., and South America. Because of their experience in Europe, Victor and Christiane have been able to inspire and encourage many of the other vintners in the area. Daughter Stéphanie, who studied oenology at Montpellier, in the south of France, appears ready to carry on the family tradition. This is *the* Québec winery to watch.

Vignoble Dietrich-Jooss

Are these people crazy or what? Victor Dietrich and Christiane Jooss already had a winery in Alsace, France, when they decided to come to Québec. They arrived in 1986 with their daughter, Stéphanie, and settled in Iberville, on the Richelieu River. They knew the weather would be a challenge, but they were ready to protect their vines by hilling them up. The Richelieu Valley gets lots of sun in the summer, and this vineyard is situated in a well-drained area where the soil dries out and warms up quickly. Dietrich and Christiane have made a careful selection of grape types, mostly Maréchal Foch for red, De Chaunac for rosé, and Seyval and Cayuga for white.

- ✔ Vignoble Dietrich-Jooss Cuvée Spéciale
- ✔ Vignoble Dietrich-Jooss Rosé
- ✔ Vignoble Dietrich-Jooss Storikengold

Vignoble du Marathonien

Jean Joly's winemaking philosophy is: "Never stop learning." A full-time engineer, he still has ample energy to tend his vineyard and winery. Much of this vitality may come from his training as a marathon runner, the concept for which the winery is named. Vignoble du Marathonien is one of the southernmost vineyards in Québec, just a few kilometres from the U.S. border. The Jolys are experimenting with red vinifera varieties like Pinot Noir, Cabernet Franc, and Merlot.

- ✔ Vignoble du Marathonien Seyval

Vignoble Leroyer/St-Pierre

Robert Leroyer and Lucie St-Pierre are never short of original ideas for improving their chances of success. For one, they use three different trellising techniques on one vine. Givre Noir, a name they give to one of their wines, evokes a certain mystique in French, but when translated, "Black Frost" is more reminiscent of the reality in the vineyard. So, in the fall, Robert and Lucie bury the vines under 20 inches of earth. Although both have a passion for Chardonnay, they are also studying 16 different vine varieties and varying rootstocks.

Vignoble Morou

Étienne Héroux, a retired chemical engineer, and Monique Morin started planting their vineyard in 1987. They began with 18 different varieties but narrowed them down over the years so that, in 1991 when they officially opened their winery, they had the 10 grape types that they felt best suited their location. Being fairly close to Lake Champlain, they benefit from its retained warmth in late autumn and have been able to grow Gamay, the vinifera grape best known in Beaujolais wine. They also grow a variety of hybrids including De Chaunac, which they oak-age for the "Le Closeau" label, as well as Geisenheim, Seyval, Cayuga white, Vidal, and Chancellor. They have won a number of awards in North American wine competitions.

 ✔ Vignoble Morou Clos Napierois

Vignoble Sous les Charmilles

Planted to Seyval Blanc, Vidal, Bacchus, and Maréchal Foch, Sous les Charmilles represents a passionate hobby that became a business. Alain Bélanger, a wine agent and former sommelier, made wine in Beaujolais and Alsace before he became consulting winemaker to several Québec wineries. It was his father who decided to plant a few vines "just for fun." About nine years later they opened their winery with co-founder Georges Ducharme. Alain has since left the winery to pursue other interests, leaving Georges with full responsibility.

Instead of burying his vines in winter, Georges collects leaves cleaned up from the lawns of wine-loving residents of nearby Sherbrooke. In the spring he rakes them off, composts what amounts to about 10,000 bags, and recycles them as organic fertilizer.

Natural techniques

Despite his background in chemical engineering (or perhaps because of it), Étienne Héroux, of Vignoble Morou, tries to avoid the use of chemicals in his winemaking. In fact, to avoid having to de-acidify his wine chemically, he rolls all his vats outside in –5° Celsius weather and leaves them there for a week. This cold treatment, similar to a technique used in Burgundy, reduces the acid levels in the wine naturally.

Québec City and Other Wineries

Where there's a will there's a way. A few wineries are found near Québec City, seemingly one of the most unlikely places to grow grapes.

Coopérative des Producteurs Viticole Bourg-Royal and Vignoble Bourg-Royal

One of the oldest vineyards in Québec, Bourg-Royal is located only 15 minutes from the centre of Québec City. From 1982 until 1999, it operated as a community collective. It then converted to a cooperative to facilitate commercializing the winery. The winery is jointly owned by members of the collective. Interested parties must purchase a minimum of 50 plants in order to come on board. Their investments support both the vineyard and winery operations.

Winemaker Gilles Tremblay works with some 350 different varieties of hardy grape types to find the best suited for the harsh climate. His winemaking methods include skin contact for the whites and carbonic maceration to create Beaujolais-style reds.

Vignoble Domaine Royarnois

Situated on the north shore of the St. Lawrence River, near Québec City, Domaine Royarnois enjoys the benefits of a micro-climate in an area well-suited to a variety of agricultural endeavours. Winemaker Roland Harnois makes dry and off-dry styles from the hardy Cliche and St. Croix grapes. The nearby Cap Tourmente wildlife refuge, known to attract flocks of snow geese, provides an added attraction for visitors.

Instead of burying his vines in winter, Roland instead trains them high above the ground.

Vignoble Angile

About 30 miles east of Québec City, le Vignoble Angile grows a handful of hardy hybrids in a tiny vineyard of only five and a half acres. It augments its production with fruit wines from 20 acres of strawberries and raspberries.

Wine is currently aged in stainless steel instead of oak.

Vignoble Îsle de Bacchus (Île d'Orléans)

In 1534, when Jacques Cartier first discovered the Île d'Orléans in the St. Lawrence River just off Québec City, he named it l'Isle de Bacchus for the vines (thought to be *Vitis riparia*) he found growing there. Then he had second thoughts, and renamed the island in honour of the son of his royal patron, the king of France.

This new winery, founded by partners Alexandre Bouchard, Donald Bouchard, Jean-Louis Crête, and Pierre Lemieux, celebrates the island's historic roots. The vineyard, situated on the slopes of the west side of the island, was originally planted in 1986 by Donald Bouchard. This location is slightly warmer than average and is frost free from mid-May to mid-October, giving the grapes a longer growing season. Harvesting normally lasts from mid-September to mid-October.

The owners rely on low trellising and snow coverage for winter protection. They have not had to bury the vines.

Vignoble le Moulin du Petit Pré

(Opening to the public in the Spring of 2001.)

Located about 15 minutes east of Québec City, Petit Pré was founded by a group of like-minded individuals all with agriculture-related careers, mostly in honey and honey-based products. They founded their company, Moulin du Petit Pré Inc., in 1997 to unite under one umbrella the activities of the vineyard, the berry fields, and the ancient mill located on the property.

History lives on in the Mill at Petit Pré

The old mill that is part of the Vignoble le Moulin du Petit Pré has a fascinating history. Built in 1695 by the Seminary of Québec, it was destroyed by fire 10 years later. It was rebuilt only to be destroyed again during the siege of Québec, in 1759. Rebuilt once more in 1763, it lasted until 1877, when yet another fire struck.

The mill was zealously erected a fourth time, and stuck to its old-fashioned practises: in 1938, it was still using stone wheels to grind wheat. Québec's Ministry of Cultural Affairs eventually took it over, undertaking further restorations. A part of the original wall from 1695 still exists and can be seen by visitors to the winery.

Julien Bédard, an agronomist, is in charge of the vineyards and berry patches. He has worked for 25 years as a financial consultant for a federal organization and has travelled throughout the agricultural regions of Québec, including those specializing in berry production. He planted his first vine in his own garden in 1982 and joined the community vineyard group of Bourg Royal (now a winery co-op) in 1994.

Two men are in charge of winemaking: Pierre Rousseau, a home winemaker for 20 years, is a biochemist with a particular interest in yeast. He is responsible for production and quality control at Rucher Promiel Inc., a producer of honey-based liqueurs. For the past three years he has also overseen the winemaking at nearby Domaine Royarnois. Redmond Hayes, also experienced in winemaking, has taken on the responsibility for sales and marketing as well.

About ten hectares are planted to Cliche-Vandal, a hardy hybrid that does not need to be buried in the winter.

The grape's hardiness is reinforced by a high-trellis system called the Geneva Double Curtain.

The land is a well-drained slope close to the St. Lawrence River. This proximity to the water delays budding long enough to avoid early spring frosts. At the end of the season it prevents early freeze-ups, giving the grapes a little longer to ripen. The vines are planted north to south, on a diagonal with the slope to maximize exposure to the sun.

The winery produces several styles of wine including white dry, white semi dry, a sparkling wine, a rosé, and a red.

Vignoble de Sainte-Pétronille (Île d'Orléans)

This vineyard on Île d'Orléans, in the middle of the St. Lawrence River, was the first commercial planting to use renowned nurseryman J.O. Vandal's newly developed cross, Cliche. It covers about 90 percent of this property, with St. Croix filling in the remaining 10 percent.

Although the climate may require owner Jean Larsen to *chaptalize* (add sugar to increase alcohol for body) his wine, he never allows the percentage alcohol to rise above 10 percent. He waits for malolactic fermentation, which may take up to two months, to soften the acids, refusing to use any chemical de-acidifiers. He produces a white, a rosé, and a Champagne-method sparkler.

Vignoble de la Vallée de l'Outaouais

Only 20 minutes out of Ottawa, just north of the town of Gatineau, Normand Dessureault and Gisèle Mitrow grow several varieties of grapes on 220 acres of partially forested land. The Vignoble de la Vallée de l'Outaouais began producing wine in 1995, and opened to the public in late 1999.

The varieties are split between Seyval, Maréchal Foch, Vidal, Cayuga, and Chambourcin. The soil is rich and composed primarily of slate. The surrounding woods protect the vineyard from the harshest elements, and they also provide a breeding ground for beneficial insects. The fallen leaves are a good source of compost.

Atlantic Province Wineries: Not a Fish Story

As you can see by looking at the map in Figure 20-2, the very young wine industry in the Atlantic region is limited to Nova Scotia, though one grape grower defies the odds on Prince Edward Island. Winemaking in Nova Scotia dates back to only 1978, when one determined individual named Roger Dial planted the first vineyard. Dial lectured in political science at Dalhousie University, but as a student in California had worked as a wine sales representative and became involved in a small winery there. He caught the bug. See Chapter 17 for more on Dial's pioneering efforts in Nova Scotia and the part he played in the evolving Canadian wine industry.

Once this first Nova Scotia winery opened its doors, the search was on for micro-climates in which vinifera grapes could thrive. Today, there are early-ripening varieties grown with increasing frequency in Nova Scotia, but they must be hilled up with earth or mulch during the winter. For the most part, winemakers rely on such reds as Michurinetz and Maréchal Foch, with Seyval Blanc, New York Muscat, and L'Acadie Blanc for whites.

Grape-growing wineries are found in two regions of Nova Scotia: the Annapolis Valley and the Northeast Shore. Both cling to the coast of a large, protected waterway that offers some respite from the frigid cold.

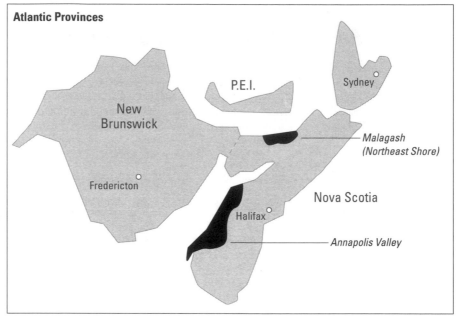

Figure 20-2:
Atlantic
province
wine
regions.

Annapolis Valley Wineries

The Annapolis Valley faces New Brunswick across the Bay of Fundy. Winters here are harsh and snowy, but the huge bay does provide a much-needed warming influence. The wineries in this region are clustered around Grand Pré, in Kings County, at the mouth of the Avon River. This location provides a little added protection.

The ups and downs of Nova Scotia's first winery

Grand Pré is the "grande dame" of Nova Scotia wineries. Roger Dial founded it in 1978, when no one thought it could be done. When the enterprise flourished, Dial was termed a visionary. He was the first to plant the Russian grape varieties Severnyi and Michurinetz, in an interesting experiment. While these varieties made palatable wine in the cool climate of Nova Scotia, they were never seriously taken up by other winemakers in Canada.

Dial over-extended himself in his efforts to bring Nova Scotia wines to the consuming public and eventually ran out of money. Grand Pré floundered in 1988, was taken over by new owners, and failed again. In 1993, prominent Swiss businessman Hanspeter Stutz purchased the property and started it back on the road to glory. He has restored the original farmhouse, which dates from 1826, executed a multimillion-dollar project for rebuilding the winery, and opened a restaurant.

Jost Vineyards finds gold on the Northeast Shore

The Northeast Shore of Nova Scotia looks out over the Northumberland Strait, towards Prince Edward Island. The only winery established there to date is Jost Vineyards, located in Malagash, on the sheltered shore of Amet Sound.

After the death of founder Hans Jost in 1988, the winery passed into the hands of his son, Hans Christian. The younger Jost went to Geisenheim, in Germany, where his family was originally from, to study winemaking and bring what he learned back to his Northeast Shore vineyard.

He aims to produce crisp, clean wines that exemplify the characteristics of a long, sunny but cool growing season. He works with a number of hybrids from the Jost vineyards and buys grapes from Ontario and Washington State as needed.

He must be doing something right. Jost Vineyards won the "Wine of the Year Award" at the 2000 All-Canadian Wine Championships with its 1999 Vidal Icewine. The wine beat out 594 other entries — it was the first time a wine from a province other than Ontario or British Columbia had won.

Domaine de Grand Pré

When Hanspeter Stutz from Switzerland bought the Grand Pré property, it had fallen into ruin. But Hanspeter had the vision and the financial resources to give it a second life. He restored and rebuilt the buildings, tackling the vineyards with equal energy. He replanted the original estate vineyard and a new, south-facing 15-acre vineyard in the Gaspereau Valley, only a short distance away. Working with the Agriculture Canada station in Kentville, the winery now features grape varieties that are best suited to the Nova Scotia environment.

Hanspeter's son Jürg, a graduate in oenology and marketing, is winemaker. In their first year of production they bottled Seyval Blanc, l'Acadie Blanc, New York Muscat, and Maréchal Foch, all well-priced, pleasant, and accessible wines.

- ✔ Grand Pré Maréchal Foch
- ✔ Grand Pré New York Muscat
- ✔ Grand Pré Seyval Blanc

Habitant Vineyards

For the time being, the wines are made from imported California wine and concentrates, as well as from Ontario wine. But Peter and Laura McCain Jensen have other irons in the fire. They have faith that Chardonnay and Pinot Noir can grow well enough in Nova Scotia to make sparkling wine, and they have a separate property dedicated to this project. They also own Creekside Winery in Ontario. The Habitant Vineyards location is under the supervision of Wayne Macdonald, a grape grower and former intelligence officer with the Royal Canadian Mounted Police. Habitant shares the winemaking skills of Marcus Ansems, of the Jensens' Niagara property.

Sainte-Famille Wines

Sainte-Famille completes the trio of Annapolis Valley wineries. It is located in Falmouth, known as the "gateway" to the valley. The spot where Doug and Suzanne Corkum's winery now sits was home to an Acadian village in the late 17th century, called "La Paroisse Sainte-Famille de Pisquit." The name of the winery pays tribute to this moment in Canadian history. The vineyards are well placed; they face south, and are protected from extreme cold in winter by the waters of the Avon River. The recent addition of a barrel cellar provides more opportunity for oak aging and barrel fermentation.

Grapes, not potatoes

Rossignol Estate Winery is the only grape-growing winery on Prince Edward Island. Owner John Rossignol obtained the use of greenhouses formerly used by tobacco farmers to shelter his tender vinifera vines. Hardier hybrids, like Seyval Blanc, Maréchal Foch, and Valient, are relegated to the vineyards. John designs some of the bottle labels himself. A neighbour and folk artist, Nancy Perkins, designs others.

Try Rossignol Seyval Blanc.

Chapter 21

Fruit Wineries

● ●

In This Chapter

▶ Defining fruit wine

▶ Forming a national association

▶ Choosing the fruit

▶ Touring Canada's fruit wineries

● ●

Although we believe that the only real wine is made from grapes, the interest in wine made from other fruits has grown so much that even we feel it would be an omission not to let you in on these "new wave wines."

The number of fruit wineries in Canada has increased to such an extent that in 1999 a national industry association, called Fruit Wines of Canada (the first of its kind in the world), was established to develop standards for the production of quality wine from fruits other than grapes. At the time of writing we counted 53 facilities across Canada that produce fruit wines. By the time you read this, the number will probably have grown.

The federal government came up with some funding for this effort to help raise the profile of this suddenly burgeoning sector through the Agri-Trade 2000 program. Ontario's provincial government did its bit too, injecting more support via the Ontario Rural Job Strategy Fund.

A Fruity Phenomenon

You only have to visit Canada's fruit-growing regions to see how abundant and diversified are the ingredients available to the winemaker. Some wineries make both grape and fruit wines (Southbrook Farms, Stoney Ridge, and Magnotta, in Ontario). Others, like Sunnybrook Farms, Archibald Orchards, and Bellamere Country Wines (also in Ontario) are dedicated solely to the production of fruit wines.

Based on the model of the VQA (Vintners Quality Alliance — Canada's appellation for wines made from grapes), Fruit Wines of Canada guarantees the products of its members with the Quality Certified (QC) standards seal.

"Just as no winery in the world would add fruit to their wine, we will have no grapes in our fruit," says Bill Redelmeir, vice-chairman of Fruit Wines of Ontario, the organization founded in 1998 to promote Ontario fruit wines. "Fruit wines must be 100-percent Ontario-grown."

There is as yet no legal definition as to what a fruit wine is. It can be made from fruit as commonplace as apples or as esoteric as gooseberries. It can have an alcoholic strength as low as 4 percent (for cider) and as high as 20 percent (for brandy-enhanced cassis or framboise). The flavours can range from tartly dry to honeyed sweet.

Winemakers will tell you that to make great wine you have to start with great grapes. Not so with fruit wines; in fact, the fruit that is fermented for fruit wine is the stuff that's cosmetically challenged — it wouldn't look good on a supermarket shelf. Basically, you can make wine out of anything that has sugar in it, and if it doesn't, you can always add it. But the best fruit wines start from produce that is ripe and flavourful.

Fruit wineries have an advantage over grape wineries in that their source material — the fruit — ripens at different times during the year. This makes their fermentation schedule less hectic. The fruit can be stored instead of having to be fermented immediately after harvesting. Growers are also permitted to freeze their fruit to extract more concentrated, sweeter juice. This practise is prohibited in the making of Icewine.

Picking the best

Tony learned a lot about fruit wine in a very short time recently, when he was invited to judge the first ever all-Canadian Fruit Wine Competition. Competitors entered 161 wines from eight provinces, making it the world's second largest fruit wine competition after New Zealand (and this in its first year!).

The competition was organized by Peter Pigeon, a partner in the newly opened St. Jacob's Country Market Winery & Cidery, in Waterloo. He told the 20 assembled judges, "The challenge you're going to face is that you'll be somewhat assaulted by a range of flavours and sweetness. You'll taste a host of different styles. You're likely to taste fruit you've never tasted before or never even heard of." (He was right. Tony had never tasted a cloudberry and had never in his life come across a bench berry.)

Which Fruit Where

Unlike Canada's grape wine industry, which is pretty much concentrated in four provinces, there are nine provinces in which fruit wine is made: Newfoundland, Nova Scotia, Prince Edward Island, New Brunswick, Québec, Ontario, Saskatchewan, Alberta, and British Columbia. Here, we look at the four major contributors to Canada's fruit wine portfolio: Ontario, B.C., Nova Scotia, and Newfoundland.

Fruit wine flavours you're likely to come across:

- Apple
- Blackcurrant
- Blueberry
- Cherry
- Cranberry
- Gooseberry
- Peach
- Pear
- Plum
- Raspberry
- Strawberry

Ontario Fruit Wineries

The fruit wineries of Ontario are scattered in different areas of the province, but most are within a two-hour drive of Toronto. A few fruit wineries grow grapes as well, but their emphasis is on a broad variety of berries and fruit.

Archibald Orchards & Estate Winery

Although the orchard and farmland has been in the Archibald family for four generations, the winery was only opened in 1997. But with 20 different varieties of apples growing, Fred and Sandy Archibald had a great selection from which to pick fruit for their wines. And they have some original ideas, too — oak-aged apple wine, for instance. These wines, made from Ida Red and McIntosh apples, are robust and dry with a distinctive oaky character. They select all the fruit for their wines from their own property.

The Archibald property provides a great environment for a family visit. Besides the winery, there are tours, a play area, a barnside theatre, a farm market featuring Sandy's pies made from her Mennonite grandmother's recipes, and a pick-your-own-apples operation.

> ✔ Archibald Orchards & Estate Winery Apple Peach
> ✔ Archibald Orchards & Estate Winery Sweet Apple Cherry

Bellamere Country Market & Winery

Bellamere's portfolio combines a variety of fruit wines with wine from grapes brought in from Niagara. Winemaker Jim Patience, who worked with the London Winery until it was bought by Vincor, brings experience and expertise to Bellamere. The winery was built next to the existing Bellamere Market and is housed in a lofty fir and pine frame structure lit by skylights during the day.

Fruit wines are made from 100-percent-Ontario produce, much of it from the Bellamere farm itself. A variety of styles and sweetness levels are made from apples, peaches, cherries, and berries. Grape wines include Vidal and barrel-aged Chardonnay from the Lailey vineyard for whites. Reds are all barrel-aged and include Baco Noir, Cabernet, and Merlot.

The County Cider Company

This estate winery specializing in hard ciders operates in Prince Edward County, often referred to simply as "The County." The promontory stretching into the north side of Lake Ontario enjoys a climate that has made it of recent interest to winemakers and, in fact, County Cider's owner, Grant Howes, has planted an experimental three acres of grapes.

Grant makes his ciders according to Bavarian purity laws, using only high-quality juice, no concentrates, no artificial flavours, and no heating. The County Cider Company's Web site is particularly informative about cider making and the environs. Log on to www.countycider.com.

Cox Creek Cellars Estate Winery

Named after the creek that runs through this picturesque farmland, Cox Creek is the first estate winery in the Guelph area. A variety of fruit and grape wines are made from the 3,450 grapevines on the property. Before starting up the winery, Adrian Trochta consulted with leading grape-growing experts in both the Niagara Peninsula and in Europe. He opted to plant the hardy Seyval and Baco Noir varieties, both of which have excellent potential in cold climates.

▮ ✔ Cox Creek Cellars Red Velvet

Meadow Lane Winery Ltd.

Meadow Lane is located in St. Thomas, in western Ontario, and produces both fruit- and grape-based wines. They currently grow a variety of berries but are in the process of developing a vineyard on the property. Owner Walter Myszko first learned about making fruit wine as a young boy in Poland. He came to Canada at the age of 15 to work on his uncle's tobacco farm. This combined experience eventually led him to winemaking.

Norfolk Estate Winery

Shirley and George Benko switched their emphasis from tobacco to apples and, in 1995, opened Ontario's first apple winery. Located in St. Williams, southeast of Tillsonburg, the winery makes a broad range of styles from the 100-acre property that the Benkos have worked since 1946. Their most successful product is Ice Apple Wine, which is an Icewine based on apples instead of grapes. They also make an intriguing Ice Apple Ginseng that features a ginseng root in the bottle.

▮ ✔ Norfolk Estate Winery Ice Apple Wine

Ocala Orchards Farm Winery

Northeast of Toronto, on the way to cottage country, this tiny winery owned by Irwin and Alissa Smith exists outside Ontario's designated wine regions. Actual vineyard land is less than that devoted to orchards, but the Smiths purchase fruit to fill their needs. The winery's philosophy is to "produce appealing wines from orchard fruit as well as grapes." Their first bottlings were limited to Chardonnay and Riesling, but they have since added a number of other whites, including an Icewine as well as a limited selection of reds.

▮ ✔ Ocala Orchards Farm Winery Blackcurrant
▮ ✔ Ocala Orchards Farm Winery Raspberry

Rush Creek Wines Ltd.

Kim and Wendy Flintoff's 57-acre farm and tender fruit orchard is located in Aylmer, between St. Thomas and Tillsonburg, not far from the north shore of Lake Erie. They grow many varieties of berries, as well as peaches, nectarines, and plums. The Flintoffs opened their winery after reading articles about similar enterprises and felt it was a natural extension of their farming activities.

They make 24 varieties, from dry, dinner-style wines to sweet wines for dessert. They also produce some kosher wines.

▮ ✔ Rush Creek Wines Blackcurrant

St. Jacob's Country Market Winery & Cidery

In its first year of operation, St. Jacob's won two gold medals at the Fruit Wines of Canada national competition. As a cidery, their principal product is Barn Owl Hard Cider, one of only a few apple ciders marketed in both draft kegs and 341-ml bottles. It is available through the LCBO as well as on site at the winery retail store.

In addition to the cider, St. Jacob's features a wide selection of wines produced from grapes purchased under contract from some of Niagara's best growers, as well as from a variety of other fruit. Grape wines include Chardonnay fermented in new French oak, Sauvignon Blanc and Gewürztraminer among whites, and Cabernet Sauvignon, Cabernet Franc, Merlot, and Gamay Noir among reds. Three partners own and operate the business: Peter Pigeon and Graham Murphy are the winemakers and Rob Schultz is business manager.

▮ ✔ St. Jacob's Country Market Winery & Cidery Blackcurrant
▮ ✔ St. Jacob's Country Market Winery & Cidery Ice Apple

Sunnybrook Farm Estate Winery

Sunnybrook is the only winery in Niagara to be dedicated entirely to fruit wine. Its stated philosophy is "to make wine from fruit other than grapes." Just the same, it makes its wine from 100-percent Ontario fruit, much of it from the farm. Gerald and Vivien Goertz had long been fruit growers and hobbyist winemakers when they turned to their hobby to solve a problem. In 1992, a nasty hailstorm bruised their peaches so badly that they couldn't sell them.

Their solution was to turn them into wine. The Goertzes are every bit as quality-conscious as any grape winemaker, allowing the fruit to ripen on the trees to enhance the natural flavours. They even make an "Icewine" by freezing a mix of berries and fruits.

- ✔ Sunnybrook Farm Golden Peach
- ✔ Sunnybrook Farm Spiced Apple
- ✔ Sunnybrook Farm Winter Peach

British Columbia Fruit Wineries

The Columbia Valley, just one-and-a-half hours east of Vancouver, benefits from a sunny summer climate and rich soil, making it perfect for growing a variety of fruit.

Bonaparte Bend Winery

Joanne and Gary Armstrong opened their new fruit winery in December 1999, on the Trans-Canada Highway near Cache Creek. Their initial releases were cranberry, blueberry, blackcurrant, and rhubarb wine.

Columbia Valley Classics Winery

Located at the south end of Cultus Lake, Columbia Valley Classics Winery is an offshoot of the Bertrand Creek Farm owned by John Stuyt. John has made a career of growing fruit and producing jams, jellies, syrups, and hazelnut-based products. The winery is a new initiative. It officially opened in January 1998, with Dominic Rivard as winemaker. Each wine is handcrafted to express the unique flavour and aroma of each fruit. Although the farm grows a couple of hybrid grapes, fruit wines are the main emphasis. John and Dominic believe that their whitecurrant wine is the only commercially made one in the world. This very rare berry results in an almost dry wine with a low sugar code of one.

- ✔ Columbia Valley Classics Raspberry

Elephant Island Orchard Wines

Miranda Griffiths and Del Halliday's new winery opened in 2000, debuting with a cherry wine. The wine consultant is Christine Leroux.

Merridale Estate Cidery

This Cobble Hill fruit winery on Vancouver Island specializes in cider. Proprietor Albert Piggott also produces Scrumpy, a rough farmhouse product beloved of inhabitants of southwest England. He also makes an interesting honey and apple-fermented product, called Cyser.

⬛ ↙ Merridale Estate Normandy Select Dry

Nova Scotia Fruit Wineries

The Nova Scotia fruit wineries grew out of well-established, family-owned fruit farms. For these quality-conscious growers, branching out into wine was a natural evolution.

Lunenburg County Winery

With names like Dis Dat Thuther, a grape-cherry blend, and Mushamush Muscat, made from Muscat grapes, who could resist trying one of these wines? Lunenburg County Winery is located on the Hackmatack Farm, a 100-acre commercial blueberry farm that has been family-owned for three generations. The farm also grows grapes, blackcurrants, and elderberries. Wine is made by traditional methods (mostly from home-grown fruit), although some of the fruit used comes from neighbouring farms and the Annapolis Valley in Nova Scotia.

Telder Berry Farm and Winery

Only 10 minutes from the Halifax airport, Brian and Lisa Telder's farm and winery is a welcome respite for the tired traveller. Relax on their licensed patio and sample one of their dozen different wines.

Telder-Berry Farms opened in 1975 as a vegetable u-pick, and then branched out into strawberries. The winery was added on in 1993 to deal with surplus fruit. Founded by Brian's parents, Robert and Barbara, Telder Berry is the province's first all-fruit winery.

Berries in Newfoundland

You may not be able to grow grapes in Newfoundland, but berries thrive in abundance. Hilary and Marie-France Rodrigues, of Rodrigues Winery, make wine from a wide variety of wild fruit, including blueberries, partridgeberries, and bakeapples. The berries are free from pesticides and other chemical pollutants because they're harvested in their natural habitat.

The winery is housed in a picturesque building that was once a hospital, and produces around 25,000 cases in a year — no small operation.

Part VI
The Part of Tens

The 5th Wave   By Rich Tennant

WORSE THAN "WINE SNOBS" ARE "WINE TOUGHS"

Hey! You call this a varietal?!

In this part . . .

You'll find quick answers to those pesky, persistent questions you may have about wine. Think of this part as instant advice that you can share with your friends and colleagues — or prove to an overbearing wine waiter that he's not the only one who knows something about the subject.

Chapter 22

Ten Frequently Asked Questions about Wine

● ●

*A*s wine writers for newspapers and magazines, we receive a lot of questions in the mail. The most popular question by far is one we really can't answer here: "What's a good wine for under $10?" That depends on what's available in your region — although you can find top-notch Rieslings in this price range. The other question we get a lot has to do with "found" bottles. Someone has come across an old bottle of wine or spirits in an attic trunk.

They wonder if it's

- ✔ Valuable
- ✔ Drinkable
- ✔ Saleable

The answer is usually no on all three counts — unfortunately. Single bottles are usually kept for sentimental reasons rather than economic ones. Such "treasures" are invariably stored in the worst possible conditions, and the wine has probably oxidized. Can you sell it? Not legally in Canada: Provincial governments have a monopoly on the sale and distribution of alcohol.

Here are 10 questions (and answers) that cover many of the concerns consumers have when it comes to purchasing and drinking wine.

Where Do I Start If I Want to Get into Wine?

First off, read this book! The best way to introduce yourself to wine is to drink something that is immediately pleasing to your palate. As kids, most of us were brought up on soft drinks that were on the sweet side and were served cold. To make the transition from soft drinks to wine, choose a white wine or rosé with some residual sweetness that you can chill.

When Tony started to drink wine, he tried a sparkling rosé from Portugal, Mateus Rosé. Mateus was Barb's second wine experience, and it became the only wine she would drink for about a year. Her first experience was Madeira, the fortified wine from the island of the same name. She enjoyed it on a picnic with her first serious boyfriend, and, for some reason she has long since forgotten, an old school friend of his as well!

Beginner wines:

- White Zinfandel from California (a medium-sweet white)
- Liebfraumilch from Germany (a sweetish white)
- Lambrusco from Emilia-Romagna in Italy (a fizzy, off-dry red)

Why Are Some Wines More Deeply Coloured Than Others?

Wine comes in three colours: white, red, and rosé. But as descriptive terms for a wine's colour, "white" and "red" are not technically correct. Milk is white. Bedsheets can be white. "White" wine is pale yellow or straw-coloured. Similarly, no red wines are red in the fire-engine sense; they range from cherry to purple-black in colour.

White wines range in colour from water white to old gold. In some rare instances, a white wine can take on a deep brown colour. White wines start off life almost water white (they might have a lime tint); but as they age they go deeper in colour. Sweet whites have a deeper colour than dry whites. Wines that have been fermented or aged in oak barrels are more deeply coloured than those made in stainless-steel tanks. Some varieties, such as Pinot Gris and Gewürztraminer, add a pinkish-grey hue to the wine.

There's a greater range of colours when it comes to red wine. They range from rose and cherry to purple-black. Unlike whites that gain colour with age, reds start off purple and actually begin to *lose* colour as they age.

What is a vintage wine?

"Vintage" has two meanings, neither of which has to do with the quality of the wine in question.

The term can either refer to:

- The harvest and winemaking process itself
- A wine made with grapes that were all picked in the same year

The expression "vintage year" means a good harvest that will produce potentially very fine wine. What the winemakers do with top-quality grapes determines the ultimate quality of the product. The year printed on the label means that the grapes were harvested in that year, not that the wine was bottled in that year. If there is no year stated on the label, neck label, or back label, then the wine is most likely a blend of two different years. Lack of a vintage date is not necessarily a mark of inferiority. When a disastrous year occurs in cool-climate regions, the resulting wines can only be improved by blending them with some of the previous year's reserves.

Tony was once asked what a vintage wine was by a woman sitting next to him at a dinner party. His meal got cold as he explained this complicated term. Hopefully it hasn't taken this long here!

What Wine Should I Bring to a Dinner Party?

Ask yourself: Do you want to give your host a present that she can put in the cellar to enjoy on another occasion, or do you want the wine to be drunk that night? There's no greater disappointment than seeing a cherished bottle you brought specially be whisked away, its contents never to pass your lips! It's even worse if the wine served is inferior to the one you brought.

Here are three "ploys" you can try to make sure yours is the bottle served.

- ✔ **Plan A:** Phone your host in advance and tell her you'd like to bring a bottle of wine for the meal. Ask about the menu and the number of guests invited. If this strategy doesn't work and the wine you brought never makes an appearance at the table, revert to Plan B, as explained next.

- ✔ **Plan B:** If you bring white wine, chill it down to the desired serving temperature beforehand and present it to the host, saying, "I don't think you'll have to put it in the fridge. It's already been chilled." If the host still doesn't take the hint, next time you're invited over take extreme action, as follows:

- ✔ **Extreme Action:** Choose a desirable red wine and pour it into a decanter — one that has enough style to grace any dinner table. Present the decanter to the host on arrival, explaining, "I had to decant the wine because it had thrown a lot of sediment." (Make sure you remember to recoup the decanter on the way out.)

There are two categories of wine that do a good job with just about every meal: Sparkling wine, especially champagne if you can afford it, and port. Also very acceptable are dessert wines — late harvest Riesling, or, for special dinners, Icewine.

How Can I Tell When Wine Is Ready to Drink?

This is perhaps the most perplexing question of all. Some 90 percent of the wines produced around the world are made to be table-ready. That is, they're fermented with low tannins so that they taste appealing right when you buy them. This is particularly true of white wines that are at their best when they're young and fresh, within a year or two of their vintage date. There are exceptions to this rule (such as fine white Burgundy). But in most instances, the fresher the better.

Red wines, because of their tannins, require a year or two of bottle age to soften up. Certain grapes require longer because of their high tannin content: Cabernet Sauvignon, Nebbiolo, and Tempranillo, for example.

New World–style wines that are made to be immediately accessible do not generally age as well as Old World–style wines that have more acidity and tannin.

How Can I Tell When a Wine Is "Off"?

By "off" we mean that the wine smells odd and is disagreeable on your palate. The reason serving staff in restaurants pour you a sample of the wine you ordered is for you to test it by eye, nose, and palate to see if it's drinkable — before you buy it.

When the server first presents the bottle, inspect it carefully, before the cork is even removed. Look for any leakage around the capsule or a cork that has risen above the level of the lip (this suggests the wine has been subjected to excessive heat or been frozen — both conditions will force the cork upwards). If the label is stained with wine or badly scuffed, it is not a good sign. It means the wine has been mistreated at some time during its aging or transportation.

Inspect the cork carefully when the waiter hands it to you. You can spot signs that suggest the wine may be off.

1. The cork is stained along its length.
2. The cork is spongy and wine-soaked when you squeeze it.
3. The cork is as hard as oak when you press it.
4. The cork smells mouldy or musty.

Pay attention to the colour of the wine when the server pours it. If the wine is cloudy or dull and hazy, that suggests a fault. If it's browning at the edge, it could be oxidated. Any foreign bodies floating or sinking in your glass are also unacceptable. The major test that will tell you whether the wine is "off" is nosing it. If it smells bad it will taste bad, simple as that. It won't improve with air, so don't wait. Send it back immediately. A "corky" smell reminds you of a damp basement. You only have to smell it once to never forget it!

How Long Can I Keep a Bottle of Wine after I've Opened It?

When you open a bottle of wine, you are exposing the contents to air for the first time since it was bottled. A little air is good because it lets the wine "breathe," allowing it to release its bouquet and flavour. An hour or two is enough for most red wines; whites require much less time.

The less wine in the open bottle, the more air it's subjected to when you recork it. The best method to store an open bottle of wine is to exclude as much air as possible. Keep a spare, clean half-bottle handy and pour the unused wine into it until the level is two inches below the top of the neck. Then, insert the cork. You can keep this half-bottle refrigerated for a week or two with little loss of bouquet and flavour. By cooling the wine down you slow down oxidation.

Some wine enthusiasts will tell you to preserve wine by *freezing* the contents in the recorked bottle. Neither Tony nor Barb has ever done this (it sounds much too traumatic for the wine) but others swear you can't tell the difference when the wine thaws out!

Why Do I React Badly When I Drink a Certain Wine?

We are assuming the reaction is not prompted by the volume of wine ingested! Some people react badly to wine because they're sensitive to certain components of it, mostly sulphites (a term that includes all sulphur compounds) and/or tannin.

White wines generally contain more sulphites than red. Some people may find that the sulphur component irritates their air passages, causing them to wheeze. If you're allergic to sulphites, look for organically grown wines with as low a sulphur content as possible. The tannins in red wines can cause headaches if you're allergic to histamines. Migraine sufferers are particularly prone since histamines are what trigger an attack. The best strategy is to select a red wine that is low in tannins (and therefore low in histamines). Wines made by carbonic maceration are good bets: Beaujolais, Beaujolais Villages and the named villages of Beaujolais.

Which Region of Canada Produces the Best Wines?

We'll get into real trouble if we say that the part of Canada where we live (Ontario) makes the best wines; but we would only be rooting for the home team. Good wines are being made in the four provinces that currently have a viable, commercial wine industry: Ontario (where 75 percent of Canadian wines are produced), British Columbia (around 20 percent), and the rest divided between Québec and Nova Scotia.

Grapes that work best in Ontario

- ✔ White
  - Chardonnay
  - Riesling
  - Sauvignon Blanc
  - Vidal/Riesling Icewine
- ✔ Red
  - Cabernet blends (Cabernet Sauvignon, Merlot, Cabernet Franc)

Grapes that work best in British Columbia

- ✔ White
  - Chardonnay
  - Gewürztraminer
  - Pinot Blanc
  - Pinot Gris
- ✔ Red
  - Merlot
  - Pinot Noir
  - Bordeaux-style blends

How Do Canadian Wines Compare to Those of Other Countries?

You can't compare the wines of Ontario and British Columbia to those of California, Australia, or Chile. We don't enjoy the same long, hot growing seasons as those regions do. A fairer comparison would be to the wines of Burgundy, Bordeaux, Loire, Champagne, Germany, and New Zealand — all of which are cool-growing regions.

Try this out. Taste these pairings blind (make sure they're within the same price range). We think you'll be pleasantly surprised at just how well Canadian wines fare against their international counterparts.

- ✔ Ontario Chardonnays against white Burgundies
- ✔ Ontario Rieslings against German Rieslings
- ✔ B.C. Pinot Blanc against Alsace Pinot Blanc
- ✔ B.C. Pinot Gris against Alsace Pinot Gris
- ✔ Ontario/B.C. Cabernet blends against Bordeaux châteaux wines

Chapter 23

Ten Ontario Winemakers to Watch

● ●

*T*here are many talented winemakers currently working in Ontario. It's difficult for us to select some and leave out others. But if you don't have the time or inclination to visit some 60 wineries in the province, you can get a great overview of what's going on by dropping in on these ladies and gentlemen. But call first. Winemakers are very hospitable people by nature and love to share their enthusiasm for their product. But remember, they're really busy most of the time. Another option: Turn to Chapter 18 for more detailed sketches of 46 wineries in Ontario. We hope you end up hopping in the car and heading out to visit at least a few of them.

Marcus Ansems: Creekside Estate Winery and Habitant Vineyards, N.S.

He may look like a weightlifter, but this big guy has a feather-light touch. Marcus arrived in Canada from Australia at the end of 1999, and within a year had proven that Australian-trained winemakers don't all make intense, blockbuster wines. Marcus brings out the best from the fruit and has a flair for delicacy without sacrificing complexity.

Derek Barnett: Southbrook Farm & Winery

Derek's a quiet, shy kinda guy, but you should have seen the smile on his face when he received the Winemaker of the Year Award at the Air Ontario Wine Awards 2000. And this wasn't the first time his talent and contribution to the Canadian wine industry had been recognized, either. He has won awards for his wines made from grapes, as well as for his fortified wines using other fruit, notably cassis and framboise.

Pierre-Jean Bosc: Château des Charmes

Pierre-Jean is one of a new breed of winemakers — a second generation in the Ontario wine industry. He followed in his father's footsteps by studying viticulture and oenology at the University of Burgundy at Dijon. Drawing on his father's accumulated experience and his own grasp of wine technology, he is in a position to continue and improve on a tradition of excellence.

Ray Cornell: Hernder Estates Winery

Soft-spoken and seemingly reticent, Ray comes alive when he gets onto the subject of Hernder wine. Trained by Jim Warren at Stoney Ridge, Ray's skills grew with Hernder's production. In 2000, his wines won no less than 13 medals. Ray's specialty is Riesling, both dry and late harvest.

Philip Dowell: Inniskillin Wines

Philip was appointed general manager of Inniskillin Wines at the end of 1998 and took charge of all winery operations. He came to Canada from Australia with extensive winemaking experience in the Yarra Valley, another cool-climate region. His international perspective is bringing a new dimension to Inniskillin Wines.

Ron Giesbrecht: Henry of Pelham Family Estate Winery

Ron completes the quartet of modern young men that has brought Henry of Pelham into the 21st century. The other three are Paul, Matthew, and Daniel Speck, sons of the winery's founder, Paul Speck Sr. Ron's wines are consistent award-winners. He has shown the Canadian wine industry that Baco Noir can be much more than wine from a simple hybrid grape.

J-L Groux: Hillebrand Estates Winery

J-L (which stands for Jean-Laurent) hails from the Loire region of France, and he studied in Burgundy and Bordeaux before striking out to Niagara's "new frontier" of wine in 1989. The main attraction for him was the freedom to experiment. Since that time he's received many awards for his wines, including the Air Ontario Winemaker of the Year Award and several international awards. In 1997, the Hillebrand Estates' Unfiltered Cabernet Sauvignon 1995 won the prestigious Grand Gold Award at the Vinitaly International Wine Competition.

Brian Schmidt: Vineland Estates

Brian succeeded his brother Allan to the post of winemaker at Vineland Estates while Allan moved into a more managerial capacity. When they're not at the winery, these brothers are likely to be off on an adventure. They once took their Icewine by dogsled to the magnetic North Pole to test the effect on the wine. Building on Vineland's reputation for Riesling, Brian is putting new emphasis on varietals such as Pinot Gris, Gewürztraminer, Merlot, Cabernet Franc, Cabernet Sauvignon, and Pinot Noir. His efforts have been well received in competitions in Europe and North America.

Ann Sperling: Malivoire Wine Company

Originally from British Columbia, Ann had a number of consulting contracts before taking on full-time winemaking duties at Malivoire. In only a short time she's shown that she can bring out the best from the winery's gravity-fed system (which allows the wine to flow gently from press to tanks rather than be subjected to pumping). She produces only a handful of wines, but they all show elegance and beautiful balance. One of her creative touches is to add a very small amount of Cabernet Franc to the Old Vines Foch. This minute addition effectively rubs the rough edges off the Old Vines Foch, resulting in an intense, yet elegant wine.

Jim Warren: Daniel Lenko Estate Winery and Nesher Wines

Founder of Stoney Ridge and industry leader in creativity, Jim has now freed himself from the shackles of winery administration to do what he does best — make wine. He is consulting for two new start-up wineries — Daniel Lenko Estate Winery, whose just-released wines cleaned up at the All Canadian Wine Championships in 2000, and Nesher Wines, specializing in kosher table wines. He's also working with a number of new fruit wineries. Jim is renowned in the industry for the number of small-batch wines he produces. He made 51 at Stoney Ridge.

Chapter 24

Ten British Columbia Winemakers to Watch

Although B.C. is a quarter the size of Ontario in terms of vineyard acreage and wine production, there are nevertheless more wineries — though most of them are fairly small. As with Ontario, it's hard for us to single out just 10 B.C. winemakers, but the individuals we've chosen are very distinctive in their style and produce some of the best wines currently being made out west. See Chapter 19 for more on the wineries where these talented folks ply their trade.

Olivier Combret: Domaine Combret

Outspoken and, some say, flamboyant, Olivier channels his energies into drawing out the characteristics of the terroir in his wines. He produces only small quantities, making them difficult to obtain — but well worth the search. He brings a special French style to his winemaking activities.

Roger Dosman: Alderlea Vineyards

In the prime of his life, Roger Dosman traded in his body shop in Vancouver for a vineyard on Vancouver Island. He admits he acted on impulse. But since he opened Alderlea Vineyards in 1998, Roger has proven his skills with hybrids as well as with Pinot Noir and Pinot Gris.

Bill Dyer: Burrowing Owl Vineyards

"Cellar rat" is the winery-speak equivalent of the term "gofer." That was Bill Dyer's first job at Charles Krug winery, in the Napa Valley. A few years later he became the cellar master at mega-winery Sterling Vineyards, and was promoted to assistant winemaker and eventually to winemaker. For more than 10 years, he oversaw the winemaking operations at Sterling, until he was invited to help set up a new winery in B.C. — Burrowing Owl. He jumped at the opportunity to discover an intriguing new wine region.

Ian Mavety: Blue Mountain Vineyard & Cellars

Ian's bread-and-butter wine is a bubbly (Blue Mountain Brut), but he has extraordinary talent for working with Pinot Noir (Burgundy's difficult grape), leading Blue Mountain to be the first Canadian winery to be invited to the annual Oregon Pinot Noir festival, International Pinot Noir Celebration. He also has a way with whites — his Pinot Gris, Pinot Blanc, and Chardonnay are not to be missed.

Alex Nichol: Nichol Vineyard & Farm Winery

Alex, with his wife Kathleen, manages the vineyard and performs all the winemaking procedures. Their winery is small, but attention to detail is large. This adds up to wines of increasing quality. Alex introduced the Syrah grape into the Valley.

Bruce Nicholson: Vincor/ Jackson-Triggs Vintners

Bruce is a major cog in the wheel of Jackson-Triggs' move into the premium wine category, up from the commercial table wine level. For two years in a row, he was B.C.'s winningest winemaker, taking home many awards in international competitions. As the grapevine speaks, Bruce is definitely the man to watch.

Sandra Oldfield: Tinhorn Creek

Sandra, who trained at the University of California at Davis, instills a distinctly California style to her wines at Tinhorn Creek, but never loses a sense of balance and elegance. She has a special affinity for Chardonnay and Pinot Gris. Her reds are a delight.

Howard Soon: Calona Vineyards

With 20 years' experience in winemaking, Howard has not only created the award-winning Calona Artist Series Chardonnays, but he has also spent countless hours educating the public in wine. He received the Okanagan Wine Festival Founder's Award in 1999 for his portfolio of wines.

Artist Robb Dunfield, a quadriplegic as a result of an accident at the age of 19, began painting the designs for Calona's labels in 1987. Remarkably, Robb paints only eight pictures a year — holding the brush in his mouth. His landscapes have graced the bottles of Calona's Artist Series ever since.

Frank Supernak: Hester Creek Estate Winery

Frank transformed the former Divino winery property into Hester Creek in 1996. This former Vincor winemaker has garnered much-deserved attention for his Pinot Blanc and Merlot.

Erik von Krosigk: Hillside Estate Winery, Pinot Reach Cellars, Red Rooster Winery, Saturna Vineyard

Erik is a consulting winemaker who brings nine years of experience and education in Germany to his work with a variety of small B.C. wineries. He even spent six years as a member of the German quality-tasting panel. His first love is for Champagne-method sparkling wines, but he also has a talent for still Pinot Noir wines and a range of other varietals. Erik is the busiest winemaker in B.C., consulting to more wineries than you can shake a stick at.

Part VII
Appendixes

The 5th Wave   By Rich Tennant

"LOOK KIDS, MOMMY AND DADDY NEED A THERMOSTATICALLY CONTROLLED ENVIRONMENT FOR THEIR WINE UNTIL THE CELLAR IS FINISHED - WE'RE TALKING BORDEAUXS HERE, KIDS - OVER 60 YEARS OLD."

In this part . . .

Here's where we get technical and ultra-detailed. See a word that you don't understand? Look it up in the glossary of wine terms. Found a couple of wineries that you'd like to visit? We've got all the contact information you need in the directory of wineries, including phone numbers, e-mail, and Web site addresses. Want to bone up on the VQA and what it really takes for a Canadian wine to get that special seal of approval? We've included the highlights of the VQA's national wine standard. Oh yeah, what about that gift you have to buy for your in-laws (who aren't too shabby themselves in the wine knowledge department)? We think you'll find what you're looking for in our list of retailers. Read on!

Appendix A

Glossary

● ●

*T*he terms that appear in *italic type* throughout the book are defined in this glossary.

acetic acid: A *volatile acid* caused by the acetobacter bacteria. In small amounts, acetic acid contributes to a wine's refreshing quality or zestiness, but too much of it causes the wine to smell and taste of vinegar.

acidify: To adjust the wine's acid content by the addition of tartaric, citric, or malic acid; usually only performed in warm growing regions where the grape sugars overbalance the acids.

acidity: Also known as total acidity. This refers to the combination of both *fixed* and *volatile* acids in wine. Acid is necessary to create balance in the wine and contributes to the capacity of a wine to age.

aerate: To introduce air into a wine by pouring into a decanter or jug. Aeration releases more of the wine's bouquet and flavour.

aftertaste: The flavour left in the mouth after the wine has been swallowed. The mark of a good wine is how long the flavour remains on your palate.

alcohol: In wine this refers to ethyl alcohol. It is a natural by-product of the fermentation process.

apéritif: A wine you drink before a meal. A dry white wine will stimulate appetite.

appearance: The look of the wine relative to colour, clarity, and brightness. In sparkling wines this includes the concentration and frequency of the bubbles and how active they are.

appellation: From the French term "appellation contrôlée," meaning "controlled name." Regulations and standards regarding the naming of wines are designed to indicate the quality of the wine and to prevent fraud. See *Vintners Quality Alliance.*

aroma: Also known as a wine's aromatics. The odours in wine derived directly from the fruit. Not to be confused with *bouquet,* which describes odours resulting from the vinification and aging process.

assemblage: French term meaning to make a final blend of different wines, or casks of the same wine, prior to bottling.

Bacchus: The Roman god of wine (all 'round good chap!), also known as *Dionysus* in the ancient Greek tradition.

barrique: A small oak barrel containing 225 litres, used for the *maturation* of wine.

Baumé: A scale for measuring the sugar in grapes at time of picking, used in much of Europe and Australia.

best expression: The most representative example of a particular wine style.

bitterness: An astringent taste in wine caused by *tannins* or poorly seasoned oak barrels.

Blanc de Blancs: A white wine made from a blend of white grapes. The term is often used for champagne (Chardonnay only) and other sparkling wines. See *Blanc de Noirs.*

Blanc de Noirs: A white wine made from black grapes. The term often denotes a champagne made from Pinot Noir or a blend of Pinot Noir and Pinot Meunier. See *Blanc de Blancs.*

blend: A combination of wines to create the final product. Blends may be of different grape types or of the same grape type but with different characteristics.

Blush: A wine style developed in California from Zinfandel grapes. In trying to make a white wine, the faintest tinge of pink coloured the wine. Unwilling to market the wine in the less-than-popular rosé category, the producers called it "Blush" and left in a little *residual sugar.*

body: The sensation of weight in the mouth when tasting wine. The impression of body results from the concentration of fruit, from the *alcohol* and *glycerin.* The more of these elements there are in the wine, the more full-bodied the wine appears. A light-bodied wine is light in colour and low in alcohol and extract (fruit flavour). A medium-bodied wine has more weight and substance, whereas a full-bodied wine is deeply coloured and fills the mouth with a higher concentration of taste and feel.

Bordeaux blend: A blend made to emulate Bordeaux wine by combining two or more of the Cabernet Sauvignon, Merlot, Cabernet Franc, Petit Verdot, and Malbec grapes for red, and the Sauvignon Blanc and Sémillon grapes, for white.

bottling: A wine is bottled when the wine-maker decides that it has finished its fermentation and aging process in barrel or tank. Once a wine is bottled, its development slows down dramatically. White wines to be enjoyed young and fresh are bottled a few months after fermentation. Red wines for aging can spend up to two years or more in barrel before being bottled. In olden days, winemakers bottled by hand. Currently, they use elaborate bottling lines that can fill thousands of bottles an hour.

Botrytis cinerea: Also known as "noble rot." A fungus that attacks the skins of grapes in warm damp conditions, allowing water to evaporate, thereby concentrating the berry's sugar and acidity. Desirable in ripe grapes intended for sweet wines as it dehydrates the fruit, thereby increasing the ratio of sugar to fluid.

bouquet: The perfume of a wine that results from the vinification process, and which becomes more intense when the glass is swirled. See *aroma.*

breathing: Exposing the wine to air to allow it to release its bouquet and flavour. Best done by pouring into a decanter. See *aerate.*

Brix: A scale used to measure the percentage of sugar in grape juice or wine. Brix measurements are a determining factor, along with measurements of acid, as to when to pick the grapes. See *Baumé* and *Oechsle.*

Brut: A term used most often to describe the driest champagne and other sparkling wines.

B.Y.O.B.: Bring Your Own Bottle. Some restaurants in Québec allow you to do this.

capsule: The tin or plastic cap that covers the top of a wine bottle.

carbon dioxide: A gas that results from the action of yeast on sugar. It usually escapes into the atmosphere, but if retained in the wine creates bubbles, as in a sparkling wine.

carbonic maceration: Also known as whole berry fermentation. A process in which grapes are maintained intact and fermentation takes place inside each berry. For this to occur, the fruit must be contained in an anaerobic atmosphere usually created by excluding oxygen by the use of carbon dioxide. The technique, used primarily in Beaujolais, especially for *vin nouveau*, produces fresh, fruity wines for early consumption.

cask: A large wooden container for wine.

caudalie: A French measurement for the length of time a wine's flavour lasts on your palate. Measured in seconds.

cava: Spanish term for a sparkling wine made by the Champagne method.

cellar book: A book in which you record details about the wine you store in your wine cellar.

champagne: A sparkling wine made in the region of Champagne, France, by inducing a secondary fermentation in the bottle. See *Champagne method.*

Champagne method: The process used to make sparkling wine by inducing a secondary fermentation in the bottle. When used outside the Champagne region, it is invariably termed "traditional method." See *méthode traditionelle.*

chaptalization: The addition of sugar or syrup to grape juice prior to fermentation to raise the level of alcohol. Named after Napoleon III's minister of agriculture, Jean-Antoine Chaptal, who introduced legislation to legalize the practise in France.

Charmat process: A less costly method of making sparkling wine. It is fermented in pressurized stainless-steel tanks rather than giving it a secondary fermentation in bottle.

claret: A term first used in England to describe red wine from the Bordeaux region of France. See also *Bordeaux blend* and *Meritage.*

clone: A variety of grapevine created by taking a cutting from another vine. The second vine has characteristics identical to the first.

clos: A French vineyard enclosed by a wall.

cluster thinning: A manual process by which bunches of unripe grapes are removed from the vine. This technique causes the remaining bunches to ripen more quickly. Also used to concentrate the bouquet and flavour of the remaining bunches.

comparative tasting: Tasting two or more wines at a time to compare and contrast their characteristics.

cooper: A person who makes barrels by hand. The place where the work is done is called a cooperage.

cork: Bark taken from the cork tree and used to make stoppers for wine bottles.

corked: A term used to describe wines affected by moulds or bacteria that cause an unpleasant, musty smell and flavour.

cross: A grapevine resulting from the union of two or more vines from the same species.

cru: French for "growth" with specific reference to a French vineyard recognized as being superior, as in Grand Cru.

crushing: The procedure by which grape skins are broken to allow the yeast to come in contact with the juice. The first effective crushing device was the human foot. See *pressing*.

cryo-extraction: Artificially freezing grapes to concentrate their sugars when pressed.

decanter: A container into which wine is poured from the bottle, and from which it can be served. See *decanting*.

decanting: The act of pouring wine out of the bottle into a separate container. Removes sediment from the wine and exposes it to air. See *decanter*.

digéstif: A wine or spirit you drink after a meal to help you digest.

destemming: The process of removing the stems from the bunches of grapes. It usually occurs during or immediately after crushing. The stems are removed by means of a strainer or sieve.

Dionysus: The Greek god of wine. See also *Bacchus*.

dry: Technically, a wine in which nearly all the sugar has been converted to alcohol; however, many wines containing small amounts of residual sugar may appear dry to the palate because of their high levels of acidity.

Eiswein: The German term for *Icewine*.

farm (gate) wineries: Small winery operations with a minimum of five acres of grapes, usually producing under 10,000 cases, selling from their own premises.

fermentation: The effect of yeast cells on sugar resulting in alcohol and carbon dioxide in almost equal amounts.

filtration: A sometimes overused procedure to remove solid particles from the wine. Extensive filtering can rob the wine of *bouquet* and flavour.

fining: An alternative to *filtration* whereby agents are added to the wine to attract floating particles floating and cause them to fall to the bottom of the container.

finish: The overall impression the wine leaves in your mouth once the taste has disappeared, indicating the length and balance of a wine's different elements.

fixed acids: Acids, including tartaric, malic, succinic, and lactic acids, that are not affected by *oxidation* or evaporation.

flight: During a wine tasting, a group of wines tasted together for comparative purposes, usually lined up left to right.

fortified wine: A wine to which alcohol has been added. Examples are sherry, port, and Madeira.

fruit-set: The point at which the flower on a grapevine develops into a grape.

fruit wines: Wines made from fruits and berries other than grapes.

futures: Wine sold by the producer before bottling — sometimes while the grapes are still hanging on the vine. The sale price at this time is lower than the price asked at time of bottling or release.

glycerin: A by-product of *fermentation* that contributes a sensation of smoothness and sweetness to wine.

grafting: Process by which a preferred grape variety, such as Chardonnay, is grafted onto a disease-resistant rootstock to combat the possibility of *phylloxera*.

hectare: A metric measurement used commonly in Europe to describe the square measure of a vineyard and equal to 2.471 acres. For simplicity's sake, reckon it as two-and-a-half times the size of one acre.

hectolitre: Equal to 100 litres or approximately 22 Imperial gallons.

helix: The spiral prong of a corkscrew that is inserted into the cork.

hermetic seal: An airtight closure.

Hock: An English expression for the wines of the Rhine Valley in Germany (after the town of Hochheim in the Rheingau).

house wine: A wine usually bought in bulk by a restaurant and sold by the glass or carafe at the lowest cost on the wine list.

hybrid: A vine created by interbreeding vines from different species to result in a "superior" vine that will ripen earlier, yield more berries, and resist disease.

Icewine: A sweet wine made from grapes left on the vine to freeze and pressed in their frozen state.

initial taste: The first sensations interpreted by the tongue as the wine enters the mouth.

Jeroboam: A large bottle equivalent to four standard bottles of 750 ml.

laying down: The act of placing wine in storage for the purpose of aging it (on its side so that the cork remains wet at all times).

lees: The sediment that falls from wine during fermentation, made up mostly of dead yeast cells and grape particles. Certain white wines benefit from extended contact with these solids that give additional flavour and a prickle on the tongue. Muscadet sur Lie from the Loire Valley in France is a good example. See *sur lie*.

legs: The trail left by droplets of wine as they fall down the side of the glass after the wine in the glass has been swirled.

length: The period of time that the taste of a wine lingers in the mouth after swallowing.

macerate: To soak the grape skins in their juice. This process is carried out in red wines to extract colour.

maderization: The effect of heat and oxygen on wine, usually the result of poor storage and/or over-aging. This effect is deliberately sought in madeira wine.

magnum: A large bottle equal to two standard 750-ml bottles.

malolactic fermentation: A chemical process in which harsh tasting malic acid (green apple taste) is transformed into the smoother tasting lactic acid (milk taste). This process may be encouraged or inhibited, depending on the style of wine desired.

maturation: The aging of wine in wood as opposed to bottle aging.

meniscus: The top surface of liquid in a bottle or tube.

Meritage: A term coined in the U.S. and adopted by Canadian winemakers to denote a wine made with the traditional varieties of Bordeaux, both red and white. See also *Bordeaux blend*.

méthode traditionelle: A term describing the champagne method of inducing bubbles in wine by causing a *secondary fermentation* in the bottle.

Methuselah: A very large bottle equal to eight standard 750-ml bottles.

millésime: French word for *vintage*.

mousse: Bubbles in sparkling wine.

mouthfeel: Tactile sensations derived from the wine as it is held in the mouth.

must: A mixture of grape juice and grape solids. The wine is in this state before *fermentation* occurs.

Nebuchadnezzar: A very, very large bottle equivalent to 20 standard 750-ml bottles.

négociant: French term for wine merchant or shipper.

New World: A modern style of winemaking that promotes the fruitiness in wines rather than producing wines that require long aging. Emphasis is on *varietal* labelling rather than labelling based on the name of the place where the grapes were grown. See *Old World*.

nose: The organ you employ most when it comes to assessing a wine. Also used as an expression for the smell of a wine.

NV: Short for "Non Vintage" (which means the wine will be a blend of two or more years).

oak: The preferred wood for making barrels and other containers used for the maturation of wine.

Oechsle: A scale used in Germany and Austria for the measurement of sugar in grapes at the time of harvest. See *Baumé* and *Brix*.

oenology (enology): The study of wine. This book helps you in this pursuit.

oenophile: A person who loves wine. If you're reading this book — you're on your way to becoming one.

Old World: A winemaking style that relies on traditional methods and the use of oak barrels for maturation of wine. See *New World*.

organic wines: Wines made without the addition of *sulphur* products in the vineyard or the cellar.

overcropping: Taking too many bunches of grapes off a grapevine. Overcropping makes for diluted flavours in the wine.

oxidation: A change in the character of wine derived from exposure to oxygen.

palate: Literally, the roof of the mouth, but as a tasting term refers to the effect of wine on the whole mouth — the tongue, inside cheeks, gums, and back of the throat.

pasteurization: The practise of flash heating wines to kill off any bacterial activity.

pH: A measurement of the active acidity in a wine. The lower the pH, the sharper the wine will taste. Wines generally have a pH between 4 and 3. The pH of lemon juice is 2.3.

photosynthesis: A biochemical reaction in which the energy of the sun causes sugar to form in the vines.

Phylloxera (vastatrix): An aphid that feeds on the roots of the vine and eventually causes it to die. Most grapevines must be grafted to specific rootstocks that have a natural resistance to this pest.

plonk: An English term for an everyday, cheap and cheerful wine. Probably a corruption of the French, "blanc" (white).

pomace: The grape solids left over after *pressing*. These can be refermented and distilled to make a spirit, such as grappa.

port: A sweet *fortified wine*, both red and white, made in the Douro Valley of Portugal.

pour: *n.* In restaurant terms this is the amount of wine you get if you order by the glass. Usually 4 to 6 ounces. The exact amount of the pour should be posted on the wine list.

provenance: Geographic origin of a wine or of the grapes used to make it.

pressing: Applying pressure to the grapes to squeeze out the juice. In red wine, this normally occurs after fermentation, once the wine has acquired sufficient colour. In white wine, it's done before *fermentation*. Originally effected by the human foot, but nowadays by hydraulic or bladder presses. See *crushing*.

pruning: Cutting back canes in winter and trimming leaves in summer to encourage more growth in the grape clusters. See cluster thinning.

punt: The indentation in the bottom of a wine bottle, very pronounced in sparkling wines to strengthen the glass against the pressure within. Originally designed to catch sediment.

racking: Draining the wine off the *lees* and transferring it to a clean barrel, vat, or tank.

racking system: Shelving or supports in which to store wine.

refractometer: Instrument for measuring the sugar in a grape berry. Usually carried into the vineyard for on-site assessment as to when to start the harvest. Light passes through a puddle of juice and the angle of refraction determines the amount of sugar.

reserve: A wine of superior quality.

residual sugar: Sugar that remains in the wine after fermentation.

resveratrol: A substance that occurs naturally in grapes and some other plants that has been shown to reduce the risk of heart disease and cancer. (Warning: Don't overmedicate yourself!)

secondary fermentation: A second fermentation induced in still wines by adding a small amount of sugar and yeast dissolved in wine. The bottle is then resealed and the action of the yeast on the sugar creates *alcohol* and *carbon dioxide*. Since the gas has nowhere to go, it becomes bound in with the wine, creating a sparkling wine. This activity can occasionally occur spontaneously in a bottled wine, spoiling it or causing the bottle to explode because of the build-up of gas.

secondary taste: The second of three stages of taste, when the wine has been warmed by the mouth and has come in contact with the entire palate. See *aftertaste* and *initial taste*.

sediment: Solids that precipitate from the wine and fall to the bottom of the container. Sediment should be decanted from the wine before serving.

Sekt: The German term for sparkling wines made by the champagne method.

sherry: A fortified wine made in the Jerez region of Spain. It ranges in style from bone dry to very sweet.

soak: The skins of the grapes are left in their juice for the purpose of extracting colour.

sommelier: A person trained in the selection, cellaring, and service of wine. Can be an intimidating presence in snooty restaurants.

sparkling: A wine in which the trapped carbon dioxide gas as a result of fermentation produces bubbles in a wine.

spraying: Farmers spray vineyards to protect the vines against mildew, pests, diseases, and weeds. In these environmentally sensitive times, minimal amounts of agro-chemicals are used. In some warm, damp-free regions, grapes grown without recourse to these products are termed *organic wines*.

spumante: The Italian term for sparkling wine.

stainless steel: The most widely used storage tank for wine. Also used for fermentation. Production of wine in stainless steel is less expensive than using *barriques*.

staves: Slats of curved wood assembled by hand to make the body of a barrel.

still: A wine that does not have bubbles.

sulphur: An element used as a fungicide in the vineyard and an antibacterial and antioxidant agent in the winery.

sur lie: French term denoting a wine that has spent extended time on its *lees*, in the tank or barrel, before bottling.

Süssreserve: A German term for unfermented grape juice that is used to sweeten some wines prior to bottling.

table wine: A wine with average alcoholic content (12.5 percent).

tannins: Substances derived from grape skins, seeds, stalks, and oak storage containers. They contribute to the wine's structure and ability to age.

tartrates: Harmless crystalline deposits that precipitate from the wine and fall to the bottom of the bottle or cling to the cork. They indicate a wine that has not been subjected to unnecessary filtration. In most cases, the winemaker will remove them at the winery by flash-chilling the wine to encourage precipitation of these crystals.

tastevin: The small silver cup worn by *sommeliers* in the fancier restaurants to sample wine. It resembles a silver ashtray. Once used extensively in Burgundian cellars to taste wines when the producer and buyer got together. The silver would reflect what little light there was.

tasting: *n.* Also known as a wine tasting. An event, usually held in a group, where participants analyze a wine using the visual, olfactory, and gustatory senses.

tasting, ambulatory: *n.* A wine tasting where participants move from station to station around a room to obtain samples of different wines.

tasting, blind: *n.* A wine tasting where the labels are covered so that participants know nothing about the wines they are sampling. A humbling experience for those who think they can identify wines by smell and taste alone. (Hint: One glance at the label is worth 25 years' experience.)

terroir: French term denoting the vine's growing environment including soil, location, and climate.

typicity: True to the nature of the grape's inherent flavour.

trellising wires: Wires strung between posts in the vineyard to support the canes of vines. Used to maximize sunlight to ensure greater ripeness and higher sugar levels in the grapes.

ullage: The loss of wine from leakage or evaporation. Visible in older bottles by the level of the wine in the neck of the bottle.

vanillan: An aromatic element in wine derived from storage in oak.

varietal: A specific variety of grape. Also, a wine that is named after the grape variety from which it is made. This is a practise used in Alsace, France, and in most New World wine regions.

vinification: The process of making wine.

Vin Nouveau: The first wine of the year, made a few weeks after the harvest. The most famous is Beaujolais Nouveau, which is released on the third Thursday of November.

vintage: Also known as vintage date. The year in which the grapes were harvested.

Vintners Quality Alliance (VQA): The Canadian system of standards for labelling wine to denote its origins and quality. See *appellation.*

Vitis labrusca: A species of table grape native to North America. No longer used for Canadian table wines. The best-known variety of this species is the Concord grape.

Vitis vinifera: A species of wine grape native to Europe and now grown in many countries around the world. Well-known varieties in this species are Riesling, Chardonnay, Pinot Noir, and Cabernet Sauvignon.

volatile acid: Acid in wine that is susceptible to oxidation and evaporation, as represented by carbonic and *acetic acid.*

wine agent: A person who represents a winery and is responsible for the sales and marketing of its wines in a particular location or territory.

wine producer: A person responsible for the making of wine, usually the owner of a winery. (This person may not be the actual winemaker.)

yeast: A single-celled organism that causes fermentation by consuming sugar and converting it to alcohol and carbon dioxide.

Appendix B

Directory of Canadian Wineries

• •

Ontario

Niagara Bench wineries

13th Street Wine Company
3983 13th Street, Jordan, ON, L0R 1S0
phone 905-562-9463, fax 905-562-5900

Andrés Wines Ltd.
P.O. Box 10550, 697 South Service Road,
Winona, ON, L8E 5S4
phone 905-643-4131, fax 905-643-4944
e-mail info@andreswines.com
web site www.andreswines.com

Birchwood Estates Wines
4679 Cherry Street, Beamsville, ON, L0R 1B1
phone 905-562-8463, fax 905-562-6344
e-mail green@bokawines.com
web site www.birchwoodwines.com

Cave Spring Cellars
3836 Main Street, Jordan, ON, L0R 1S0
phone 905-562-3581, fax 905-562-3232
web site www.cavespringcellars.com

Creekside Estate Winery
2170 4th Avenue, Jordan Station, ON, L0R 1S0
phone 905-562-0035, fax 905-562-5493
e-mail wineryinfo@creeksideestatewinery.com
web site www.creeksideestatewinery.com

Crown Bench Estates
3850 Aberdeen Road, Beamsville, ON, L0R 1B7
phone 905-563-3959, fax 905-563-3441
e-mail winery@crownbenchestates.com
web site www.crownbenchestates.com

Daniel Lenko Estate Winery
5246 Regional Road 81, Beamsville, ON, L0R 1B3
Opening autumn 2000

EastDell Estates
4041 Locust Lane, Beamsville, ON, L0R 1B2
phone 905-563-9463, fax 905-563-4633
e-mail winery@eastdell.com
web site www.eastdell.com

Harbour Estates Winery Limited
4362 Jordan Road, Jordan Station, ON, L0R 1S0
phone 905-562-6279, 1-877-HEW-WINE,
fax 905-562-3829
e-mail info@hewwine.com
web site www.hewwine.com

Henry of Pelham Family Estate Winery
1469 Pelham Road, R.R. #1, St. Catharines, ON,
L2R 6P7
phone 905-684-8423, fax 905-684-8444
e-mail visits@henryofpelham.com
web site www.henryofpelham.com

Hernder Estates Winery
1607 8th Street, St. Catharines, ON, L2R 6P7
phone 905-684-3300, fax 905-684-3303
e-mail email@hernder.com
web site www.hernder.com

Kittling Ridge Estate Wines & Spirits
297 South Service Road, Grimsby, ON, L3M 4E9
phone 905-945-9225, 416-777-6300,
fax 905-945-4330
e-mail admin@kittlingridge.com
web site www.kittlingridge.com

Lakeview Cellars Estate Winery
R.R. #1, 4037 Cherry Avenue, Vineland, ON,
L0R 2C0
phone 905-562-5685, fax 905-562-0673
e-mail info@lakeviewcellars.on.ca
web site www.lakeviewcellars.on.ca

Malivoire Wine Company
4260 King Street East, P.O. Box 475, Beamsville,
ON, L0R 1B0
phone 905-563-9253, fax 905-563-9512
e-mail ladybug@malivoirewineco.com
web site www.malivoirewineco.com

Peninsula Ridge Estates Winery
5600 King Street, P.O. Box 550, Beamsville, ON,
L0R 1B0
phone 905-563-0900, fax 905-563-0995
e-mail info@peninsularidge.com
web site www.peninsularigde.com

Royal deMaria Wines Co. Ltd.
4551 Cherry Avenue, Vineland, ON, L0R 1B0
phone 905-563-9692, fax 905-563-9001
e-mail royald@idirect.com
web site www.royaldemaria.com

Stoney Ridge Cellars Ltd.
3201 King Street, Vineland, ON, L0R 2C0
phone 905-562-1324, fax 905-562-7777
e-mail srcellar@vaxxine.com
web site www.stoneyridge.com

Thirty Bench Vineyard & Winery
4281 Mountainview Road, Beamsville, ON,
L0R 1B0
phone 905-563-1698, fax 905-563-3921
e-mail wine@thirtybench.com
web site www.thirtybench.com

Thomas & Vaughan Vintners
4245 King Street, Beamsville, ON, L0R 1B1
phone 905-563-7737, fax 905-563-4114
e-mail exec_power@yahoo.com
web site www.thomasandvaughan.com

Vineland Estates Wines Ltd.
R.R. #1, 3620 Moyer Road, Vineland, ON,
L0R 2C0
phone 905-562-7088, 1-888-VINELAND
(1-888-846-3526), fax 905-562-3071
e-mail wine@vineland.com
web site www.vineland.com

Willow Heights Estate Winery
3751 Regional Road 81, Vineland, ON, L0R 2C0
phone 905-562-4945, fax 905-562-5761
e-mail Willow.Heights@sympatico.ca
web site www.willowheights.on.ca

Niagara-on-the-Lake wineries

Château des Charmes Wines Ltd.
P.O. Box 280, 1025 York Road, St. David's, ON,
L0S 1P0
phone 905-262-4219, HOSPITALITY LINE
905-262-5202, 905-262-4210, toll free
1-800-263-5124, fax 905-262-5548
e-mail sjanke@chateaudescharmes.com
web site www.chateaudescharmes.com

Domaine Vagners
1973 Four Mile Creek Road, R.R. #3, Niagara-on-
the-Lake, ON, L0S 1J0
phone 905-468-7296
e-mail mvagners@netcom.ca

Hillebrand Estates Winery
1249 Niagara Stone Road, R.R. #2, Niagara-on-
the-Lake, ON, L0S 1J0
phone: 905-468-7123, 1-800-582-8412,
fax 905-468-4789
e-mail info@hillebrand.com
web site www.hillebrand.com

Inniskillin Wines Inc.
S. R. #66, R.R. #1, Niagara Parkway, Niagara-on-
the-Lake, ON, L0S 1J0
phone 905-468-2187, 1-888-466-4754,
fax 905-468-5355
e-mail inniskil@inniskillin.com
web site www.inniskillin.com

Jackson-Triggs Estate Winery
2145 Niagara Stone Road (Highway 55),
R.R. #3, Niagara-on-the-Lake, ON, L0S 1J0
Opening Spring 2001

Joseph's Estate Wines
1811 Niagara Stone Road (Hwy 55), R.R. #3,
Niagara-on-the-Lake, ON, L0S 1J0
phone 905-468-1259, fax 905-468-9242
e-mail info@josephsestatewine.com
web site www.josephsestatewines.com

Konzelmann Estate Winery
R.R. #3, 1096 Lakeshore Road, Niagara-on-the-
Lake, ON, L0S 1J0
phone 905-935-2866, fax 905-935-2864
e-mail wine@konzelmannwines.com
web site www.konzelmannwines.com

Marynissen Estates Limited
R.R. #6, Concession 1, Niagara-on-the-Lake,
ON, L0S 1J0
phone 905-468-7270, fax 905-468-5784
e-mail marynisn@netcom.ca
web site www.islandnet.com/dining/wine/

Peller Estates
290 John Street, Niagara-on-the-Lake, ON,
L0S 1J0
Opening Spring 2001
phone N/A, fax N/A
e-mail N/A, web site www.peller.com

Pillitteri Estates Winery
1696 Niagara Stone Road (Highway 55),
Niagara-on-the-Lake, ON, L0S 1J0
phone 905-468-3147, fax 905-468-0389
e-mail winery@pillitteri.com
web site www.pillitteri.com

Reif Estate Winery
15606 Niagara Parkway, Niagara-on-the-Lake,
ON, L0S 1J0
phone 905-468-7738, fax 905-468-5878
e-mail wine@reifwinery.com
web site www.reifwinery.com

Stonechurch Vineyards
1270 Irvine Road, R.R. #5, Niagara-on-the-Lake,
ON, L0S 1J0
phone 905-935-3535, fax 905-646-8892
e-mail wine@stonechurch.com
web site www.stonechurch.com

Strewn Inc.
1339 Lakeshore Road, Niagara-on-the-Lake,
ON, L0S 1J0
phone 905-468-1229, toll free 1-888-4strewn,
fax 905-468-8305
e-mail strewnwines@sympatico.ca
web site www.strewnwinery.com

Vincor International Inc.
Niagara Cellars, 4887 Dorchester Road,
P.O. Box 510, Niagara Falls, ON, L2E 6V4
phone 905-358-7141, fax 905-358-7750

Wine Rack, retail division of Vincor
International Inc.
Corporate Head Office, 441 Courtneypark Drive
East, Mississauga, ON, L5T 2V3
phone 905-564-6900, 1-888-793-9999,
fax 905-564-6181
web site www.winerack.com

Lake Erie North Shore wineries

Colio Estate Wines
P.O. Box 372, 1 Colio Drive, Harrow, ON,
N0R 1G0
phone 519-738-2241, 1-800-265-1322,
fax 519-738-3070
Head Office, Sales & Marketing Office
2300 Haines Road, Mississauga, ON, L4Y 1Y6
phone 905-896-8512, 1-800-263-0802,
fax 905-949-4269
e-mail colio@total.net
web site www.lsol.com/colio

D'Angelo Estate Winery
5141 Concession #5, R.R. #4, Amherstburg,
ON, N9V 2Y9
phone 519-736-7959, 1-888-598-8317,
fax 519-736-1912
e-mail dangelowines@on.aibn.com
web site N/A

LeBlanc Estate Winery
4716-4th Concession, R.R. #2, Harrow, ON,
N0R 1G0
phone 519-738-9228, fax 519-738-2609
e-mail info@leblancestatewinery.com
web site leblancestatewinery.com

Pelee Island Winery
455 Seacliff Drive (County Road #20)
Kingsville, ON, N9Y 2K5
phone 519-733-6551, 1-800-597-3533,
fax 519-733-6553
e-mail inquiries@peleeisland.com
web site www.peleeisland.com

Toronto/GTA wineries

Cilento Wines
672 Chrislea Road, Woodbridge, ON, L4L 8K9
phone 905-264-9463, 1-888-245-9463,
fax 905-264-8671
e-mail vinbon@ica.net
web site www.vinbon.ca

De Sousa Wine Cellars
Exit #64 Beamsville, 3753 Quarry Road,
Beamsville, ON, L0R 1B0
phone 905-563-7269, fax 905-338-9404
Toronto address:
802 Dundas Street West, Toronto, ON, M6G 1V3
phone 416-603-0202, fax 905-338-9404
web site www.desousawines.com

Magnotta Winery Estates
271 Chrislea Road, Vaughan, ON, L4L 8N6
phone 905-738-9463, 1-800-461-WINE,
fax 905-738-5551
e-mail mailbox@magnotta.com
web site www.magnotta.com

Milan Wineries
6811 Steeles Avenue West, Toronto, ON,
M9V 4R9
phone 416-740-2005, fax 416-740-8747
e-mail milan@milanwineries.com
web site www.milanwineries.com

Southbrook Farm & Winery
(Mailing) P.O. Box 147, Richmond Hill, ON,
L4C 4X9
(Location) 1061 Major McKenzie Drive West,
Maple, ON, L6A 1R9
phone 905-832-2548, fax 905-832-9811
e-mail office@southbrook.com
web site www.southbrook.com

Vinoteca
527 Jevlan Drive, Woodbridge, ON, L4L 8W1
phone 905-856-5700, fax 905-856-8208
web site www.toronto.com/vinoteca

Other areas

Quai du Vin Estate Winery
45811 Fruit Ridge Line, R.R. #5, St. Thomas,
ON, N5P 3S9
phone 519-775-2216, fax 519-775-0168
e-mail info@quaiduvin.com
web site www.quaiduvin.com

British Columbia

Okanagan Valley wineries

Bella Vista Vineyards
3111 Agnew Road, Vernon, BC, V1H 1A1
phone 250-558-0770, Toll free 1-888-221-0222,
fax 250-549-7017
e-mail bvv@workshopbc.com
web site www.webtec.com.au/bvv/

Black Hills Estate Winery
30880 Black Sage Road, R.R. #1, S52 C22, Oliver,
BC, V0H 1T0
phone 250-498-0666 fax 250-498-0690
e-mail info@blackhillswinery.com
web site www.blackhillswinery.com

Blue Mountain Vineyard & Cellars
R.R. #1, S3 C4, Okanagan Falls, BC, V0H 1R0
phone 250-497-8244, fax 250-497-6160
e-mail jmavety@vip.net
web site www.bluemountainwinery.com

Burrowing Owl Vineyards
100 Burrowing Owl Place, R.R. #1, Site 52
Comp 20, Oliver, BC, V0H 1T0
phone 250-498-0620, toll free 877-498-0620,
fax 604-984-2753, 250-498-0621
e-mail info@bovwine.com
web site www.bovwine.com

Calona Vineyards
1125 Richter Street, Kelowna, BC, V1Y 2K6
phone 250-762-3332, WINE SHOP 250-762-9144,
ORDER LINE 1-800-663-5086, fax 250-762-2999
e-mail wineboutique@cascadia.ca
web site N/A

Carriage House Wines
32764 Black Sage Road, R.R. #1, S46 C19,
Oliver, BC, V0H 1T0
phone/fax 250-498-8818

CedarCreek Estate Winery
5445 Lakeshore Road, Kelowna, BC, V1W 4S5
phone 250-764-8866 or 1-800-730-9463,
fax 250-764-2603
e-mail info@cedarcreek.bc.ca
web site www.cedarcreek.bc.ca

Domaine Combret
P.O. Box 1170, Road 13, Oliver, BC, V0H 1T0
phone 250-498-8878, fax 250-498-8879
e-mail domaine_combret@telus.net
web site http://www.winesnw.com/
  domainecombret.htm

Fairview Cellars
13147 334th Avenue (Old Golf Course Road,
R.R. #1, S66 C15), Oliver, BC, V0H 1T0
300 Yards North of Fairview Golf Course
phone/fax 250-498-2211
e-mail beggert@img.net
web site www.winecountry.net/faircella.htm

Gehringer Brothers Estate Winery
Road 8, R.R. #1, S23 C4, Oliver, BC, V0H 1T0
phone 250-498-3537, 1-800-784-6304,
fax 250-498-3510
web site www.oliverchamber.bc.ca/
business/gehringe.htm

Gersighel Wineberg
29690 R.R. #1, S40 C20, Oliver, BC, V0H 1T0
phone/fax 250-495-3319

Golden Mile Cellars
13140 316a Avenue, Road 13, R.R. #1, S28A C4,
Oliver, BC, V0H 1T0
phone 250-498-8330, fax 250-498-8331

Gray Monk Estate Winery
1055 Camp Road, Okanagan Centre, BC,
V4V 2H4
phone 250-766-3168 or 1-800-663-4205,
fax 250-766.3390
e-mail mailbox@graymonk.com
web site www.graymonk.com

Hainle Vineyards Estate Winery
5355 Trepanier Bench Road, Box 650,
Peachland, BC, V0H 1X0
phone 250-767-2525 or ORDERS 1-800-767-3109,
fax 250-767-2543
e-mail tilman@hainle.com
web site www.hainle.com

Hawthorne Mountain Vineyards
Green Lake Road, Box 480, Okanagan Falls, BC,
V0H 1R0 (5.8 km North of Okanagan Falls)
phone 250-497-8267, fax 250-497-8073,
e-mail info@hmvineyard.com
web site www.hmvineyard.com

Hester Creek Estate Winery
13163 326th Avenue, Box 1605, Oliver, BC,
V0H 1T0
phone 250-498-4435, fax 250-498-0651
e-mail hestercreek@img.net
web site www.hestercreek.com

Hillside Estate Winery
1350 Naramata Road, Penticton, BC, V2A 8T6
phone 250-493-6274, toll free 1-888-923-9463,
fax 250-493-6294
e-mail info@hillsideestate.com
web site www.hillsideestate.com

House of Rose Vineyards
2270 Garner Road, Kelowna, BC, V1P 1E2
phone 250-765-0802, fax 250-765-7762
e-mail arose@shuswap.net

Inniskillin Okanagan Vineyards Inc.
Road 11, R.R. #1, S24 C5, Oliver, BC, V0H 1T0
phone 250-498-6663 or 1-800-498-6211,
fax 250-498-4566
e-mail inniskil@inniskillin.com
web site www.inniskillin.com/okanagan/
inkamep.html

Kettle Valley Winery
2988 Hayman Road, R.R. #1, S2 C39, Naramata,
BC, V0H 1N0
phone 250-496-5898, fax 250-496-5298
e-mail KettleValleyWinery@telus.net

Lake Breeze Vineyards
930 Sammet Road, P.O. Box 9, Naramata, BC,
V0H 1N0
phone 250-496-5659, fax 250-496-5894
e-mail lakebreeze@telus.net

Lang Vineyard
2493 Gammon Road, R.R. #1, S11 C55,
Naramata, BC, V0H 1N0
phone 250-496-5987, fax 250-496-5706
e-mail langwines@img.net

Larch Hills Winery
110 Timms Road, Salmon Arm, BC, V1E 2P8
phone 250-832-0155, fax 250-832-9419
e-mail lhwinery@shuswap.net
web site www.larchhillswinery.bc.ca

Mission Hill Winery
1730 Mission Hill Road, Westbank, Okanagan
Valley, BC, V4T 2E4
phone 250-768-7611,1-800-957-9911,
fax 250-768-2267
e-mail info@missionhillwinery.com
web site www.missionhillwinery.com

Nichol Vineyard & Farm Winery
1285 Smethurst Road, R.R. #1, S14 C13,
Naramata, BC, V0H 1N0
phone 250-496-5962, fax 250-496-4275

Pinot Reach Cellars
1670 Dehart Road, Kelowna, BC, V1W 4N6
phone 250-764-0078, toll free 1-877-764-0078,
fax 250-764-0771
e-mail pinot@direct.ca

Poplar Grove Farm Winery
1060 Poplar Grove Road, Penticton, BC, V2A 8T6
phone 250-492-4575, fax 250-492-9162
e-mail poplargrove@img.net

Prpich Hills
378 Parsons Road, R.R. #1, S30 C8, Okanagan
Falls, BC, V0H 1R0
phone 250-497-1125, fax 250-497-1126

Quails' Gate Estate Winery
3303 Boucherie Road, Kelowna, BC, V1Z 2H3
phone 250-769-4451, 1-800-420-WINE,
fax 250-769-3451
e-mail info@quailsgate.com
web site www.quailsgate.com

Recline Ridge Vineyards & Winery Ltd.
2640 Skimikin Road, R.R. #1, S12 C16, Tappen,
BC, V0E 2X0
phone 250-835-2212, fax 250-835-2228
e-mail inquiry@recline-ridge.bc.ca
web site www.recline-ridge.bc.ca

Red Rooster Winery
910 De Beck Road, Naramata, BC, V0H 1N0
phone 250-496-4041, fax 250-496-5674
e-mail redrooster@img.net

St. Hubertus Estate Winery
5225 Lakeshore Road, Kelowna, BC, V1W 4J1
phone 250-764-7888 or 1-800-989-9463,
fax 250-764-0499
e-mail wine@st-hubertus.bc.ca
web site www.st-hubertus.bc.ca

Scherzinger Vineyards
7311 Fiske Street, Summerland, BC, V0H 1Z0
phone/fax 250-494-8815
e-mail scherzi@telus.net

Slamka Cellars Winery
2815 Ourtoland Road, Kelowna, BC, V1Z 2H5
phone 250-769-0404, 604-327-9164,
fax 250-763-8168
e-mail slamka@silk.net
web site www.slamka.bc.ca

Stag's Hollow Winery & Vineyard
R.R. #1, S3 C36, 2237 Sunvalley Way, Okanagan
Falls, BC, V0H 1R0
phone/fax 250-497-6162
e-mail stagshollow@vip.net
web site www.stagshollowwinery.com

Sumac Ridge Estate Winery Ltd.
17403 Highway 97, P.O. Box 307, Summerland,
BC, V0H 1Z0
phone 250-494-0451, fax 250-494-3456
e-mail info@sumacridge.com
web site www.sumacridge.com

Summerhill Estate Winery
4870 Chute Lake Road, Kelowna, BC, V1W 4M3
phone 250-764-8000 or 1-800-667-3538,
fax 250-764-2598
e-mail summerhill@summerhill.bc.ca
web site www.summerhill.bc.ca

Tinhorn Creek Vineyards
32830 Tinhorn Creek Road, P.O. Box 2010,
Oliver, BC, V0H 1T0
phone 250-498-3743 or 1-888-4-TINHORN,
fax 250-498-3228
e-mail winery@tinhorn.com
web site www.tinhorn.com

Vincor/Jackson-Triggs Vintners
Highway 97, P.O. Box 1650, North Oliver, BC,
V0H 1T0
phone 250-498-4981, fax 250-498-6505

Wild Goose Vineyards
R.R. #1, S3, C11, Lot 11, Sunvalley Way,
Okanagan Falls, BC, V0H 1R0
phone 250-497-8919, fax 250-497-6853
e-mail wildgoose@img.net

Similkameen Valley wineries

Crowsnest Vineyards
Surprise Drive, R.R. #1, S18 C18, Cawston, BC,
V0X 1C0
phone 250-499-5129, fax 250-499-5129
e-mail crowsnest@img.net
web site www.crowsnestvinyards.com

St. Laszlo Vineyards
R.R. #1, S95 C8, Highway 3, Keremeos, BC,
V0X 1N0
phone/fax 250-499-2856 (tasting is open from 9
to 9 every day)

Greater Vancouver and Fraser Valley wineries

Andrés Wine (BC) Ltd.
2120 Vintner Street, Port Moody, BC, V3H 1W8
phone 604-937-3411, 1-800-663-6483,
fax 604-937-5487
e-mail info.bc@andreswines.com

Domaine de Chaberton Estates Limited
1064 216th Street, Langley, BC, V2Z 1R3
phone 604-530-1736 or 1-888-332-9463,
fax 604-533-9687
e-mail cviolet@direct.ca
web site www.domainedechaberton.com

Vancouver Island wineries

Alderlea Vineyards
1751 Stamps Road, R.R. #1, Duncan, BC,
V9L 5W2
phone 250-746-7122, fax 250-746-7122

Blue Grouse Vineyards & Winery
4365 Blue Grouse Road, Duncan, Vancouver
Island, BC, V9L 6M3
phone 250-743-3834, fax 250-743-9305
e-mail www.bluegrousevineyards.com
web site skiltz@bluegrousevineyards.com

Chateau Wolff
2534 Maxey Road, Nanaimo, BC, V9S 5V6
phone 250-753-9669, fax 250-753-0614

Cherry Point Vineyards
840 Cherry Point Road, R.R. #3, Cobble Hill,
BC, V0R 1L0
phone 250-743-1272, fax 250-743-1059
e-mail info@cherrypointvineyards.com
web site www.cherrypointvineyards.com

Divino Estate Winery
1500 Freeman Road, Cobble Hill, BC, V0R 1L0
phone 250-743-2311, fax 250-743-1087

Saturna Vineyard
Saturna Island, BC, V0N 2Y0
phone 250-539-5139, fax 250-539-5157
e-mail wine@saturnavineyards.com
web site www.saturnavineyards.com

Venturi-Schulze Vineyards
4235 TransCanada Hwy, R.R. #1, Cobble Hill,
BC, V0R 1L0
phone 250-743-5630, fax 250-743-5638
e-mail info@venturischulze.com
web site www.venturischulze.com

Vigneti Zanatta Winery and Vineyards
5039 Marshall Road, Duncan, BC, V9L 6S3
phone 250-748-2338, fax 250-748-2347
e-mail zanatta@zanatta.bc.ca
web site www.zanatta.bc.ca

The Vineyard at Bowen Island
687 Cates Lane, CH 6, Bowen Island, BC, V0N 1G0
phone 604-947-0028, fax 604-947-0693
e-mail staff@vineyard.bc.ca
web site www.vineyard.bc.ca

Québec

Eastern Townships wineries

Domaine Félibre
740 Bean Road, Stanstead, QC, J0B 3E0
phone/fax 819-876-7900
e-mail felibre@abacom.com
web site www.produitdelaferme.com/felibre

Vignoble de l'Aurore Boréale
1421 rang Brodeur, St-Eugène de Grantham,
QC, J0C 1J0
phone 819-396-7349, fax 819-396-7349
e-mail aurore.boreale@sympatico.ca

Vignoble de la Sablière
1050 chemin Dutch (Route 235), St-Armand,
QC, J0J 1T0
phone/fax 450-248-2634
e-mail lasabliere@acbm.net

Vignoble Domaine de l'Ardennais
158 Ridge, Stanbridge East, QC, J2J 2H0
phone/fax 450-248-0597

Vignoble Domaine des Côtes d'Ardoise
889 Bruce (Route 202), Dunham, QC, J0E 1M0
phone 450-295-2020, Fax 450-295-2309

Vignoble l'Orpailleur
1086 Bruce (Route 202), C.P. 339, Dunham,
QC, J0E 1M0
phone 450-295-2763, fax 450-295-3112
e-mail info@orpailleur.ca
web site www.orpailleur.ca

Vignoble la Bauge
155 des Érables, Brigham, QC, J2K 4E1
phone 514-266-2149, 514-263-7157,
fax 514-263-2035
e-mail bauge@virtuel.qc.ca
web site www.la-bauge.com

Vignoble le Cep d'Argent
1257 chemin de la Rivière, Canton de Magog,
QC, J1X 3W5
phone 819-864-4441, fax 819-864-7534
e-mail info@cepdargent.com
web site www.cepdargent.com

Vignoble les Arpents de Neige
4042 Principale, Dunham, QC, J0E 1M0
phone 450-295-3383, fax 450-295-1102
e-mail arpents@qc.aira.com

Vignoble les Blancs Coteaux
1046 Bruce (Route 202), Dunham, QC, J0E 1M0
phone 450-295-3503, fax 450-295-3503
e-mail govino@acbm.qc.ca

Vignoble les Chants de Vignes
459 chemin de la Rivière, Canton de Magog,
QC, J1X 3W5
phone 819-847-8467, fax 819-847-2940

Vignoble les Pervenches
150 chemin Boulais, Farnham, QC, J2N 2P9
phone 450-293-8311, fax 450-293-8311,
e-mail lespervenches@ekno.com

Vignoble les Trois Clochers
341 Bruce (Route 202), Dunham, QC, J0E 1M0
phone 450-295-2034
e-mail abq@qc.aira.com

Montérégie wineries

Clos Saint-Denis, Verger-Vignoble
1149 chemin des Patriotes, Saint-Denis-sur-
Richelieu, QC, J0H 1K0
phone 450-787-3766, fax 450-787-9956
e-mail info@clos-saint-denis.qc.ca
web site www.clos-saint-denis.qc.ca

Vignoble Angell
134 rang St-Georges, St-Bernard de Lacolle,
QC, J0J 1V0
phone 450-246-4219

Vignoble Cappabianca
586 St-Jean-Baptiste, Mercier, QC, J6R 2A7
phone 450-691-1515, fax 450-691-4212

Vignoble Clos de la Montagne
330 de la Montagne, Mont-St-Grégoire, QC,
J0J 1K0
phone 450-358-4868, fax 450-358-5628
e-mail aryden@qc.aira.com

Vignoble des Négondos
7100 Rang Saint-Vincent, Saint-Benoit de
Mirabel, QC, J7N 3N1
phone 450-258-2099, toll free 1-877-309-2099,
fax 450-437-7234
e-mail vignoble.negondos@sympatico.ca

Vignoble des Pins
136 Grand Sabrevois, Sabrevois, QC, J0J 2G0
phone 450-347-1073, fax 450-347-1073
e-mail vigdespins@aol.com
web site www.sud-quebec.com/despins.htm

Vignoble Dietrich-Jooss
407 chemin de la Grande Ligne, Iberville, QC,
J2X 4J2
phone 450-347-6857, fax 450-347-6857
e-mail vignobledietrich-jooss@qc.aira.com

Vignoble du Marathonien
318 Route 202, Havelock, QC, J0S 2C0
phone 450-826-0522, fax 514-321-9347

Vignoble Leroyer/St-Pierre
182, route 221, St-Cyprien de Napierville, QC,
J0J 1L0
phone 450-245-0208, fax 450-245-0388
e-mail robertleroyer@sprint.ca

Vignoble Morou
238 route 221, Napierville, QC, J0J 1L0
phone 450-245-7569, fax 450-245-7550
e-mail morou@sympatico.ca
web site www3.sympatico.ca/morou/

Vignoble Sous les Charmilles
3747 chemin Dunant, Rock-Forest, QC, J1N 3B7
phone 819-346-7189, fax 819-346-0620

Québec City and other wineries

Coopérative des Producteurs Viticoles
Bourg-Royal and Vignoble Bourg-Royal
1910 des Érables, Charlesbourg, QC, G2L 1R8
phone 418-622-2230, fax 418-623-2434
e-mail bourg-royal@bigfoot.com
web site www.multimania.com/vignoble

Vignoble Domaine Royarnois
146 chemin du Cap-Tourmente, St. Joachim de
Montmorency, QC, G0A 3X0
phone 418-827-4465, fax 418-827-5002
e-mail domaineroyarnois@sympatico.ca

Vignoble Angile
267, 2ème Rang Ouest, St-Michel de
Bellechasse, QC, G0R 3S0
phone/fax 418-884-2327
web site www.quebecweb.com/angile/

Vignoble Îsle de Bacchus
1071 chemin Royal, Saint-Pierre-de-l'Île
d'Orléans, QC, G0A 4E0
phone 418-828-9562

Vignoble le Moulin du Petit Pré
7007 avenue Royale
Château-Richer, QC, G0A 1N0
phone 418-824-4411 fax 418-824-4422
e-mail rhayes@musee-abeille.qc.ca
web site www.moulin-petitpre.com (under
construction)

Vignoble de Sainte-Pétronille
1A, chemin du Bout de l'Ile, Ste-Pétronille, QC,
G0A 4C0
phone 418-828-9554, fax 418-828-1253
e-mail vsp@orecom.ca

Other Areas

Vignoble de la Vallée de l'Outaouais
828 Rang 6, Gatineau, QC, J8R 3A4
phone 819-669-2020, fax 819-669-3060
e-mail normand.dessureault@bigfoot.com

Nova Scotia

Annapolis Valley wineries

Domaine de Grand Pré
11611 Highway 1, P.O. Box 105, Grand Pre, NS,
B0P 1M0
phone 902-542-1753, fax 902-542-0060
e-mail mail@grandprewines.ns.ca
web site www.grandprewines.ns.ca

Habitant Vineyards
10318 Highway 221, Canning, NS, B0P 1H0
phone 902-582-7565, 1-877-582-7565,
fax 902-582-3661
e-mail therese@ns.sympatico.ca
web site www.habitant.ca

Jost Vineyards
48 Vintage Lane, R.R. #1, Malagash, NS, B0K 1E0
phone 902-257-2636, toll free 1-800-565-4567,
fax 902-257-2248
e-mail info@jostwine.com
web site www.jostwine.com

Sainte-Famille Wines
9 Dudley Park Lane, Falmouth, NS, B0P 1L0
phone 902-798-8311, toll free 1-800-565-0993,
fax 902-798-9418
e-mail s.corkum@st-famille.ns.ca
web site www.st-famille.com

Prince Edward Island

Rossignol Estate Winery
Little Sands, R.R. #4, Murray River, PEI, C0A 1W0
phone/fax 902-962-4193
web site www.rossignolwinery.com

Fruit wineries

Ontario

Archibald Orchards & Estate Winery
6275 Liberty Street, North Bowmanville, ON,
L1C 3K6
phone 905-263-2396, fax 905-263-4263
e-mail archibalds@archibalds-estatewinery.
  on.ca
web site www.archibalds-estatewinery.on.ca

Bellamere Country Market & Winery
1260 Gainsborough Road, London, ON, N6H 5K8
phone 519-473-2273, fax 519-473-5312
e-mail farm@bellamere.com
web site www.bellamere.com

The County Cider Company
County Road #8 (10 miles East of Picton),
R.R. #4, Picton, ON, K0K 2T0
phone 613-476-6224, TASTING ROOM
613-476-1022
e-mail countycider@reach.net
web site www.countycider.com

Cox Creek Cellars Estate Winery
R.R. #5, Guelph, ON, N1H 6J2
phone 519-767-3253, fax 519-824-0808
e-mail information@CoxCreekCellars.on.ca
or tours@coxcreekcellars.on.ca
web site www.coxcreekcellars.on.ca

Meadow Lane Winery Ltd.
44892 Talbot Line, R.R. #3, St. Thomas, ON,
N5P 3S7
phone 519-633-1933, fax 519-633-1355
e-mail wines@meadowlanewinery.com
web site www.meadowlanewinery.com

Norfolk Estate Winery
R.R. #1, St. Williams, ON, N0E 1P0
phone 519-586-2237, fax 519-586-7995
e-mail newine@kwic.com
web site www.kwic.com/~newine

Ocala Orchards Farm Winery
971 High Point Road, Port Perry, ON, L9L 1B3
phone 905-985-9924, fax 905-985-7794
e-mail ocala@sympatico.ca

Rush Creek Wines Ltd.
48995 Jamestown Line, R.R. #2, Aylmer, ON,
N5H 2R2
phone 519-773-5432, fax 519-773-5431
e-mail rushcreek@amtelecom.net
web site www.elgin.net/RUSHCREEKWINES/

St. Jacob's Country Market Winery & Cidery
40 Benjamin Road East, Waterloo, ON, N2J 3Z4
phone 519-747-2337, Fax 519-747-5594
e-mail sales@stjacobswinery.com
web site www.stjacobswinery.com

Sunnybrook Farm Estate Winery
1425 Lakeshore Road, R.R. #3, Niagara-on-the-
Lake, ON, L0S 1J0
phone 905-468-1122, fax 905-468-1068
web site www.sunnybrookfarmwinery.com

British Columbia

Bonaparte Bend Winery
Box 47, Highway 97 North (Cariboo Highway),
Cache Creek, BC, V0K 1H0
phone 250-457-6667

Columbia Valley Classics Winery
1385 Frost Road, Lindell Beach, BC, V2R 4X8
phone/fax 250-858-5233
e-mail info@cvcwines.com
web site www.cvcwines.com

Elephant Island Orchard Wines
2730 Aikens Loop
R.R. #1, S5 C18, Naramata, BC, V0H 1N0
phone 250-496-5522, fax 250-496-5522

Merridale Estate Cidery
1230 Merridale Road, Cobble Hill, BC, V0R 1L0
phone 250-743-4293, toll free 1-800-998-9908,
fax 250-250-743-9310
e-mail janet@merridalecider.com
web site www.merridalecider.com

Nova Scotia

Lunenburg County Winery
R.R. #3, Mahone Bay, Lunenburg County,
Newburne, NS, B0J 2E0
phone 902-644-2415, fax 902-644-3614
e-mail winery@istar.ca
web site www.canadian-wine.com

Telder Berry Farm and Winery
Site 8, Box 28, R.R. #1, Elmsdale, 1251 Enfield
Road, Nine Mile River, Hants County, NS,
B0N 1M0
phone 902-883-8433, fax 902-883-1625
e-mail telwines@ns.sympatico.ca
web site www3.ns.sympatico.ca/telwines/
index.htm

Newfoundland

Rodrigues Winery
Box 98, Whitbourne, NF, A0B 3K0
phone 709-759-3003, fax 709-759-2086
e-mail hillary@rodrigueswinery.com
web site www.rodrigueswinery.com

Useful Web sites for more wine information

www.tonyaspler.com
Wine and food matching, wine reviews, and
general, global information

www.travelenvoy.com/wine
Lots of information and links to wines across
Canada and the world

www.winesofcanada.com
Varied information with links to wineries

www.wineroute.com
Operated by the Wine Council of Ontario, lists
wineries and addresses

www.wineward.com
Guide to wineries, news, touring and
accommodation

www.bcwine.com
General information on British Columbia wines
and links to travel suggestions, wine growers
associations, etc.

www.winegrowers.bc.ca
Association of British Columbia Winegrowers
Web site, with mailing addresses and e-mail
addresses

www.brocku.ca/ccovi
Cool Climate Oenology and Viticultural
Institute Brock University
Describes academic programs and research
projects

www.owfs.com
Okanagan Valley wine festivals

www.niagarafest.on.ca
Niagara region wine festivals

winefest.bc.sympatico.ca
Vancouver Playhouse Wine Festival

www.vignerons-du-quebec.com
Québec winery Web sites

www.geocities.com/NapaValley/
Vineyard/3765
Click on the VQA logo for news about Ontario
wineries

We'd like to make a special mention of the
Canadian Sommelier Guild, which offers inten-
sive diploma courses as well as lectures and
training at all levels for both the wine lover
and professional:

20 Mullet Drive, Streetsville, ON, L5M 2G3
phone 905-858-1217
fax 905-858-3440
e-mail canadiansommelierguild@
sympatico.ca
Web sites: www.canadiansommelierguild.com
www.canadiansommelierguild.org,
www.cellarmasters.org

Appendix C
Coolers & Corkscrews

*T*his is where to go to get good wine stuff and some wine education.

Wine accessories

A Step Up Distinctive Gifts
1226 Hollis Park Lane
5657 Spring Garden Road
Halifax, NS, B3J 1T6
phone 902-422-9155
Glasses and wine accessories

Aux Plaisirs de Bacchus
1225 rue Bernard,
Outremont, QC, H2V 1V7
phone 514-273-3104
toll free 1-888-777-3104
fax 514-273-3161
e-mail auxplaisirs.debacchus@sympatico.ca
Cellars, glasses, and accessories

C.A. Paradis
1314 Bank Street
Ottawa, ON, K1S 3Y4
phone 613-731-2866
fax 613-731-8439
e-mail info@caparadis.com
web site www.caparadis.com
Various accessories

Cavavin
2910 boul. Losch,
Saint-Hubert, QC, J3Y 3V8
phone 450-676-6447
toll free 1-877-676-6447
fax 514-525-1912
e-mail info@cavavin.com
web site www.cavavin.com
Refrigerated coolers

The Cookbook Store
850 Yonge Street
Toronto, ON, M4W 2H1
phone 416-920-2665, 1-800-268-6018,
fax 416-920-3271
e-mail cooking@ican.net
web site www.cook-book.com
The best store in the country for wine books

Dream Cellar Design
416-410-4492
Cellar designs

Lesley Stowe Fine Foods
1780 West 3rd Avenue
Vancouver, BC, V6J 1K4
phone 604-731-3663
fax 604-731-3666
e-mail catering@lesleystowe.com
web site www.lesleystowe.com
Wine magazines and extra-virgin olive oils

Robilan Imports
phone 506-859-4133, fax 506-859-4233
e-mail robilan@nbnet.nb.ca
Distributor of the Private Preserve wine preserver in Atlantic provinces.

Rosehill Wine Cellar & Renovation Group Inc.
32 Howden Road, Unit 3
Toronto, ON, M1R 3E4
phone 416-285-6604, 1-888-253-6807,
fax 416-285-6605
e-mail info@rosehillwinecellars.com
web site www.rosehillwinecellars.com
Wineracks and cellar design

Tapisseries de France Inc.
371, rue Corot
Ile-Des-Soeurs, QC, H3E 1K8
phone 514-766-5672
fax 514-362-1387
e-mail aubusson@darwin.qc.ca
web site www.royalaubusson.com
Woven tapestries with wine motifs

The Toronto Foundation for Student Success
49 Cluny Drive
Toronto, ON, M4W 2R1
phone 416-922-2237, fax 416-925-5676
e-mail lifeiswine@aol.com
*One art poster of the 11 vineyards of the
Primum Familiae Vini (First Families of Wine)
(non-profit)*

Toscan vini
phone 514-341-2368, fax 341-4465
e-mail david@toscan.qc.ca
web site www.toscan.qc.ca
Distributor of the Private Preserve in Québec.

Vinifera Wine Services
1055 Yonge Street, Suite 306
Toronto, ON, M4W 2L2
phone 416-924-4004
fax 416-924-1449
Wine accessories and wines

Vintage Keeper
5648 McAdam Road,
Mississauga, ON, L4Z 1T2
phone 905-501-8582, 1-888-274-8813
fax 905-501-0889
e-mail info@vintagekeeper.com
web site www.vintagekeeper.com
Climate-controlled cellar units

Vinum Design
1480 City Councillors
Montréal, QC, H3A 2E5
phone 514-985-3200
fax 514-985-9802
e-mail (ORDERING) achats@vinumdesign.com
web site www.vinumdesign.com
Cellars, glasses, and accessories

The Wine Environment (coming soon)
Cellar designs
2 Roxborough Street East
Toronto, ON, M4W 3V7
phone 416- 657-2486
fax 416-480-1240
web site www.thewineenvironment.com
(under construction)

The Wine Establishment Ltd.
250 The Esplanade, Courtyard Suite 104
Toronto, ON, M5A 1J2
phone 416-861-1331,1-800-268-8418
fax 416-861-1098
e-mail mail@thewineestablishment.com
web site www.thewineestablishment.com
*A one-stop-shop for all wine-related accessories
and cellar designs*

Wineworld
phone 416-487-7147
toll free 1-800-246-7167
fax 416-487-7140
e-mail wineworld@attglobal.net
web site www.wineworldimporters.com
*Distributor of the Private Preserve in Ontario and
Western provinces.*

Wine magazines (English)

Enoteca
P.O Box 37
Concord, ON, L4K 1B2
phone 905-760-1724
fax 905-760-1718

Vines Magazine
159 York Street
St. Catharines, ON, L2R 6E9
phone 905-682-4509, 1-888-883-3372
fax 905-682-8219
e-mail editor@iaw.on.ca
web site www.vinesmag.com

Wine Access
162 John Street
Toronto, ON, M5V 2E5
phone 416-596-555
fax 416-596-1520
e-mail wineaccess@warwickgp.com
web site www.wineaccessmag.com

Winetidings
5165 Sherbrooke Street West, #414
Montreal, QC, H4A 9Z9
phone 514-481-5892
fax 514-481-9699
e-mail winetidings@netcom.ca

Wine magazines (French)

La Barrique
5165 Sherbrooke Street, West
Montréal, QC, H4A 1T6
phone 514-481-5892
fax 514-481-9699
e-mail barrique@netcom.ca

Vins & Vignobles
8250, boul. Décarie, #205
Montréal, QC, H4P 2P5
phone 514-735-5191
fax 514-342-9406
e-mail montreal@mcgown.com

Computer software: Cellar programs

These programs are great for keeping track of the bottles in your cellar. Most of them allow you to download sample software for testing.

Cellar! The Software for Wine Enthusiasts
web site www.collectware.com

Cellarmaster Wine Database
web site www.quandt.com

Robert Parker's Wine Advisor and Cellar Manager Software
web site www.winetech.com

Wine Cellar Book for Windows
web site www.primasoft.com/wb.htm

Catalogue shopping for wine

Three provincial liquor boards have an Internet presence with links to their specialty wine catalogues, but you must phone or fax your order. www.canwine.com has links to these sites.

Manitoba

web site www.mlcc.mb.ca
Delivery within the city of Winnipeg only.

Ontario

phone 416-365-5767
toll free 1-800-266-4764
web site www.vintages.com/classics
Delivery to specific stores across the province.

Québec

phone 514-864-3253
toll free 1-800-317-9317
web site www.saq.com
Delivery to specific stores across the province.

Canada's largest wine society, Opimian, works exclusively by catalogue orders.
phone 514-483-5551
fax 514-481-9699
web site www.opim.ca

Highlights of the Vintners Quality Alliance (VQA) National Wine Standard

• •

The Vintners Quality Alliance — VQA Canada — is an Appellation of Origin system by which consumers can identify quality wines of Canada based on the origin of the grapes from which they are produced.

The National VQA Standards constitute the base for the establishment of provincial VQA Rules and Regulations for wines produced exclusively from grapes grown in recognized Canadian geographical indications.

Mission Statement

The Vintners Quality Alliance (VQA) Canada is a subcommittee of the Canadian Wine Institute, with a mandate to harmonize wine quality standards among provincially based VQA organizations in Canada, through the establishment of a body of national rules and regulations.

Geographical Indications (G.I.)

Under the VQA, Geographical Indications (appellations of origin) are divided into two categories: provincial and viticultural areas.

Provincial areas

A VQA provincial designation shall be the name of the province from which the wine originates. Currently, only Ontario and British Columbia are recognized by VQA Canada, as VQA provincial designations.

A wine produced in accordance with this standard shall be entitled to a VQA provincial designation if it is produced exclusively from grapes grown within the political boundaries of Canada; and

1. Not less than 85 percent of the wine's content is derived from grapes grown within the political boundaries of the named province in which the wine is bottled.

2. It meets all standards set out herein and all applicable provincial VQA standards (provincial standards may be more stringent).

3. It is approved through a provincial VQA certification process.

Viticultural areas

The Viticultural Areas (VA's) currently recognized by VQA Canada are:

✔ In British Columbia:

- Fraser Valley
- Okanagan Valley
- Similkameen Valley
- Vancouver Island

✔ In Ontario:

- Lake Erie North Shore
- Niagara Peninsula
- Pelee Island
- Prince Edward County

The Viticultural Area identified on the principal display panel (the label on the wine bottle) denotes the origin of the grapes, not the location of the processing facility.

Vineyard Designation

Where a vineyard is designated on the principal display panel, the wine must be derived exclusively from grapes grown in the designated vineyard.

The designated vineyard shall be located within a Viticultural Area.

Estate Bottled Declaration

The word *estate* may be used in place of the word *vineyard* if the wine meets all of the *Estate bottled Declaration* requirements.

Where an estate-bottled designation is declared on the principal display panel the wine shall be derived exclusively from grapes grown on land owned or controlled by the bottling winery, which must be located within a Viticultural Area.

The bottling winery shall have harvested and crushed the grapes, fermented the resulting must, finished, aged, and bottled the wine.

The finished wine shall have at no time left the winery prior to being bottled.

The Viticultural Area within which the land is owned or controlled by the bottling winery shall be declared on the principal display panel.

No designation other than "Estate Bottled" may be used on a principal display panel to indicate combined growing and bottling conditions.

Wine Categories

All categories of wine shall be produced from the complete or partial alcoholic fermentation of fresh grapes, grape juice, or grape must.

Wine or Table Wine shall be an alcoholic beverage produced by the complete or partial alcoholic fermentation of fresh grapes, grape juice, or grape must obtained from one or more authorized grape varieties, and grown within a VQA Canada approved geographical indication. Wine or table wine shall have an actual alcoholic content not less than 8.5 percent and not greater than 14.9 percent by volume.

Icewine shall be a wine produced exclusively from grapes that have been harvested, naturally frozen on the vine, and pressed in a continuous process while the air temperature is –8° Celsius or lower.

Artificial refrigeration of the grapes or artificial refrigeration of the juice, must, or wine is prohibited at any point in the manufacturing process except for tank cooling during fermentation and/or during cold stabilization prior to bottling;

Late, Select Late, and Special Select Late Harvest Wines Each category of "late harvest" wine shall be produced entirely from fresh ripe grapes of which a significant portion has been desiccated under natural conditions in a manner that favours the concentration of sugars in the berries.

The addition of sweet reserve to any category of "late harvest" wine is prohibited.

Nouveau Wine shall be a wine produced exclusively from fresh grapes that have been naturally harvested. Vinification shall involve at least partial carbonic maceration

Blanc de Noirs Wine shall be a wine produced exclusively from fresh grapes, of which 85 percent shall be a red variety.

1. The juice shall be separated from the skins prior to fermentation and vinified using processes and treatments suitable for the production of white wine.

2. The term *Blanc de Noirs* shall appear on the principal display panel directly above or below the named grape variety(s) in letters at least half the size but no larger than twice the size of those specifying the grape variety(s).

Fortified Wine shall be the product obtained by adding alcohol, derived from the alcoholic fermentation of a food source and distilled to not less than 94 percent alcohol by volume, grape brandy and/or fruit spirit to wine, or grape juice or grape must in fermentation. In addition, a fortified wine shall have an actual content greater than 14.9 percent but not greater than 20 percent by volume;

Liqueur Wine shall be the product obtained exclusively from the alcoholic fermentation of fresh grapes, grape juice, grape must, or wine. In addition a liqueur wine:

1. Shall have an alcohol content greater than 14.9 percent but not greater than 20 percent by volume.

2. May be designated *natural* if the residual sugar results exclusively from the sugar of the grapes.

Sparkling Wine shall be a wine surcharged with carbon dioxide gas to a pressure not less than 300 kPa at 10° Celsius; which:

1. Has an actual alcoholic strength, including the alcohol contained in any "expedition liqueur" added, of not less than 8.5 percent by volume.

2. Derives its effervescence exclusively from a primary or secondary alcoholic fermentation in a closed vessel.

3. Is produced exclusively using either the Traditional Method or the Charmat Method.

Cuvée is grape must in fermentation or wine, or a mixture of grape musts in fermentation or wines, intended for the preparation of sparkling wine, having a total alcoholic strength of not less than 9 percent by volume.

Tirage Liqueur is the product added to the "cuvée" to provoke a secondary alcoholic fermentation. It is produced exclusively from grape must, grape must in fermentation, or wine suitable for yielding the same quality VQA sparkling wine as that to which the "tirage liqueur" is added.

Expedition Liqueur is the product added to sparkling wine to enhance specific flavour qualities and/or to maximize fill levels after dégorgement.

Traditional Method is a method of producing sparkling wine by a secondary fermentation in a glass bottle having a capacity not exceeding five litres, in accordance with the following:

1. It shall be made exclusively from grapes of the species *Vitis vinifera*.

2. The finished wine shall be sold in the bottle in which the secondary fermentation took place.

3. The wine shall at no time have left the bottle prior to final corking.

Charmat Method is a method of producing sparkling wine by a primary or secondary fermentation in a closed vessel having a capacity exceeding five litres, in accordance with the following:

1. The duration of the process to make sparkling wine from the start of the alcoholic fermentation designed to make the wine sparkling, including aging at the undertaking where the wine was made, shall not be less than six months.

2. The duration of the alcoholic fermentation process designed to make the "cuvée" sparkling and the duration of the presence of the "cuvée" on the lees shall not be less than 80 days, or 30 days if the fermentation took place in a tank with a mixer.

3. The resulting wine will only be entitled to a provincial designation.

Labelling

All VQA-approved wines shall meet the packaging and labelling requirements for alcoholic beverages and other relevant requirements under the Food and Drugs Act and Regulations and the Consumer Packaging and Labelling Act and Regulations.

Varietal wines

Except where otherwise indicated, a wine bearing a varietal designation shall have the predominant character of a wine produced from the designated grape variety(s), as determined by a VQA tasting/evaluation panel.

In the case of single-varietal wines, where the variety is indicated on the principal display panel, not less than 85 percent of the wine shall be made from the named individual grape variety.

In the case of dual-varietal wines, where the varieties are indicated on the principal display panel, not less than 90 percent of the wine shall be made from the two varieties named, with the second being not less than 15 percent of the total.

In the case of triple-varietal wines, where the varieties are indicated on the principal display panel, not less than 95 percent of the wine shall be made from the three varieties named, with the second being not less than 15 percent and the third not less than 10 percent of the total.

In every case, the declared varieties shall be listed on the principal display panel in descending order of quantity, in identical type and identically displayed.

In every case, the declared varieties shall appear immediately before or after the geographical indication. Nothing shall be permitted to be written between the designated variety(s) and the geographical indication.

Blended wines (proprietary names)

A VQA-approved wine not labelled as a varietal, in accordance with the provisions listed in this document, shall be identified by a proprietary name on the principal display panel. When grape varieties are declared, all varieties used to produce the blend must be declared and must appear in descending order of quantity, in identical type and identically displayed.

"Meritage" may be used as a proprietary name providing its use is in accordance with provisions specifically established in the applicable provincial VQA Rules and Regulations.

Vintage dating

Vintage dating is to be mandatory for all VQA wines, with the exception of sparkling, fortified, liqueur wines, and wines produced and packaged with a private label, beginning with the 1996 vintage.

Not less than 85 percent of the wine must be derived from grapes grown in the designated vintage year.

Foreign geographical indications

A wine approved through a VQA certification process, that bears a VQA declaration as part of its package, shall be prohibited from using a "customary" (generic) wine name listed in section 11.18 (3) of the Trademarks Act.

Synonyms

In cases where the name of a grape variety has a synonym containing a numerical designation only the prime name shall be used on the principal display panel.

Addition of water

The addition of water for the purpose of increasing yield is prohibited.

Chaptalization

Chaptalization is defined as enrichment by the addition of sugar to fresh grapes, grape juice, or grape must prior to or during fermentation.

Chaptalization is permitted for all VQA wines, unless otherwise prohibited within this standard.

Sweet reserve

Sweet reserve shall be defined as single strength grape juice that is added to wine as a sweetener.

The use of sweet reserve is permitted for all VQA wines, unless otherwise prohibited within this standard. When used its volume shall not exceed 15 percent of the total.

Certification process

Each provincial VQA authority shall be responsible to set up a certification process for the purpose of certifying wines for VQA.

Label approval

Each VQA participating winery shall be responsible to ensure that their VQA approved wines are labelled in accordance with this standard, the Food and Drugs Act and Regulations, and the Consumer Packaging Act and Regulations.

Tasting/evaluation panel — composition

Each provincial VQA authority shall be responsible to provide a panel to organoleptically evaluate wines submitted for VQA approval.

Each VQA tasting/evaluation panel shall normally consist of a minimum of six (6) members, of which not more than 50 percent shall normally be representatives of the Canadian wine industry. To qualify for membership to a VQA tasting/evaluation panel, candidates must pass a written test and a sensory evaluation tasting.

Packaging

The following regulations apply to packaging.

VQA label declaration

A wine that meets the minimum production and geographical indication standards set out herein, which is also passed by the applicable VQA tasting/ evaluation panel, shall display either the letters "VQA," the VQA medallion, or both, as part of its package.

One of the following forms of the VQA medallion shall appear on the bottle as part of the package:

1. A self-adhesive sticker applied to the front shoulder or neck of the bottle or to the capsule.
2. Printed on a shoulder label, body label, or neck label.
3. Printed three times around the capsule.
4. A gold-painted outline on a dark bottle.

Maintenance of This Standard

Changes to this standard must be approved by the VQA Canada Sub-Committee. Proposals may only be submitted by a provincial VQA authority.

Changes to this standard shall be incorporated into all provincial VQA standards. Provincial VQA authorities reserve the right to adopt standards that may be more stringent than those set out herein, but may not adopt standards less stringent.

Establishment of New Provincial Authorities

A proposal can be presented by a provincially-based, recognized organization, to VQA Canada to become authorized to use the VQA designation. A decision on acceptance of a responsible authority as a provincial VQA authority will be based on the conformity of the proposal with VQA Canada standards in both content and application.

Index

• N •

• O •